Whitehead's Radically Different
Postmodern Philosophy

SUNY series in Philosophy
George R. Lucas Jr., editor

Whitehead's Radically Different Postmodern Philosophy

An Argument for Its Contemporary Relevance

David Ray Griffin

STATE UNIVERSITY OF NEW YORK PRESS

Cover photo: black and white photograph / portrait of Alfred North Whitehead
courtesy of the Center for Process Studies, Claremont, CA

Published by
State University of New York Press, Albany

For information, address State University of New York Press,
194 Washington Avenue, Suite 305, Albany, NY 12210–2384

Production by Marilyn P. Semerad
Marketing by Anne M. Valentine

Library of Congress Cataloging-in-Publication Data

Griffin, David Ray, 1939–
    Whitehead's radically different postmodern philosophy : an argument
for its contemporary relevance / David Ray Griffin.
        p. cm.
    Includes bibliographical references and index.
    ISBN-13: 978–0–7914–7049–7 (hardcover : alk. paper)
    ISBN-13: 978–0–7914–7050–3 (pbk. : alk. paper)
    1. Whitehead, Alfred North, 1861–1947. 2. Postmodernism.
    3. Process philosophy. I. Title

B1674.W354G75 2007
192—dc22

                                                                    2006017525

10 9 8 7 6 5 4 3 2 1

Contents

INTRODUCTION   vii

ABBREVIATIONS   xi

PART 1. WHITEHEAD'S PHILOSOPHY AS POSTMODERN

1. Whitehead's Philosophy as Postmodern Philosophy   3

2. Whitehead's Philosophy and the Enlightenment   15

PART 2. WHITEHEAD ON CONSCIOUSNESS, ECOLOGY, TRUTH, TIME, AND ETHICS

3. Consciousness as a Subjective Form: Interactionism without Dualism   51

4. Whitehead's Deeply Ecological Worldview:
   Egalitarianism without Irrelevance   70

5. Truth as Correspondence, Knowledge as Dialogical:
   Pluralism without Relativism   86

6. Time in Physics and the Time of Our Lives:
   Overcoming Misplaced Concreteness   106

7. Whitehead and the Crisis in Moral Theory:
   Theistic Ethics without Heteronomy   139

PART 3. THE COHERENCE OF WHITEHEADIAN THEISM

8. Relativity Physics and Whiteheadian Theism:
   Overcoming the Apparent Conflicts   166

9. Whiteheadian Theism: A Response to Robert Neville's Critique   186

APPENDIX: Whitehead's Subjectivist Principle:
   From Descartes to Panexperientialism   215

NOTES   242

BIBLIOGRAPHY   276

INDEX   297

Introduction

When thinkers started using the term *postmodern* with some regularity in the 1960s and 1970s, its meaning was such that its application to the philosophy of Alfred North Whitehead was eminently appropriate. In those days, in fact, the idea of "postmodern thought" was associated with Whitehead more often than not.

In later decades, however, this term came to be used with a radically different meaning, one that made Whiteheadian philosophy seem more an opponent than an exemplification of postmodernism. For example, in an essay entitled "Postmodernism" in the *Cambridge Dictionary of Philosophy*, Bernd Magnus, an expert on Nietzsche, says that postmodernism is characterized by three central concepts: 'anti-realism,' 'opposition to transcendental arguments and transcendental standpoints,' and 'rejection of truth as correspondence to reality.' Whitehead, far from exemplifying any of these positions, explicitly argues against them (although this is true in relation to the second one only under some of the possible meanings of the word *transcendental*). Many philosophers, accordingly, would find the use of the term *postmodern* to characterize Whitehead's philosophy misleading or even illegitimate.

To draw that conclusion, however, is to commit the common fallacy of equating a genus with one of its species. This fallacy is, to be sure, quite commonly committed. For example, evolutionism is widely equated with the *neo-Darwinian* theory of evolution; theism is widely equated with *traditional* theism; and mind-body interactionism is widely equated with *dualistic* interactionism. The fact that the fallacy is widely committed does not, however, remove its fallacious nature and its possible perniciousness.

The equation of a genus with one of its species can be pernicious because if that species is widely regarded as deeply problematic, those problems will be used to reject the genus as such. Christian fundamentalists, for example, commonly use problems in neo-Darwinism as a basis for arguing that evolutionism as such should be rejected; atheists use problems in traditional theism, such as its insoluble problem of evil, as a basis for rejecting theism of every type; and materialist identists, who regard the mind as identical with the brain, use problems in dualistic interactionism as the basis for rejecting mind-brain interactionism altogether. These fallacious rejections are especially pernicious if it is the case, as I believe, that a true account of the nature of reality would involve a species of evolutionism, a species of theism, and a species of mind-brain interactionism.

In a similar way, the fallacious equation of postmodernism as such with the species of postmodernism that became prevalent in the 1980s and 1990s has led many thinkers to argue, from the fact that that form of postmodernism is deeply problematic (being even self-stultifying), that postmodernism as such should be left behind. But that attitude, besides being fallacious, is also pernicious if it is the case, as I believe, that the best way to overcome the incoherence and irrelevance of mainstream modern philosophies is by means of an approach that is most accurately termed "postmodern," even though it disagrees radically with many of the central theses widely thought to be inextricably connected with that term.

This radical disagreement about what kind of approach is most deserving of the term 'postmodern' is intimately related to the question of which dimensions of distinctively *modern* philosophy need to be transcended. Whitehead had very definite ideas about this question and developed his philosophy as a solution to some very basic ontological and epistemological premises that are distinctive to the "modern worldview." He believed there was no hope for significant progress in philosophy apart from a rejection of those premises. His philosophy is properly called "postmodern" insofar as it provides a reasoned critique of, and alternative to, those premises while retaining the clear advances associated with modernity (rather than returning to a *pre*modern worldview).

Besides being fallacious and pernicious, the contention that Whitehead's philosophy cannot legitimately be called "postmodern" is possibly even self-contradictory. That is, this contention seems to entail the claim that Whitehead's philosophy conflicts with the essence of postmodernism—even though one of the features of the kind of postmodernism in question is the rejection of essentialist thinking.

Be that as it may, I believe that the characterization of Whitehead's philosophy as postmodern helps bring out important dimensions of his philosophy that would otherwise be missed or at least underemphasized. I also suspect that Whitehead's philosophy, in addition to being one species or version of postmodernism, is the superior species in the sense of best dealing with the commonly recognized problems created by distinctively modern philosophy. I will not, however, engage in the kind of comparative analysis that such an argument will require. I will simply show that Whitehead's philosophy can in fact deal with a wide range of those problems. I leave to others the issue of whether there is another kind of postmodernism that can do a better or at least comparable job.

The first part of this book looks at Whitehead's philosophy from this point of view. The use of 'postmodern' to describe Whitehead's philosophy is explored most fully in chapter 1. The second chapter looks at the closely related issue of the relation of Whitehead's philosophy to the movement commonly known as "the enlightenment."

The second part of the book examines five issues that have been widely recognized as deeply problematic for modern philosophy. The first four problems have resulted from one of the distinctive premises of modern thought, namely, the idea that the most elementary units of the world are what Whitehead calls "vacuous actualities"—meaning entities that are fully actual and yet wholly devoid of experience. These four problems are (1) the inability to explain (apart from the supernaturalism presupposed by Descartes) the existence of conscious experience and its capacity to interact with the physical world, including the brain; (2) the existence of an antiecological worldview, in which "nature" is regarded as devoid of intrinsic value; (3) the inability to articulate our presupposition that truth means "correspondence"; and (4) the inability to reconcile time as we experience it with the only kind of time that can exist in the world studied by physicists, if that world is indeed comprised of vacuous actualities (as both dualists and materialists assume). I argue that Whitehead's panexperientialism, arguably the most fundamental of his postmodern doctrines, provides the basis for solving all four of these problems.

The fifth problem, the current crisis in moral theory, is shown to have resulted primarily from taking the modern insistence that ethics cannot be heteronomous—that is, based on an appeal to authority—to entail that it must be independent of theism. I show that Whitehead's philosophy, especially his version of theism, can, while fully rejecting all appeals to authority, overcome the central problems responsible for the current crisis in moral theory.

In the third part of the book, I defend Whitehead's version of theism, often called "panentheism," which is another of his postmodern doctrines (being an alternative to the three modern possibilities of supernaturalistic theism, pantheism, and atheism). I defend this panentheism against two kinds of criticism. Chapter 8 argues that, contrary to widespread belief, special relativity physics creates no difficulties for Whitehead's temporalistic theism or even the more fully temporalistic theism of Charles Hartshorne. Chapter 9 defends Whiteheadian theism against the "challenge to process theism" issued by Robert Neville, who has argued that Whitehead's position could be made more adequate and coherent by replacing Whitehead's doctrine of God with a radically different doctrine.

The appendix examines in some detail Whitehead's treatment of the major methodological move—the "subjectivist turn"—made by the archetypal modern philosopher, René Descartes. Whitehead argued that if Descartes, whose name is virtually synonymous with ontological dualism and its notorious mind-body problem, had carried his subjectivist turn to its logical conclusion, he would have been led to panexperientialism, in which this problem does not arise.

Although this chapter is very important for understanding the methodological basis for Whitehead's panexperientialism and hence his postmodern alternative to modern philosophy, it is relegated to the appendix because it is not essential to the book's argument and also because of its highly technical and primarily textual nature.

The book as a whole is an argument for the contemporary relevance of Whitehead's philosophy, understood as a version of postmodern philosophy. I make this argument primarily by showing how it provides solutions to a range of problems that, besides being created by distinctively modern philosophy, have proved insoluble by philosophers who have continued—perhaps even while considering their own approach postmodern—to accept the modern assumptions that created the problems in the first place.

Abbreviations

AI   *Adventures of Ideas* (orig. 1933). New York: Free Press, 1967.

ESP   *Essays in Science and Philosophy*. New York: Philosophical Library, 1947.

FR   *The Function of Reason* (orig. 1929). Boston: Beacon, 1968.

MT   *Modes of Thought* (orig. 1938). New York: Free Press 1968.

PR   *Process and Reality: An Essay in Cosmology* (orig. 1929), corrected edition, ed. David Ray Griffin and Donald W. Sherburne. New York: Free Press, 1978.

RM   *Religion in the Making*. New York: Fordham University Press, 1996 (reprint of original 1926 edition).

S   *Symbolism: Its Meaning and Effect* (orig. 1927). New York: Capricorn, 1959.

SMW   *Science and the Modern World* (orig. 1925). New York: Free Press 1967.

Part 1. Whitehead's Philosophy as Postmodern

1

Whitehead's Philosophy as Postmodern Philosophy

CALLING WHITEHEAD'S PHILOSOPHY "POSTMODERN"

I, along with several others, have long referred to Whitehead's philosophy as "postmodern," but the hitherto dominant connotations of this term can make this usage seem inappropriate, perhaps opportunistic. In this chapter, I explain why referring to Whitehead's philosophy as postmodern is not only appropriate but also illuminating, calling attention to aspects of his philosophy that challenge several distinctively modern tenets. This chapter, by introducing these aspects and pointing to the subsequent chapters in which they are developed and applied, thereby serves as an introduction to the book as a whole.

Although 'postmodern' was not used by Whitehead himself, the notion was implicit in his 1925 book, *Science and the Modern World*, in which he said that recent developments in both physics and philosophy had superseded some of the scientific and philosophical ideas that were foundational for the modern world.

Whitehead's most explicit statement about the end of the modern epoch occurred in a discussion of William James's 1904 essay "Does Consciousness Exist?" Whitehead took the crux of this essay to be the denial that consciousness is a stuff that is essentially different from the stuff of which the physical world is composed. Whitehead suggested that just as Descartes, with his formulation of a dualism between matter and mind as different kinds of substances, could (with some exaggeration) be regarded as the thinker who inaugurated the modern period, James, with his challenge to Cartesian dualism, could (with similar exaggeration) be regarded as having inaugurated "a new stage in philosophy."

Combining this challenge with that offered to "scientific materialism" by physics in the same period, Whitehead suggested that this "double challenge marks the end of a period which lasted for about two hundred and fifty years" (SMW 143).[1] Having described the scientific and philosophical thought of that period as distinctively modern, Whitehead thereby implied that his own philosophy, which sought to unite the philosophical implications of relativity and quantum physics with the Jamesian rejection of dualism, was distinctively postmodern, although he did not use the term.

The term itself was applied to Whitehead's philosophy in a 1964 essay by John Cobb entitled "From Crisis Theology to the Post-Modern World," which dealt with the emerging discussion of the "death of God."[2] Arguing that the dominant modern mentality, which equates the real with the objects of sensory perception, excludes the possible causality and even reality of God and thereby leads to relativism and nihilism, Cobb portrayed Whitehead's philosophy as distinctively postmodern by virtue of three features: its epistemology rejected the primacy of sense perception, its ontology replaced material substances with events having intrinsic value and internal relations, and these ideas were developed through reflections on problems in modern science.

Cobb restated his argument that Whitehead provides a postmodern vision in several subsequent writings,[3] most importantly in his 1975 book *Christ in a Pluralistic Age*, in which he enlarged his use of 'postmodern,' now employing it to refer to a pluralistic method and mind-set that goes beyond the idea of a single truth without falling into complete relativism.[4] Cobb's writings provided the stimulus for my own first use of the term in an essay on Cobb's theology written in 1972.[5]

Cobb was not the only one who was thinking of Whitehead's philosophy as postmodern. In the same year as Cobb's seminal essay (1964), Floyd Matson, who was also influenced by Whitehead, advocated a "postmodern science," by which he meant one that overcame mechanistic, reductionistic, and behaviorist approaches.[6] In 1973, a "post-modern science" was advocated at greater length and with more explication of Whitehead's position by Harold Schilling.[7] In that same year, Charles Altieri argued that it is Whitehead's philosophy, even more than Heidegger's, that best explains the connection between fact and value suggested by a number of American poets considered distinctively postmodern by Altieri.[8] And in a 1976 book subtitled *Resources for the Post-Modern World*, Frederick Ferré, besides following Schilling in speaking of the need for the kind of "post-modern science" provided by Whitehead, also suggested that Christian process theology presents a "post-modern version of Christianity" that could help overcome the ecological crisis engendered by modernity.[9]

Having long considered 1964 the year in which 'postmodern' began to be applied to the Whiteheadian approach, I subsequently learned that this application had actually been made as early as 1944. In that year, John Herman Randall Jr., writing of the emergence of "'post-modern' naturalistic philosophies," referred to Whitehead as "one of the pioneers" of this movement. The great advantage of this postmodern naturalism, said Randall, was that by rejecting the modern, mechanistic, reductionistic type of naturalism, it overcame the modern conflict of scientific naturalism with moral, aesthetic, and religious values[10]—a description that accords completely with the stated purpose of Whitehead's philosophy (SMW vi, 156, 185; PR 15).

In any case, whether the use of 'postmodern' to refer to Whiteheadian process philosophy is said to have begun in 1944 or 1964, it is ironic that some critics, understanding the term in light of meanings it took on in the 1980s, have considered the Whiteheadian use of the term opportunistic. Noteworthy in this regard is the fact that in a 1995 volume on early "postmodernism," in which Altieri's 1973 article was reprinted, editor Paul Bové's introductory essay draws attention to the great difference between this early postmodernism and the type of thought with which the term later became associated.[11]

We have here historical evidence that postmodernism is a genus with more than one species. In light of the fact that Whitehead's thought was being called "postmodern" long before the term became fashionable, it would very strange to argue that the application of the term to Whitehead's philosophy is illegitimate. But it would be equally strange to argue that the use of the term for the later type of postmodernism is illegitimate. Postmodernism needs to be understood as a generic phenomenon, which can and does have more than one species.

In any case, although the idea of Whiteheadian postmodernism can claim legitimacy by virtue of historical priority, the more important questions are substantive: Does thinking of Whiteheadian process philosophy as postmodern help to illuminate central doctrines of distinctively modern thought that have led to intractable problems? Do the central doctrines of Whitehead's philosophy provide a way to overcome these problems? I will suggest that an affirmative answer can be given to both questions. First, however, I need to address the widespread assumption that any philosophy that affirms the ideal of reason and engages in metaphysics is ipso facto not postmodern.

THE QUESTIONS OF METAPHYSICS AND RATIONALITY

Whereas Whitehead affirms the need for a metaphysical cosmology, "metaphysics" is one of the things that most discussions of postmodernism assume that we now are—or at least should be—beyond. This difference is to some extent terminological, in that many of the characterizations of "metaphysics" presupposed in this widespread rejection do not apply to Whitehead's thought.

Many postmodernists, for example, presuppose the Kantian conception, according to which metaphysics is the attempt to talk about things beyond all possible experience. Whitehead, by contrast, understood metaphysics as the endeavor to construct a coherent scheme of ideas "in terms of which every element of our experience can be interpreted," adding that the "elucidation of immediate experience is the sole justification for any thought" (PR 3, 4).

Sometimes metaphysics is understood as an approach that necessarily does violence to experience for the sake of a tidy system. But Whitehead, who praised the intellectual life of William James as one long "protest against the dismissal of experience in the interest of system" (MT 3), insisted repeatedly on the need to consider the "whole of the evidence" and *every* type of experience, adding that "[n]othing can be omitted" (SMW vii, 187; AI 226).

Thinkers influenced by Martin Heidegger sometimes portray metaphysics as necessarily committed to the domination of nature. Whitehead's metaphysical analysis, however, led him to say that our experience of actuality is "a value experience. Its basic expression is—Have a care, here is something that matters!" (MT 116).

Still another reason for rejecting metaphysical systems is that they allegedly claim to attain certainty. But Whitehead regarded a metaphysical system as a tentative hypothesis, an "experimental adventure," adding that "the merest hint of dogmatic certainty as to finality of statement is an exhibition of folly" (PR 8, 9, xiv). Closely related is the widespread assumption that metaphysics is necessarily "foundationalist" in the sense now widely discredited, according to which the philosopher begins with a few indubitable basic beliefs, from which all other beliefs are to be deduced. Whitehead, however, explicitly rejected the idea "that metaphysical thought started from principles which were individually clear, distinct, and certain" (FR 49).

Nevertheless, although most of the apparent differences between Whiteheadians and other types of postmodernists can be dismissed in these ways, a real difference does remain. Whitehead's philosophical work was oriented around the conviction that we must and can reconcile religion and reason, which in our time largely means religion and science. Whitehead, in fact, said that philosophy's most important task is to show how religion and the sciences—natural and social—can be integrated into a coherent worldview (PR 15). Many other postmodernists, by contrast, reject any attempt at a comprehensive account of things, whether the attempt be called a "metaphysics," a "metanarrative," or something else, considering all such attempts to be ideological efforts to impose one's will on others. Whiteheadian postmodernists, while recognizing that every attempt at a comprehensive account will involve distortions due to ignorance and bias, deny that the very effort to engage in such thinking necessarily involves hegemonial intentions.[12] They argue, furthermore, that the human need for stories or narratives orienting us to reality as a whole cannot be removed by declaration.[13]

The differences here involve fundamentally different ideas about modernity's fatal flaw. While these other postmodernists see modernity as afflicted by rationalistic pretensions, Whitehead regarded modernity as an essentially *antirational* enterprise. Whitehead's view here depended on his conviction that the ideas that we inevitably presume in practice should be taken as the ultimate criteria for rational thought. "Rationalism," said Whitehead, "is the search for the coherence of such presumptions" (PR 153). Rationalism, thus understood, is not opposed to empiricism. It is simply the attempt to combine into a self-consistent theory all the ideas that we find inevitably presupposed in our experience—ideas that I have come to call "hard-core commonsense ideas."

A precedent-setting instance of modern antirationalism was Hume's acknowledgment that in living he necessarily presupposed various ideas, such as a real world and causal influence, that could find no place in his philosophical theory. Whitehead argues that rather than resting content with a philosophical theory that had to be supplemented by an appeal to "practice," Hume should have revised his philosophy until it included all the inevitable presuppositions of practice of which he was aware (PR 13).

The reason that it is antirational to deny in theory ideas that one necessarily presupposes in practice is that one thereby violates the first rule of reason, the law of noncontradiction. It is irrational simultaneously to affirm and deny one and the same proposition. And this is what happens when one denies a hard-core commonsense idea. That is, one is denying the idea explicitly while affirming it implicitly. This point has been made by Karl-Otto Apel and Jürgen Habermas in their critique of "performative contradiction," in which the very act of performing a speech act contradicts its semantic content, its meaning.[14]

Let us take, for example, our assumption that we live in a real world, consisting of other things and other people. Hume agreed that he could not help presupposing this in practice. As a philosopher, however, he said that he had to remain skeptical, because his theory provided no basis for affirming a real world. Let us assume then that Hume told an audience that he was a solipsist—that, as far as he knew, he was the only actual being, with everything and everyone else being mere elements in his imagination, like characters and things in a dream. In saying that to other people, Hume would have shown by the very fact of addressing them that he did not really doubt their existence. The meaning of his statement would have been contradicted by the very act of making it. Such a self-contradiction is "absolutely self-refuting" in the sense clarified by John Passmore: "The proposition *p* is absolutely self-refuting, if to assert *p* is equivalent to asserting *both p and not-p*."[15]

It is impossible, accordingly, for one to deny the existence of a real world beyond oneself without being guilty of this kind of self-refuting inconsistency. The same is true of all our other hard-core commonsense ideas.

OVERCOMING PROBLEMATIC MODERN ASSUMPTIONS

From a Whiteheadian perspective, it lies at the heart of the task of postmodern thinking to overcome the assumptions that led to the modern dualism between the ideas affirmed in theory and those presupposed in practice. The crucial assumptions are the *sensationist view of perception*, according to which our sensory organs provide our only means of perceiving things beyond ourselves, and the *mechanistic view of nature*, according to which the ultimate units of nature are devoid of all experience, intrinsic value, internal purpose, and internal relations. It is these correlative ideas that led to the modern divorce of theoretical from practical reason and thereby to the Humean-Kantian conviction that metaphysics, which would show how the two sets of ideas can be integrated into a self-consistent worldview, is impossible.

Causation, the World, the Past, and Time

The sensationist theory of perception is responsible for many of the problems, including those involving causation, a real world, and a real past. With regard to causation, Hume famously pointed out that although we have usually thought of causation as involving some sort of *necessary connection* between the cause and the effect because the "cause" is thought to exert *real influence* on the "effect," sensory data provide no basis for this idea, so that causation, to be an empirical concept, must be redefined to mean simply *constant correlation* between two types of phenomena. Although Hume continued to presuppose in practice that causation involves real influence—that his wine glass moved to his lips because he used his hand to lift it—he said that he qua philosopher could not employ that meaning.

Hume even said, as mentioned earlier, that he as philosopher could not affirm the reality of the world. He could not help, he pointed out, being a realist in everyday life, necessarily presupposing that he lived in a world with other people and things, such as tables and food. According to his analysis of perception, however, he did not perceive such things but only sense data, such as colors and shapes. As a philosopher, therefore, he had to be a solipsist, doubting the existence of an external world, even though in practice, including the practice of using a pen to record his skeptical ideas on paper, he had no doubts.

At the outset of the twentieth century, George Santayana showed that the Humean brand of empiricism leads not simply to solipsism but also to "solipsism of the present moment."[16] That is, because sense perception reveals only various data immediately present to our consciousness, he concluded, we must be agnostic about the reality of the past and therefore of time.

Empiricist philosophy was said, accordingly, to be unable to support four of the most fundamental presuppositions of the empirical sciences—the reality of causal influence, the reality of time, the reality of the past, and even the reality of the world as such. Having no basis for saying that causal relations observed in the past will hold true in the future, this kind of empiricist philosophy obviously could not justify the principle of induction. Much postmodernism has drawn the conclusion that science, generally taken to be the paradigm of rationality, is itself rationally groundless.

Normative Values

The sensationist version of empiricism leads to the same conclusion about normative values. Philosophers had traditionally affirmed the existence of logical, aesthetic, and moral norms. Sensory perception, however, can provide no access to such norms. Early modern philosophers, such as John Locke and Francis Hutcheson, said that we know such norms because they were divinely revealed (Locke) or because they were divinely implanted in our minds (Hutcheson). But late modernity, having rejected supernatural explanations, concluded that all such norms are our own creations. Most forms of postmodernism have emphasized the implications of this conclusion, saying that we must regard even our most basic moral convictions as local conventions with no rational grounding, even while continuing to presuppose, in the very act of writing such things, that various moral norms—such as the idea that we should not repress "difference" and oppress the "other"—are universally valid. The apparent necessity to presuppose various ideas even while criticizing them is sometimes justified by referring to them as "transcendental illusions" in the Kantian sense.[17]

Whitehead on Causation, the World, the Past, and Time

Whiteheadian postmodernism, rather than accepting the inevitability of such contradictions, follows the "radical empiricism" of William James in rejecting the sensationist view of perception. At the heart of Whitehead's epistemology is a deconstruction of sensory perception, showing it to be a hybrid composed of two pure modes of perception. Hume and most subsequent philosophy noticed only "perception in the mode of presentational immediacy," in which sense data are immediately present to the mind. If this were our only mode of perception, we would indeed be doomed to solipsism of the present moment. But this mode of perception, Whitehead argues at great length—much of *Process and Reality* and virtually all of *Symbolism* are devoted to this point—is derivative from a more fundamental mode, "perception in the mode of causal efficacy." In this more fundamental mode, we directly perceive other actualities as exerting causal efficacy upon us—which explains why we know that other actualities exist and that causation is more than Humean constant conjunction. One example of this mode of perception, or "prehension," is our awareness that our sensory organs are causing us to have certain experiences, as when we are aware that we are seeing a tree *by means of* our eyes. Such prehension, while presupposed in sensory perception, is itself nonsensory. In seeing a tree, I do not see my brain cells or my eyes, but I do prehend them and hence the data they convey.

Another example of this nonsensory perception is our prehension of immediately prior moments of our own experience, through which we know the reality of the past and thereby of time.

This point depends on a third idea deconstructed by Whitehead. This is an idea about the things that are the most fundamental actual entities. Such actual entities, traditionally called "substances," are those things that are regarded as both actual and not analyzable into entities that are more fully actual. Whitehead rejected the idea, common to modern and premodern Western thought (although rejected long ago by Buddhists), that the world's most fundamental actual entities, or substances, are individuals that endure through time. According to Whitehead's alternative account, an enduring individual, such as an electron, a living cell, or a human soul, is analyzable into *momentary* actual entities, which he calls "actual occasions."

To remember a previous moment of one's own experience, therefore, is to prehend an actual entity that is numerically different from the actual occasion that is doing the remembering (AI 220–21). This prehension of previous occasions of our own experience gives us our idea of time. Modern and (non-Buddhist) premodern thought, by regarding the soul or mind as numerically one through time, had blinded philosophers to the primary experiential basis for our category of time.

The significance of these explanations of the origin of our basic categories, such as *time, causality,* and *actuality* (which combines the Kantian categories of *existence* and *substance*), would be hard to overstate. Besides the fact that Hume denied the empirical basis for these concepts, Kant's "Copernican revolution," which lies behind most forms of idealism, phenomenology, structuralism, poststructuralism, and postmodernism, was based on the need to explain such categories while assuming, with Hume, the sensationist doctrine of perception.

Whitehead on Norms and Scientism

Equally important to the distinction between Whitehead-based and Kant-based forms of postmodernism is the fact that Whitehead, by insisting on the reality of nonsensory perception, allows our apparent awareness of normative values to be accepted as genuine. Our moral and aesthetic discourse, accordingly, can be regarded as *cognitive*, capable of being true or false (or somewhere in between). This fact—that the Whitehead-based type of postmodernism affirms, while the other type denies, our direct apprehension of normative ideals, such as truth, beauty, and justice—is the most important difference between them in relation to social-political-cultural issues.

The distinction between Kant-based and Whitehead-based forms of postmodernism is fundamental to the question of the appropriate strategy for overcoming modern scientism. Kantian forms of postmodernism, such as Richard Rorty's, put moral and aesthetic discourse on the same level with scientific discourse by denying that either type tells us about reality. This denial supports the widespread equation of postmodernism with an antiscience bias. Whiteheadian postmodernism, by contrast, achieves parity by showing how all three types of discourse can express real, if partial, truths about the nature of things—partial truths it is the cultural role of philosophy to harmonize.

Freedom

Whereas the sensationist view of perception led to contradictions between theory and practice with regard to realism, causation, the past, time, and normative values, the mechanistic view of nature led to such a contradiction with regard to freedom. Early modernity reconciled human freedom with the mechanistic view of nature by means of a Cartesian soul, different in kind from the stuff of which the body is composed. However, the relation of such a soul to its body could only be explained—Descartes, Malebranche, Thomas Reid, and many others agreed—by means of a Supernatural Coordinator. As William James said: "For thinkers of that age, 'God' was the great solvent of all absurdities."[18]

The late modern demise of supernaturalism, accordingly, entailed the transmutation of Cartesian dualism into a full-fledged materialism, in which the soul, mind, or self is taken to be merely a property, or at best an epiphenomenon, of the body's brain, not an entity with any agency of its own. Whatever the "self" is, it has no power of *self*-determination. Freedom must be denied or—which comes to the same thing—redefined to make it compatible with determinism. Some late modern philosophers explicitly admit that they must continue to presuppose freedom in practice while not being able to make sense of it in theory.[19] Much postmodernism accentuates this contradiction, proclaiming the "disappearance of the (centered) self" while exhorting us to use our freedom to overcome oppressive views and practices.

Whiteheadian postmodernism, instead of accepting materialism or antirationalism or returning to early modern dualism, rejects the mechanistic view of nature at the root of these stances. Its alternative view—again, anticipated by

James[20]—is panexperientialism, according to which experience and thereby spontaneity, intrinsic value, and internal relations go all the way down to the most primitive units of nature. Besides referring to actual entities as actual "occasions," accordingly, Whitehead also calls them "occasions of experience." On the basis of this panexperientialism, the unanswerable questions faced by materialists as well as dualists—*Where* and *how* did things with experience, spontaneity, intrinsic value, and internal relations emerge out of bits of matter wholly devoid of these?—need not be asked. Evolution involves real emergence, but it is the emergence of higher types of spontaneous experience out of lower types.

All such doctrines, usually under the name *panpsychism*, have been widely rejected as patently absurd. Such rejections often rest on characterizations that do not apply to Whiteheadian-Hartshornean panexperientialism. Critics rightly say, for example, that it would be absurd to attribute any freedom and thereby any experience to sticks and stones. But it is essential to the Whiteheadian-Hartshornean position, the more complete characterization of which is "panexperientialism with organizational duality," to distinguish between aggregational organizations, which as such have no experience or spontaneity, and "compound individuals," which do.[21]

Even after becoming aware of this distinction, however, modern thinkers tend to consider panexperientialism to be obviously false—a fact that suggests that one of modernity's most basic assumptions is being challenged. The same is true of the Jamesian-Whiteheadian endorsement of nonsensory perception, as evidenced by the fact that most admiring treatments of James's thought virtually ignore the fact that he endorsed the reality of telepathy and devoted much of his time to psychical research.[22] In any case, these distinctively postmodern views about being and perceiving, besides solving various philosophical problems, also provide the basis for a distinctive type of postmodernism.

WHITEHEAD'S PHILOSOPHY AND THE DOMINANT IMAGE OF POSTMODERNISM

'Postmodernism' is commonly associated with a wide variety of ideas that together constitute what can be called the "dominant image" of postmodernism. Whiteheadian postmodern thought exemplifies this dominant image in many respects. It rejects foundationalism and with it the quest for certainty. It accepts the need to deconstruct a wide range of received ideas, including the substantial self, history as having a predetermined end, and the "ontotheological" idea of God (in which a Supreme Being is identified with Being Itself). It seeks, moreover, to foster pluralism and diversity, both human and ecological.

But the Whiteheadian type of postmodernism also involves many radical differences from the dominant image of postmodernism. For example, whereas most postmodernists speak derisively of the "correspondence theory of truth" and the idea of language as "referential," Whiteheadian philosophers defend these notions, partly by pointing out that their denials lead to performative contradictions, partly by showing how Whitehead's philosophy, with its panexperientialist ontology and nonsensationist view of perception, overcomes the standard objections, as shown in chapter 5 of this book.[23]

Other differences are implicit in the differing ideas about just which distinctively "modern" ideas and practices need to be overcome. One extreme view is that a genuinely postmodern view must overcome *all* modern ideas and practices. This extreme idea is rarely if ever explicitly stated, but it is implicit in many critiques, in which a particular position calling itself postmodern is said not to be *really* postmodern because it still affirms X, Y, and Z, all of which are modern ideas.

At least most forms of postmodern thought, however, portray themselves as involving a critique of some of modernity's *pernicious* ideas and concerns, with the intent thereby to defend and extend modernity's *valuable* ideas and concerns. For example, in a summary account of my own Whiteheadian position, I speak of the need for an emancipation from modernity but then add: "The term *postmodern*, however, by contrast with *premodern*, emphasizes that the modern world has produced unparalleled advances that must not be lost in a general revulsion against its negative features."[24]

One of these advances, especially emphasized in Jürgen Habermas's defense of modernity, is its aspiration to universal human liberation. Habermas rejects postmodernism in large part because the versions of it with which he is familiar undercut the conceptual basis for this aspiration. Whitehead's philosophy, as I show in chapter 7, recovers this basis—while also providing, as chapter 4 shows, the basis for a more inclusive, ecological liberation.

Another modern advance, which Franklin Gamwell has labeled "the modern commitment," is the insistence that ideas are no longer to be accepted on the basis of authority but are instead to be defended solely on the basis of experience and reason.[25] Whitehead's defense of empirical rationalism is an exemplification of that commitment.

In light of its strong agreement with these two modern emphases, in fact, the Whiteheadian position could well be called "postmodern modernism."

Another feature of Whiteheadian process philosophy that differentiates it from the dominant image of postmodernism is its theism—which, as chapter 7 shows, is essential to its defense of the objectivity of moral norms. Some postmodernists seem to take it as self-evident that a position that is theistic could not be appropriately called "postmodern." From a Whiteheadian perspective, however, the decline of theism is based partly on the fact that early modern theism retained a premodern idea of God—one that could *not* be defended on the basis of experience and reason—and partly on modernity's mechanistic idea of nature and its sensationist version of empiricism. From a Whiteheadian perspective, therefore, the return to theism—albeit of a significantly different type, best called "panentheism"—is part and parcel of the overcoming of modernity's fatal flaws, flaws that prevented the development of a worldview that could be defended in terms of the ideals of rational empiricism (or empirical rationalism). Chapter 9 deals with the question of the rational need for, and defensibility of, the kind of theism to which Whitehead pointed.

As indicated at the outset of this chapter, the fact that Whitehead provides the basis for a "postmodern science" has been central to references to his philosophy as postmodern from the beginning. This concern to develop a postmodern framework for science is partly for the sake of reconciling science with our moral, aesthetic, and religious intuitions. But it is also for the sake of science itself. This twofold point is developed most fully in chapters 3 through 6. At the center of these chapters is the idea of panexperientialism.

The appendix shows that Whitehead's "subjectivist principle," the correct interpretation of which had long baffled Whitehead scholars (including myself), most basically refers to Descartes' famous "subjectivist bias." This chapter also shows that Whitehead's argument was that if the implications of this subjectivist turn are properly thought through, we are led to panexperientialism. This argument hence says that panexperientialism, the central ontological idea of postmodern philosophy (of this type), is implicit in the methodological turn introduced by Descartes, the generally recognized founder of modern philosophy. Descartes and his modernist successors could not see this implication, of course, because of other assumptions they held. But once those assumptions are relinquished, we can see that the step from a modern to a postmodern worldview is not as great as it had seemed.

2

Whitehead's Philosophy and the Enlightenment

Charles Hartshorne, reflecting upon the fact that Whitehead said that we need a New Reformation, added: "We need a New Enlightenment."[1] In this chapter, I argue that Whitehead's philosophy—as Hartshorne would have agreed—provides the basis for a new enlightenment, one that actually illumines our experience more than it obscures it. This argument requires reflection upon the relation of Whitehead's philosophy to the seventeenth-and-eighteenth-century intellectual movement to which the label "the enlightenment" usually refers. Because this movement is generally regarded as definitive of distinctively modern thought, the idea of being "postmodern" is generally thought to involve being "postenlightenment." I will, accordingly, discuss the extent to which Whiteheadian philosophy—here often called simply "process philosophy"—reflects enlightenment assumptions and the extent to which it rejects them. More pointedly: Is process philosophy basically proenlightenment or antienlightenment? Is it better understood as a present-day instance of enlightenment philosophy or as part of the present-day revolt against enlightenment philosophies?

No quick and easy answer to this question is possible. This is so partly because the movement generally referred to as "the enlightenment" was an extremely complex movement with many dimensions, some of which were in tension with others. Because of this complexity, every characterization of the "essence of the enlightenment" is necessarily subjective, involving selection bias as well as value judgments. If this is true of well-informed, richly nuanced portrayals, such as those of Ernst Cassirer and Peter Gay,[2] it is all the more true of those brief characterizations involved in blanket endorsements of the enlightenment, which were still common only a few decades ago,[3] or blanket rejections, which are common today. To say whether process philosophy is more pro- or

15

antienlightenment, accordingly, requires specifying which dimensions of the movement, and under what characterization, are in view. I will lay out my perspective in terms of seven features that have been widely thought to characterize the enlightenment: ontological naturalism, epistemic naturalism, empiricism, rationalism (including foundationalism), individualism, belief in universal truths and values, and belief in progress. First, however, it is necessary to pave the way for understanding the enlightenment by seeing it in historical context.

THE ENLIGHTENMENT IN HISTORICAL CONTEXT

The enlightenment, although recognized to be a historical movement in the sense of having occurred in Europe in the seventeenth and eighteenth centuries, is often otherwise portrayed in ahistorical terms. In particular, insofar as it is regarded as a movement involving naturalism, rationalism, and empiricism, it is often portrayed as if it involved an emphasis upon reason, nature, and empiricism *in general*, rather than reason based upon *nature and experience understood in highly specific ways*. Widely recognized, to be sure, is the fact that the enlightenment was based upon the rise of "the new mechanical philosophy" in the seventeenth century. But the rise of this philosophy is often understood naively, as if it had been derived inductively from the unbiased perception of empirical facts. And, insofar as the emergence of this new worldview is recognized to have involved a battle, the only opponent has generally been understood to have been a decrepit Aristotelianism. In recent decades, however, historians of the period have provided a new understanding of the rise of the "modern scientific worldview," thereby affording us a better grasp of some of the distinctive assumptions of the enlightenment.

The Three-Cornered Battle of the Worldviews

At the root of this new understanding is the recognition that the proponents of the mechanistic view of nature had been battling even more vigorously against a third movement, which arose out of Neoplatonic, Hermetic, and Cabalistic (also spelled Kabbalistic) traditions. For example, Brian Easlea, referring to these Neoplatonic-magical-spiritualist movements as simply the "magical cosmologies," argues against the old idea that the mechanical cosmology simply took the place of a crumbling Aristotelian cosmology:

> [P]rotagonists of very different and rival cosmologies engag[ed] in a bitter and protracted struggle for supremacy, both with each other and

against the entrenched proponents of Aristotelian-Thomistic cosmology. "Modern science" emerged, at least in part, out of a three-cornered contest between proponents of the established view and adherents of newly prospering magical cosmologies, both to be opposed in the seventeenth century by advocates of revived mechanical world views. Scholastic Aristotelianism versus magic versus mechanical philosophies.[4]

In giving a summary of this "three-cornered contest,"[5] I will focus on the victory of the mechanistic tradition over the Neoplatonic-magical-spiritualist tradition. Although these two traditions had some features in common against Aristotelianism, especially the twofold emphasis on experimentation and the importance of mathematics, I will focus on their differences, which can be grouped under three main headings: the relation of God to the world, the possibility of influence at a distance, and the relation between God's "two books" (Nature and Scripture).

The Relation of God to the World: Those in the Neoplatonic-magical-spiritualist traditions generally held an animistic view of nature, according to which it is replete with aims, powers, sympathies, and antipathies. Part and parcel of this conception was their account of the human being as a microcosm. They generally portrayed deity as present in the world and the world as present in deity, with this idea sometimes understood more pantheistically, sometimes more panentheistically. And they generally regarded the behavior of things as rooted in their divine or divinely implanted powers. All of these ideas were rejected by the representatives of the view of nature that was to become victorious, which Eugene Klaaren has called the "legal-mechanical" view, because it combined the mechanism of the Greek atomists, especially Democritus, with legal ideas of nature based upon the voluntarist theologians, such as Scotus, Occam, and Calvin. "Legal" points to the idea that the order of nature was said to be due entirely to divinely imposed laws.[6]

From this perspective, Robert Boyle, used by Klaaren as the main bridge from the voluntarist theological tradition to the legal-mechanical philosophy of nature, believed that the views of the spiritualists involved the worst of all intellectual errors, confusing God and the world. Against the view that God is present in all things, Boyle said that God cannot be unified with matter.[7] Against the view, common to spiritualists and Aristotelians, that creatures have "internal principles of motion," Boyle said that these "vulgar" views make nature "almost divine." Rather than motion being inherent in matter, Boyle insisted, the laws of motion exist only as imposed by God.[8] All of this imposed motion, furthermore, is *loco*motion, as opposed to internally motivated becoming. Although God causes some things to act *as if* they had appetition, they in reality do not.[9] The world's order, in short, manifests no inherent rationality but is completely imposed by the arbitrary fiat of God.[10] Only this view, Boyle held, respects the absolute difference between the creator and the created, the absolute transcendence of God over the world.

This absolute transcendence meant that, some spiritualists to the contrary, God is not the soul of the world but is completely transcendent over it, having created it ex nihilo. For example, Isaac Newton, Boyle's follower in many respects, said that God "governs all things, not as the soul of the world, but as Lord over all; . . . *Deity* is the dominion of God not over his own body, as those imagine who fancy God to be the soul of the world, but over servants."[11]

The Possibility of Influence at a Distance: A central feature of the Neoplatonic-magical-spiritualist traditions, from which the designation "magical" partly derives, was the idea that nature has the inherent capacity, perhaps on the basis of "sympathies" and "antipathies," to exert influence at a distance. Gravitational attraction seemed an obvious example, and Gilbert's discoveries with regard to magnetism occurred within this tradition. No aspect of this tradition was more strongly rejected by the mechanical philosophers. For example, Descartes wrote that "nothing is more absurd than the assumption . . . that a certain property is inherent in each of the parts of the world's matter and that, by the force of this property, the parts are carried towards one another and attract each other."[12] According to Descartes' mechanistic view, by contrast, "there exist no occult forces in stones or plants, no amazing and marvellous sympathies and antipathies, in fact there exists nothing in the whole of nature which cannot be explained in terms of purely corporeal causes, totally devoid of mind and thought."[13] This denial of influence at a distance, far from being an incidental feature of the mechanists' view, lay at its heart: "[T]he fundamental tenet of Descartes' mechanical philosophy of nature," says Richard Westfall, was "that one body can act on another only by direct contact."[14]

This rejection of influence at a distance usually involved the denial of non-sensory perception. Given a dualistic view of human beings, this denial did not follow logically: the idea that matter operated only by contact left open the possibility that the mind, being different in kind, might be able to perceive noncontiguous things, such as other minds, directly, rather than only through the mediation of the body. Nevertheless, the dominant view among dualists, including both rationalists such as Descartes and empiricists such as Locke, was to affirm that all perception of actualities beyond ourselves is by means of our sensory organs.

The Relation between God's Two Books: These substantive differences were partly rooted in a formal difference about method. Against the Aristotelian theologians, who distinguished absolutely between *natural* theology, based on (universal) experience and reason, and *revealed* theology, based solely on Scripture, those in the Neoplatonic-magical-spiritual traditions generally advocated interpreting God's "two books" (Nature and Scripture) in terms of each other, so as to produce a unified, "pansophist" view. They were very critical of the refusal of the medieval Aristotelian philosophers to develop a "Christian philosophy." Those in the mechanical tradition, by contrast, tended to side with the two-level approach of the Aristotelians. Boyle, holding with Francis Bacon that the two books are to be kept separate, said that theology is to be based on Scripture alone, not diluted with natural philosophy, and that theologians are not, on the basis of Scriptural revelation, to interfere with natural philosophy.[15]

Why the Legal-Mechanical Movement Won

Now that we have before us these differences between the two movements, we need to ask: why did the legal-mechanical view emerge victorious? Although the usual assumption has been that it did so because its views were obviously superior, a historical investigation shows that this is not so. The main reason for the victory of the legal-mechanical view, now commonplace among historians of the period, is summarized by Easlea: "[T]he victory of this extraordinary [mechanical] philosophy over its equally extraordinary rival cannot be understood in terms of the relative explanatory successes of each basic cosmology but rather in terms of the fortunes of the social forces identified with each cosmology."[16] This answer, in a nutshell, is that the legal-mechanical view won the battle of the worldviews because it seemed to support the social-political-economic status quo and thereby the interests of the wealthy and the powerful, whereas the worldview of the Neoplatonic-magical-spiritualist traditions seemed to threaten those interests.

This latter tradition became associated in the public mind with the intent to "turn the world upside down."[17] In some cases, the intent to do this was explicit. For example, Paracelsus, who advocated a general spiritual and social reformation, supported the peasants' uprising of 1525.[18] More generally, Morris Berman says, "ties between occult and revolutionary thought can be seen in a whole spectrum of leading radicals." The essential point, however, is that whatever the actual influence of "occult" and "enthusiastic" beliefs on the lower classes and radical groups, this association was widely made, especially by representatives of the establishment. "[T]he popular impression that communism, libertinism, heresy, and Hermeticism were part of some vast conspiracy," reports Berman, "is amply documented in the numerous statements made on the subject by clergymen."[19]

Much of the polemic against this tradition was carried on at the theological level. However, the idea that this worldview was a threat to the status quo, with its social, political, economic, and ecclesiastical hierarchies, underlay most of the theological reasons for preferring the legal-mechanical view. I will illustrate this point with regard to three notions of the alternative view that were rejected by the legal-mechanical school: self-moving matter, influence at a distance, and nonsensory perception.

The Rejection of Self-Moving Matter: The animistic idea of matter as self-moving was threatening to belief in both a transcendent God and an immortal soul. With regard to the former, some thinkers argued that the world, being composed of self-moving parts, could be a self-organizing whole. In other words, rather than having been ordered by an external creator, the world could have ordered itself. Sometimes the resulting worldview was atheistic, thereby confirming the widespread association of animism with the atheism of Epicurus;[20] sometimes it was pantheistic; and sometimes it was closer to what today would be called "panentheism." Denied, in any case, was the wholly transcendent deity who had created the world ex nihilo and therefore exercised absolute dominion over it. In these alternative cosmologies, there was no place for a God who, having created a heaven with arbitrary admission standards, had then, with equal arbitrariness, given the "keys to the kingdom" to a particular institution, delegating to it the power to guarantee admission to its faithful, obedient members while consigning others to hell. The immanent deity of the pantheists and panentheists, furthermore, could be directly experienced by the masses, not known only through the ecclesiastical hierarchy. Given the almost universal assumption that the authority of the government depended upon the support of the church with its power over people's extramundane status, we can understand why this worldview was threatening to those who favored stability in terms of the social-political-economic status quo. What would prevent rebellion if the church were no longer regarded as having such power?

    The belief that the church had such power depended, of course, not only on the belief in a transcendent, voluntaristic deity, but also on the belief that the soul *would have* an extramundane existence. The animistic view of matter was seen as threatening to this belief as well. The main argument for the belief in life after death had been the Platonic idea that the soul, unlike the matter of which the body is composed, is self-moving. Given this idea, the fact that the body decomposes at death provides no reason to think that the same fate awaits the soul, because its unique power of self-motion shows it to be different in kind from the matter making up the body. This argument was undermined by the idea that matter is self-moving: if matter is self-moving and yet decomposes, the fact that the soul is a self-moving thing provides no reason to think it will not also decompose. Not all advocates of this position actually denied life after death. Some simply pointed back to Pietro Pomponazzi (1462–1525), whose treatise *On the Immortality of the Soul* argued that the doctrine of the soul's immortality, while valuable for maintaining social order, can be affirmed only on the basis of faith, not reason.[21] But some thinkers, such as Henry Stubbe, explicitly affirmed mortalism as part of a comprehensive attack on traditional Christianity.[22]

To many of those wanting to defend a transcendent creator and an immortal soul against these threats, the mechanistic idea of matter seemed a godsend. With regard to a transcendent creator, for example, Boyle wrote: "[S]ince motion does not essentially belong to matter..., the motions of all bodies, at least at the beginnings of things, ... were impressed upon them, ... by an external immaterial agent, God."[23] Newton, having pointed out that inertia is merely a passive principle, declared: "By this Principle alone there never could have been any Motion in the World. Some other Principle was necessary for putting Bodies into Motion." The necessity of thinking of matter as moved by "certain active Principles," Newton added, leads to the conclusion that there is "a powerful ever-living Agent" who "in the Beginning form'd Matter in solid, massy, hard, impenetrable, moveable Particles."[24]

The mechanical view of matter was seen as equally helpful with regard to defending the soul's immortality. By portraying matter as wholly insentient and inert, it showed clearly that one's mind or soul, being conscious and self-moving, must be different in kind from the matter comprising one's body. The fact that the body decayed after death, therefore, was no reason to think that the soul would too. This argument, formulated by Boyle,[25] among others, was evidently central to the conversion of Walter Charleton, a Royalist physician, who had written three books reflecting magical ideas. Later, saying that atheists plotted to "undermine the received belief in an omnipotent *eternal being*, to murder *the immortality of the Soul* (the basis of all religion) and to deride the *Compensation of good and evil actions after death*," Charleton renounced his magical views in favor of Cartesianism.[26]

Descartes himself had connected his radical dualism between matter and the human mind to belief in the "compensation of good and evil actions after death." Having stated the conservative conviction that "present institutions are practically always more tolerable than would be a change in them," he asked why people rebel against divinely appointed rulers. His answer was that "after the error of those who deny God ..., there is none that leads weak minds further from the straight path of virtue than that of imagining that the souls of beasts are of the same nature as ours, and hence that after the present life we have nothing to fear or to hope for, any more than flies or ants."[27] Although many mechanists were uncomfortable with Descartes' particular way of formulating the dualism between mind and matter, his more general point—that the mechanistic view of nature supports the teaching of the church and thereby the social, political, economic status quo—was widely appreciated.

The Rejection of Influence at a Distance: The fact that the mechanistic philosophy also denied to nature the inherent capacity to exert or receive influence at a distance is equally important for explaining its victory. This importance can be seen in relation to arguments about miracles, God, and witchcraft.

The miracles of the New Testament, and for Roman Catholics the miracles in the lives of the saints, had provided the main evidence that Christianity, alone among the religions of the world, had been ordained by God as *the* vehicle of ultimate truth and salvation. Without the evidence of divine favor provided by these supernatural interventions, the church's claim to possess the keys to the kingdom would have seemed groundless. This evidence would have been undermined, of course, if it had been concluded that the miracles did not happen. But it would also have been undermined if it was believed that the miracles could be given a naturalistic interpretation. The latter was argued by some of those who considered the power to exert and receive influence at a distance to be a natural capacity. For example, Thomas Fludd and later Henry Stubbe argued that the miracles of Jesus and the apostles were not different in kind from extraordinary occurrences that have been performed in non-Christian religious traditions.[28]

This issue was fundamental to the introduction of the mechanistic philosophy into France. Fr. Marin Mersenne, having come to see the magical tradition as "public enemy number one" by virtue of its denial of the supernatural character of the Christian miracles,[29] published in 1623 a critique of the Hermetic-Cabalistic-Paracelsian philosophy. His critique dealt especially with Giordano Bruno, whom he called "one of the wickedest men whom the earth has ever supported...who seems to have invented a new manner of philosophizing only in order to make underhand attacks on the Christian religion," and Thomas Fludd, whom he called "Bruno's vile successor and principal enemy of Christian religion."[30] When Fludd replied, Mersenne, realizing that he needed an alternative system to defeat Fludd's Cabalistic philosophy, appealed to Pierre Gassendi, who introduced him to the Democritean mechanistic philosophy, which had recently been revived in Italy by Galileo.[31] Seeing that this mechanistic philosophy denied influence at a distance even more clearly than did Aristotelianism, Mersenne enthusiastically adopted it, employing it to defend the supernatural character of the Christian miracles.[32]

This debate was replayed later in the century in England. Stubbe's attempt to give a naturalistic explanation for the biblical miracles depended, Boyle said, upon his false view of an "animated and intelligent universe."[33] Against all such attempts, Boyle recommended the mechanical philosophy, saying that people who accept it will "frankly acknowledge, and heartily believe, divers effects to be truly miraculous, that may be plausibly ascribed to other causes in the vulgar philosophy." Given the importance of this issue to Boyle, we can understand why he so often stressed, against the "vulgar philosophy," that matter interacts only by contact.[34]

The rejection of a natural capacity for action at a distance was also, in conjunction with the phenomenon of gravitation, used to provide another argument for a transcendent deity, as illustrated by Richard Bentley, an admirer of Newton. Bentley was coached by Newton to reject the Epicurean idea that gravitation is "innate, inherent, and essential to matter," which would imply that "inanimate brute matter should . . . operate upon and affect other matter without mutual contact." Having learned his lessons well, Bentley argued that "mutual gravitation or spontaneous attraction can neither be inherent and essential to matter, nor ever supervene to it, unless impressed and infused into it by a divine power." The phenomenon of gravitation, Bentley concluded, provides "a new and invincible argument for the being of God, being a direct and positive proof that an immaterial living mind doth inform and actuate the dead matter."[35]

The witch craze, which was arguably the chief social problem of the sixteenth and seventeenth centuries, provided yet another reason for favoring the mechanical philosophy of nature, with its denial of the possibility of influence at a distance. Given the association of action at a distance with the Neoplatonic-magical-spiritualist philosophy, the desire of humane people to put an end to the witch hunts led to revulsion against that philosophy. This reaction was actually unfair. What made witchcraft an "exceptional crime," worthy of an inquisition, was the charge that the extraordinary powers attributed to witches to do harm resulted from a pact with the devil.[36] The magical tradition, affirming influence at a distance as a natural capacity, had no need for this satanic hypothesis. Also, many of the chief critics of the persecutions were adherents of the magical tradition. In the public mind, nevertheless, the idea of witchcraft was associated with this worldview, and this guilt by association undermined its image.[37] The spread of the mechanistic worldview of Mersenne and Descartes, by contrast, was associated with the ending of the witch persecutions, so its image was enhanced.[38]

The Rejection of Nonsensory Perception: The rejection of nonsensory perception, about which the mechanists agreed with the Aristotelians against the magical philosophies, was involved in several of the issues discussed above. The denial that one could contact Satan or other "demons" was often based on a sensationalist doctrine of perception, according to which all perception is by means of the physical sensory organs. Likewise, the defense of the supernatural character of some of the Christian miracles, such as Jesus' knowledge of the contents of other minds, presupposed that human beings have no natural capacity for nonsensory perception. Finally, the affirmation of a wholly transcendent deity, in place of a divine reality that is immanent in the world, was often part and parcel of the rejection of "enthusiastic" sects, which affirmed God's direct presence in the human mind. This rejection of "enthusiasm" and "mysticism" was supported by the limitation of perception to sensory perception.

It is in the light of the above considerations that I stress the fact that the enlightenment did not involve simply an emphasis upon experience, reason, and nature in some vague, general sense. Rather, being based upon a worldview that had only recently vanquished its foes, it involved a very definite, even polemical, understanding of the nature of nature and the nature of experience. Enlightenment reason, accordingly, had to work within the constraints of those understandings of nature and experience. The implication for religion was that, if it was to be considered rational, it would have to conform to the limits of reason thus constrained. In *Religion within the Limits of Reason Alone*, for example, Kant said that religion had to be understood within the limits of reason based on a sensationist doctrine of perception, in terms of which any affirmation of "a feeling of the immediate presence of the Supreme Being" would be a "fanatical religious illusion."[39]

I turn now to the relationship of enlightenment thought, thus understood, to Whiteheadian process philosophy.

PROCESS PHILOSOPHY AND ENLIGHTENMENT THOUGHT

The complexity of the enlightenment, as I indicated earlier, is part of the reason that no simple answer can be given to the question of whether process philosophy accepts the enlightenment. One would have to specify which of the various dimensions of enlightenment thought was in view—its ontological naturalism, epistemic naturalism, empiricism, rationalism, individualism, belief in universal truths and values, or belief in progress. I now add another reason why no simple answer is possible. If one specifies any of these dimensions and asks whether process thought accepts it, the answer will be both yes and no. The answer in each case is yes with regard to the general notion but no with regard to the way in which enlightenment thinkers typically construed the notion, due to one or more of the assumptions discussed above.

Ontological Naturalism

Naturalism, understood as the rejection of supernaturalism, has both ontological and epistemic dimensions. *Ontological* naturalism is, minimally, the doctrine that there are no supernatural interventions into the world's most fundamental causal principles. The world's basic causal nexus is never interrupted. In scientific circles, this doctrine was originally called "uniformitarianism," which said that scientists are not to explain events in the past by affirming any form of causation then that is not operative today. Although there was a specifically geological version of this doctrine—which has now been repudiated—uniformitarianism in the ontological sense, under the name *naturalism*, is now virtually an official doctrine of the scientific community.

Naturalism in this sense was *not* affirmed, as we saw above, by most of the seventeenth-century founders of the modern worldview. They, to the contrary, were interested in undergirding supernaturalism.

Nevertheless, the trajectory they began soon became naturalistic, with the three options being deism, pantheism (as in Spinoza), or complete atheism. Deists still affirmed the ontological presupposition behind supernatural interventions, insofar as they retained the belief that the world had been created ex nihilo. But they said that the creator never exercised the option of intervening—at least almost never. The rejection of supernatural interventions, insofar as it was held to be completely without exceptions, meant the denial of any present divine influence in the world.

More precisely, this rejection of supernatural intervention meant the denial of any *variable* divine influence. This specification is necessary to take account of a position that can be called "semideism." This view says that the world cannot accurately be described as a self-sustaining machine, because it requires the ongoing sustaining power of God.[40] However, this semideism, like strict deism, pantheism, and atheism, says that the world has required no variable divine causation since it was created. If God exists, in other words, God has not done anything new since creating the world.

This denial of variable divine influence seemed to be implied by the rejection of supernatural interventions because of a generally accepted way of distinguishing special from ordinary divine activity. This way, inherited from medieval theologians, involved a distinction between "primary" and "secondary" causation. According to most medieval theologians (such as Thomas Aquinas), God is the primary cause of all events. But ordinarily, they added, God works through secondary causes, also called "natural causes." These secondary or natural causes were said to be sufficient to explain the event, as long as attention is focused only upon the content, or "whatness," of the event. If, by contrast, we wish to explain the event's "thatness"—the very fact that it exists, along with the whole chain of secondary causes leading up to it—we need to refer to God's primary causation. But insofar as we prescind from this ultimate question, there is no need to refer to divine causation to explain ordinary events. Reference to divine causation is necessary to explain the whatness only of *extraordinary* events—that is, miracles—which are produced immediately by God's primary causation, without using natural causes. Most events, however, can be fully accounted for in terms of natural (secondary) causes alone, with no reference to divine causation.

On the basis of that scheme of primary and secondary causation, the move to naturalism—according to which there are no supernatural miracles, so there are *no* events without natural causes—implied that reference to ongoing divine influence is unnecessary altogether, except perhaps in the semideistic sense. In other words, given the equation of special divine influence with supernatural interventions, the denial of the latter meant that the category of "special divine acts" became empty.

Of course, given this background, according to which any affirmation of variable divine influence in the world entailed a supernatural intervention, the complete and consistent rejection of supernaturalism was not easy. This fact was illustrated by Charles Lyell. Although Lyell was known as—and, in supernaturalist circles, damned as—the "father of uniformitarianism," he believed that fresh divine influence was necessary to explain one thing: the origin of the human mind. Divine intervention, he said, added "the moral and intellectual faculties of the human race, to a system of nature which had gone on for millions of years without the intervention of any analogous cause." This assertion meant, Lyell added, that we must "assume a primeval creative power which does not act with uniformity."[41]

Lyell's qualified deism could not, however, be accepted by those who saw the need for science to be based on a fully consistent naturalism. The move to a consistently deistic position was made by Lyell's younger friend, Charles Darwin. In a letter to Lyell, Darwin rejected the idea of divine additions to explain the distinctive capacities of the human mind, saying: "I would give nothing for the theory of natural selection, if it requires miraculous additions at any one stage of descent."[42]

Since the time of Darwin, the scientific community has rejected even Darwin's deism in favor of a completely atheistic worldview. Such a worldview is generally seen as necessary for a full-fledged affirmation of naturalism. For example, biologist Richard Lewontin, while admitting the "patent absurdity" of many of the explanations required by that worldview, insists that scientists must maintain it. "[W]e cannot allow a Divine Foot in the door," says Lewontin, because "[t]o appeal to an omnipotent deity is to allow that at any moment the regularities of nature may be ruptured, that miracles may happen."[43] This atheistic worldview, on behalf of which Lewontin speaks, is now generally considered, by both admirers and detractors, to be necessary for a naturalistic worldview.

I turn now to (Whiteheadian) process philosophy's yes-and-no response to ontological naturalism. On the one hand, process philosophy fully endorses ontological naturalism. There neither are, nor conceivably could be, any supernatural interruptions of the world's normal pattern of causal relations.

On the other hand, process philosophy does not agree with the assumption that naturalism necessarily means atheism, pantheism, or at least deism (including semideism). It instead endorses a naturalistic theism that affirms ongoing divine influence, even variable divine influence. Process philosophy's acceptance of a form of theism, however, in no way mitigates the denial that supernatural interventions are possible.

The possibility of such interventions in traditional theism presupposed the idea that the world had been created ex nihilo, with *nihil* understood to mean absolute nothingness, a complete absence of finite entities. Having been thus created, the world was regarded as *wholly* contingent, so that it embodied no principles that are truly metaphysical, in the sense of being eternal, necessary principles inherent in the very nature of things. In particular, our world's basic causal principles were said to be merely contingent, so they could be interrupted. Having been freely created, they could be freely interrupted.

Whitehead explicitly rejected this "theory of a wholly transcendent God creating out of nothing an accidental universe" (PR 95).[44] He therefore rejected the idea of "one supreme reality, omnipotently disposing a wholly derivative world" (AI 166). Rather than portraying a God who is wholly transcendent, in the sense of being able to exist apart from the world, Whitehead's philosophy portrays not only "the World as requiring its union with God" but also "God as requiring his union with the World." In contrast with extreme voluntarism, according to which the entire nature of the world—even the bare fact that there *is* a world of finite existents—is contingent upon the divine will, Whitehead's theism holds that "the relationships of God to the World . . . lie beyond the accidents of will," being instead "founded upon the necessities of the nature of God and the nature of the World" (AI 168).

As this reference to the "necessities of . . . the nature of the World" indicates, the world's existence is not "wholly derivative," not entirely contingent. This denial does not mean that *our* world, with its electrons, protons, and inverse square law of gravitational attraction, exists necessarily. This world came into existence at some point in the past—evidently, it now seems, about 14 billion years ago.[45] Its coming into existence, however, was "not the beginning of [finite] matter of fact, but the incoming of a certain type of order" (PR 96). That is, the creation of our particular world, which Whitehead called our "cosmic epoch," involved bringing order out of chaos, or at least inducing the rise of a new type of order out of a previous type. Accordingly, when Whitehead spoke of "the World" (capitalized) as necessary, he meant only that *some* world of finite actualities must exist and that whatever particular world, or cosmic epoch, does exist will exemplify certain metaphysical principles. Because these principles obtain necessarily, not through a contingent act of will, they cannot be violated.

Whiteheadian naturalistic theism can also, with Hartshorne, be called "panentheism." This term, which literally means that "all things are in God," indicates that the world—in the sense of *some* realm of finite actualities—is an essential part of the divine existence. God could not exist without a world. This point can be made by referring to God, again with Hartshorne, as "the soul of the world." If God is by definition soul of the world, then the world's existence is not contingent but is an essential part of the divine existence.[46] *Our* world is, to be sure, contingent. But the fact that *some* world exists is not.

Implicit in this distinction between the two meanings of "world" is a distinction between (necessary) metaphysical principles and (contingent) laws of nature. In supernaturalistic theism, no such distinction is made: all the principles by which the world normally runs were freely created by God, so they are all equally contingent. This is why the God of traditional theism can interrupt not only the law of gravity but also the very principle of causation, according to which finite events are usually conditioned by prior finite events. In Whitehead's naturalistic theism, by contrast, there are, beneath the contingent laws of our particular cosmic epoch, some metaphysical principles, which obtain necessarily.

Stated otherwise, the ultimate reality, which Whitehead called "creativity," is always embodied in both God and a multiplicity of finite events. Creativity is the twofold power of a unified event—which Whitehead calls an "actual occasion"—to exercise self-determination (final causation) and then to exert causal influence (efficient causation) on subsequent events. The metaphysical principles are *causal* principles in terms of which these events actualize themselves and causally influence each other. These causal principles are inherent in the very nature of things. Indeed, because God is necessarily related to a world embodying them, they belong to the very nature of God. Given the self-evident truth, endorsed by traditional theists, that God cannot act contrary to the divine nature, the doctrine that these principles belong to the very nature of God means that any suggestion that God could interrupt them would be self-contradictory.

This denial of supernatural interventions is combined, however, with process philosophy's affirmation of ongoing divine influence, even *variable* divine influence, in the world. Divine influence occurs not as an interruption of the normal causal processes but as a regular, necessary dimension of those processes. According to Whitehead's description of this divine influence, every actual occasion begins with a divinely derived "initial aim." This doctrine means a rejection of the view that the whatness of all, or at least most, finite events is in principle explainable apart from reference to divine causation. Reference to initial aims from God is essential to understanding the content as well as the existence of all events. And, because the contents of events vary enormously, the contents of their initial aims, which are toward the best possibilities open to them,[47] vary enormously.

To put this discussion in terms of uniformitarianism: process theism affirms this principle formally, in that God always acts by means of providing initial aims. Negatively, this doctrine means the denial of occasional interruptions of the world's basic causal processes. Those process theists who say that "God acts in the same way always and everywhere" emphasize this aspect of the doctrine. With regard to the content of the initial aims, however, uniformitarianism is denied: God provides vastly different initial aims for electrons and human beings, even different aims for human beings in different situations. Unlike most postenlightenment liberal theologians, accordingly, process theologians can speak of God's doing new things in particular moments of both evolutionary and human history. Reference to divine causation is necessary, I have argued elsewhere, to explain the directionality, novelty, and jumps in the evolutionary process.[48]

Many Christian theologians have, of course, believed that an even stronger form of exceptional divine activity needs to be affirmed in relation to creation, christology, miracles, and eschatology. They believe, in other words, that uniformitarianism needs to be denied even in the formal sense, so as to allow occasional supernatural interventions. The attempt to modify process philosophy to allow for such interventions, however, would be not to modify it but to reject it, insofar as its naturalistic form of theism belongs to its core doctrines. Allowing for even a single divine interruption of the normal pattern of causality would imply a rejection of the fundamental principles summarized above—the denial of creation ex nihilo, the necessary embodiment of (nonoverridable) creativity in a realm of finite existents, and the distinction between metaphysical and merely cosmological principles. Such a modification would undermine the basis provided by Whitehead for a form of theism that is not shipwrecked on the problem of evil and that is not inconsistent with the ontological naturalism that is now irreversibly presupposed by science.

Besides rejecting the atheism of late modern thought, process philosophy also says no to the other dimensions of the form of naturalism with which it is generally associated. I call that doctrine "naturalism$_{sam}$," with "sam" indicating a sensationist-atheist-materialist version of naturalism. The sensationist doctrine of perception is one of the elements of the early modern view that was retained in later modern thought. The other element was the mechanistic doctrine of nature. In early modern thought, as we saw, this mechanistic doctrine of nature was part of a dualistic view of human beings, which were understood to be spiritual souls inhabiting machinelike bodies. But in later modern thought, the soul, like God, was rejected, so that the human being as a whole was to be understood in mechanistic terms. It is this later doctrine, with its mechanistic-materialistic account of everything, including human beings, to which the "materialism" of naturalism$_{sam}$ refers.

The naturalism of process philosophy, by contrast, can be called "naturalism$_{ppp}$," meaning a prehensive-panentheist-panexperientialist version of naturalism. The atheism of naturalism$_{sam}$ is replaced, as we have seen, by panentheism. Naturalismsam's sensationist doctrine of perception is replaced by a *prehensive* doctrine of perception, and its materialism is replaced by a *panexperientialist* ontology. These later two doctrines will be explained below. For now the important point is that process philosophy's naturalistic theism, or panentheism, is not a doctrine that can intelligibly be affirmed in isolation. It is instead an integral part of a new, overall worldview. Nothing but incoherence would result from the attempt to affirm naturalistic theism while retaining sensationism and the mechanistic-materialistic view of nature, because those doctrines, as we saw, were designed precisely to rule out any but a supernaturalistic version of theism.

In any case, given the theistic dimension of Whiteheadian naturalism, it is very different from the kind of worldview that is now commonly called "naturalistic." The term *naturalism* is often not defined simply in the way that I have defined it here, as the rejection of a worldview that allows for the supernatural interruptions of the world's normal causal patterns. Instead, 'naturalism' is often defined much more sweepingly as the doctrine that "nature is all there is," with "nature" here understood to be the totality of finite things and events. Using "*nati*" to stand for "nature is all there is," we can call naturalism in this sense "naturalismnati." Since "nature" in this phrase is explicitly equated with the totality of *finite* things, 'naturalism' thus defined entails atheism. This more sweeping definition is commonly employed by both advocates and critics of atheism alike. For example, Gilbert Harman, an advocate, defines 'naturalism' as "the sensible thesis that *all* facts are facts of nature," adding that this worldview "has no place for gods." And theist Philip Johnson says that, according to naturalists, nature is understood "to be 'all there is.'"[49]

One problem with this sweeping definition of 'naturalism' is that, if it is used, then the label *supernaturalism* must be applied to every form of theism that distinguishes God from the totality of finite events and processes, even forms of theism that rule out the possibility that God could interrupt the world's normal causal processes. The resulting confusion can be illustrated by the case of William James. Having defined 'naturalism' as the view that there is nothing beyond the world known through sensory perception (which is another way of saying that nature is all there is), James rejected naturalism, because he believed in an "unseen region" from which ideal impulses come. James said, accordingly: "If one should make a division of all thinkers into naturalists and supernaturalists, I should undoubtedly have to go...into the supernaturalist branch."[50]

Given James' equation of naturalism with atheism, he had to call himself a "supernaturalist" simply because he believed in a divine reality that is distinct from the world known through sensory perception. James also affirmed real divine influence in the world, even variable divine influence in the world. This affirmation led him to call his view "piecemeal supernaturalism" to distinguish it from the "universal supernaturalism" of the Hegelians, according to which God (or the Absolute) acts on the world only in a "wholesale" manner. James, holding that the divine reality, by means of the ideal impulses, "interpolate[s] itself piecemeal between distinct portions of nature," affirmed that it entered into "transactions of detail."[51] This doctrine was, accordingly, an anticipation of Whitehead's doctrine of variable divine influence by means of initial aims. James's doctrine was, therefore, a version of naturalistic theism in the same sense in which Whitehead's doctrine is. James did *not* mean that the world's most fundamental causal principles could be occasionally subverted.

Nevertheless, the very fact that James used the term *supernaturalism* for his position has led many interpreters to assume that he affirmed supernatural interruptions of the world's basic causal processes. For example, John Mackie, having defined miracles as "divine interventions which have disrupted the natural course of events," explicated James's piecemeal supernaturalism to mean that "the supernatural must enter into 'transactions of detail' with the natural—in other words, the sorts of interventions that we have defined miracles to be."[52]

It is confusing, therefore, to define naturalism as the doctrine that "nature is all there is."[53] There is no need to use 'naturalism' for that doctrine, moreover, because there is already a perfectly good word for it: *atheism*. 'Naturalism' can thereby be saved for the doctrine that the term more readily suggests, the rejection of supernaturalism. And with this definition, we can see that Whitehead's worldview is, in spite of its theism, a version of ontological naturalism.

Epistemic Naturalism

I turn now to epistemic naturalism, according to which all claims to truth are to be judged in terms of experience and reason. What is thereby rejected is *epistemic supernaturalism*, according to which some doctrines are considered true because they are thought to have been revealed so that they need not be defended in terms of their adequacy to the facts of experience and self-consistency with other beliefs. Epistemic supernaturalism presupposed infallibility and inerrancy in the human beings through which the revelation came. It thereby presupposed supernatural intervention through which the normally fallible processes of human beings was overridden. Given process philosophy's ontological naturalism, accordingly, it says yes to the enlightenment's epistemic naturalism.

This acceptance is illustrated by process theist Franklin Gamwell, who fully endorses, as mentioned in chapter 1, what he calls the "modern commitment," defined as the "increasing affirmation that our understandings of reality... cannot be validated or redeemed by appeals to some authoritative expression or tradition or institution" but "only by appeal in some sense to human experience and reason."[54] This modern commitment is also reflected in the writings of Whitehead, who, as Gamwell points out, said: "The appeal to reason is the appeal to that ultimate judge... to which all authority must bow."[55] Gamwell is right to highlight this doctrine's centrality to modernity. It was at the very heart of the enlightenment, being embodied in Kant's famous statement—made in his essay "What Is Enlightenment?"—that enlightenment is thinking for oneself, rather than relying on the authority of others. In other words, enlightenment is embodying autonomy, rather than heteronomy, in one's intellectual life. This doctrine is also one that has, as Gamwell indicates, received "increasing affirmation" (with the exception, we should add, of one strand of thought that is sometimes called "postmodern" but is more accurately called "postliberal").

The full-fledged acceptance of this modern commitment can, Gamwell rightly suggests, be part of a postmodern position. We can distinguish "the modern commitment in its formal sense," he points out, from any "material or substantive meaning of modernity" that has been historically associated with it. Most uses of "postmodern," he adds, "involve a contrast with some material or substantive meaning of modernity, rather than with the [modern] commitment in its formal sense."[56] This is precisely the distinction presupposed in the treatment of Whiteheadian philosophy as postmodern. As I suggested in the previous chapter, we could call it "postmodern modernism," since the formal commitment of modernity to defending all ideas in terms of experience and reason is combined with a critique of certain substantive ideas that are also distinctively modern.

The denial of epistemic supernaturalism does not necessarily entail the denial of divine revelation. The idea that God influences all events, therefore every occasion of human experience, means that revelation from God can occur through human beings. What is denied is only the notion that the affirmation of revelation can be used epistemically—that the idea that a book embodies divine revelation can be used to argue that its teachings are true, regardless of whether these teachings can be verified by experience and reason. Given this caveat, a theologian working from within, say, the Jewish, Christian, or Islamic tradition could employ Whiteheadian philosophy to develop a doctrine of revelation.[57] In any case, having said that epistemic naturalism judges all propositions in terms of experience and reason, I turn now to these two concepts under the rubrics of 'empiricism' and 'rationalism,' beginning with the former.

Empiricism

Empiricism has many meanings, some of which Whitehead endorsed. "The elucidation of immediate experience," he declared, "is the sole justification for any thought" (PR 4). He affirmed adequacy to the various facts of experience as a central criterion for philosophy, saying that the goal is to develop a system of ideas "in terms of which every element of our experience can be interpreted" (PR 3). And he even affirmed Hume's *conceptual* empiricism, according to which "nothing is to be received into the philosophical scheme which is not discoverable as an element in subjective experience"—which means that "Hume's demand that causation be describable as an element in experience is...entirely justifiable" (PR 166–67). In his most explicit endorsement of empiricism, Whitehead said: "[A]ll knowledge is derived from, and verified by, direct intuitive observation. I accept this axiom of empiricism as stated in this general form" (AI 177). In saying that he accepted this doctrine "as stated in this general form," Whitehead illustrated my earlier point, that he affirmed the central doctrines of the enlightenment in a general form, which is susceptible to various specifications, but he rejected the specific forms that these doctrines have taken in the dominant trajectory coming out of the enlightenment.

With regard to the doctrine at hand, Whitehead emphatically rejected "enlightenment empiricism" insofar as it involves the sensationist doctrine of perception, according to which "direct intuitive observation" of things beyond our own minds is equated with sensory perception (AI 177). Whereas ancient thinkers asked "What have we experienced?"—which Whitehead regarded as the right question—"moderns asked what can we experience," with the assumption that this question is identical with the question of "what data are directly provided by the activity of the sense-organs?" (AI 224–25). It is this assumption that has been behind most of the shallowness and inadequacy of postenlightenment philosophy and theology. If perceptual experience is equated with sensory perception, then we have no perceptual experience of causation, the actual world, or the past. There can be no religious experience, in the sense of a direct awareness of a divine reality. There can be no perceptual experience of normative ideals, whether moral, aesthetic, or logical. And there can be no telepathy, which, besides providing an empirically verifiable analogue for theistic religious experience, is also involved in the various kinds of empirical evidence for life after death.[58] Whitehead himself explicitly affirmed the reality of telepathy (SME 150; PR 253, 308–09; AI 248) and our direct perception of God (RM 155–56; PR 244). It is by means of this nonsensory perception of God, furthermore, that our awareness of normative ideals is explained (AI 11; MT 103).

This idea of nonsensory perception is central to Whitehead's prehensive doctrine of perception, mentioned earlier. Whitehead used the term *prehension* to refer to a mode of taking account of other things that could be either sensory or nonsensory. Sensory perception, rather than being our basic mode of perception, is a mixed mode, which involves two pure modes.

One of these pure modes, which can be called "pure" sense perception, is called "prehension in the mode of presentational immediacy." It is sense perception as defined by Hume, according to which the content of perception is limited to sense data, such as colored shapes. This mode is called "presentational immediacy," because the data are immediately present to you, telling nothing about the past or the future. Whitehead, in fact, derived the name from Hume's statement that "the mind [cannot] go beyond what is immediately present to the senses, either to discover the real existence or the relation of objects" (S 32).[59] For example, when you look at the clear night sky, you see various points of light. Although you know that they are stars that exist millions of light years away, this is information you have learned from other sources. From the data immediately present to you, you know only that you see colored shapes. Similar visual experiences might be produced, in fact, by using electrodes to stimulate your visual cortex. This fact makes it clear that the sense data as such do not tell you anything about actual existence beyond your own consciousness. They do not tell you what is causing you to experience them.

The knowledge of the causal efficacy of actual things beyond our own experience comes from the other pure mode of perception, which Whitehead called, logically enough, "perception in the mode of causal efficacy." It is always involved in any instance of *full-fledged* sensory perception. Hume's description of sensory perception as giving us no information except sense data is very incomplete. When I look at the night sky, I am aware not only of the points of light that I call "stars" but also of the fact that I am seeing them *with my eyes*. It is true that pure sensory perception, or perception in the mode of presentational immediacy, tells me nothing more than that these points of light are immediately present to my conscious experience. But full-fledged sensory perception tells me much more. It tells me that my experience is not the only actual thing that exists, so I need not suffer the solipsistic worry that everything else might simply be figments of my imagination, like creatures of my dreams. Full-fledged sensory perception tells me, for starters, that I have a body, made of things as actual as my experience is, and that at least parts of my body, such as my eyes, exert causal efficacy on my experience. And, knowing that my bodily parts are actual and capable of exerting causal efficacy, I then have an analogical basis for thinking of other things, beyond my body, as also actual and causally efficacious. I thereby have a basis for attributing actual existence to the stars and, closer to home, the other items of my visual field, such as, well, my home.

Whitehead's name for this full-fledged sensory perception is "perception in the mode of symbolic reference." The point of this name is that the data from one mode are used as symbols to refer to, and hence interpret, the other mode. For example, I may take a green shape to mean that there is a tree in the region at which my eyes are directed. The green shape is hence understood not only as qualifying a region external to my body but also as somehow involved in my eyes as imposing themselves on my experience. That is, we see the green tree out there *by means of* our eyes. "Thus perception in the mode of causal efficacy discloses that the data in the mode of sense-perception are provided by it" (S 50).

Given this analysis of full-fledged sensory perception as a mixed mode, involving two pure modes, what needs to be emphasized now is that the mode of causal efficacy is a *nonsensory* mode of perception. In being aware that I see the tree by means of my eyes, I do not see my eyes. Rather, I—the experiences constituting my "mind" at that moment—grasp my eyes in a more fundamental way. My experience, of course, receives the data from my eyes through my brain. My brain is the part of my body that my experience grasps most directly. But I do not see my brain. And yet if I were unable to apprehend the brain, with its billions of neurons, I would not be able to see the tree. Sensory perception, therefore, presupposes this more fundamental, nonsensory mode of perceiving or grasping things.

Whitehead used the term *prehension* for this more fundamental way of grasping things. He then distinguished between different types of prehensions, depending on their data. When the data are other actual things—such as one's eyes—the prehensions are called "physical" prehensions. There are also "conceptual" prehensions, "propositional" prehensions, and so on. So Whitehead's doctrine of perception as a whole can be called a "prehensive doctrine of perception." I primarily use this name, however, to point to the fact that this doctrine says that our most fundamental mode of perception is a nonsensory mode. Whitehead's doctrine of perception is, therefore, a nonsensationist doctrine, since it rejects the idea that perception by means of our senses is our only, or even our most fundamental, mode of perception.

This nonsensationist theory of perception lies behind Whitehead's main criticism of modern philosophy, which is directed against its penchant for "boldly denying the facts," for destroying its usefulness by indulging in "brilliant feats of explaining away" (PR 6, 17). This criticism is contained in Whitehead's brief characterization of the eighteenth-century thinkers most often identified with the enlightenment:

> *Les philosophes* were not philosophers. They were men of genius, clear-headed and acute, who applied the seventeenth century group of abstractions to the analysis of the unbounded universe.... Whatever did not fit into their scheme was ignored, derided, disbelieved. Their hatred of Gothic architecture symbolises their lack of sympathy with dim perspectives. It was the age of reason,... but, of one-eyed reason, deficient in its vision of depth. (SMW 59)

The final sentence of this quotation shows the connection, in Whitehead's mind, between the enlightenment's superficial view of experience and its limited rationalism. I turn now to this latter issue.

Rationalism

Deconstructive postmodern thinkers commonly lift up rationalism—in the sense of the attempt to develop an adequate, self-consistent set of ideas for interpreting the world—as one of the dominant features of enlightenment modernity. Genuinely postmodern thinkers, they suggest, would give up that quest. Whitehead, by contrast, saw modern science and thereby the enlightenment as having originated in a "historical revolt" against the unbridled rationalism of the middle ages (SMW 8–9, 16). This historical revolt, involving a focus on origins and efficient causes, was an "anti-rationalistic movement," being devoid of any interest in justifying its assumptions, such as the principle of induction (SMW 42–44). In contrast with the medieval period, which was "the age of faith based upon reason," the eighteenth century was "the age of reason, based upon faith" (SMW 57). Whitehead's criticism here was that enlightenment *philosophes* failed to apply reason to the examination of their ultimate assumptions, simply taking them on faith.

By characterizing modern thought as antirationalistic, Whitehead's main point was that the historical revolt led to "the exclusion of philosophy from its proper role of harmonising the various abstractions of methodological thought." That is, the supreme task of reason, in Whitehead's view, is to compare "the various schemes of abstraction which are well founded in our various types of experience," showing how they can be fitted together in a harmonious way (SMW 18). Whitehead's commitment to rationalism in this sense is shown by the indication, on the first page of his first metaphysical book, that he was going to suggest a cosmology based on aesthetic, ethical, and religious intuitions as well as scientific intuitions (SMW vii). He later said, more simply, that philosophy's most important task is to fuse religion and science into one rational scheme of thought (PR 15). He differed from enlightenment-based modes of philosophy on this score primarily because of his nonsensationist doctrine of perceptual experience, which allowed him to regard religious experience—in the inclusive sense, understood to include moral and aesthetic experience—as a source of knowledge that has something of importance to contribute to metaphysics (RM 57, 84).

Modernity's antirationalism is manifested within scientific thought by its tendency to be "ardently rationalistic within its own borders, and dogmatically irrational beyond those borders" (PR 5). In modern thought more generally, this antirationalism is illustrated by the tendency to obtain a self-consistent philosophy by denying the reality of everything that does not fit: "It is easy enough to find a theory, logically harmonious and with important applications in the region of fact," chided Whitehead, "provided that you are content to disregard half your evidence" (SMW 187). The chief example of this tendency is the divorce, articulated most clearly by Hume, between theory and the necessary presuppositions of practice, with the result that the former is considered satisfactory even though it admittedly does not include the latter (PR 133, 156). Explicitly rejecting this Humean antirationalism, Whitehead stated: "Whatever is found in 'practice' must lie with the scope of the metaphysical description. When the description fails to include the 'practice,' the metaphysics is inadequate and requires revision. There can be no appeal to practice to supplement metaphysics" (PR 13).

Diametrically opposing this anti-rational appeal, Whitehead enunciated the "metaphysical rule of evidence," namely, "that we must bow to those presumptions, which, in despite of criticism, we still employ for the regulation of our lives....Rationalism is the search for the coherence of such presumptions" (PR 151).

In taking the inevitable presuppositions of practice as the chief criterion to which a philosophy must be adequate, Whitehead was echoing the "common-sense philosophy" of Hume's chief antagonist in the Scottish Enlightenment, Thomas Reid. There is, however, a crucial difference. Both agreed that our philosophies must include beliefs in such principles as causal efficacy, the external world, the past, and the distinction between better and worse possibilities. Reid, however, spoke of these as principles "which we are under a necessity to take for granted in the common concerns of life, without being able to give a reason for them."[60] Reid thought that we could give no reason for them—beyond supposing them to have been supernaturally implanted in our minds by God—because he shared with Hume the sensationist doctrine of perception.

By contrast, Whitehead, on the basis of his doctrine of a more fundamental, nonsensory mode of perception, could say that we inevitably presuppose such notions because of direct perceptions in which they are rooted. That we derive the notion of causation as real influence from this mode of perception is emphasized by calling it "perception in the mode of causal efficacy." Through the fact that we thereby perceive other actualities—not simply forms, such as sensory data—we know of the existence of an actual world beyond our present experience. Through the fact that the actualities thus perceived are always antecedent to the percipient occasion, and especially through our prehension of our own prior occasions of experience, we know of the reality of the past and therefore of time. Through the nonsensory prehension of God, who envisages normative ideals, we experience such ideals, thereby obtaining our notion of better and worse possibilities (MT 103). Even our presupposition about the existence of other minds, Whitehead suggested, is rooted partly in a direct (albeit usually unconscious) perception of these minds, rather than being based entirely on inference from sensory data (SMW 150).

Given this difference between Whitehead and Reid, process philosophy's use of the inevitable presuppositions of practice is very different from that of the "reformed epistemology" associated primarily with Alvin Plantinga and Nicholas Wolterstorff. These reformed epistemologists regard these presuppositions as "basic beliefs," meaning beliefs that are rightly presupposed even though they are, as Reid said, not based on evidence. They use this doctrine to conclude that other beliefs of a particular community, such as Christian beliefs in an omnipotent deity and inerrantly inspired scriptures, can be considered properly basic.[61] From the perspective of Whiteheadian epistemology, by contrast, the inevitable presuppositions of practice are grounded in experience. Our acceptance of them can provide no license, accordingly, for presupposing the truth of notions that cannot justify themselves in terms of the normal criteria of rationality.

It might be thought, however, that the acceptance of such presuppositions as the ultimate criteria for philosophy and theology involves "foundationalism." But that is not the case, unless the term *foundationalism* is stretched far beyond its original meaning to designate any philosophy that rejects complete relativism. Our inevitable presuppositions, as understood by process philosophy, do share one feature with foundational beliefs in the original sense of the term: They are taken to be truly universal, in the sense of being inevitably presupposed in practice by *all* human beings, including those who deny them verbally. As such, these beliefs provide process philosophy with a basis for avoiding complete relativism, a goal of enlightenment thought that it affirms. But foundationalism, in the original sense of the term, involves the acceptance of certain beliefs as "basic," meaning beliefs from which thought is to begin and from which all nonbasic beliefs are to be deduced. In process philosophy, by contrast, the universal presuppositions of practice function not as a foundation for a building but simply as a compass for a voyage, warning us when we have gotten off course.

I should perhaps add that, although Whitehead supported rationalism in the sense described above, he did not support every attitude sometimes suggested by the term. Whitehead rejected, for example, the rationalistic tendency to achieve consistency at the expense of experiential inclusiveness. And he rejected that form of rationalism that is yoked with static dogmatism. "Rationalism," he declared, "is an adventure in the clarification of thought, progressive and never final" (PR 9). In any case, having discussed several formal issues—epistemic naturalism, empiricism, and rationalism—I return now to substantive, ontological matters.

Individualism

Another commonly listed feature of the enlightenment is individualism. Process philosophy, again, says both yes and no. It affirms individualism insofar as this means that there are real individuals, prior to our perception and conception of such. In fact, Whitehead's ontological principle, which says that only actual entities can act, means that all causation—be it efficient or final—is rooted in individuals. Whitehead's eighteenth category of explanation is that

> every condition to which the process of becoming conforms in any particular instance has its reason *either* in the character of some actual entity in the actual world of that concrescence, or in the character of the subject which is in process of concrescence. This category of explanation is termed the "ontological principle." It could also be termed the "principle of efficient, and final, causation." This ontological principle

means that actual entities are the only *reasons*; so that to search for a *reason* is to search for one or more actual entities. (PR 24)

Individuals, in other words, are the only agents. One implication of this principle is that, if there is any causal influence on the world beyond that of the totality of finite individuals, there must be a nonfinite individual. It was Whitehead's realization of this implication that led him to see that, if mathematical, logical, aesthetic, and moral norms are to have any influence on the world, they must be lodged in a divine individual.

Process philosophy also affirms individualism insofar as it means that all intrinsic value is resident in individuals. Although process philosophy can be considered communitarian in some respects, it insists that communities finally exist for the sake of their members, not vice-versa. A community has value for its individual members. But a community, such as a nation, has no value for itself, because it is not an experiencing individual. A political philosophy, therefore, should not say that the individual exists for the sake of the state. Rather, the state exists finally for the sake of its individual members. This doctrine stands behind, for example, the U.S. Bill of Rights, which gives American citizens protection from the power of the national state. Insofar as Hegelianism rejects this principle, Whiteheadian process philosophy rejects Hegelianism, and political philosophies derivative from it, in the name of individuals.

Whitehead rejects individualism, however, in the sense of the ontological doctrine of individual substances that "require nothing but themselves in order to exist." That was Descartes' definition of a substance. This definition was also filled by Leibniz's "windowless monads," which had no openings through which influences from other monads could enter. An individual monad was, therefore, related only externally to other individuals, meaning that its "relations" to other things did not enter into it. In other words, although Leibniz defined each monad as having experiences, including *perceptions*, he did not mean that a monad actually perceived other monads. To use Whitehead's language, there was no perception in the mode of causal efficacy, in which one monad directly perceived the actuality and causal efficacy of other monads. Rather, the perception was limited to perception in the mode of presentational immediacy, in which various sense data are projected outward, so that one *seems* to perceive other things. These projected percepts could correspond to what was really going on thanks to the "pre-established harmony" between percepts and reality that had been programmed into all the monads by God at creation.[62]

Whitehead developed his ontology by installing windows in the Leibnizian monads. That is, he agreed with Leibniz that the world is composed exclusively of individuals with experience. Whitehead thus endorsed panexperientialism, according to which all true individuals have experience. But, pointing out that Leibniz "did not discriminate the event, as the unit of experience, from the enduring organism as its stablisation into importance" (SMW 155), Whitehead built his own system around this distinction by "toning down [Leibniz's] monads into the unified events in space and time" (SMW 70). Whitehead's doctrine that the ultimate individuals of the world are momentary events is announced terminologically, as indicated earlier, by saying that the *actual* entities—the entities that are individuals in the fullest sense of the term, being "monads" or "atoms" and hence indivisible—are actual *occasions* (AI 177).[63] Given the fact that all actual occasions have experience, they can also be called "occasions of experience." Each individual that endures through time, such as an electron or a human mind, is a temporal *society* of these momentary experiences. "The real actual things that endure are all societies. They are not actual occasions. It is the mistake that has thwarted European metaphysics from the time of the Greeks, namely, to confuse societies with the completely real things, which are the actual occasions" (AI 204).[64]

By means of this doctrine, Whitehead could portray each monad—each actual occasion—as beginning with an open window, into which the influences from the past world rush. These influences from prior actual occasions are, from the point of view of the present occasion, its prehensions of them, through which it takes aspects of them into itself. It is thereby internally related to, and thereby partially constituted out of, prior individuals.

Unlike some doctrines of internal relatedness, however, this one does not vitiate the notion of distinct individuals. In some doctrines, any two individuals, which we can call "A" and "B," influence *each other*. This means that not only does A influence B, but B-as-influenced-by-A influences A, which means that it was A-as-influenced-by-B-as-influenced-by-A that influenced B, and so on infinitely. With this infinite mutual influence, it is hard to see how A and B could remain distinct. It seems that everything would become an undifferentiated mush. Allowing internal relations into a pluralistic system thereby seemed to threaten to turn the pluralism into monism. Many philosophers insistent on keeping pluralism, therefore, have affirmed that all relations are external, meaning that they are not *real* relations at all, because they make no difference to the individual. Cartesian substances and Leibnizian monads were externally related to everything else (except for God).

Whitehead's view that the ultimate units are momentary events allowed him to affirm both internal and external relations. Each occasion of experience is internally related to all prior events. But it is externally related to contemporary and future occasions. *Contemporary* occasions are those that have their moment of becoming at the same time. Whitehead's technical term for becoming is *concrescence*, which means "becoming concrete." Because neither actual occasion is yet concrete, it is not yet anything determinate, so it cannot be prehended. So neither of two contemporary occasions can influence the other. With regard to future occasions, it belongs to each occasion that there *will be* future occasions, because "anticipation" is a part of each occasion, in the sense that it anticipates that it will exert causal influence on the future. But the actual nature of that influence—which means the exact way in which the present occasion is prehended by future occasions—is external to the present occasion. For example, when I decide to speak to someone, I may anticipate that my speaking will have a particular effect. But the effect it actually has is external to the occasion of experience in which I made the decision. The way in which my speaking is received does not go back and affect that decision. It is forever what it was. Therefore, because present occasions are externally related to both contemporary and future occasions, no actual occasion is influenced by any actual occasion that it had influenced. All influence between actual occasions goes only in one direction.[65] A genuine pluralism of distinct individuals is thereby maintained.

The doctrine that all enduring individuals, such as electrons and human souls, are really temporally ordered *societies* of events provides the basis for process philosophy's rejection of individualism in the ethical sense. This sense is the doctrine called "ethical egoism," according to which everything we do is ultimately based on self-love, because it is not really possible for us to care about the welfare of others (except as it will help us). The ontological presupposition behind this egoistic doctrine is that we as enduring individuals are enduring substances, being strictly the one self-same individual from moment to moment. Given this assumption, one's relation to one's own past and future states would be a relation of absolutely identity, whereas one's relationship to other individuals would be a relation of absolute difference. The call to love our neighbors "as we love ourselves," accordingly, would be urging us to do the metaphysically impossible.

The Whiteheadian view that enduring individuals are really temporally ordered societies of distinct occasions of experience undermines this argument. According to this view, your present experience, being a distinct event, is not strictly (numerically) identical with any of your past or future experiences. Likewise, because influences from other individuals enter into your experiences, helping to constitute them, and because your present experiences will enter into the experiences of other individuals, helping to constitute them, we are not absolutely different from other individuals. By seeing that our relations to our own past and future experiences are different only in degree from our relations to the past and future experiences of other people, we see that altruism—genuinely caring for others—is not metaphysically impossible. "On this ground alone," said Hartshorne, "I would not give up the event doctrine without the most rigorous proofs of its erroneousness."[66]

Closely related to ethical egoism is the view of life as a primarily competitive, rather than a cooperative, affair, which is the implication of "individualism" upon which Whitehead focused (SMW 111–12, 194–96; AI 28, 30–31, 35).

Modern nationalism, militarism, capitalism, and Social Darwinism, he argued, all reflect the one-sided enlightenment view of individuals with merely external relations to their environment, including other people. Whitehead intended his own doctrine, by emphasizing internal as well as external relations, to lead to a healthier and more realistic balance between strife and harmony, competition and coordination. The universe has "its aspects of struggle and of friendly help," so that "romantic ruthlessness is no nearer to real politics, than is romantic self-abnegation" (SMW 112). Expressing the ideal he meant his philosophy to support, Whitehead said: "The antithesis between the general good and the individual interest can be abolished only when the individual is such that its interest is the general good" (PR 15).[67]

This event doctrine of the enduring self, according to which it is a temporal society of occasions of experiences, is also important for reconciling the belief that all events are part of a closed causal nexus with the assumption that human behavior is significantly free, which is one of the inevitable presuppositions of human practice (SMW 75–79). Commenting upon the overstressing of efficient causes in the modern period, which followed upon the overstressing of final causes in the Middle Ages, Whitehead declared: "One task of a sound metaphysics is to exhibit final and efficient causes in their proper relation to each other" (PR 84).

At the root of Whitehead's effort to fulfill this task was the doctrine that the ultimate individuals of which the world is composed are momentary occasions of experience. As we saw earlier, each occasion begins as an open window to the past, into which rush causal influences from the past world. This reception of efficient causation constitutes what Whitehead called the "physical pole" of the occasion of experience. With this pole constituted, the occasion's window is closed, as it were, while the occasion has its "mental pole," during which it exercises final causation, in the sense of self-determination. The occasion of experience decides, in other words, precisely how to form itself out of the influences it received. Finally, the occasion, having become fully determinate, fully concrete, becomes one of the many efficient causes upon subsequent occasions of experience, and the process continues.

Given this conceptualization, we do not have to wonder how something can exert efficient causation on other things while it is still indeterminate because it is exercising self-determination. It does not. Nor must we wonder how it exercises self-determination while it is being influenced by other things. It does not. The doctrine of temporal atomicity means that final and efficient causation occur sequentially, never simultaneously. An occasion of experience first exercises self-determination, and then it exercises efficient causation on others. Being composed of very brief occasions of experience, an enduring individual, such as an electron or a human mind, oscillates between efficient and final causation many times a second. In this way, Whitehead shows how enduring individuals can, while participating in the universal causal nexus, be truly self-determining. This reconciliation of efficient and final causation provides one of the ways in which Whitehead's philosophy is postmodern in the sense of reconciling modern and premodern emphases.

Belief in Universal Truths and Values

Another feature of enlightenment thought that is often mentioned today is its belief in universal truths and values. The belief in universal truths is widely rejected by deconstructive postmodern thinkers who urge, however paradoxically, that the (universal) truth is that all truths are local, because the criteria for truth, being culturally conditioned or even created, are relative to a particular culture. A similar position is taken with regard to values, such as the traditional axiological trinity of Truth, Beauty, and Goodness.

Behind this relativism lies a concern to undermine the bases for Euro-American cultural imperialism, in which Euro-American ideas of what is true, beautiful, and good—with regard to, for example, economic development—are imposed on other peoples, whether by force or by seduction. Whiteheadian process thinkers support the intent behind this relativism—the intent to subvert this imperialistic elevation of parochial truths and values into universal ones. Whiteheadian postmodernists do not, however, reject the idea of universal truths and norms as such.

With regard to truth, Whitehead avoids relativism without falling into dogmatism by emphasizing the complexity of the universe in general and of every event in particular. Because each event embodies, to some extent, the whole universe within itself, any statement about the event will involve an enormous abstraction. An indefinite number of abstractions about an event, formulated from diverse perspectives, can all express something true about the event. Whitehead used this point to support the enlightenment virtue of tolerance. Attributing this idea to Plato, Whitehead said:

> His Dialogues are permeated with a sense of the variousness of the Universe, not to be fathomed by our intellects.... The moral of his writings is that all points of view, reasonably coherent and in some sense with an application, have something to contribute to our understanding of the universe, and also involve omissions whereby they fail to include the totality of evident fact. The duty of tolerance is our finite homage to the ... complexity of accomplished fact which exceeds our stretch of insight. (AI 51–52)

With regard to values, Whitehead affirmed pluralism by rejecting "the notion of the one type of perfection at which the Universe aims" (AI 291). The notion of "one ideal 'order' which all actual entities should attain," he said, "arises from the disastrous overmoralization of thought under the influence of fanaticism, or pedantry" (PR 84). Likewise, saying that the divine reality of the universe aims at "importance," he rejected the tendency to equate importance as such with any of its species, such as morality, logic, religion, or art. By this false equation, he said, "the ultimate aim infused into the process of nature has been trivialized into the guardianship of mores, or of rules of thought, or of mystic sentiment, or of aesthetic enjoyment" (MT 12). On the basis of this pluralism with respect to ultimate ideals, Whitehead pointed to the greatness that can be present in very different styles of life, such as the "stern self-restraint" of the Puritans or the "aesthetic culture" of the Italian Renaissance and modern Paris (PR 337–38). There is not only one right way to be human.

At the same time, Whitehead's position has bases for resisting a complete relativism of truth and value. Whitehead's dipolar theism, with its distinction between God's primordial nature and consequent nature—which distinguishes between God as influencing and God as being influenced by the world, respectively—is relevant to this issue. The primordial nature of God, which is God's appetitive envisagement of eternal possibilities or forms, lies behind Whitehead's support of universal values. Although no culture's particular ideas of beauty are to be universalized, "The teleology of the Universe is directed to the production of Beauty," defined as experience characterized by harmonious intensity (AI 264). Expressing this point in the even more general language of "importance," Whitehead stated: "The generic aim of process is the attainment of importance, in that species and to that extent which in that instance is possible" (MT 12). With regard to morality in particular, Whitehead commented upon the parochial nature of all moral codes: "There is no one behaviour system belonging to the essential character of the universe, as the universal moral ideal" (MT 8–11). But he added that there *is* something that is universal: a "spirit," a "general ideal," that "should permeate any behaviour system," namely, the aim to maximize the importance that is possible in every particular situation (MT 14–15). This ultimately nonrelativistic stance was possible because of Whitehead's doctrine of the primordial nature of God, conjoined with his non-sensationist doctrine of perception, which allows us to experience God. For example, having said that we have experiences of ideals, "of ideals entertained, of ideals aimed at, of ideals achieved, of ideals defaced," he added: "This is the experience of the deity of the universe" (MT 103).

Whitehead's ultimately nonrelativistic stance on truth depends on both natures of God. On the one hand, our prehension of the primordial nature lies behind our sense of the importance of truth (MT 8–11, AI 11). On the other hand, the doctrine of the consequent nature supports our (inevitable) presupposition that there is such a thing as "the truth" about anything, because it exists somewhere: "The truth itself is nothing else than how the composite natures of the organic actualities of the world obtain adequate representation in ... the 'consequent nature' of God" (PR 12). Without this doctrine, Whitehead would have had a Nietzschean perspectivalism, in which, by the ontological principle, there could be no truth because there would be no actuality in which it could subsist.

Whitehead, therefore, gave due weight to the postmodern emphasis on cultural relativity with regard to both values and perceptions of truth, but without rejecting the idea of universal values and truths. As a postmodern modernism, his position does not undermine the enlightenment's aspiration, emphasized in Habermas's modernism, for universal human liberation.[68]

Belief in Progress

The statement—or accusation—that someone "believes in progress" is ambiguous. The belief in progress can mean the belief (1) that progress is possible, (2) that it has occurred, (3) that it is promoted by some power in the universe, or (4) that it is inevitable. Whitehead believed in progress in the first three senses but not the fourth.

One of his reasons for believing that progress is at least possible was stated in the previous point. That is, one of the main reasons for rejecting the idea of progress is the conviction that there are no objective criteria by which to call anything an improvement over what existed earlier. It is common in neo-Darwinian evolutionary circles, for example, to deny that the evolutionary process is progressive in any objective sense, because there is thought to be no general criterion—other than evolutionary success, defined as survival—by which to judge excellence. In recent years, this idea was pushed by the late Stephen Jay Gould.[69] This kind of complete relativism with regard to truth and value, however, would lead to the conclusion that not only is no social system objectively better than any other, but also that no worldview is better than any other—which would undermine the reason for accepting neo-Darwinism as an advance over prior views. This kind of complete relativism is hence self-refuting.

Whitehead, in any case, could affirm the possibility of progress because he rejected, as the "evolutionist fallacy," the "belief that fitness for survival is identical with the best exemplification of the Art of Life" (FR 4). For Whitehead, by contrast, the cosmic aim is "a three-fold urge: (i) to live, (ii) to live well, and (iii), to live better," with the latter meaning "to acquire an increase in satisfaction" (FR 8). The criterion for progress is, therefore, richness of experience. This criterion is closely related to the criterion of maximizing importance, previously discussed. On this basis, Whitehead affirmed the possibility of progress in social organization as well as in biological evolution (PR 14; AI 15; SMW 107; FR 4, 9, 89–90).

He also believed that, given this criterion, it was impossible to deny that progress has occurred. This denial can be made, to be sure, by stipulating extreme criteria. With regard to biological evolution, for example, some thinkers have assumed that we could affirm evolutionary progress only if it is *uniform*, going on without interruption, and *general*, occurring in all lines and from the beginning to the end of each line. As Francisco Ayala points out, however, to affirm that progress has occurred it is necessary only to say that *net* progress has occurred in *some* lines. And by any reasonable criterion of progress, such as Whitehead's criterion, or Ayala's criterion ("the ability of an organism to obtain and process information about the environment"),[70] net progress has certainly occurred in the line that has produced mammals.

As indicated earlier, Whitehead also believed that, thanks to the primordial nature of God, the universe as a whole promotes progress. In perhaps his most explicit statement on this subject, he says: "Apart from the intervention of God, there could be nothing new in the world.... The course of creation would be a dead level of ineffectiveness.... The novel hybrid feelings derived from God with the derivative sympathetic conceptual valuations, are the foundations of progress" (PR 247). Whitehead, in sum, believed that progress is possible, that it occurs, and even that the universe promotes it.

Most criticisms of the "enlightenment's belief in progress," however, are directed at the optimistic enlightenment belief, central to the systems of both Hegel and Marx, that progress is inevitable, being somehow built into the very nature of things. Whitehead emphatically did not accept belief in progress in this sense. He pointed out, for one thing, that progress is far from universal: "[I]f we survey the universe of nature, mere static survival seems to be the general rule, accompanied by a slow decay. The instances of the upward trend are represented by a sprinkling of exceptional cases" (FR 29).

Whitehead's primary basis for saying that progress is not inevitable, although it is favored by God and hence the universe, was his naturalistic theism, with its distinction between God and creativity. The creatures, in Whitehead's pluralistic universe, necessarily have their own creative power vis-à-vis God (whereas the finite things in Hegel's more monistic system had little, if any, power of their own vis-à-vis the Absolute Geist). Accordingly, the divine lures result in progress only if the creatures respond positively. Enlightenment deists, by contrast, still largely presupposed an omnipotent creator, who had built in an overriding drive toward progress. Even Darwin retained that presupposition, which lay behind his belief in inevitable biological and civilizational progress.[71] Whitehead rejected that view without, like most neo-Darwinists, rejecting the belief in divine directivity altogether.

A second basis for process philosophy's rejection of the idea of inevitable progress is the principle that every condition increasing the possibilities for good also proportionately increases the possibilities for evil. Process philosophy does not construe this principle to mean that every increase in good is necessarily accompanied by an actual and correlative increase in evil—a doctrine that would imply the impossibility of social progress. But the mere fact that every advance increases the possibilities for evil is sufficient to render progress far from inevitable. Having made this principle central to my development of a process theodicy, I have more recently employed it to show how, at the human level, creaturely creativity can, besides being diametrically opposed to divine creativity, be sufficiently powerful to threaten divine aims.[72] The development of a civilization with the power to destroy itself and all other higher forms of life—forms of existence that it has taken our creator billions of years to bring about—is the ultimate revelation in our time of this potentiality and, thereby, of the fact that progress, while possible, is not inevitable.

CONCLUSION

Whiteheadian process philosophy cannot be said to be primarily proenlightenment or antienlightenment. In general, it favors the formal commitments with which we usually associate the enlightenment, insofar as those commitments reflect the acceptance of universal truths and values and the rejection of supernaturalism, both ontological and epistemic. The enlightenment, however, was based upon substantive ideas about the natural world and human experience that are strongly rejected by Whitehead. This fact is no coincidence, I have suggested, because Whitehead's philosophy can be considered a postmodern reemergence of the kind of philosophical theology that was rejected by the leading opinion makers of the late seventeenth century. In this kind of approach, the effort is made to combine scientific experience, religious experience, and philosophical reflection to produce an integral, "pansophist" worldview that is equally adequate for the scientific, religious, and philosophical communities. Substantively, this approach rejects the modern options of regarding God as either omnipotent or nonexistent. It attributes spontaneity, experience, and internal relations to all individuals. As a corollary of its panexperientialism, it attributes nonsensory perceptual experience to human beings, through which they are open to the whole universe, thereby being able to know all sorts of things that enlightenment-based thought had to attribute to a deistic implantation or deny that we can know at all. Building on these beliefs, this Whiteheadian type of philosophy regards God as present in all things and the whole world as present in God. For these reasons, this kind of philosophy opposes most of the substantive ideas that have been identified with enlightenment modernity. It can best be summarized, therefore, as post-modern modernism.

I began this chapter with Hartshorne's suggestion that we need a new enlightenment. My friendly amendment to this suggestion is that the kind of new enlightenment needed should involve a postmodern incorporation of several ideas that were, for dubious reasons, rejected at the outset of the previous enlightenment. In the following five chapters, I show how this type of postmodern philosophy can solve several problems of modern thought, beginning with the mind-body problem.

Part 2. Whitehead on Consciousness, Ecology, Truth, Time, and Ethics

3

Consciousness as a Subjective Form: Interactionism without Dualism

Whitehead's position on consciousness differs radically from that of the approaches that have dominated modern philosophy: Cartesian dualism and reductionist materialism. But its postmodern approach, based on carrying through Descartes' subjectivist principle to its logical conclusion (see the appendix), does share aspects of these two positions. Part of its novelty, in fact, is that it can combine ideas that had previously seemed irreconcilable.

With dualists, Whitehead agrees that consciousness belongs to an entity—a mind or psyche—that is distinct from the brain. Partly for this reason, he agrees that genuine freedom can be attributed to conscious experience.

With materialists, Whitehead shares a naturalistic sensibility, thereby eschewing any even implicitly supernaturalistic solution to philosophical problems. Partly for this reason, he rejects any dualism between two kinds of actualities. Like materialists, in other words, he affirms a pluralistic monism. He thereby regards consciousness as a function of something more fundamental.

And yet he, like dualists, rejects the reductionism involved in functionalism as understood by materialists. He can thereby affirm genuine interaction between the brain and the mind.

All of these features of Whitehead's position are implicit in his doctrine that *consciousness is the subjective form of an intellectual feeling, which arises, if at all, only in a late phase of a moment of experience*. It will be the purpose of this chapter to explain this idea and show how it enables us to solve a number of philosophical problems associated with consciousness.

SOME CRITERIA FOR AN ADEQUATE DOCTRINE OF CONSCIOUSNESS

In listing the criteria by which to judge the success of any metaphysical theory, Whitehead includes "adequacy" as well as self-consistency and coherence (PR 3).

Although it is now fashionable in some circles to argue that there can be no universal, tradition-transcendent criteria in terms of which to judge the adequacy of theories, Whitehead disagreed. The "metaphysical rule of evidence," he said, is "that we must bow to those presumptions which, in despite of criticism, we still employ for the regulation of our lives" (PR 151).

In affirming this view, Whitehead was explicitly rejecting Hume's dualism between theory and practice, according to which we have various "natural beliefs," such as the belief in an external world, that we necessarily presuppose in practice but cannot affirm in philosophical theory. Whitehead, in response, said: "Whatever is found in "practice" must lie within the scope of the metaphysical description. When the description fails to include the 'practice,' the metaphysics is inadequate and requires revision. There can be no appeal to practice to supplement metaphysics" (PR 13).

Some advocates of deconstruction, using a Kantian description, refer to ideas that we cannot help presupposing, even though we must consider them false, as "transcendental illusions."[1] As pointed out in chapter 1, however, to call false an idea that we cannot help presupposing is to violate the law of noncontradiction, usually considered the first rule of reason, because one is both (implicitly) affirming and (explicitly) denying one and the same proposition.[2] Jürgen Habermas and Karl-Otto Apel, as we saw, call such a self-contradiction a "performative contradiction," because the performance of making the statement contradicts the statement's meaning.[3] For example, if I say that I doubt your existence, the fact that I am addressing you contradicts my professed doubt. Whitehead makes the same point by saying that we must avoid "negations of what in practice is presupposed" (PR 13).

In enunciating this criterion, Whitehead thereby stood, as we have seen, in the tradition of "commonsense" philosophy. The term *common sense*, however, is now often used to refer to ideas that, although widely held at a certain time and place, are false. Science, in fact, is often described as a systematic assault on common sense, undermining such "commonsense" ideas as the flatness of the earth, its centrality in the universe, and the solidity of matter. I distinguish between these two meanings, accordingly, by referring to common sense in the latter sense as "soft-core" common sense, while referring to those ideas that we all inevitably presuppose as "hard-core" commonsense ideas. It was common sense in the hard-core sense that Whitehead had in mind in referring to his "endeavor to interpret experience in accordance with the overpowering deliverance of common sense" (PR 50). Commonsense notions of this hard-core type are "overpowering" because we cannot help presupposing them, even in the act of verbally denying them.

With regard to conscious experience, four of these overpowering notions are (1) that conscious experience exists, (2) that it exerts influence upon the body,

(3) that it has a degree of self-determining freedom, and (4) that it can act in accord with various norms. The fact that all four of these notions are inevitably presupposed in practice is widely recognized by contemporary philosophers.

First, the impossibility of doubting the existence of one's own conscious experience was famously emphasized by Descartes. Now Jaakko Hintikka, in an essay titled "Cogito, Ergo Sum," has shown that Descartes' argument involved the notion of a performative self-contradiction. If I say, "I doubt herewith, now, that I exist," then, explains Hintikka, "the propositional component contradicts the performative component of the speech act expressed by that self-referential sentence."[4] Insofar as the extreme version of materialism known as "eliminative materialism" seeks to eliminate all references to conscious experience, it is involved in this kind of self-refuting contradiction.

With regard to our second notion, the efficacy of conscious experience for bodily behavior, William Seager observes that "it presents the aspect of a datum rather than a disputable hypothesis."[5] Ted Honderich, explicitly bringing out the hard-core commonsense status of this belief, says that its main recommendation is "the futility of contemplating its denial." With regard to epiphenomenalism, which is the doctrine that conscious experience does *not* exert causal efficacy on the body, Honderich says: "Off the page, no one believes it."[6] Suggesting a *reductio ab absurdum* of epiphenomenalism, Jaegwon Kim says: "If our reasons and desires have no causal efficacy at all in influencing our bodily actions, then perhaps no one has ever performed a single intentional action!"[7] One's theory, Kim insists, must have room for the reality of psychophysical causation, as when, feeling a pain, one's decision to call the doctor leads one to walk to the telephone and dial it.[8] John Searle, in a similar vein, includes "the reality and causal efficacy of consciousness" among the "obvious facts" about our minds and endorses the "commonsense objection to 'eliminative materialism' that it is 'crazy to say that . . . my beliefs and desires don't play any role in my behavior.' "[9]

Our third idea, that such actions are based on a degree of self-determining freedom, is equally recognized to be an inevitable presupposition. Searle, pointing out that people *have* been able to give up some commonsense beliefs, such as the beliefs in a flat earth and literal "sunsets," says that "we can't similarly give up the conviction of freedom because that conviction is built into every normal, conscious intentional action. . . . [W]e can't act otherwise than on the assumption of freedom, no matter how much we learn about how the world works as a determined physical system."[10] Similarly, Thomas Nagel, in spite of seeing no way to give a coherent account of freedom, says: "I can no more help holding myself and others responsible in ordinary life than I can help feeling that my actions originate with me."[11] To be sure, some philosophers, such as William Lycan, try to make this *feeling* of freedom compatible with complete determinism by redefining freedom. According to this compatibilist definition, to say I did X freely is *not* to say that I could have acted otherwise.[12] But to speak of freedom only in this compatibilist, Pickwickian sense, both Nagel and Searle see, is not to speak of freedom as we presuppose it.[13]

Fourth, it is also widely recognized that we presuppose that our actions can be shaped by various norms. Kim, in emphasizing the importance of affirming the efficacy of our decisions for our bodily actions, says that otherwise we "would render our moral and cognitive life wholly unintelligible" because we could no longer affirm that "our norms and beliefs regulate our deliberations and decisions."[14] Charles Larmore likewise recognizes that both moral and cognitive norms somehow exercise authority over our conscious experience. He says, for example, that it would be ridiculous to suggest "that even so basic a rule of reasoning as the avoidance of contradiction has no more authority than what we choose to give it."[15]

INADEQUACIES OF DUALISM AND MATERIALISM

It would seem to be widely agreed, therefore, that for any theory of conscious experience to be deemed even minimally adequate, it would have to do justice to these four notions. But both dualism and materialism have difficulty affirming these notions in a self-consistent way, at least without appealing to supernatural assistance. I will discuss their difficulties with these four notions in order.

First, for Descartes, there was no problem in asserting *the existence of consciousness*, as he simply assumed that God, in creating the world, had created minds as well as bodies ex nihilo. But philosophers today presuppose a naturalistic, evolutionary worldview. Materialists and dualists, both presupposing a materialistic view of the ultimate units of nature, must affirm that conscious experience somehow emerged out of entities wholly devoid of experience. For dualists, this means the emergence of minds, as a new kind of *actuality* (or *substance*); for materialists, this means the emergence of consciousness as a new *property* of matter. In either case, this kind of emergence is hard to make intelligible.

From the side of dualism, Karl Popper and H. D. Lewis implicitly admitted that they could not explain it.[16] Geoffrey Madell, more candidly, has explicitly admitted that "the appearance of consciousness in the course of evolution must appear for the dualist to be an utterly inexplicable emergence of something entirely new, an emergence which must appear quite bizarre."[17] Some materialists think that this problem uniquely exists for dualism. J. J. C. Smart, for example, said: "How could a nonphysical property or entity suddenly arise in the course of animal evolution? . . . [W]hat sort of chemical process could lead to the springing into existence of something nonphysical? No enzyme can catalyze the production of a spook!"[18] Smart failed to see, however, that the idea that an *apparent* spook is produced out of wholly insentient stuff creates an equal difficulty. But Colin McGinn, another materialist, does see this, saying that "we do not know how consciousness might have arisen by natural processes from antecedently existing material things. Somehow or other sentience sprang from pulpy matter, giving matter an inner aspect, but we have no idea how this leap was propelled." McGinn's reference to "natural" processes is essential to his point. "One is tempted," he says, "to turn to divine assistance: for only a kind of miracle could produce *this* from *that*. It would take a supernatural magician to extract consciousness from matter. Consciousness appears to introduce a sharp break in the natural order—a point at which scientific naturalism runs out of steam."[19] At least one contemporary philosopher, Richard Swinburne, succumbs to this temptation, arguing thus: "[S]cience cannot explain the evolution of a mental life. That is to say,...there is nothing in the nature of certain physical events...to give rise to connections to [mental events]....God, being omnipotent, would have the power to produce a soul."[20] But McGinn, speaking for most contemporary philosophers by insisting that naturalism must be presupposed, cannot countenance such an answer.[21]

McGinn is far from the only materialist to see the difficulty of how, as McGinn puts it, "the aggregation of millions of individually insentient neurons [constituting the brain could] generate subjective awareness."[22] Thomas Nagel, using *en soi* for a being that exists merely "in itself" and *pour soi* for one that, having experience, exists "for itself," has said: "One cannot derive a *pour soi* from an *en soi*....This gap is logically unbridgeable. If a bodiless god wanted to create a conscious being, he could not expect to do it by combining together in organic form a lot of particles with none but physical properties."[23] The problem here for both dualists and materialists is not that they deny the existence of consciousness. It is that their positions cannot account for this existence.

Second, a similar problem obtains with our hard-core commonsense presupposition that *our conscious experience exerts causal efficacy upon our bodies*, thus directing our bodily actions. Although dualists and materialists inevitably presuppose that such efficacy occurs, as we have seen, they cannot explain how. For dualists, one reason for this difficulty is simply the problem of understanding how a mental or spiritual entity could influence physical entities, understood to be completely different in kind. As Madell admits, "the nature of the causal connection between the mental and the physical, as the Cartesian conceives of it, is utterly mysterious."[24] Descartes himself was not embarrassed by this mysteriousness, because for him the problem was solved by appeal to divine omnipotence, an appeal that was brought out more explicitly in the doctrine of "occasionalism" enunciated by his followers Nicolas Malebranche and Arnold Geulincx.[25] As William James said, "For thinkers of that age, 'God' was the great solvent of all absurdities."[26] Aside from a few throwbacks to that age such as Swinburne, dualists today cannot employ this solvent, so they cannot explain our conviction that the mind affects the body.

Epiphenomenalists, like dualists, think of the mind as a mental or spiritual entity, distinct from the brain, but they use the impossibility of understanding how it *could* affect the brain as a basis for denying that it *does*. This denial, however, involves arbitrariness. At least one advocate of epiphenomenalism, Keith Campbell, admits that it is arbitrary, because it "rejects only one half of the interaction of matter and spirit." That is, epiphenomenalism denies "the action of spirit on matter" while accepting the idea that the spiritual mind emerged out of a wholly materialistic universe, thereby affirming "the action of the material on the spiritual."[27] Campbell's twofold motive for this arbitrariness, he says, is that it allows him, on the one hand, to admit that the mind exists, so that he need not, with materialists, think of psychological states, such as pains, as simply properties of the brain,[28] and yet, on the other hand, to "preserve the completeness of the physical accounts of human action."[29]

This latter part of Campbell's motive reflects a widespread conviction held by materialists as well as epiphenomenalists, the conviction that, as Jaegwon Kim puts it, the bottom layer of nature is controlled by the laws of physics and chemistry so that it cannot be influenced by higher levels of nature. Given this conviction, our thoughts cannot influence our bodily behavior, because the latter must in principle be fully understandable in terms of the laws of physics and chemistry. But this view rules out Kim's affirmation, which he had made in opposition to epiphenomenalism, that we walk to the telephone *because* we have decided to make a call. Upon seeing this contradiction, Kim admitted that materialism seems "to be up against a dead end."[30]

Third, materialists have even greater difficulty with freedom than with downward causation. Searle, for example, believes that science "allows no place for freedom of the will."[31] This denial follows from Searle's materialistic assumptions, which he summarizes thus: "Since nature consists of particles and their relations with each other, and since everything can be accounted for in terms of those particles and their relations, there is simply no room for freedom of the will."[32]

Scientific explanation, Searle further argues, is bottom-up explanation, which explains the behavior of all complex things in terms of their most elementary constituents.[33] The idea of statistical indeterminacy at the quantum level provides no basis for affirming freedom, Searle adds, because all such indeterminacy is canceled out in macroobjects, such as billiard balls and human bodies.[34] So, although Searle admits that we cannot help presupposing that we and others act freely, the fact that freedom is not reconcilable with scientific materialism means that our feeling of freedom must be an illusion built into the structure of human experience by evolution.[35] Searle explicitly admits his failure, saying that although "ideally, I would like to be able to keep both my commonsense conceptions and my scientific beliefs ... [,] when it comes to the question of freedom and determinism, I am ... unable to reconcile the two."[36]

Searle's inability to affirm genuine freedom is echoed by many other materialists, such as Colin McGinn, Thomas Nagel, and Daniel Dennett.[37]

This inability to affirm freedom, furthermore, undermines the claim by materialists to have endorsed our second notion, downward causation from conscious experience to the body. This is at least the case if we accept, as I do, Mortimer Taube's careful definition of an efficient cause: "An event A causes event B, when B results partly from some activity or influence originating in A."[38] In other words, if an event in the life of my mind helps bring about an event in my body, I can rightly refer to my mind as a cause upon my body only if the bodily event resulted partly from some activity that originated in the mind-event itself. Materialists cannot say this because for them the mind, not being an entity distinct from the brain, cannot be a locus of power.

Searle is explicit about the fact that his denial of human freedom depends on this assumption that we do not have a mind that could, as he puts it, force the particles of the brain to "swerve from their paths."[39] Because consciousness is merely an emergent property of the brain, it cannot "cause things that could not be explained by the causal behavior of the neurons."[40] Dualists, by contrast, do affirm the existence of a mind that, being distinct from the brain, can be affirmed as the locus of self-determining freedom. Dualists, however, cannot explain how the mind, being different in kind from the neurons of the brain, can influence them. Searle, driving home this problem, says: "How could something mental make a physical difference? Are we supposed to think that our thoughts and feelings can somehow produce chemical effects on our brains...? How could such a thing occur? Are we supposed to think that thoughts can wrap themselves around the axons or shake the dendrites or sneak inside the cell wall and attack the cell nucleus?"[41] Dualists, not being able to answer this question— as Madell and others admit—can, therefore, really do little more justice than can materialists to our inescapable assumption that our bodily actions reflect a degree of freedom.

Fourth, the same inability obtains with regard to our presupposition that we can *consciously act in terms of norms*. McGinn points to the difficulty of this problem for his materialist position by asking "how a physical organism can be subject to the norms of rationality. How, for example, does *modus ponens* get its grip on the causal transitions between mental states?"[42] The problem is that causation involving norms, which are *abstract* (rather than physical) entities, would be wholly different from billiard-ball causation, which McGinn, in line with his materialism, takes to be paradigmatic for causation in general.[43] "[C]ausal relations between...abstract entities and human minds," says McGinn, would be "funny kinds of causation."[44] Another way to state the problem is to point out that if norms—whether cognitive, moral, or aesthetic—are to have some authority over our experience, there must be some way for us to apprehend these norms. But materialists, equating the mind with the brain, hold that all perception is through the body's physical senses, which cannot be activated by nonphysical things such as norms.

Again, dualists, by virtue of distinguishing between the mind and the brain, are able in principle to affirm the reality of nonsensory perception, through which norms could be apprehended, and some dualists do make this affirmation.[45] But they still have the problem of being unable to explain how a nonphysical mind can affect the physical body, so dualists cannot really explain how norm-guided behavior is possible.

Dualism and materialism, in sum, are complete failures with regard to our hard-core commonsense assumptions about our own conscious experience. They, accordingly, must be regarded as woefully inadequate. This woeful inadequacy suggests that the world must in reality be radically different from the world as portrayed by both dualists and materialists.

WHITEHEAD'S PANEXPERIENTIALISM

Such a radically different worldview was proffered by Whitehead. Part of this difference involves the fact that Whitehead became a theist of sorts, in order to explain various features of our world that seemed otherwise inexplicable. But this adoption of a theistic perspective did not involve any recursion to supernaturalism. He rejected the earlier "appeal to a *deus ex machina* who was capable of rising superior to the difficulties of metaphysics" (SMW 156). In line with his complete eschewal of supernaturalism, he rejected any doctrine that implied a dualism between two types of actualities.[46] Positively, this rejection took the form of the acceptance of panexperientialism, according to which all actualities have experience.

Accepting this view implied the rejection of what he called "vacuous actualities," meaning things that are fully actual and yet wholly devoid of experience (PR 29, 167). Because the assumption that the ultimate units of nature are indeed vacuous actualities was, as we saw in chapter 2, one of the founding dogmas of modern thought, which is common to both dualism and materialism, Whitehead's rejection of it in favor of panexperientialism is one of the most important ways in which his philosophy is postmodern.

Panexperientialism is, to be sure, still thought in many circles to be self-evidently absurd. But this is partly because the *pan* in panexperientialism is often taken to mean that literally *all* things, including aggregations such as sticks and stones, have experience. Whitehead's doctrine, however, is only that all *genuine individuals* have experience. Genuine individuals are of two types. There are simple individuals, which are the most elementary units of nature (whether these be thought to be quarks or even simpler units). And there are what Charles Hartshorne, in developing Whitehead's panexperientialism more fully, called "compound individuals,"[47] which are compounded out of simpler individuals, as when atoms are compounded out of subatomic particles, molecules out of atoms, living cells out of macromolecules, and animals out of cells.

These compound individuals are true individuals because the experience of their members gives birth to a highest level experience, which is the "dominant" member of the organism as a whole. This dominant member gives the compound individual a unity of experience and a unity of action, so that it can act purposively with a degree of freedom. These compound individuals hence *differ in kind* from mere aggregations of individuals, such as rocks and telephones, in which the experiences of the individual molecules do not give rise to a higher level, inclusive experience. For this reason, I emphasize that Whitehead's doctrine should be called not simply "panexperientialism" but "panexperientialism with organizational duality."[48]

A second reason for considering doctrines of this type absurd is the assumption that they attribute not just experience, but *conscious* experience, to all things, or at least all individuals. This assumption has been based partly on the older term for such doctrines, *panpsychism*, which, by implying that all things are psyches, suggests that they all have high-grade, conscious mentality. Whitehead himself evidently rejected 'panpsychism' for this reason.[49] Although he did not propose the term *panexperientialism* as an alternative, it is suggested by many of his statements, such as his rejection of the concept of an actuality "void of subjective experience," his statement that "apart from the experiences of subjects there is nothing," and his denial that there is any meaning of "togetherness" other than "experiential togetherness" (PR 167, 189).[50] Whitehead's panexperientialism, in any case, holds that all individuals have experience, but that *consciousness is a very high-level form of experience*, enjoyed by relatively few individuals. With these clarifications, we can see that the standard rejections of panexperientialism as absurd—such as McGinn's claim that it attributes thoughts to rocks[51]—do not apply to Whitehead's version of it.[52]

There are still, to be sure, other reasons for resisting the doctrine, chief among which is probably pointed to by Nagel's statement that "if one travels too far down the phylogenetic tree, people gradually shed their faith that there is experience there at all."[53] This reason, however, is an example of *soft-core* common sense, which science has repeatedly undermined.

The scientific undermining of this particular assumption, that experience could not go all the way down, is, in fact, already well advanced. Whereas Descartes denied experience to all earthly creatures except humans, some leading ethologists now posit experience at least as far down as bees.[54] Going much further down, there is now a wide range of evidence suggestive of the idea that single-cell organisms, such as amoebae and paramecia, have a primitive type of experience.[55] Going still further, to the prokaryotic level, some biologists have provided evidence for a rudimentary form of decision making, based on a rudimentary form of memory, in bacteria.[56] Furthermore, although DNA molecules were originally pictured in mechanistic terms, later studies suggested a more organismic understanding.[57] Going all the way down, quantum physics has shown entities at this level not to be analogous to billiard balls,[58] and, as physicist David Bohm and philosopher William Seager have said, quantum theory implies that the behavior of the elementary units of nature can be explained only by attributing to them something analogous to our own mentality.[59] Accordingly, the prejudice that experience cannot go all the way down, far from being supported by any scientific evidence, is being increasingly undermined by the relevant evidence—this being one of the ways in which modern science is becoming postmodern.

I have, in any case, argued elsewhere that this empirical support for panexperientialism is only one of many lines of argumentation pointing toward its truth.[60] Another of those lines is that panexperientialism, and apparently *only* panexperientialism, can do justice to the four hard-core commonsense assumptions about conscious experience examined earlier. A basis for this argument can be provided by spelling out Whitehead's panexperientialism as the doctrine that the actual world is comprised of *creative, experiential, physical-mental events.* I will deal with each of these terms in reverse order, beginning with the fourth term, *events.*

All the world's actual entities in the fullest sense are momentary *events.* These are all spatiotemporal events with a finite inner duration, ranging perhaps from less than a billionth of a second at the subatomic level to a tenth or twentieth of a second at the level of human experience. All *enduring* individuals, such as electrons and minds, are temporal societies of such events. This feature provides another reason why 'panexperientialism' is a better term for this doctrine than 'panpsychism.' The latter term, being based on the word *psyche*, suggests that the ultimate units of the world are enduring individuals, whereas 'panexperientialism' suggests that they are experiences, which are momentary.

In any case, each such event has both *physical* and *mental* aspects, with the physical aspect always being prior. The physical aspect is the event's reception of the efficient causation of prior events into itself. This receptivity is called "physical prehension," or "physical feeling," which is a mode of perception more basic than sensory perception. An event originates with a multiplicity of physical prehensions, each of which has two aspects: an *objective datum*, which is *what* is felt, and a *subjective form*, which is *how* that datum is felt. To say that every unit-event (in distinction from an aggregational event)[61] has a mental aspect means that it has a degree—however slight in the most elementary events—of spontaneity or self-determination. Although the event's physical pole is *given* to it, its mentality is its capacity to decide precisely what to make of its given foundation. Its physicality is its relation to past actuality; its mentality involves its prehension of ideality or possibility, through which it escapes total determination by the past.

Each event, the second of our terms indicates, is *experiential* from beginning to end, which means that, in distinction from usage reflecting dualism, the physical aspect of the event is not devoid of experience, hence the mental aspect is not uniquely associated with experience. An event's mentality is simply its experience insofar as it is self-determining. Whitehead emphasizes the experiential nature of unit-events by calling them "occasions of experience."

With regard to the first term, *creative*, we have already seen that each event is, in its mental pole, *self*-creative, deciding precisely how to respond to the efficient causation exerted upon it. A second dimension of an experience's creativity, which comes after its self-determination, is its efficient causation on subsequent events, through which it shares in the creation of the future. This transition from self-creation to efficient causation betokens another distinction to be made with regard to each unit-event. Each occasion of experience exists first as a *subject* of experience, with its physical and mental poles. But then its subjectivity perishes, and it becomes an *object* for subsequent subjects. In each enduring individual, accordingly, there is a perpetual oscillation between two modes of existence: subjectivity and objectivity.[62] Put in causal language, there is a perpetual oscillation between final causation (in the sense of self-determination) and efficient causation.

Whitehead's postmodern solution to the modern mind-body problem depends partly on this doctrine of creative, experiential, physical-mental events and partly on the idea of compound individuals, one crucial point of which is that the dominant members of increasingly complex compound individuals have an increasing degree of mentality and thereby an increasingly greater capacity for both richness of experience and self-determination. The occasions of experience constituting a squirrel's psyche, for example, enjoy a much more complex, sophisticated mode of experience, and far more power for self-determination, than the occasions of experience constituting any of the cells in its body.

WHITEHEAD'S EXPLANATION OF OUR HARD-CORE COMMONSENSE ASSUMPTIONS ABOUT CONSCIOUSNESS

I turn now to the question of how Whitehead's panexperientialism can do justice to our hard-core commonsense assumptions about conscious experience.

With regard to the existence of consciousness, we can begin with Whitehead's discussion of William James's essay "Does Consciousness Exist?" In this essay—which, as we saw in chapter 1, Whitehead saw as inaugurating a new era in philosophy, beyond the one inaugurated by Descartes—James rejected the existence of consciousness in the sense of an "aboriginal stuff [to be] contrasted with that of which material objects are made, out of which our thoughts of them are made" (SMW 144). Besides endorsing this point,

Whitehead also endorsed James's contention that consciousness is a particular *function* of experience.

To understand James and Whitehead correctly here, it is important to see that they are *not* saying that consciousness is a function of the brain. Rather, consciousness is called a function of *experience*. It is also important not to take the denial that consciousness is an "aboriginal stuff" to mean that experience is not. Experience *is* an aboriginal stuff—for James, who affirmed panpsychism,[63] and for Whitehead. But it is not, of course, an aboriginal stuff *different in kind* from the stuff out of which material things are made. The whole point of panexperientialism is that creative experience is the aboriginal stuff out of which human experience and what we call "material objects" are both made. However, in human beings and other highly complex compound individuals, experience can give rise to conscious thoughts, which have a function that is not enjoyed in the experience of low-grade individuals. This function, said James, is "knowing." Whitehead agreed, saying that consciousness is "the function of knowing" (SMW 144, 151).

Given Whitehead's panexperientialist ontology, the main reasons for denying the full-fledged reality of conscious experience disappear. If we hold that neurons are sentient, the insoluble problem of how conscious experience could emerge out of insentient neurons does not arise. Even McGinn grants this point, saying that if we could suppose neurons to have "proto-conscious states," it would be "easy enough to see how neurons could generate consciousness."[64]

The problem of mental or downward causation—how one's decisions can affect one's brain and thereby one's bodily behavior—is overcome for the same reason. Hartshorne explains panexperientialism's solution to both sides of the problem of interaction by saying that "cells can influence our human experiences because they have feelings that we can feel. To deal with the influences of human experiences upon cells, one turns this around. *We* have feelings that *cells* can feel."[65] As this statement shows, panexperientialism involves a radically new conception of causation. Rather than, with materialists, thinking of billiard-ball collisions as paradigmatic or, with dualists, thinking in terms of two radically different kinds of causation—that between minds, and that between bodies—and then wondering how minds and bodies can interact, panexperientialism conceives of all causation as involving causation that is analogous to the transference of feeling between two moments of our own experience.[66] Accordingly, to hold that "our thoughts and feelings can somehow produce chemical effects on our brains," we do not have to imagine, as Searle suggests, thoughts "wrap[ping] themselves around the axons or shak[ing] the dendrites [of the brain's neurons]."

The other standard reason for denying downward causation from conscious experience to the body—the idea that the behavior of things in the physical world is determined by laws of nature—also does not apply. For Whitehead's panexperientialism, the laws of nature are not to be thought of as prescriptive—the interpretation of them that derives, as we saw in chapter 2, from the "legal-mechanical" worldview of the seventeenth-century supernaturalists. Whitehead, like James and Peirce before him, instead regards the so-called laws of nature to be descriptive of the widespread *habits* of nature (MT 154–55).[67] And, just as we feel and act differently in different environments, so do cells, molecules, and electrons. After a molecule migrates from the soil through a carrot to a human body, it is subject to different influences—including influences from the body's living cells and its dominant member, the mind—and hence behaves differently (SMW 78–80). This fact is itself one of the "laws of nature." Holding that our conscious experiences, with their degree of freedom, guide our bodies, therefore, does not violate any laws of nature.

I have just mentioned our third hard-core commonsense assumption about our own experience, namely, that we act with a degree of freedom. One dimension of Whitehead's explanation of this assumption is the idea that all individual events are *creative* events, exercising at least some slight iota of self-determination. He thereby rejects another founding dogma of modern thought—the contention, originally insisted on by Boyle and other advocates of the legal-mechanical worldview, that the ultimate units of nature had to be wholly inert. By rejecting this modern dogma, Whitehead did not have to try to explain how our experience, with its great capacity for self-determination, could have arisen out of entities that interact in a wholly deterministic way. Freedom did not suddenly appear at some point in the evolutionary process. Rather, compound individuals with increasingly more mentality emerged out of ones with less.

It is, of course, one thing to assert that all individuals have a degree of freedom; it is another thing to *explain how* freedom is conceivable in a world in which all events are enmeshed in a universal nexus of efficient causation. The key to this explanation is the idea, discussed above, that every enduring individual, such as a molecule or a human psyche, perpetually oscillates between subjectivity and objectivity. Each occasion of experience in an enduring individual exists first as a subject. In this mode, it begins as an effect of prior events, receiving efficient causation from them. This is the subject's physical pole. Then the event exercises its self-determination, deciding precisely how to respond to the various causal influences upon it. This is the subject's mental pole, during which it exercises final causation. But then the event becomes an object, at which time it exerts efficient causation on future subjects. This efficient causation is based upon the event's final causation, its self-determination. The event's freedom, in other words, is exercised *between* its reception of efficient causation from the past and its exertion of efficient causation on the future. In Whitehead's words, each "occasion arises as an effect facing its past and ends as a cause facing its future. In between there lies the teleology of the universe" (AI 194).

We need only apply this idea to the human mind or psyche, understood as a temporal society of dominant occasions of experience, to understand its freedom in relation to its body. In each moment, the dominant occasion arises out of causal influences from the past world—most immediately its own past experiences and its bodily parts, as mediated through its brain. It then exercises its self-determination in deciding how to respond to these influences. This decision then influences its future experiences and its brain cells, which then transmit the decisions to the relevant parts of the body. Therefore, our bodily action does, as we assume, reflect our free choices.

Implicit in this discussion of the psyche—as a temporal series of dominant occasions of experience—is the major way in which Whiteheadian panexperientialism agrees with dualism. Materialists cannot even begin to do justice to our freedom because of their view that the mind is numerically identical with the brain. As I emphasized earlier, this identification entails the denial that the mind is a locus of power that could exercise self-determination. Structurally, therefore, a human being or a dog is not different in kind from a toaster or a computer. Searle brings out this fact by saying that human and canine behavior must be explained in terms of bottom-up causation just as it is in those other things, because there is nothing in a human being or a dog to exert any top-down causation, at least not causation that reflects self-determination. Dualists have always rejected this account, insisting that the human mind, being a numerically distinct entity, is a locus of self-determining power. Structurally, therefore, humans are different in kind from rocks, toasters, and computers. Whiteheadian panexperientialism, with its distinction between compound individuals and non-individualized aggregational societies, agrees with dualists on this score. Both views affirm human freedom, and both views, thereby, affirm the mind's efficient causation on the body in Taube's sense. Both views, more generally, endorse interactionism—that the mind and the brain, being numerically distinct, interact, with each exerting causal efficacy on the other.[68]

The only difference is that dualism, in addition to affirming this numerical distinctness, affirms that the mind is ontologically different in kind from the brain's components, being composed of different stuff. So, although dualism's numerical thesis provides a necessary condition for making interaction intelligible, its ontological thesis makes this interaction *un*intelligible. Whiteheadian panexperientialism keeps the numerical thesis while rejecting the ontological thesis. And it is the ontological thesis, not the numerical thesis by itself, that makes the position dualistic and hence problematic.[69] Whitehead's position, therefore, can be called "nondualistic interactionism."[70] This doctrine is essential to his defense of human freedom.

Our fourth hard-core assumption is that our action, besides embodying freedom, also involves acting in accord with norms. Part of the Whiteheadian vindication of this assumption has already been given—namely, that in exercising final causation, we are aiming at a goal, and this goal can well involve some ideal, such as the ideal to be moral or self-consistent. Implicit in this position, however, is the idea that we can be aware of norms. Whitehead's panexperientialism speaks to this issue as well. The modern belief that we could not perceive cognitive, moral, and aesthetic norms, even if such norms exist, is based on the belief that we experience things beyond ourselves only by means of our sensory organs. However, the idea that perceptual experience is enjoyed by all individuals, including all individuals without sense organs, implies that there is a mode of perception more basic than sensory perception. And this is Whitehead's doctrine—that sensory perception is a high-level form of perception, derivative from a more primitive, nonsensory mode of perception, which he calls "prehension" or "feeling." It is through this nonsensory prehension that we apprehend norms.[71]

I have been explaining how Whitehead's panexperientialism, with its nonreductionistic naturalism, allows us to do justice to four of our hard-core commonsense assumptions about conscious experience that have been problematic for both dualists and materialists. One ingredient in this explanation is the Jamesian demotion of consciousness from the status of an entity or a stuff to that an emergent function.[72] In the final section, I will explain Whitehead's development of this Jamesian notion into the doctrine that consciousness is the subjective form of a feeling of a certain type. I will also point out some other ways, in addition to its being a necessary ingredient in Whitehead's solution to the mind-body problem, that this doctrine is important.

THE DOCTRINE OF CONSCIOUSNESS AS A SUBJECTIVE FORM: ITS MEANING AND IMPORTANCE

Consciousness for Whitehead, to recall, is the subjective form of an intellectual feeling, which arises, if at all, only in a late phase of an occasion of experience. Thus far the discussion of different phases of experience has been limited to two: the physical and the mental poles. In an occasion of experience that attains consciousness, however, the mental pole itself has phases.

Intellectual Feelings

According to Whitehead's more detailed analysis of a conscious occasion of experience, there are four phases altogether. The first phase is the physical phase, which feels past actual occasions. In the second phase, various pure possibilities (eternal objects) are felt conceptually or appetitively. In the third phase, these possibilities are conjoined with the actualities felt in the physical pole, resulting in the feeling of propositions. In the fourth phase, these propositions are compared with the original physical feelings, resulting in "intellectual feelings" (PR 241, 266, 277, 344). What is unique about an intellectual feeling is that it involves a contrast between a fact and a proposition (or theory)—between what is and what might be. This is called the "affirmation-negation contrast."

Like all other feelings, intellectual feelings have, besides an objective datum, also a subjective form, which is how that datum is felt. The objective datum of an intellectual feeling is an affirmation-negation contrast; the subjective form is consciousness. Consciousness, in other words, involves awareness both of something definite and of potentialities that "illustrate *either* what it is and might not be, or what it is not and might be. In other words, there is no consciousness without reference to definiteness, affirmation, and negation. Consciousness is how we feel the affirmation-negation contrast" (PR 243).

To explain more fully the difference between experience that is and is not conscious: experience is present whenever there is any awareness of what *is*; but we should not speak of *conscious* experience, Whitehead proposes, except where there is also an awareness of what *is not*. "Consciousness is the feeling of negation: in the perception of 'the stone as grey,' such feeling is in barest germ; in the perception of 'the stone as not grey,' such feeling is in full development. Thus the negative perception is the triumph of consciousness" (PR 161).

Consciousness, according to this analysis, is provoked into existence by, and only by, the right type of datum, this being an affirmation-negation contrast. Without this datum, there can be no consciousness. This explains why consciousness can appear only in a late phase of experience: an intellectual feeling is a complex feeling, involving the integration of feelings arising in earlier phases, so it can arise only in a late phase. This idea lies behind Whitehead's well-known statement that "consciousness presupposes experience, and not experience consciousness" (PR 53). Consciousness, if it occurs, lights up experience that preceded it, a level of experience that can exist without consciousness. Whitehead says, accordingly, that "consciousness is the crown of experience, only occasionally attained, not its necessary base" (PR 267).

In saying that consciousness is only occasionally attained, Whitehead means partly that those enduring individuals that are capable of attaining consciousness do not do so in every occasion of their experience (as in dreamless sleep). But he is mainly referring to the fact that most of the occasions of experience in the universe are too simple to go beyond the third phase. They are hence incapable of creating any full-fledged propositions, which are necessary conditions for intellectual feelings. Whitehead thereby explains how there can be experience without consciousness and also how compound individuals capable of consciousness could have emerged out of ones without this capacity.

An explanation of how consciousness could have emerged is an essential component in the theory's adequacy. Panexperientialism, as we saw earlier, avoids what has rightly been seen as an insoluble problem: how conscious experience could have emerged out of entities wholly devoid of experience. But one could accept panexperientialism and still not find it self-evident how experience of our type could have emerged out of entities such as quarks and photons. Whitehead's account of the phases of concrescence provides an abstract scheme that shows what kind of experiences the intervening steps might have had. This scheme can be described in terms of the language of "intentionality," which many philosophers of mind have used to express the problem of how consciousness could have emerged. That is, consciousness involves "intentionality" in the sense of "aboutness"; it has "intentional objects." These intended objects may be actual things, such as food, or ideal things, such as numbers or propositions. In any case, the puzzle is how beings such as us, with our intentionality, could have emerged out of things such as quarks and photons, which, even if we grant them some type of experience, cannot be supposed to have anything approaching the intentionality that we enjoy.

The abstract line of development suggested by Whitehead's analysis says that: very elementary occasions of experience are not able to synthesize physical and conceptual feelings into propositional feelings, but they do synthesize them into rudimentary analogues, which Whitehead calls "physical purposes" (PR 267, 276). These experiences, not being able to focus on a possibility qua possibility, have only, we can say, *incipient* intentionality. Somewhat higher level occasions of experience, complex enough to have propositional (but not intellectual) feelings, have, we can say, *proto*intentionality. Only very high-level experiences have *full-fledged, conscious* intentionality, because only they are sophisticated enough to contrast propositions, as possibilities, with the perceived facts. Given the idea of evolution as involving increasingly complex compound individuals, which can provide their dominant occasions with increasingly complex data, we can see how experiences of our type could have gradually arisen out of extremely trivial experiences.

Whitehead's Perceptual Law

Whitehead's analysis of consciousness, I have shown, is part and parcel of his explanation of how conscious beings could have emerged evolutionarily and of his justification of our hard-core commonsense assumptions about our experience. I will conclude by pointing out how it also lies behind Whitehead's explanation of why, although our hard-core commonsense beliefs have an empirical basis, philosophers have tended to overlook this basis.

The main idea in this explanation is that consciousness, arising only near the conclusion of an occasion of experience, fails to shed its light upon the origins of that experience and thereby its most basic ingredients. In Whitehead's words: "Consciousness only arises in a late derivative phase of complex integrations" and "primarily illuminates the higher phase in which it arises." Accordingly, "consciousness only dimly illuminates the...primitive elements in our experience." Whitehead even refers to this point as a "law"—"that the late derivative elements are more clearly illuminated by consciousness than the primitive elements" (PR 162). We can call this "Whitehead's perceptual law."

On the basis of this law, we can understand why philosophers, at least since the time of Hume, have worried about the empirical basis of our beliefs about causation and the "external world." We do, Whitehead says, directly perceive the existence of actual things beyond ourselves and also their causal efficacy on us. Whitehead, in fact, refers to this as a distinct mode of perception, which he calls "perception in the mode of causal efficacy" (this being a synonym for "physical prehension"). This mode stands in contrast with another mode, which he calls "perception in the mode of presentational immediacy," because in this latter mode various data are immediately present to our consciousness. The perception of sense data, such as colored shapes, is the most obvious example of perception in this mode. Full-fledged sense perception always involves a synthesis of these two modes, which Whitehead calls "perception in the mode of symbolic reference."[73] In our conscious experience, however, the data of perception in the mode of causal efficacy tend to drop out so that sensory perception gets virtually equated with perception in the mode of presentational immediacy. This is especially the case with philosophers insofar as they focus on the "clear and distinct" data of perception, presuming them to be basic. Accordingly, Hume, while admitting that in "practice" he could not help presupposing a real world and causation as real influence, said that in his philosophical "theory," which was to be based rigidly on perceptual experience, he could not refute solipsism and could define causation only as the "constant conjunction" of two types of phenomena.

Whitehead's perceptual law—"that the late derivative elements [in an occasion of experience] are more clearly illuminated by consciousness than the primitive elements"—explains why Hume, focusing on the clear and distinct elements in perceptual experience, came to that conclusion. "[C]onsciousness only dimly illuminates the prehensions in the mode of causal efficacy," says Whitehead, "because these prehensions are primitive elements in our experience." By contrast, "prehensions in the mode of presentational immediacy...are late derivatives"; they, accordingly, "are among those prehensions which we enjoy with the most vivid consciousness" (PR 162).

Whitehead's perceptual law presupposes his idea that the mind or psyche is not an enduring "substance," or even "stream," numerically one through time, with consciousness as the stuff of which it consists. Accordingly, *consciousness is not simply waiting there, as it were, to be filled by this or that content.* If it were, we would expect it to light up early arrivals as clearly as, or even more clearly than, latecomers. This seemed to be Hume's assumption. But the mind or psyche is, instead, a serially ordered society of distinct (albeit intimately interconnected) occasions of experience, and consciousness is a subjective form that arises, if at all, only in a late phase of these occasions. It is not lying in waiting, but *must be provoked into existence.* And this provocation, as we have seen, can occur only in a late phase. Consciousness, accordingly, primarily illuminates the latecomers, which have been *constructed* by the occasion of experience itself, rather than the early arrivals, which were *given* to the occasion of experience from beyond itself.

If this were the only implication of Whitehead's perceptual law, it would be of importance only to philosophers, who seem to be the only ones tempted to solipsism and phenomenalist definitions of causality. A more general cultural problem of modernity, however, is the widespread doubt that normative ideals are given to our experience. Max Weber called modernity's transition to seeing the world as not embodying such ideals "the disenchantment of the world." The existential implication of this disenchantment is the relativistic belief that ideals are invented, not discovered.[74] The political implication is that "might makes right."[75]

The denial that we perceive normative ideals is closely related to the equation of perception with sensory perception. Because ideals are not the kinds of things that can be detected by means of our physical sense organs, the belief that we can perceive only by means of our senses can persuade us that we do not perceive ideals. But this denial is also due in part to the fact that this perception is generally at the fringes of the conscious portion of our experience. This fringiness of ideals does not mean that they are absent or secondary in our experience. The exact contrary is the case: they are secondary or even tertiary in consciousness because they are *primary* in experience.

To explain this point more fully would require a discussion of Whitehead's theism, God's provision of an "initial aim" for each finite occasion of experience, and our direct perception of God (in whom, by the "ontological principle," the normative ideals must subsist if they are to exist and be perceivable). A complete account of Whitehead's psychology, in other words, is not possible in abstraction from his theology. I have discussed this connection elsewhere.[76] For now I simply repeat the main points of the present account—that Whitehead defines consciousness as the subjective form of an intellectual feeling; that this conception of consciousness is part and parcel of Whitehead's panexperientialist worldview; that this postmodern worldview, with its nonreductionistic naturalism, is far more adequate to our inevitable presuppositions than either of the modern options, dualism and materialism; and that this conception of consciousness can help us understand that our inevitable presuppositions have a basis in our perceptual experience even though modern philosophers, and our conscious experience more generally, tend to overlook this basis.

4

Whitehead's Deeply Ecological Worldview: Egalitarianism without Irrelevance

Whitehead once described Christianity as "a religion seeking a metaphysic" (RM 50). It can equally be said that the environmentalism is a movement seeking a worldview. Valuable ideas for an appropriate worldview can be drawn from many philosophies, theologies, and traditions, including modern-becoming-postmodern science. After this is realized, however, the question still remains as to which overall worldview provides the best standpoint from which to appropriate elements from the others.

My own judgment is that Whitehead himself went far toward providing the kind of worldview that the environmental movement needs. The kind of worldview that is needed, I believe, is one that is deeply ecological; one that is pragmatic, in the sense of providing a livable guide for action; one that can be commended, because of its coherence and relative adequacy, as at least not obviously false; and one that, as part of the evidence for its relative adequacy, can reconcile tensions between other positions, doing justice to the elements of truth in each. Whitehead's cosmological philosophy has, I believe, all these virtues.

Before beginning the exposition of Whitehead's worldview in relation to this issue, I will explain, in a preliminary way, how I am using the term *deeply ecological*, then point out how Whitehead's position can reconcile a central conflict between various philosophies that legitimately can be called "deeply ecological."

DEEP ECOLOGY

The term 'deep ecology' is ambiguous, even embattled.[1] In its most general use, it refers to any environmental ethic that is not purely anthropocentric—to any ethic that bases its call for environmental preservation and restoration not solely on enlightened human self-interest but also on the intrinsic value of other species.[2] We can call this "deep ecology$_{na}$" (nonanthropocentric deep ecology). In this most general sense, those who focus on the rights of animals are deep ecologists.

But that is not the way the term is usually employed: "animal liberationists" have usually been contrasted with "deep ecologists."[3] Animal liberationists, as the name implies, typically focus only on animals, rather than on other forms of life, and on individuals rather than on ecosystems. Most of them also limit their concern primarily to the highest forms of animal life, especially fellow mammals. Most of them, furthermore, draw a line below which there is assumed to be no reason for ethical concern.

Deep ecologists, by contrast, are typically concerned with the biosphere as a whole and do not draw a line beneath which there is assumed to be no inherent value to be respected. We can call this "deep ecology$_b$" (biospheric deep ecology).

For some deep ecologists, finally, even this stipulation is not sufficiently precise. To be a truly deep ecologist, say some followers of Arne Naess (who coined the term 'deep ecology'), one must affirm "biospherical (or biological) egalitarianism," rejecting any type of hierarchy of value according to which some beings have more intrinsic value than others. We can call this "deep ecology$_e$" (egalitarian deep ecology).[4]

In speaking of Whitehead's worldview as deeply ecological, I mean, in the first place, that his position supports deep ecology in the first two senses: deep ecology$_b$ as well as deep ecology$_{na}$. Nevertheless, while supporting biospheric deep ecology over against any dualistic line drawing and any exclusive focus on individuals in distinction from ecosystems, Whitehead's position also implies that the animal liberationist position, in presupposing that the higher animals are worthy of special concern, is rooted in a sound intuition. A synthesis of deep ecological$_b$ and animal liberationist positions is thereby achieved.

This synthesis is possible, however, only because Whiteheadian philosophy rejects deep ecology$_e$ as it has hitherto usually been understood, a rejection that has led Whiteheadian philosophy to be *contrasted* with deep ecology by both Naessian deep ecologists and Whiteheadians.

The basis for this contrast and the basis for reconciliation can best be approached by examining an eight-point platform for deep ecology written by Arne Naess and George Sessions:

1. The well-being and flourishing of human and nonhuman life on Earth have value in themselves (synonyms: intrinsic value, inherent value). These values are independent of the usefulness of the nonhuman world for human purposes.
2. Richness and diversity of life forms contribute to the realization of these values and are also values in themselves.

3. Humans have no right to reduce this richness and diversity except to satisfy *vital* needs.

4. The flourishing of human life and cultures is compatible with a substantial decrease of the human population. The flourishing of nonhuman life requires such a decrease.

5. Present human interference with the nonhuman world is excessive, and the situation is rapidly worsening.

6. Policies must therefore be changed. These policies affect basic economic, technological, and ideological structures. The resulting state of affairs will be deeply different from the present.

7. The ideological change is mainly that of appreciating *life* quality (dwelling in situations of inherent value) rather than adhering to an increasingly higher standard of living. There will be a profound awareness of the difference between big and great.

8. Those who subscribe to the foregoing points have an obligation directly or indirectly to try to implement the necessary changes.[5]

MUTUAL PERCEPTIONS OF OPPOSITION

After quoting this platform, two Whiteheadians, Herman Daly and John Cobb, say: "We find ourselves in basic agreement with the principles of deep ecology as thus interpreted." However, they add, "For Naess and Sessions our position is in fact excluded from deep ecology despite our acceptance of the eight basic propositions." The reason for this exclusion, they explain, is that the first point of the platform is "interpreted in terms of 'biocentric equality,' the intuition 'that . . . all organisms and entities in the ecosphe . . . are equal in intrinsic worth.'" Daly and Cobb then suggest that deep ecology, interpreted in terms of biological egalitarianism, is deeply irrelevant:

> We do not share this view. We believe there is more intrinsic value in a human being than in a mosquito or a virus. We also believe that there is more intrinsic value in a chimpanzee or a porpoise than in an earthworm or a bacterium. This judgment of intrinsic value is quite different from the judgment of the importance of a species to the interrelated whole. . . . We believe that distinctions of this sort are important as guides to practical life and economic policy and that the insistence that a deep ecologist refuse to make them is an invitation to deep irrelevance.[6]

This judgment that Naessian deep ecology and Whiteheadian ecophilosophy are deeply opposed echoes the previous exclusion of Whiteheadians from the ranks of deep ecologists by Bill Devall and George Sessions. In *Deep Ecology*, Devall and Sessions had said that Whiteheadians "fail to meet the deep ecology norm of 'ecological egalitarianism in principle.'"[7]

OVERCOMING THE APPARENT OPPOSITION

In spite of this mutual perception of opposition, however, Whitehead's philosophy, with its different levels of intrinsic value, and Naessian deep ecology, with its egalitarianism of value, are not necessarily opposed. There are two reasons behind this claim.

In the first place, although Daly and Cobb say that they as Whiteheadians were excluded from the ranks of deep ecologists by "Naess and Sessions," this exclusion was in fact made only by Devall and Sessions. Naess himself distinguishes clearly between deep ecology as such, which he understands very broadly to include all ecophilosophies that are not anthropocentric, and his own personal preference, which is a Spinoza-inspired position affirming biological egalitarianism.[8] It is Devall and Sessions who collapsed this distinction, simply equating deep ecology$_e$ with deep ecology as such. Under Naess's own big-tent definition of deeply ecological philosophers, by contrast, Whitehead is specifically *included*—as shown by a statement quoted by Devall and Sessions themselves (although with no acknowledgment of the conflict with their own narrow definition).[9]

In the second place, Whitehead's philosophy is not even necessarily opposed to the intuition on which egalitarian deep ecology is based. I said earlier that it is opposed to deep ecology$_e$ "as it has hitherto usually been understood." Whitehead's intuition that there are different levels of intrinsic value may be compatible with the intuition of egalitarian deep ecologists that all things, at least all living things, have equal inherent value. The possibility of reconciliation arises from the fact that what the advocates of deep ecology have meant in speaking of "inherent" value—whether they use the term *inherent* or *intrinsic*—differs greatly from what Whiteheadians mean in referring to "intrinsic" value.

Given this introduction, I shall, in the following sections, show that Whitehead's worldview is deeply ecological in the following senses: (1) it portrays all individuals as having intrinsic value; (2) it portrays all things as internally related to their environments; (3) it portrays the self in particular as an ecological self; (4) it portrays the divine reality as ecologically interconnected with the world and shows that the support given to an ecological consciousness by this portrayal of the divine reality is not undermined by the problem of evil; and (5) it shows how a special concern for human beings and other higher animals is not inconsistent with concern for the biosphere as a whole and with the intuition that, in some sense, all forms of life have (roughly) equal inherent value.

INTRINSIC VALUE

Although the term *intrinsic value* was used only occasionally by Whitehead himself, it has been widely used by Whiteheadians as a technical term for the value that something has in and for itself. The only things that are anything *for* themselves are, of course, things with experience. 'Intrinsic value' stands in contrast with *extrinsic value*, which means value something has for anything else. The term *instrumental value*, which has been widely used in this inclusive sense, is better saved for only one of the many kinds of extrinsic value.

And there are, indeed, many kinds of extrinsic value. A most important dimension of the extrinsic value of something—the dimension mainly of interest to Naessian deep ecologists—is its *ecological value*, meaning its value for sustaining the cycle of life. Its value as food for other beings would be part of this ecological value, but so would many other functions, such as the function of worms in aerating the soil and that of certain soil bacteria in nitrogen fixation. Other forms of extrinsic value are *companion value*, *instrumental value* (in the narrow sense, such as a stick's value to a bird in ferreting out bugs from a tree limb), *aesthetic value*, and *medicinal value*. Some other forms of extrinsic value are such only to human beings, such as *scientific value*, *monetary value*, and *symbolic* (including *moral* and *religious*) *value*. From these examples it can be seen that anything, whether or not it has intrinsic value (value for itself), can have extrinsic value (value for others).

The fact that only those things with experience can have intrinsic value does not, for Whitehead, mean that the world is divided into two kinds of actual things—those with and those without intrinsic value. Descartes and other dualists, of course, have assumed otherwise. For Descartes, the line (among earthly creatures) was to be drawn between human beings and everything else; other dualists draw the line further down, attributing experience to all animals with central nervous systems, or still lower. Whitehead believes, for various reasons, that no such line can be drawn. This attribution of intrinsic value to all levels of nature is part and parcel of his panexperientialism.

ABOLISHING "VACUOUS ACTUALITIES"

One reason for affirming this position is theoretical. It is impossible, as we saw in the prior chapter, to understand how experiencing things and nonexperiencing things could interact. It is also impossible to understand, apart from an appeal to supernatural causation, how experience could have evolved out of things wholly devoid of experience.

This twofold theoretical difficulty with the dualistic hypothesis is buttressed by an empirical difficulty, which is that science, as we saw in the prior chapter, has increasingly been removing the bases for assuming absolute discontinuity anywhere in the evolutionary process, whether with the rise of humans, the rise of animals, the rise of life, or somewhere else.

In any case, Whitehead attributes experience to individuals all the way down. He does not mean, of course, that all types of individuals have the level of experience enjoyed by human beings, or even that enjoyed by dogs and cats. Even the kind of experience enjoyed by a living cell is already a fairly high-level experience, compared with that of macromolecules, ordinary molecules, atoms, and subatomic entities such as protons and electrons. The experience of such entities must be assumed to be very trivial. The point remains, however, that they should be thought to be only different in degree from us, however greatly, not wholly different in kind. Whitehead believed, as we have seen, that the notion of "vacuous actuality"—the idea of something that is actual and yet "void of subjective experience" (PR 167)—should be abolished.

Whitehead realized that this move had ethical implications. Kant had said that we should treat other human beings as ends in themselves, not merely as means to our own ends. The implication was that all other beings could be treated as simply means to our ends. "But if we discard the notion of vacuous existence," Whitehead points out, "we must conceive each actuality as attaining an end for itself" (FR 30–31). In a chapter in which he expresses agreement with the romantic poets, Whitehead says: "'Value' is the word I use for the intrinsic reality of an event" (SMW 93).

The idea of vacuous actuality, according to Whitehead's analysis, results from the "fallacy of misplaced concreteness," in which an abstraction from some actuality is equated with the concrete actuality itself (SMW 51; PR 7–8). "In physics there is abstraction. The science ignores what anything is in itself. Its entities are merely considered in respect to their extrinsic reality" (SMW 153). Modern science, with its "Cartesian scientific doctrine of bits of matter, bare of intrinsic value" (SMW 195), has had negative consequences, said Whitehead, because it fostered "the habit of ignoring the intrinsic worth of the environment which must be allowed its weight in any consideration of final ends" (SMW, 196).

To abolish the notion of vacuous actuality would be to establish the basis for replacing this bad habit with the habit of reverence: "Everything has some value for itself. . . . By reason of this character, constituting reality, the conception of morals arises. We have no right to deface the value experience which is the very essence of the universe" (MT 110).

PANEXPERIENTIALISM WITH ORGANIZATIONAL DUALITY

Given its denial of actualities devoid of experience, Whitehead's worldview can, as we have seen, be called "panexperientialism." But, as we have also seen, the "pan" must not be understood to mean literally everything to which one can refer, but only all *actual individuals*. Only they have experience. Excluded are not only things with merely *ideal* existence, such as numbers, concepts, and propositions, but also *aggregational societies* of individuals that are not themselves individuals, such as rocks.

As we saw in chapter 3, Whitehead's position is best called "panexperientialism with organizational duality,"[10] because there are two basic ways in which individuals can be organized. On the one hand, individuals at one level can be organized so as to give rise to a higher level individual that turns the whole into what Charles Hartshorne called a "compound individual."[11] Humans and squirrels are obvious examples, as the trillions of cells constituting the body give rise to a much higher level individual, which we call the "mind" or "soul," which turns this aggregation of cells into an individual. Cells, organelles, macromolecules, ordinary molecules, and atoms can also be considered compound individuals.

On the other hand, a multiplicity of individuals may be organized in such a way so as not to give rise to a higher level experience, in which case we have an aggregational, nonindividuated society. Sticks, stones, chairs, and mountains provide obvious examples. The only experiences in the stone are the experiences of the various molecules making it up; the stone qua stone—in contrast with the living squirrel qua squirrel—has no experience.

Making this distinction acknowledges the obvious distinction on which Descartes' dualism was based but does so without falling prey to the problems created by that dualism. The obvious distinction is between those objects of our sensory experience that do and those that do not seem to be capable of initiating activity and making a unified response to their environments—the distinction between sticks, stones, and stars, on the one hand, and squirrels, snakes, and seagulls, on the other. We instinctively, and reasonably, assume that the latter, like ourselves, have a unified experience and that the former do not. Descartes' dualism is based on the assumption that the ultimate units of the world are tiny things that are more like stones than like squirrels. Whitehead avoids this dualism by making the opposite assumption—that molecules are more analogous to squirrels and humans than to stones. Through this analogy, what we call "nature" is viewed as permeated by value: "We have only to transfer to the very texture of realisation in itself," suggested Whitehead, "that which we recognise so readily in terms of human life" (SMW, 93).

INTERNAL RELATIONS

Besides intrinsic value all the way down, the other central point of any deeply ecological philosophy is a strong doctrine of internal relations, meaning relations that are internal to, and thus constitutive of, the things in question. Modern thought has been as unecological in this regard as the former. It has seen the world as comprised of substances that, in Descartes' notorious phrase, "need nothing but themselves in order to exist." Accordingly, Whitehead complains, in modern philosophies "the relations between individual substances constitute metaphysical nuisances: there is no place for them" (PR 137). In Whitehead's postmodern philosophy, by contrast, relations are fundamental. Each thing arises out of its social relations and is internally constituted by these social relations. To see how fundamental social relations are in Whitehead's worldview, we need a more precise notion of his view of individuals.

ENDURING INDIVIDUALS AS SOCIETIES

I have thus far written of *enduring* individuals, such as electrons, molecules, cells, and squirrels. For Whitehead, however, the things that are most fully actual are not enduring individuals but momentary events, which he calls "actual occasions" or "occasions of experience." These occasions have a more-or-less brief existence, lasting anywhere from less than a billionth of a second, in the case of electronic or photonic occasions, to perhaps a tenth of a second, in the case of an occasion of human experience. Although this doctrine was discussed in Chapter 2, we need to look at it here in relation to our present concerns.

The doctrine that the actual entities of the world are momentary occasions means that things that endure, such as electrons, molecules, and minds, already exemplify a type of social existence. Whitehead, accordingly, calls them "societies": "The real actual things that endure are all societies. They are not actual occasions. It is a mistake...to confuse societies with the completely real things which are the actual occasions" (AI 204). Enduring individuals are "temporally ordered societies": the social relations are purely temporal, because only one member exists at a time. Any given occasion of experience belongs to that temporal society that consists of all those members that came before it and all those that will come after it.

This doctrine makes social relations fundamental while making "enduring substances" derivative. What appears to be an independent substance, such as a proton, is in reality a pattern of social relations, with perhaps a billion such relations occurring in each second. Each actual occasion, however, does not simply arise out of its predecessor in the temporally ordered society to which it belongs. Each occasion is also influenced, even if less significantly, by other past occasions. In fact, each occasion is influenced, to some slight degree, by the whole past universe. "The whole world conspires to produce a new creation" (RM 113).

CAUSATION AS INFLUENCE

In being affected by previous events, furthermore, an occasion of experience is not simply affected in some external way, as billiard-ball images of causation suggest. Rather, the causal influence of the past upon the present is in-fluence, a real in-flowing, which affects the present experience internally. We know that our own experience is influenced in this way. The causal influence of my parents on me, for example, is nothing like the impact of two billiard balls upon a third. Rather, I am who I am in large part because of attitudes, values, and habits that I internalized from them. By thinking of all enduring individuals as series of occasions of experience, we can think of all causal influence between individuals in those terms.

Prehension is Whitehead's term for this internal appropriation of causal influences from the past. He said: "I use the term 'prehension' for the general way in which the occasion of experience can include, as part of its own essence, any other entity" (AI 234). "The essence of an actual entity," he also said, "consists solely in the fact that it is a prehending thing" (PR 41). That is, far from requiring nothing else to be, an actual entity must, by its very nature, appropriate influences from prior actualities into itself. This idea—that occasions of experience are taken up into later occasions of experience—is at the very heart of Whitehead's cosmology. His philosophy, he said, "is mainly devoted to the task of making clear the notion of 'being present in another entity'" (PR 50).

TWO MODES OF EXISTENCE, TWO TYPES OF VALUE

This notion brings us to another distinctive feature of Whitehead's cosmology, the idea that each actual entity exists in two modes. It exists first as a subject of experience. In this mode, it prehends prior experiences, then makes a self-determining response to them. After existing as a subject, its subjectivity perishes; it then exists as an object for subsequent subjects.

This twofold mode of existence is correlated with the previous distinction between intrinsic and extrinsic value. In referring to the intrinsic value of something, we are referring, strictly speaking, to the momentary actual occasions, not the enduring individuals. While it is a subject enjoying experience, an actual occasion has intrinsic value, value for itself. When it becomes an object for others, it has extrinsic value, value for others. It cannot have both kinds of value at the same time: it does not become an object for others until its moment of subjectivity, with its intrinsic value, is over. Only individual occasions can enjoy intrinsic value. But anything that can be prehended—an individual experience, a temporally ordered society of occasions, or an aggregation of occasions—can have extrinsic value.

THE ECOLOGICAL SELF

Given the fact that human experience is taken as paradigmatic for actual entities, some aspects of the ecological nature of the self have been established by what has been said earlier. The enduring self is a temporally ordered society of occasions of experience, each of which arises out of its relations to former occasions of experience and then contributes itself to later occasions. Each moment of experience is a microcosm, taking into itself, at least to some slight degree, all prior events. For the momentary self to realize its true nature is to realize that it is akin to all other things. What remains here is to explain, if this is the true nature of the self, why this is not more obvious.

SOURCES OF DUALISTIC ILLUSIONS

One reason for the perceived opposition between self and world has already been explained: Low-grade actual occasions can be organized into aggregational societies in which evidence of their spontaneity, and thus of their experience, is masked.

This ontological basis for the illusion that we are different in kind from "nature" is supported by an epistemological basis: in sensory perception, we do not perceive individual actualities, but only blurred masses. The things that we see and touch, accordingly, seem to be passive, hence entirely different from what we know ourselves to be—individuals with spontaneous energy (AI 213, 218).

The illusion that the "physical world" is entirely different from us is also promoted by the fact that sensory perception is a derivative form of perception. Sensory perception is so prominent in consciousness not, as modern philosophy has assumed, because it is our fundamental form of perception but precisely because it is not. This is so because consciousness is itself a derivative form of experience.

As we saw in the prior chapter, each occasion of experience consists of several phases, and consciousness is a special way of experiencing objects—a way that may or may not be evoked in a late phase. Because consciousness arises, if at all, only in a late phase, it *tends to illuminate only those elements of experience that themselves arise in a late phase*. The negative point here is that consciousness therefore does *not* cast a bright searchlight upon those elements of experience that are truly fundamental in the sense of arising in the initial phase of experience: "Consciousness only dimly illuminates the...primitive elements in our experience" (PR 162). The "primitive elements" in experience are those that enter through our (nonsensory) prehension. Because they occur before consciousness arises, they are generally only illuminated dimly, if at all.

The reason why we are not generally conscious of the "physical world" (or "nature") as filled with intrinsic value is that it is only in nonsensory prehension that we experience other things as value laden. For example, we directly prehend our prior occasions of experience and "remember" them with their joys, sufferings, and desires. We also directly experience, if in more blurred fashion, our bodily members, feeling their excitement, their enjoyment, their suffering, their thirst and hunger. If we would generalize this knowledge of what the "physical world" is like, we would not think of it as devoid of values but as a throbbing multiplicity of energetic, passionate, appetitive events striving for, and realizing, values.

We have instead assumed, especially in the modern world, that it is our sensory perception, especially vision, that tells us what the physical world is really like. This assumption has had such fateful consequences because, in sensory perception, the element of value is virtually lost. What was received in prehension is transmuted, and the transmutation involves playing down the subjective, emotional nature of the data and playing up the objective, purely geometrical aspects.

WHITEHEAD ON SYMPATHETIC PERCEPTION

In Whitehead's alternative account, "the primitive, element [in experience] is *sympathy*, that is, feeling the feeling *in* another and feeling conformally *with* another" (PR 162). Whitehead's account thereby reminds us that we directly know, through prehensions of our own bodies, that the world is comprised of beings with which we can sympathize and that sympathy is our natural response. His account is also designed to remove the tendency produced by consciousness to see ourselves as cut off from the world.

Whitehead in an important passage described the task of philosophy as "the self-correction by consciousness of its own initial excess of subjectivity." What consciousness would thereby correct, he said, was its tendency, by focusing on its own products, to obscure "the external totality from which [the individual] originates and which it embodies." The self-correction, Whitehead said, involves the individual's reminder to itself that, deep down, it "has truck with the totality of things" (PR 15).

A central purpose of Whitehead's cosmology is to remind us, in other words, of what we essentially are, below the superficialities of consciousness and sensory perception, with the hope that "the intellectual insight" will be converted "into an emotional force correct[ing] the sensitive experience in the direction of morality" (PR 15). The epistemological revolution suggested by Whitehead could help promote a moral revolution.

AN ECOLOGICAL DEITY

A complete account of Whitehead's ecological worldview would require an extensive account of his view of the God-world relation. That relation is described in other chapters. Here I will simply mention the points that are most germane to the development of an ecological worldview.

At the center of the difference between Whitehead's God and that of traditional theism is his dictum that "God is not to be treated as an exception to all metaphysical principles" but as "their chief exemplification" (PR 343). On the one hand, God enters into all other actualities: "The world lives by its incarnation of God in itself" (RM 156). On the other hand, all other actualities enter into God: "It is as true to say that the World is immanent in God, as that God is immanent in the World" (PR 348). Because of this mutual influence, Whitehead's doctrine of God is sometimes called "panentheism." Unlike pantheism, God is not simply identical with the world; unlike traditional theism, God could not live apart from a world. God is essentially the soul of the world.[12]

Equally important is that God's power is not coercive but persuasive, which means that God cannot unilaterally determine what happens in the world. Besides the fact that this idea of divine power means that the idea of God's goodness and love for the world is not undermined by the problem of evil, it also means that belief in God is no basis for complacency. We cannot simply ignore the ecological crisis on the basis of the assumption that if things get bad enough, God will intervene to save us from our foolish ways.

Besides not being undermined by belief in this God, ecological commitment is actually reinforced. Our sense of the importance of our actions in relation to other creatures is reinforced by the idea that God is immanent in all beings so that each species is a unique mode of divine presence, as Thomas Berry says,[13] and by the idea that all creatures contribute value to the divine life.

Finally, this doctrine of God counters an ethical skepticism that suspects terms such as *good* and *right* to be purely emotive, with no real meaning. The panentheist view implies that that which is right in any situation is that which God, as the all-inclusive sympathetic participant, prefers.

BIOLOGICAL EGALITARIANISM

I come now to the issue mentioned at the outset: whether Whitehead's cosmology, besides being deeply ecological in the above-mentioned ways, can also, in some sense, affirm the idea that has been the most controversial feature of the position to which the label *deep ecology* is usually applied, the idea of biological egalitarianism. I suggest that it can, thereby removing the major reason why this idea has been so divisive. The basis for the reconciliation is the recognition that when Whiteheadians affirm and Naessians deny that various species of life have different degrees of intrinsic value, 'intrinsic value' is being used differently.

INTRINSIC AND INHERENT VALUE

Naess himself has admitted that his intuition about biological egalitarianism is problematic. After describing his philosophy as "ecosophy," meaning "insight directly relevant to action," he has admitted that one cannot really act in harmony with statements about biological equality. He has admitted, furthermore, that he does not know "how to work this [intuition] out in a fairly precise way." Two of his most careful attempts, evidently, are that "there is a value inherent in living beings which is the same value for all" and that "every living being is equal to all others to the extent that it has intrinsic value."[14]

Note that Naess seems to use 'intrinsic' and 'inherent' value interchangeably. What he and his followers mean by these terms is different from the meaning given to 'intrinsic value' in my Whiteheadian discussion above. To minimize confusion, I suggest that in future discussions of these two positions, 'intrinsic value' be used for the Whiteheadian meaning and the term 'inherent value' for the Naessian meaning.

The difference between the two meanings involves what the contrast is with. On the one hand, the intrinsic value of something (in Whiteheadian discussions) stands in contrast with its (extrinsic) value for others—*any* others, be they plants, animals, humans, or God. The "other" can even be a later member of the same enduring individual. For example, a prior moment of my own experience, which at the time had intrinsic value for itself, now has extrinsic value for my present experience. On the other hand, the inherent value of something (in Naessian discussions) *stands in contrast solely with its (perceived) value for human beings.* That this is so is shown by the first point in the eight-point platform of the deep ecology movement written by Naess and Sessions, quoted earlier: "The well-being and flourishing of human and nonhuman life on Earth have value in themselves (synonyms: intrinsic value, inherent value). These values are independent of the usefulness of the nonhuman world for human purposes."[15]

Accordingly, 'inherent value' in the Naessian sense includes most of what counts as 'extrinsic value' in the Whiteheadian usage. In particular, an organism's inherent value includes its *ecological* value—its value for sustaining the ecosystem. Because the only kind of value that is excluded from inherent value is the (perceived) value of something for human beings, then some other kinds of extrinsic value, besides ecological value, would also be included in inherent value, such as the aesthetic and instrumental values that things may have for nonhuman animals. For the sake of this discussion, however, we can focus on ecological value as the most important type of extrinsic value (in the

Whiteheadian sense) that is included in inherent value (in the Naessian sense). In any case, the fact that Naessian inherent value includes so much more than Whiteheadian intrinsic value means that, although it would be unlivable (and hence deeply irrelevant) to affirm egalitarianism with regard to (Whiteheadian) intrinsic value, it might not be so to affirm equality with regard to (Naessian) inherent value.

Another contrast between Whiteheadian intrinsic value and Naessian inherent value is that the former applies only to individuals, while the latter, because it includes both intrinsic and extrinsic value (in the Whiteheadian sense), applies to species as well as to individuals.

EQUALITY OF INHERENT VALUE

The central implication of this terminological discussion is that a rough equality in the inherent value of the various species results from an inverse relation that exists, in general, between intrinsic value and ecological value. That is, those species whose (individual) members have the *least* intrinsic value, such as bacteria, worms, trees, and the plankton, have the *greatest* ecological value: without them, the whole ecosystem would collapse. By contrast, those species whose members have the greatest intrinsic value (meaning the richest experience and thereby the most value for themselves), such as whales, dolphins, and primates, have the least ecological value. In the case of human primates, in fact, the ecological value is negative. Most of the other forms of life would be better off, and the ecosystem as a whole would not be threatened, if we did not exist. In any case, assuming that this inverse correlation generally obtains throughout the ecological pyramid, we can say that *all forms of life have, roughly, the same inherent value.* The distinctive point of egalitarian deep ecology is, therefore, compatible with the Whiteheadian emphasis on many different levels of intrinsic value.

CONCLUSION

Recognition that the *total* inherent value of anything includes both its intrinsic and its ecological values provides a basis for reconciling the erstwhile conflict between deep ecologists and advocates of the "land ethic," on the one hand, and humanitarians and animal liberationists, on the other.

Deep ecologists and land ethicists have been focusing primarily on ecological value. Given that focus, they rightly see that the species at the base of the ecological pyramid—such as the worms, the trees, the bacteria, the plankton—are vital. If these thinkers focus exclusively on ecological value, they may regard the concern to liberate humans and other mammals from suffering to be diversionary or worse. The concern with individuals, as opposed to species, will seem misguided. The concern to protect humans from premature and massive death may even seem counterproductive, especially if the exclusive focus on ecological value leads to misanthropy. The charge of "speciesism" may be leveled.

Animal liberationists and humanitarians, on the other hand, focus primarily upon intrinsic value and therefore primarily upon individuals. Given this focus, animal liberationists rightly see that, among the nonhuman forms of life, the higher animals, especially mammals, have the greatest capacity for intrinsic value, and thereby the greatest capacity to suffer and to have their potentials for self-realization thwarted. One's ethical activity with regard to the nonhuman world is, accordingly, most appropriately directed toward preventing the suffering and ensuring the flourishing of the higher animals. Humanitarians see that the rights of our fellow human beings to live without unnecessary suffering and without unnecessary restraints on their flourishing should especially be protected. If these animal and human liberationists focus exclusively on intrinsic value, they may regard the efforts of deep ecologists as diversionary or worse. Seeing the misanthropy of some of them, they may mutter "ecological fascism."

Once we see, however, that the total inherent value of things—the total value things have in themselves—includes not only their intrinsic value but also their ecological value and that these values generally exist in inverse proportion to each other, we can see these two ethical concerns as complementary, not conflictual. Both concerns are valid and need to be addressed simultaneously. Those who wish to focus their energies on one can do so wholeheartedly, knowing that other thinkers and activists are focusing their energies on the other.

The panentheistic perspective underwrites this both/and attitude. On the one hand, God (by hypothesis) has spent billions of years coaxing along a universe that could bring forth life and presumably does not wish the whole enterprise, on this planet at least, to come to an end, or at least to be drastically reduced, billions of years prematurely. If the divine perspective finally defines what is right, it is right to try to preserve the ozone shield, to prevent severe global warming, to preserve biodiversity, and to do whatever else is necessary to protect the integrity of the global ecosystem.

On the other hand, God has not only brought forth life but has continually evoked *increasingly complex* species of life, whose individual members are capable of increasingly richer intrinsic value and are thereby capable of contributing more value to the universe as a Whole, to God. Because God not only enjoys the enjoyments of the various creatures but also suffers their sufferings, God wants the suffering of the creatures minimized, their flourishing maximized. It is right, then, to give special attention to preventing suffering and enabling flourishing, especially with regard to those creatures who can suffer the most and whose potentials can be most severely thwarted.

The Whiteheadian God, accordingly, is a deep ecologist, but one whose deep ecology includes animal and human liberation.

5

Truth as Correspondence, Knowledge as Dialogical: Pluralism without Relativism

What is truth? This provocative question, attributed to Pilate in the Gospel of John, is provocative partly because it is richly ambiguous. Even if we limit the issue to the truth of propositions, we can understand the question in different ways. One way is to understand it to be asking what it *means* to say a proposition is true. That is, does the truth of the proposition consist in its correspondence to something beyond itself, its warranted assertability, its pragmatic usefulness, its coherence with other propositions, its being the view of those in power, or something else? Alternatively, we can understand the question to refer to the concrete truth about something—about a particular issue, such as whether it is now raining somewhere in Oregon, or about the nature of reality in general. Still another way to understand the question involves the issue of knowledge, namely, how we know what the truth about anything is.

Although these questions, especially the question about the very nature of truth, surely worried the real Pilate little more than they worry most political functionaries today, they are now embattled questions at the center of our cultural controversies. Part of the reason the abstract question about the nature of truth is so embattled, I will argue, is that it has often not been properly distinguished from the question of knowledge. As a result, certain things that are true of knowledge—that it is created by humans, largely through dialogue, and is relative to time and place—are attributed to truth itself. For example, one theologian involved in interreligious dialogue suggests that we "deabsolutize truth" and think of it as "dialogic."[1] Although such suggestions are well intentioned, they result in paradoxical formulations implying relativism. I will also argue, however, that many of the things that have falsely been said about truth constitute important insights about human knowledge. These theses are implicit in the chapter title, "Truth as Correspondence, Knowledge as Dialogical."

TRUTH AS CORRESPONDENCE: A HARD-CORE COMMONSENSE NOTION

In defending the notion that truth is correspondence, I am limiting my discussion of truth to the issue of what it means to say of some proposition, idea, assertion, statement, sentence, or belief that it is true. There are, of course, other ways to use the term *truth* (and its equivalents in other languages). We can speak of a true friend, of being true to oneself, and so on. But my focus is on what it means to say of some idea that it is true.

The traditional understanding has been that it means that the idea corresponds to the reality to which it refers. For example, the proposition, former U.S. President Bill Clinton was impeached by the U.S. House of Representatives," is true if and only if there is a person named Bill Clinton who formerly was president of the United States and was, during his tenure, impeached by the U.S. House of Representatives. As this example illustrates, we presuppose in our daily lives that truth is correspondence.[2] Indeed, most people outside the academy, and even most academics outside the humanities, would wonder why anyone would find it necessary to defend the idea that truth means correspondence.

And yet the notion of truth as correspondence has been widely rejected in recent thought. Richard Rorty, for example, rejects the claim that "some nonlinguistic state of the world . . . 'makes a belief true' by 'corresponding' to it."[3] Rorty and many others write as if the issue were settled, that the idea of truth as correspondence is dead so that we need a new view of truth.

There are two broad reasons for this conclusion. One is the claim that the idea of truth as correspondence cannot be made intelligible. The other reason is the claim that the idea that truth consists in correspondence has harmful consequences, with a central claim being that this idea, being absolutist, works against the development of a pluralistic attitude. I will explain later why I do not find either of these claims persuasive.

First, however, I need to explain my basic reason for reaffirming the traditional view that truth is correspondence, even though to do so today is widely regarded as reactionary.[4]

The basic reason for reaffirming the idea of truth as correspondence is that this idea belongs to our hard-core common sense, which means that we cannot consistently deny it. That correspondence is the commonsense understanding of truth is widely recognized. For example, D. J. O'Connor says: "The correspondence theory of truth may be regarded as a systematic development of the commonsense account of truth embodied in such dictionary definitions for 'truth' as 'conformity with fact' and the like."[5] Paul Horwich says that the "common-sense notion [is] that truth is a kind of 'correspondence with the facts.'"[6]

For many philosophers, however, to say that an idea belongs to our commonsense repertoire of beliefs is not to pay it a compliment. Science has widely become understood as a systematic assault on common sense. For example, common sense took the earth to be flat and matter to be solid, but science has shown these commonsense ideas to be false. On this basis, as John Searle has pointed out,[7] many philosophers have concluded that they need not do justice to any of our commonsense notions.[8] With regard to our intuition that truth involves correspondence, Rorty admits that we have it but urges us to "do our best to *stop having* [this intuition]."[9]

The belief that all commonsense ideas can be left behind, however, fails to take account of the all-important distinction between two meanings of the expression *common sense*, which was discussed in chapter 3. It is certainly true that soft-core commonsense notions can be left behind. If the idea that truth is correspondence were merely a soft-core commonsense idea, we might indeed be able to get over it. It belongs, however, to our hard-core common sense.

Hard-core commonsense beliefs are, by definition, common to all human beings. To say this does not mean, as we have seen, that all human beings consciously affirm these ideas. But it does mean that we *really* believe them, in the sense presupposing them in practice, regardless of what we may say verbally. The criterion being used here for what we really believe is the pragmatic criterion of Charles Peirce and William James, which is that our actions, more than our theories, show what we really believe. We should not pretend to doubt in our theories, they insisted, ideas that we inevitably presuppose in practice. This criterion was endorsed by Whitehead's statement that "metaphysical rule of evidence [is] that we must bow to those presumptions which, in despite of criticism, we still employ for the regulation of our lives" (PR 151). Such assumptions, said Peirce, James, and Whitehead, should be taken as universally valid criteria for judging the adequacy of any theory, be it called a "scientific," a "philosophical," or a "theological" theory.

As we have seen, to be sure, some philosophers recognize that we might inevitably presuppose various notions and yet consider them "transcendental illusions."[10] To explain why we inevitably presuppose these assumptions, even though they are false, Rorty suggests that "[w]e have been educated within an intellectual tradition built around such claims."[11] Another possible explanation is that the evolutionary process has programmed these assumptions into us because they have been useful in the struggle for survival, which is John Searle's way of explaining why we cannot help presupposing that we have a degree of freedom even though, as we saw in chapter 3, Searle believes that freedom is ruled out by the scientific worldview.[12]

However, the problem with all such views is that if we *inevitably* presuppose these ideas, we presuppose them in the very act of criticizing them, involving us in a violation of the principle of noncontradiction. To deny any hard-core commonsense ideas verbally is, as we saw in chapter 1, to be guilty of a performative contradiction. If we wish to honor the demands of rationality, therefore, we have no choice but to honor our hard-core commonsense notions, taking a denial of any of them as a sign that the system of thought making the denial is inadequate.[13] The implication for our topic is that we cannot rationally give up the notion of truth as correspondence *if* it is one of our hard-core commonsense notions. And it certainly does seem to be.

For example, Paul Horwich, having said that the commonsense notion is that truth is "a kind of 'correspondence with the facts,'" adds that the alternatives to correspondence theories have been problematic precisely because "they don't accommodate the 'correspondence' intuition."[14]

Richard Rorty, as we have seen, urges us to give up that intuition, but he himself has been unable to do so. Having suggested the "Romantic" view that truth is made rather than found, Rorty admits that it is difficult for him "to avoid hinting that this suggestion gets something right, that my sort of philosophy corresponds to the way things really are."[15]

The task, however, seems not merely difficult but impossible. Rorty speaks, for example, of "what was true in the Romantic idea that truth is made rather than found,"[16] thereby implying that this idea corresponded to something that was already the case. Rorty also says that the "Romantic" view expressed "the realization that a talent for speaking differently, rather than for arguing well, is the chief instrument of cultural change." In speaking of this view as a "realization," Rorty implies that it corresponds to the facts about how cultural change occurs. The way the Romantics expressed this realization, he says, was in terms of "the claim that imagination, rather than reason, is the central human faculty." In making this statement, Rorty is claiming that it corresponds with a claim that the Romantics actually made. This kind of implicit correspondence claim fills Rorty's pages, even those in which he is explicitly rejecting the idea of truth as correspondence. He tells us, for example, that Peirce and James both rejected the idea of correspondence. Although this claim is arguably false,[17] this issue is irrelevant to the point at hand. What is relevant is that Rorty in making the claim implies that what he says about Peirce and James corresponds to what they really believed. Rorty's example, in sum, illustrates the fact that it is impossible to deny, without falling into performative contradiction, the idea that the truth of propositions consists in their correspondence to a reality beyond themselves.

It is for this reason that I do not follow the common practice of referring to "the correspondence theory of truth." I speak instead of "truth as correspondence." To speak of "the correspondence theory of truth" would imply that the idea that truth is correspondence were merely one theory among others, which could be given up.

We can, to be sure, meaningfully speak of *a* correspondence theory of truth. Such a theory seeks to explain what this relationship of correspondence is, how or in what sense a proposition can correspond to something else. There are, however, many such theories, such as the theory of the early Wittgenstein and that of the later Whitehead. We should, therefore, use the plural, speaking of correspondence *theories* of truth. We should not speak in the singular of "the correspondence theory of truth," thereby falsely suggesting that the idea that truth involves correspondence is merely a theory.

Now, having argued that it is impossible consistently to reject the idea of truth as correspondence, I will look at two kinds of arguments as to why we should try. The arguments of the first kind claim that the idea of truth as correspondence is unintelligible.

CRITICISMS OF TRUTH AS CORRESPONDENCE AS UNINTELLIGIBLE

Criticism Presupposing an Epistemic Conception of Truth

The most well-known argument of this type is question begging, because it depends on an epistemic conception of truth, which is precisely the conception rejected by correspondence conceptions. In an epistemic conception of truth, the truth of a statement is said to be dependent on human cognition. Truth may be said to be that which is rationally justifiable.

Rorty, for example, has endorsed Michael Dummett's identification of truth with "warranted assertability."[18] Rorty has sometimes paraphrased this definition provocatively by saying that truth is simply "what our peers will, ceteris paribus, let us get away with saying."[19] Warranted assertability is often understood in terms of the so-called *coherence* theory of truth, according to which a proposition is true if it has a place in a coherent system of propositions about reality.

Rorty has also endorsed the idea, derived from Habermas, that we should think of "truth as what comes to be believed in the course of free and open encounters."[20] Hilary Putnam at one time said that "we call a statement 'true' if it would be justified under [epistemically ideal] conditions."[21] Because it is generally agreed that ideas are justified or warranted to the extent that they have achieved widespread intersubjective agreement, this view leads to the idea that truth is dialogic, the result of dialogue.

In any case, what all these epistemic conceptions of truth have in common, as William Alston points out, is the idea that the truth of a belief "consists not in its relation to some 'transcendent' state of affairs [meaning transcendent to the belief], but in the epistemic virtues the [belief] displays *within* our thought, experience, and discourse. Truth value is a matter of whether... a belief is *justified, warranted, rational, well grounded*, or the like."[22]

In a correspondence conception of truth, by contrast, the truth of a proposition does not depend on us at all. It depends entirely on the relation of the proposition to the state of affairs to which it refers. The proposition, Alfred North Whitehead taught at Harvard, is true if and only if Whitehead taught at Harvard. Whereas the "only if" in this statement means that Whitehead's having taught at Harvard is a *necessary* condition of the proposition's truth, the "if" means that his having taught at Harvard, is a *sufficient* condition. Nothing else is relevant. It matters not whether we have reached intersubjective agreement, through dialogue, that Whitehead taught at Harvard or whether we find that the proposition fits coherently with the other things we believe about him. These matters are very relevant, of course, to whether we *believe* the proposition that Whitehead taught at Harvard and to whether our belief counts as a piece of *knowledge*. But they are irrelevant to the question of this proposition's truth, which depends simply on whether Whitehead in fact taught at Harvard. This is what it means to hold a correspondence conception of truth.

The most prevalent criticism of this conception takes off from the fact that, according to the notion of truth as correspondence, the truth of our beliefs about the world consists in their correspondence to the way the world is in itself, independently of our beliefs. But, say the critics, all our observations of the world are theory-laden, so we have no access to the world in itself, apart from our beliefs or theories about it. We cannot, therefore, get outside our belief system in order to see if the world as it is in itself corresponds to our beliefs about it.

For example, Cornel West, using this Rorty-inspired argument, "rejects Reality as the ultimate standard" of truth because "realist appeals to 'the world' as a final court of appeal to determine what is true can only be viciously circular."[23] It is, however, West's criticism that is circular, for it depends on the assumption that truth consists not simply in the relation of a belief to reality but also involves our human ability to *know* this reality. His criticism of the correspondence conception of truth already presupposes, therefore, the epistemic conception.

The question begging involved in this criticism is now being recognized by some of those originally responsible for its popularity, including two philosophers to whom Rorty had appealed for support: Donald Davidson and Hilary Putnam. Davidson had long rejected correspondence theories, he reports, because of the "usual complaint" that "it makes no sense to suggest that it is somehow possible to compare one's words or beliefs with the world." But, he now points out, "this complaint against correspondence theories is not sound [because] it depends on assuming that some form of epistemic theory is correct."[24] Likewise, Hilary Putnam now rejects epistemic theories of truth in favor of "common-sense realism," dissociating himself from Rorty's attempt to show the idea of correspondence to be empty.[25] With philosophers such as Davidson and Putnam turning away from it, we can assume that this epistemic-based criticism of truth as correspondence will die out.

Criticism Presupposing Materialism

The epistemic conception of truth, however, has not been the only basis for the claim that the correspondence notion of truth is unintelligible. This claim is also made on the basis of a materialistic ontology. This ontology, according to which nothing exists except bits and aggregations of matter, rules out the standard, traditional way of understanding what it means to speak of truth as correspondence.

According to this traditional understanding, to say that some verbal statement is true means that the proposition embodied in the sentence corresponds to the reality to which it refers. The proposition is the *meaning* of the sentence. This meaning can be the meaning that the speaker (or writer) intended to express. Or it can be the meaning that was evoked in the hearer (or reader). In either case, the proposition (meaning) is true if and only if it corresponds to the reality to which it refers.

To make clear the distinction between a sentence and a proposition, we can take the English sentence, *It is raining*. This sentence is not identical with its meaning, because this meaning can be equally expressed by the German sentence, *Es regnet*, and the French sentence, *Il pleut*. We have here three linguistic entities, three sentences, expressing the same meaning, the same proposition. What directly corresponds to reality, if it is really raining, is this proposition. It is, in other words, the proposition, not the sentence, in which the property of truth primarily inheres.

The idea that propositions are the primary bearers of either truth or falsity is supported by several philosophers, including William Alston, Paul Horwich, and Marian David.[26] Sentences and beliefs can, however, be truth bearers in a secondary sense. Sentences can be truth bearers in this secondary sense because of their capacity to *express* propositions in the mind of the speaker or writer and/or to *evoke* propositions in the minds of hearers or readers. Linguistic communication is successful insofar as the propositions evoked are similar to the propositions intended. Likewise, we often speak of a belief as corresponding to reality. But it is not the belief itself, which is a state of mind, that may correspond to the reality in question. It is instead the content of the belief, and this is a proposition.

If it is the proposition that is true by virtue of corresponding to reality, what exactly is this relationship called "correspondence"? The relationship of correspondence consists of the fact that the same state of affairs is in the proposition and in reality. This state of affairs exists in the proposition *as a mere possibility*, whereas in reality it exists *as actualized*. This explanation overcomes one of the standard objections to the notion of truth as correspondence. This objection assumes that in affirming a correspondence between a proposition and reality, one is affirming *identity*. That would clearly be nonsensical, because the proposition expressed by the statement, It is raining, is obviously not the same as the reality of rain. The proposition, for one thing, will not make one wet. Correspondence, however, does not mean identity. Although a true proposition contains the same ingredients as the reality to which it refers, it contains them in a different mode of togetherness.

Take, for example, the proposition expressed by the statement, This ball is red. The real ball is a nexus of molecules qualified by the color red. Assuming the proposition to be true, the proposition and the real world have the same elements: the same subject (the ball) and the same predicate (red). The proposition and the ball are not identical, however, because, as Whitehead explains, in the actual world, the ball and the redness are together "in the mode of realization," whereas in the proposition the ball and the redness are together in "the mode of abstract possibility." The ball and the proposition, therefore, "belong to different categories of existence" so that "[t]heir identification is mere nonsense" (AI 244–45).

Insofar as contemporary philosophy is dominated by the acceptance of a materialist ontology, however, this traditional understanding of correspondence is ruled out, because materialism rejects the existence of abstract, nonmaterial entities such as propositions.[27] There can be no distinction between a sentence and the proposition it expresses or evokes. There is only the sentence, as a material, linguistic entity. Given this view, it becomes difficult to explain what it would mean to say that truth consists of correspondence. In what sense, for example, can the sentence, It is raining, be said to correspond to what is going on outside when rain is coming down?

One problem with affirming correspondence, if all we have is language, is due to the fact that language is thoroughly indeterminate, ambiguous. Take the sentence, Caesar crossed the Rubicon. The word *Caesar* could refer to an emperor, a movie star, or a puppy. The word *Rubicon* could refer to a river in Europe, a creek in a local village, or a metaphorical boundary. We cannot say, therefore, that the sentence either corresponds, or fails to correspond, to reality. Of course, by eliminating all the ambiguities, thereby specifying what particular meaning is intended, we could say that the sentence is true or false in a secondary, derivative sense, by virtue of expressing and evoking this meaning. But to make this move would be to return to the idea that the primary bearer of truth or falsity is the meaning, the (nonlinguistic) proposition, and this is what materialism forbids.

Still another problem for the idea of truth as correspondence follows from this materialistic denial of the reality of propositions. If we cannot distinguish between sentences and propositions, then sentences are the primary—and in fact the only—bearers of truth. Rorty's case against the idea of correspondence now rests primarily on this contention that truth must be a property of sentences. Arguing that "where there are no sentences there is no truth," Rorty concludes that "[t]ruth cannot be out there—cannot exist independently of the human mind."[28] In other words, sentences only exist where there are linguistic creatures, which in our world means human beings. This insight, says Rorty, rules out the main contention of those who defend the correspondence conception, which is that truth exists independently of human beings. On this point, Rorty still has the support of Putnam, who says: "It is statements (not abstract entities called 'propositions') that are true or false."[29]

This position, however, leads to paradoxes. For example, Putnam elsewhere says: "While it is true that the stars would still have existed even if language users had not evolved, it is not the case that sentences would have existed. There would have still been a world, but there would not have been any *truths*."[30] But if it is now true that there would have been stars even if language users had never emerged, as Putnam agrees, can we avoid saying that it *was* true that there were stars even before the rise of language users? Surely not. And yet Rorty and Putnam must try to say this, because of the materialistic rejection of propositions.[31]

The rejection of propositions on the basis of materialism, however, would make sense only if materialism had proved itself to be generally adequate. As we saw in chapter 3, however, materialism is increasingly seen to be incapable of doing justice to the mind-body relation, with its various dimensions, including our hard-core commonsense belief in freedom. Materialism can, more generally, be shown to be incapable of doing justice to a wide range of notions that science necessarily presupposes.[32] From this perspective, rather than rejecting propositions in the name of materialism, we should add its rejection of propositions to the list of reasons for rejecting materialism.

Criticism Based on Atheism

The idea that truth is correspondence has also been criticized on the basis of the acceptance of an atheistic worldview. One criticism involves a Nietzschean argument from "perspectivism." To accept the implication of the death of God, says this argument, is to realize that there is no all-inclusive perspective on reality but only a multiplicity of finite perspectives, which are partial, fallible, and often contradictory of each other. There is, accordingly, no place for truth to exist.

This argument has merit, because, as is widely accepted, abstractions can exist only in concrete, actual things. Whitehead endorsed this widespread view in terms of his "ontological principle," also called the "Aristotelian principle," according to which anything that is nonactual can exist only in some actual thing. If we believe that there is no all-inclusive perspective, then it will indeed be difficult to make sense of the idea that there is such a thing as *the* truth, sometimes called "Truth with a capital T."

This argument, however, is self-stultifying, because it argues against the reality of truth on the basis of the presumed truth of atheism. The real moral of the argument, therefore, is that the fact that atheism cannot accommodate our intuition about the reality of truth is one of many reasons to reject atheism.[33] Whitehead implicitly responds to this issue with his statement that "[t]he truth itself is nothing else than how the composite natures of the organic actualities of the world obtain adequate representation in the... 'consequent nature' of God" (PR 12).

Although there are yet more reasons philosophers have had for doubting the intelligibility of the idea of truth as correspondence, at least some of which I have discussed elsewhere,[34] I must now turn to the other main complaint against the idea of truth as correspondence, namely, that it is harmful—in particular, that it is absolutist and thereby contrary to pluralism.

THE CLAIM THAT TRUTH AS CORRESPONDENCE IS ANTIPLURALIST

The present age is often called a "pluralist age." Pluralism is defined in various ways. Some of these are problematic, as when pluralism is equated with relativism, understood as the doctrine that there are no universal criteria in terms of which to judge the truth of any proposition. I take pluralism, however, to be the acceptance of the idea that no one religion, or no particular culture, has a monopoly on truth. Given this meaning, pluralism is, I hold, an attitude to be embraced and promoted with enthusiasm.[35] I would find it distressing, therefore, if the idea of truth as correspondence were antithetical to pluralism. Fortunately, that is not the case.

Some opponents of the idea of truth as correspondence, however, have assumed otherwise. One of their reasons for opposing the idea of truth as correspondence is to undercut the claims of authoritarian institutions to possess the truth. For example, Christian institutions have traditionally claimed that Christianity is the one true religion, the only one approved by God. This exclusivist claim, which has been the source of untold suffering in the past, today stands in the way of a truly pluralistic world, in which the adherents of the various religions would appreciate the distinctive truths and values in each others' traditions. This exclusivist claim is still upheld by most Christian churches today. Some critics believe that the way to undermine this claim, which assumes a cor-respondence between traditional Christian beliefs and the divine will, is to undermine the very idea that truth is correspondence.

This approach, however, is confused and self-defeating. It is confused inso-far as it confuses the question of the *meaning* of "truth" with a concrete claim to *possess* the truth. To reject a particular truth claim, one needs only to deny that it is justified by the relevant evidence; it is not necessary to deny that truth means correspondence. That latter denial is also self-defeating, because intellec-tuals who reject truth as correspondence thereby give up their main weapon for challenging harmful ideologies, which is to get them labeled false by showing that they do not really correspond to the facts. Although the desire to promote pluralism by defeating absolutist truth claims is commendable, it is unnecessary and self-defeating to do this by denying that truth means correspondence.

The desire to promote pluralistic attitudes has produced a more subtle criti-cism of the idea of truth as correspondence, which goes something like this:

> The notion that truth means correspondence means that, if your theory about something is true, there is a one-to-one correspondence between your theory and the thing. But reality seems to be indescrib-ably complex. For example, Western medical theories about the human body seem to be "true" in the sense that they lead to diagnoses and treatments that produce positive results. But we have now learned that Chinese medical theory, which is completely different, also pro-duces positive results. The Western world was unable to recognize this fact for several centuries because the idea that truth is correspondence led us to think we had the whole truth about the human body. This idea is still preventing us from realizing that although the Buddhist view of ultimate reality is very different from the Jewish or the Christian view, it also produces positive results, leading to lives of peace and compassion. If we want a pluralistic world, we must reject the idea of truth as correspondence.

Although this argument may at first glance appear to be decisive, it achieves its apparent victory only by imposing on the idea of truth as correspon-dence an assumption not entailed by it. This assumption is that if my idea of X is true, my idea captures the complete truth about X. But we do not ordinarily assume this.

For example, if I say that my copy of Whitehead's *Process and Reality* is black, I do not thereby claim to have exhausted the truth about this book. I know that it is also rectangular, fairly thick, and difficult to understand on first reading.

Likewise, the statement that Charles Hartshorne was a well-known philosopher is true, but no one would suppose that it states the full truth about him. He was also the son of an Episcopal priest, a student at Haverford and Harvard, the man who married Dorothy Cooper, a professor at Chicago, Emory, and the University of Texas, and an ornithologist famous for his antimonotony principle. And these truths do not even begin to exhaust the indefinitely rich reality that was Charles Hartshorne.

To say that a proposition is true means not that it states the full truth about its referent but only that it states *something* true about it. If Hartshorne was indescribably complex, furthermore, just think how complex God must be. And perhaps ultimate reality is more complex yet, so that Buddhist and Christian ideas about it can be equally true.

This idea that reality is far more complex than any of our theories about it is very important for promoting pluralism. But it is not in conflict with the idea that truth means correspondence. The idea that Western medicine's theory of the human body, with its notions of cells, enzymes, viruses, and bacteria, corresponds to certain dimensions of the body does not prevent us from believing that Chinese medicine's theory, with its notions of yin, yang, ch'i, and chakras, corresponds to other dimensions. Likewise, the idea that reality as a whole contains a being corresponding to what Jews, Christians, and Muslims call "God" would not necessarily prevent it from containing a reality corresponding to what Buddhists call "emptiness."

In fact, the notion that reality is indescribably complex, far from being in conflict with the idea of truth as correspondence, presupposes it. It would be self-contradictory to deny the idea of truth as correspondence on the grounds that reality is indescribably complex, because one would be presupposing that the possible characteristic, *indescribable complexity*, is in fact instantiated by reality so that the description of reality as indescribably complex corresponds to reality better than the description of it as quite simple.

With this point, I conclude my discussion of truth as correspondence and move to the issue of knowledge as dialogical.

KNOWLEDGE AS DIALOGICAL

Although the subtitle of this chapter refers to affirming pluralism without relativism, I have thus far explicitly said very little about relativism. Implicitly, however, the entire preceding discussion involved a rejection of relativism by virtue of rejecting epistemic definitions of truth, which are inherently relativistic.

The relativism inherent in such definitions can be illustrated in terms of the idea that truth is what is rationally justifiable by the intellectual leaders of a community. If this is how "truth" is defined, then what is true differs radically from time to time and place to place. For example, the idea that the earth is flat was true at one time, but it is no longer true—except perhaps within the Flat Earth Society and certain other primitive tribes. In the philosophy department at Notre Dame University, it is true that the universe was created by an omnipotent, omniscient, personal creator, but this is false in the philosophy department at the University of Pittsburgh.

Given an epistemic conception of truth, to say of some proposition that it is true can mean only that it is "true for me" or, at best, "true for us." Nothing can be true prior to being believed, so truth depends entirely on human cognition, with all its conditioning by time, place, circumstance, and interests.

To reject epistemic definitions of truth, therefore, is to reject this relativism of truth. To define truth as correspondence is to say that the truth is what it is regardless of what we or any other people happen to think. Of course, by virtue of thinking something, you create a new truth—the truth that you had that thought. But once you had it, it is true that you had it regardless of what anyone else thinks, including what you at a later time, perhaps in a "senior moment," may think. Truth is, in this sense, absolute.[36]

Knowledge, however, is another matter. Knowledge does, by definition, involve the knower, so all knowledge is knower dependent. It would be possible for one to accept the absoluteness of truth and still affirm complete relativism with regard to human knowledge.

To enter into a discussion of this question requires, of course, a definition of knowledge. I accept the traditional definition, according to which knowledge is "justified true belief." This definition means, on the other hand, that for a belief to be considered knowledge it is not sufficient for the belief to be rationally justified; it must also be true, which means, as argued earlier, that the content of the belief (the proposition) must correspond to reality. On the other hand, a belief does not count as an item of knowledge just because it happens to be true. The belief must be justified in the sense of being believed for the right reasons.

Cognitive Relativism

Given this conception of knowledge, some reasons for affirming complete relativism are excluded, but not all. One could still hold that human belief formation, even the part we call "cognition" (knowing), may be completely relativistic. In referring to "cognitive" relativism, I mean the twofold doctrine (1) that human beings inevitably conceive and even perceive reality in terms of a particular framework, nowadays often called a "cultural-linguistic" system of concepts, and (2) that there are no universally valid, framework-transcendent criteria in terms of which to adjudicate differences of opinion. Even if we conclude that the issue of the relativism of truth is a red herring (one created by epistemic definitions of truth and an atheistic, materialistic view of reality), cognitive relativism, especially this *framework* relativism, is a serious problem. I believe, nevertheless, that it is a false doctrine, because we are not completely at the mercy of the framework with which we happen to grow up.

There is, to be sure, a great deal of truth in this doctrine. The cognitive framework we assimilate from our culture does provide a perspective that heavily conditions not only the conscious judgments we make but also which things and features of the world we consciously notice and thereby take into consideration in forming our worldview. We make most of our explicit judgments on the basis of what I have called "soft-core" common sense, which consists of assumptions we have simply taken over from our culture or subculture. The frameworks or perspectives provided by different cultures, furthermore, can be very different. Insofar as Nietzsche's "perspectivism" is taken simply as a description of the human condition, it is largely correct.

Universally Valid Formal Criteria

However, if we take this perspectival relativism to be the whole truth, various paradoxes result. One such paradox is the truth claim that truth does not exist. Another one is the claim that the universal truth about the human condition is that no one can know universal truths. Some thinkers claim that we simply have to live with these paradoxes. That conclusion, however, would follow only on the assumption that we are completely devoid of any universally valid criteria for judging worldviews.

In discussing this issue, it is important to distinguish between formal and substantive criteria. Because my claim that there are some universally valid substantive criteria is the more controversial claim, I will begin with the issue of formal criteria. Although some extremists deny it, there are quite clearly some formal criteria that are universally presupposed.

One of these formal criteria is self-consistency, or noncontradiction, which I have discussed earlier. There have been some philosophers, to be sure, who have challenged the idea that even this principle has universal validity.

In a well-known essay, "Two Dogmas of Empiricism," Willard Quine rejected the idea that the law of noncontradiction is an a priori, unchallengeable truth.[37] As Charles Larmore points out, however, we cannot even imagine believing that "the avoidance of contradiction has no more authority than what we choose to give it."[38] Larmore's point, in other words, is that we cannot help assuming that the law of noncontradiction is a principle somehow inherent in the nature of things, which provides a universally valid norm for credible thought. Hilary Putnam, who at one time had endorsed Quine's position, later came to accept the same view as Larmore, arguing in an essay titled "There Is at Least One A Priori Truth" that the principle of noncontradiction is absolutely unrevisable.[39]

People with different worldviews have, therefore, at least this basis for criticizing each others' positions. It is not irrelevant, therefore, for neo-Darwinists to criticize Creation Science if they find serious inconsistencies in it. It is equally valid for Creation Scientists to criticize neo-Darwinism if they find serious inconsistencies in it.

If, however, consistency were the only universally valid test of truth, the only reason to reject a worldview would be if it contained self-contradictions. But another formal criterion that we all presuppose is adequacy to the facts. The primary reason that most scientists reject Creation Science is not that they find inconsistencies in it but because they find it grossly inadequate to a wide range of facts, such as those indicating beyond any reasonable doubt that the earth is several billion years old. The main criticism directed at neo-Darwinism, in turn, is that it is inadequate to various facts, especially the fact that the fossil record does not support the gradualism entailed by the theory.

This criterion, however, has become problematic. The main problem is the fact that adequacy, though a purely formal criterion, presupposes that there are some universally accessible facts for a theory to be adequate *to*. It assumes, therefore, that we, in spite of our culturally conditioned perspectives, have access to some facts—some data—to which other people, perceiving the world in terms of other frameworks, also have access, and much recent philosophy rejects this assumption.

One dimension of this rejection is the denial that our experience contains any "data," in the strict sense of that term, whatsoever. Data in the strict sense is information that is simply *given* to our experience, as opposed to being created by our perceptual-cognitive processes, but some philosophers deny that our experience contains anything that is given in this sense. This denial was expressed most famously in Wilfrid Sellars' critique of what he called "the myth of the given,"[40] and many other philosophers, such as Michael Williams in a book titled *Groundless Belief*, have endorsed this denial. "Evidence from the psychology of perception," says Williams, "all points to there being no such thing as a state of sensuous apprehension utterly unaffected by beliefs, desires and expectations and consequently no experience of the given as such."[41]

Having dealt with this position at some length elsewhere,[42] I will here only summarize my three main arguments against it. First, the claim that the relevant evidence shows that our experience contains no given elements is self-stultifying, because if this claim were true there could *be* no "evidence." Second, the denial of givenness, being based on the analysis of conscious sense perception, presupposes that sense perception is our only mode of perception. These first two points are both illustrated by the quotation from Williams.

My third point is that a careful analysis of experience, with attention to *all* forms of human experience, reveals that sense perception, rather than being our only mode of perception, is derivative from a more fundamental mode of perception, in which data *are* given to our experience. This third point, by suggesting that there is a preconscious, bottom layer of human experience that is basically the same—in the sense of involving the same *kinds* of data—in all human beings, is especially important for our topic of relativism.

Universally Valid Substantive Criteria

This importance can best be explained in terms of the other major issue involved in the question of whether there are any universal elements of experience to serve as framework-transcendent criteria of adequacy. This is whether there are any notions that are universally presupposed, any hard-core common-sense notions. I have, of course, already suggested that there are at least two formal notions of this type: the idea of truth as correspondence and the law of noncontradiction. However, if these purely formal notions were our only framework-transcendent criteria, we would have little basis for judging the relative adequacy of various systems of thought.

I have also, however, pointed to four hard-core notions of a *substantive* nature: the existence of an external world, of the past, of causation as real influence, and of human freedom. And elsewhere I have suggested that there are several more universally presupposed substantive notions, including the distinction between better and worse possibilities, the idea that some things are important, and the reality of something sacred or holy. It would take some time to make a convincing case for the universality of these ideas, and some readers even then might be reluctant to accept the universality of all of them. If, however, at least some of them are universally presupposed in practice, then we cannot verbally deny them without violating the law of noncontradiction.

To be rational, therefore, we must accept them as universally valid criteria for judging the adequacy of any system of thought. Insofar as my list is accepted, we could rule out, for example, any systems espousing acausalism, determinism, solipsism, nihilism, or the unreality of time.[43] Insofar as we recognize that we have these universally valid substantive criteria, we can resist the suggestion that we are condemned to a relativism of beliefs.

It might seem, incidentally, that by endorsing the existence of universally valid criteria, I am endorsing foundationalism, which is widely considered discredited. The term *foundationalism*, however, has come to be used with a wide variety of meanings. All that has been discredited, as far as I can see, is foundationalism in the strict, original sense, which involves the epistemological doctrine

(1) that a system of beliefs is distinguishable into basic and nonbasic beliefs, (2) that basic beliefs are known immediately to be true, (3) that in a rational system basic beliefs form the starting points from which all nonbasic beliefs must be derived, and (4) that the relation between basic and nonbasic beliefs is an entirely one-way relation, with basic beliefs supporting, without in any way being supported by, nonbasic beliefs.[44]

In my position, hard-core commonsense beliefs do not provide a foundation, on which all other beliefs are to be based, but a compass, which tells us when our journey of thought is heading off course. It would not be a valid criticism to claim that my position is guilty of being foundationalist in a more general sense of the term unless one can explain why foundationalism in this more general sense should also be considered discredited.

Why Increased Knowledge Requires Dialogue

I have mentioned seven substantive hard-core commonsense notions. But there may be dozens of such notions in the bottom layer of our experience, with one set of them lifted to consciousness in one religious-cultural tradition, another set in a second tradition, still another set in a third, and so on. With this hypothesis, interreligious dialogue becomes extremely important. Charles Hartshorne once suggested that philosophical theology should involve "an effort, through cooperation, to discover what the bottom layer of our common human thought really is."[45] Central to such cooperation would be interreligious dialogue, through which we would help each other achieve an increased awareness of the notions that we in practice presuppose in common.

This is one of the most important ways in which knowledge is dialogical. It is very difficult to become aware of the notions that we presuppose in every moment, in every act, in every thought. However, if each tradition has become consciously aware of a different set of these notions, which is a reasonable working hypothesis, then we can learn from each other. It seems, for example, that the Jewish, Christian, Muslim, and Confucian traditions have been especially conscious of a principle of rightness, which Confucians call the "mandate of heaven" and the others "the will of God," whereas Buddhists have been especially aware of the causal conditioning of every moment of human experience and, by extension, of all events, a feature that some Buddhists call "emptiness." Through dialogue, those in one tradition can become aware of a dimension of their own experience on which they previously had not be encouraged to focus.[46]

Dialogue is necessary, however, not only to increase our knowledge of dimensions of our own experience. It is often needed to help us see how the different insights of the various religious traditions can be reconciled. To speak of "insights" is to suggest that the various religious traditions have all expressed truths about the nature of reality in general and human experience in particular. This hypothesis, besides being a helpful one with which to begin, is simply the reverse side of the basic assumption of the pluralistic attitude, which is that one's own tradition is not the repository of all truth. The hypothesis that each of the traditions contains important insights is a reasonable assumption, because it is hard to believe that any tradition devoid of genuine insights into the nature of reality and human experience could have been sustained for a long period of time. It is also reasonable, however, to assume that the various traditions are usually more correct in what they affirm than in what they deny. Otherwise put, traditions have often exaggerated their insights in ways that exclude complementary insights.

This human tendency to exaggerate, thereby turning true insights into falsehoods, can be illustrated within Western thought. The recognition that every event, including every moment of human experience, is conditioned by the past has often been turned into the false doctrine that every event is wholly determined by the past.[47] Contrariwise, the recognition that we have genuine freedom is often exaggerated to the point of ignoring the great extent to which our thought and action are conditioned (as in the denial, discussed earlier, that our experience begins with elements that are simply given). The task of rational thought, faced with the fact that experience is both conditioned and free, is to show how these two truths are compatible. As Whitehead said, "One task of a sound metaphysics is to exhibit final and efficient causes in their proper relation to each other" (PR 84).

Another example of such exaggeration is provided by traditional theism. Insofar as it said that our experience is constantly influenced by divine causation, the same causation that has been primarily responsible for the creation of our universe, traditional theism expresses an important truth. But this truth was turned into a falsehood by theists who exaggerated divine power to the point of excluding the truth of creaturely freedom. Part and parcel of this falsehood, as suggested in chapter 2, is the exaggeration known as the doctrine of creatio ex nihilo, which understood the "nothing" out of which our world was created to be an *absolute* nothing, meaning a complete absence of finite actuality, rather than simply the *relative* nothing of a primeval chaos.[48] This exaggeration resulted in endless controversies about grace and free will and an insoluble problem of evil.[49] It also produced, by reaction, atheistic views of the universe, in which divine guidance is denied altogether. Still another consequence of the doctrine of creation out of absolute nothingness is that it put Christianity and, through its influence, Judaism and Islam in opposition to the other religious traditions. For example, this doctrine made it appear that if biblical theism is true, then Buddhism, which explicitly denies the idea that our world was created out of nothing, is false, and vice-versa.

Through dialogue, however, progress has been made in overcoming these contradictions. Forms of theism have arisen that, besides synthesizing the elements of truth in traditional theism and its denial, allow divine influence to be compatible with creaturely freedom. We process theologians believe that process theism represents such a synthesis.[50] And some Buddhists and Christians have moved toward a commonly acceptable position in which the positive insights of both traditions are affirmed.[51]

I am arguing that, although truth is absolute in the sense of being independent of our cognitive activities, none of our beliefs, even those that we think of as knowledge, should be considered absolute. Human belief formation is a thoroughly fallible process. As I suggested earlier, reality is indescribably, probably infinitely, complex, whether one is discussing reality as a whole or any particular thing, such as the human body or even a single living cell. But our minds, our cognitive processes, are thoroughly finite and fallible, prone to invincible ignorance, sinful distortions, and simple mistakes of numerous sorts. Part of our finitude and fallibility is that we necessarily perceive and think about the world in terms of the perspective or framework that we inherit from a particular tradition. As Paul Knitter says, this conclusion leads to what David Lochhead calls the "dialogical imperative,"[52] because it is through dialogue with members of other religious traditions that "we can expand or correct the truth that we have," thereby overcoming the "limitations of our own viewpoint."[53] Through such dialogue we can partly overcome the mismatch between the infinite complexity of reality and our limited perspectives.

It is not, of course, only with members of other religious traditions that we need dialogue. As much recent thought has emphasized, we need ongoing, endless dialogue with people of different genders, races, classes, countries, and cultures. We need dialogue with people who especially identify with the nonhuman world. And we academics need dialogue with people in different disciplines and even subdisciplines. If we want to approach the fullest truth of which we are capable, we need dialogue with as many perspectives as possible. In our pluralistic age, it is only with regard to those points on which we have reached intersubjective agreement with peoples of many diverse perspectives that we should be confident enough of our beliefs to call them knowledge. This is especially the case with respect to what to do about the global crises of our time, such as the long-term and increasing gap between rich and poor that is sometimes called "global apartheid." Although the old saying that "the voice of the people is the voice of God" is not literally true, it expresses the insight that it is only by taking into account the considered opinion of all peoples that we can even begin to approximate the divine perspective, in which is combined the full truth of our situation and the best solution for the mess into which the human race has gotten itself.

CONCLUSION

As these final reflections suggest, the full implications of the recognition that knowledge is dialogical are far more important for the future of our world than the philosophical point that truth is correspondence. But this philosophical point *is* important, partly for avoiding a debilitating relativism. It is important to see, therefore, that the fact that knowledge is dialogical does not contradict, and in fact presupposes, the idea of truth as correspondence.

6

Time in Physics and the Time of Our Lives: Overcoming Misplaced Concreteness

INTRODUCTION

The relation of time as experienced, or "lived time," to the ultimate nature of reality is one of the oldest topics of human thought. In traditional thought, both East and West, reflection on this topic was often made both vital and perplexing by the conviction that, while our experience is undoubtedly temporal, the divine reality is not. In late modern thought, concern with the topic has been spurred by the widespread consensus that time as known in human experience is ultimately unreal for physics and the objects and interactions it describes. This belief has led to the conclusion that time as known in human experience is ultimately unreal, period.

Three Features of Lived Time

In speaking of "time as known in human experience," at least three features are usually in view: asymmetry, constant becoming, and irreversibility in principle.

Asymmetry means that the relation of the present to the past is different in kind from the relation of the present to the future. We express this difference by saying that we "remember" the past while "anticipating" the future. Less neutrally, we "regret" or are "grateful" for the past, while we "fear" or are "hopeful" about the future. These different relations to the past and to the future express our assumptions that the past is fully settled, while the future involves potentialities still to be settled. The present, the "now" between past and future, is assumed to be the time in which potentialities are being settled.

The phrase *constant becoming* refers to the fact that "now" does not stand still, but always divides a different set of events into past and future: in each new "now" there are events in the past that in previous "nows" had not yet happened, having at most been anticipated as probable events.

Irreversibility in principle means that a series of events can only go in one direction, from past to present to future. The series of events could not conceivably turn around and go in the opposite direction. Events in my past could not also be in my future. The fact that we neither anticipate past events nor remember future events is not simply a contingent feature of our experience. Rather, it is built into the very meaning of "past" and "future." It is analytic. It would be meaningless to speak of remembering the future or anticipating the past.

Lived time, the time of our lives, involves asymmetry, constant becoming, and irreversibility in principle.

Although we can distinguish these three aspects of time as known in human experience, each of them presupposes the others. For example, part of the reason that time is irreversible in principle is that the past is comprised entirely of totally settled, determinate events. It would be self-contradictory, accordingly, to think that those events could somehow come to be in the future, for that would mean that they would be in the realm of the still partially indeterminate. Likewise, it is because the present involves the transformation of possibilities into actualities that there is constant becoming, which means that time cannot "stand still." Once some possibilities have been chosen and others excluded, one cannot again face those same options. Those decisions are, as we say, "behind us," and we now confront new options.

In any case, time in this threefold sense will henceforth be referred to not only as "time as known in human experience" and "lived time" but also as "time in the usual sense" or simply as "time" or "temporality," because this threefold description simply brings out what we usually *mean* by speaking of time.

Given this understanding of time, the question before us is how philosophers should respond to the twofold idea that time in this sense, which is the time of our lives, does not exist for physics and is, therefore, ultimately unreal.

The Claim that Physics Supports the Unreality of Time

This conclusion, that the authority of physics supports the ultimate unreality of time, has been widely disseminated through various popular books. The message of Fritjof Capra's *Tao of Physics* is that modern physics teaches the same lesson as those forms of Buddhism, such as Hua-Yen and Zen, that speak of the mutual interfusion of past, present, and future.[1] With regard to the implications of special relativity physics, Capra says: "The relativistic theory of particle interactions shows thus a complete symmetry with regard to the direction of time.... To get the right feeling for the relativistic world of particles, we must 'forget the lapse of time.'"[2] Capra supports this conclusion with a famous quotation from physicist Louis de Broglie:

> In space-time, everything which for each of us constitutes the past, the present, and the future is given in block, and the entire collection of events, successive for us, which form the existence of a material particle is represented by a line, the world-line of the particle. Each observer, as his time passes, discovers, so to speak, new slices of space-time which appear to him as successive aspects of the material world, though in reality the ensemble of events constituting space-time exist prior to his knowledge of them.[3]

Another best-selling book, *The Dancing Wu Li Masters* by Gary Zukav, conveys essentially the same message. The reader learns that the preferred interpretation of quantum field theory is to speak of antiparticles as particles traveling backward in time. Louis de Broglie is again quoted to show that the idea that events "develop" in time is an illusion.[4]

In *Space, Time and Medicine*, Larry Dossey begins a chapter on "Modern Time" with the quotation from de Broglie and another by Thomas Gold, which reads: "The *flow* of time is clearly an inappropriate concept for the description of the physical world that has no past, present and future. It just is." Dossey also draws on the ideas of Paul C. W. Davies, who said that "relativity physics has shifted the moving present out from the superstructure of the universe, into the minds of human beings, where it belongs."[5] Reflecting this statement and Davies' observation that no physical experiment detecting the passage of time has ever been performed, Dossey concludes: "The notion that time flows in a one-way fashion is a property of our consciousness. It is a subjective phenomenon and is a property that simply cannot be demonstrated in the natural world. This is an incontrovertible lesson from modern science....A flowing time belongs to our mind, not to nature. We serially perceive events that simply 'are.'"[6]

This discussion by Dossey, a medical doctor, shows the authority typically ascribed to physics to settle philosophical issues about the ultimate nature of reality. For example, Dossey cites a famous statement from Herman Weyl: "The objective world simply is. It does not happen. Only to the gaze of my consciousness crawling upward along the lifeline of my body does a section of this world come to life as a fleeting image." Dossey then comments: "This view is an affront to common sense.... [But we] must assimilate it," for "we cannot ignore what modern physical science has revealed to us about the nature of time."[7]

The Importance of this Claim for Religious and Moral Philosophy

The widespread idea that physical science has indeed "revealed" time to be ulti-mately unreal is of utmost importance for the relation between science and reli-gious thought within the context of biblically based religions.

Reality as Temporal: For one thing, the Hebrew-Christian Bible portrays reality as historical, as temporal. Much of the dynamism of Western civilization is attribut-able to this sense that the temporal process, in which we are immersed, is of ulti-mate significance. To be sure, classical Christian theology, with its subordination of biblical temporality to the atemporal eternity of Greek philosophy, implied that temporal existence is, if not illusory, somehow less than fully real, having a merely derivative, secondary type of reality. In terms of popular consciousness, however, this detemporalized theology could not overcome the influence of the biblical portrayal, with its temporal deity interacting with the world, leading from a creation at a particular time in the past to a reign of God to be realized at some particular time in the future. With the Protestant Reformation, further-more, the influence of Greek philosophy upon Christian theology was criticized, with the result that Protestant theologies generally reflect temporality of the bib-lical picture of reality more fully than did the medieval theologies.

   In any case, the message of modern physics, according to many of its leading representatives and best-selling popularizers, is that this biblically based view of reality is wrong at the level of its basic presupposition, which is that reality is ultimately temporal. Capra and Zukav address this religious issue directly, saying that the authority of physics supports instead those religious visions of the East in which time is considered illusory.[8]

Moral Freedom: A closely related issue is the reality of moral freedom. To believe in freedom is to believe that our actions in the present are not fully determined by the events that led up to this moment. Although our present actions are, of course, heavily conditioned by those antecedent events, they are not fully deter-mined by them. Although our choices are always limited, we do choose among real alternatives and, after having made the choice, it is true that we could have chosen otherwise. This freedom in the present means that the future, unlike the past, is partly open. Just as the past does not fully determine the present, the present does not fully determine the future. "The future," accordingly, does not yet exist in all its concreteness. It does already exist in the sense that there *will be* a future—that present events will be followed by subsequent events. And the future does already exist in the sense that some features of the future are already implicit in the present. But the future in all its concreteness does not exist.

For example, it is not now—on June 15, 2006, as I am editing this chapter—already determined whether I will be alive on August 8, 2009. It *is* settled that, if I am alive then, I will be 70 years old. But it is not settled where I will then be, what I will have for breakfast, what I will read in the newspaper, and how I will celebrate my birthday. In between now and then there will occur billions of partly contingent events, many of which will have some influence upon those matters. Also, even after all those intervening events have occurred, I will still have decisions to make. What my experiences will be that day will be partly decided by me, moment by moment, throughout the day. This is, at least, what is implied by our common belief that our actions are partly free.

According to some physicists and physics popularizers, however, this is all an illusion: the future is already as fully determined as the past. Speaking critically of that view, Frederick Ferré has brought out its implications for the issue of freedom and morality:

> [On that view] the future must be pictured as no less complete and determinate—and no less intractable to alteration—than the past. There is little wonder that such a conception has been called...the "block universe." Our future, could we but know it, is (in a tenseless sense of "is") inescapably part of the universe. Our efforts contribute to our future...; but in a larger sense, our very efforts themselves are fated to occur just where and when they do occur. No one is responsible; no one could have done otherwise; the illusion of personal responsibility is based on the illusion of temporal becoming.

This view, Ferré points out, can be comforting, in that it can offer "relief from guilt and stress." But this relief, he adds, comes at too high a price, because it requires "abandoning altogether the category of moral goodness."[9]

Creativity: Because the concept of 'creativity' is closely related to that of freedom, being in one of its aspects identical with it, it too is threatened by the concept of a wholly timeless universe. The tension between the two concepts is illustrated by Dossey's attempt to reconcile them: "This concept of creativity as a feature of a timeless, eternal world is hard to swallow, especially if one wishes to see his creative act as a literal making of some new thing. But in the modern context of a nonlinear time, as de Broglie states, events exist prior to us in time. We create nothing, since all things exist already."[10]

If this view of the nonreality of time for physics is true, therefore, it has devastating implications for the relation between science, on the one hand, and morality, religious thought, and the very meaning of life, on the other. It is crucial to determine, accordingly, whether this widespread picture of the implications of physics is correct.

The Fallacy of Misplaced Concreteness

The thesis of the present chapter is that this picture is false, being based upon what Whitehead called "the fallacy of misplaced concreteness." This fallacy, as we have seen in previous chapters, involves mistaking an abstraction from concrete realities—an abstraction that may be very useful for certain purposes—for the concrete realities themselves.

Sometimes called the "confusion of the map with the territory," this fallacy involves, in the case at hand, the assumption that the real electrons, protons, neutrons, photons, and other "elementary particles" at the base of nature are adequately described by the abstractions that physicists have found generally adequate for their (limited) purposes. Whitehead's view was that these abstractions, while they are adequate for most questions of interest to physicists, do not describe these entities in their concreteness. Just as the externalist concepts of psychological behaviorism abstract from what human beings are in themselves—namely, conscious individuals—the concepts of the physicist abstract from what the most elementary entities are in themselves.

One result of this fallacy is the materialistic view of the ultimate units of nature. It is this view of the objects studied by physics that leads to the conclusion that time does not exist for them. This chapter shows, accordingly, that like many of the other apparent conflicts of science with religion and morality, this one is due to the contingent fact that science is still largely associated with the materialistic view of the ultimate units of nature—which was adopted in the seventeenth century, as we saw in chapter 2, for social, political, and theological reasons.

A central part of Whitehead's version of postmodern philosophy, we have seen, is an alternative view of what these units are in themselves. One of the implications of this view is that it allows irreversible time to go all the way down. However, because this panexperientialist view is probably still difficult for many readers to accept, it will be best to look at the difficulties in the other possible positions. Having seen that the more conventional viewpoints run into insuperable difficulties in accounting for our inescapable presuppositions about time, readers may be more ready to consider Whitehead's more radical solution.

The Three Basic Positions

There are three basic positions with regard to the reality of time or temporality. The first view, which has already been introduced, is *nontemporalism*, which says that reality is thoroughly nontemporal, so that time as known in human experience is illusory. The second view is *temporal-nontemporal dualism*, which holds that the actual world is composed of two types of actual entities: temporal actual entities, for which time exists, and nontemporal ones, for which it does not.[11] The third basic doctrine is *pantemporalism,* according to which all actualities are temporal. I will advocate Whitehead's version of this third doctrine. Before doing so, however, I will look at the former two doctrines and their problems.

NONTEMPORALISM

Nontemporalism, according to which ultimate reality is devoid of time, or temporal passage, comes in both transcendental and reductionistic versions. In *transcendental* nontemporalism, the nontemporal ultimate reality transcends human experience, in the sense of being higher than it, and is usually considered divine. Transcendental nontemporalism is affirmed by Spinozism, Advaita Vedanta, some forms of Platonism and Buddhism, and most forms of thought referred to as "perennialism" (one version of which, that of Huston Smith, I have engaged in our jointly authored book, *Primordial Truth and Postmodern Theology*). In *reductionistic* nontemporalism, the nontemporal ultimate reality is described by physics, not theology.

The main problem for nontemporalism, in either version, is to explain why, if time is ultimately not real, it seems to be. If, as Advaita Vedanta holds, the ultimate and indeed only reality is Brahman, and Brahman is timeless, then time is an illusion. But how could this illusion conceivably arise? By hypothesis, the (apparent) many, with their (apparently) temporal relations, are really one. All things, including the human soul (Atman), are Brahman. If we human beings have the illusion that time is real, this would seem to mean that Brahman is confused. But that, by definition, cannot be, because Brahman is said to be perfect, timeless consciousness. How is it possible, accordingly, to explain our sense that time is real?

The reductionist version of nontemporalism, on which we will focus, has a similar problem. This reductionist version of nontemporalism is at least implicitly based on an argument that can be formulated thus:

1. Physics does not reveal time in atomic and subatomic particles.
2. Physics deals with the full, concrete reality of atomic and subatomic particles, at least to the extent that it does not abstract from anything about them that would make time (in the threefold sense of temporal asymmetry, constant becoming, and irreversibility in principle) real for them.
3. Time, therefore, does not exist for subatomic particles.
4. What does not exist for atomic and subatomic particles does not exist, period.
5. Time as experienced by us is, therefore, an illusion.

The argument will henceforth be called the "nontemporalist syllogism."

Its conclusion can be avoided, of course, by challenging any of its premises. Dualists challenge premise 4. Pantemporalists could challenge either 1 or 2. Before looking at these challenges, however, we need first to examine the non-temporalist position more fully by looking at two forms it has taken.

Extremely Reductionist Nontemporalism

The most extreme form of nontemporalism is based on the belief that time is to be ascribed no other nature, and no more reality, than it has in the fundamental laws of physics, combined with the belief that these laws provide no basis for temporal asymmetry, constant becoming, or irreversibility in principle. The so-called fundamental laws of physics are often said to require time only in the very abstract sense of the t-coordinate, on which events are strung out. Not only do these laws provide no basis for categorical distinctions between past, present, and future and no basis for constant becoming. They also do not—with possibly one minor exception (the behavior of the K meson)—even allow for "anisotropy," the phenomenon in which the order of events when read off in one direction can be objectively distinguished from the order when read off in the other direction. It is often, therefore, considered entirely a matter of convention that the vector points from the "past" to the "future."[12]

This extreme nontemporalism is reflected in the previously cited statements by Capra, de Broglie, Gold, Weyl, and Davies. It is also reflected in Einstein's famous statement, "For us believing physicists, the distinction between past, present and future is only an illusion, even if a stubborn one."[13] With Einstein's relativity theory in mind, Costa de Beauregard said:

> There can no longer be any objective and essential...division of space-time between "events which have already occurred" and "events which have not yet occurred."...Relativity is a theory in which everything is "written" and where change is only relative to the perceptual mode of living beings.[14]

Adolf Grünbaum put the point more concisely: "The theory of relativity," he said, "conceives of events as simply being."[15] Bertrand Russell, influenced by such views, said: "There is some sense...in which time is an unimportant and superficial characteristic of reality. Past and future must be acknowledged to be as real as the present."[16] Years earlier, Lewis Carroll—really, the Oxford mathematician Charles Dodgson—had the White Queen say to Alice: "It's a poor sort of memory that only works backwards." Russell echoed this whimsical idea, saying—-evidently *without* tongue in cheek—"It is a mere accident that we have no memory of the future."[17]

As brought out by the nontemporalist syllogism, the conclusion that time is ultimately unreal is based not only on the idea that time is not real for physics but also on the conviction that, if it is not real for physics, it is not real, period. This twofold conviction was stated in a book entitled *The Direction of Time* by Hans Reichenbach, who wrote: "There is no other way to solve the problem of time than the way through physics.... If time is objective the physicist must have discovered the fact. If there is Becoming, the physicist must know it.... If there is a solution to the philosophical problem of time, it is written down in the equations of mathematical physics."[18] Essentially the same perspective is reflected by Henry Mehlberg, who, in a book called *Time, Causality, and the Quantum Theory*, wrote:

> It seems to me that it would be either a miracle or an unbelievable coincidence if all the major scientific theories ... somehow managed to co-operate with each other so as to conceal time's arrow from us. There would be neither a miracle nor an unbelievable coincidence in the concealment of time's arrow from us only if there were nothing to conceal—that is, if time had no arrow.[19]

Mehlberg, of course, affirms that final statement, that time has no inherent directionality, which is simply another way of saying that time as known in human experience, the time of our lives, does not really exist.

Less Extreme Reductionistic Nontemporalism

A less extreme form of reductionistic nontemporalism grants that physical time does, in a sense, have an arrow. This form of nontemporalism shares with the first form the view that 'time,' to be a meaningful concept, must be discoverable by physics. And it agrees that the concept of time is not to be found in the fundamental laws of physics. It holds, however, that time is nonetheless rooted in one branch of physics, thermodynamics. According to this view, time is rooted in the entropic process, in which organized bodies of matter with high energy gradually move toward a state of lower energy, and thereby higher entropy.

Thermodynamics, in describing this entropic process, does provide for the arrow of time in the sense of "anisotropy," which, as we saw earlier, means that the order of events when read off in one direction can be objectively distinguished from the order when read off in the other direction. As Kenneth Denbigh says in *Three Concepts of Time*, the thermodynamic concept of 'entropy' thereby brings "the concept of 'time' a little closer to what we have from our own experience." With reference to time's arrow, Denbigh says that the thermo-dynamic "gradient of monotonically changing entropy states . . . appears to correlate completely with our own judgment of the temporal order of events."

Nevertheless, Denbigh adds, the thermodynamic description of the entropic process still does not provide any categorical distinction between past and future. "For although thermodynamics finds the two directions of time to be distinguishable, it does not display the one direction as being in any sense 'more real' than the reverse direction. . . . The question, 'Which direction along the *t*-coordinate is the real direction?' just doesn't arise in physical science."[20]

Thermodynamics also provides no irreversibility in principle. This is in part because the anisotropy it provides applies only to large aggregations of entities or events, not to the individual entities or events themselves. In the words of Paul Davies, "Nothing yet discovered in nature requires individual atoms to experience time asymmetry [which term Davies uses for what others call "anisotropy"], the very essence of which is the collective quality of complex systems, like life itself."[21] Because this time anisotropy is a collective property, it is merely a statistical matter and, as such, provides for no irreversibility in principle. Richard Feynman, for example, said that "irreversibility is caused by the general accidents of life. . . . Things are irreversible only in a sense that going one way is likely, but going the other way, although it is possible and is according to the laws of physics, would not happen in a million years."[22]

As Denbigh noted, this entropic process seems in fact to correlate perfectly with lived time, with its distinction between memory (of the past) and anticipation (of the future). But those who root time in entropy see no necessary correlation. Thinkers such as Davies and Feynman, who derive the irreversibility of time from entropy, typically hold that our memory is irreversible only because we are ourselves complex systems, exemplifying entropic principles.[23] If thermodynamic systems were to reverse directions, therefore, our memory would reverse, too, with the result that, while we would be capable of only predicting the past, we would—as Bertrand Russell and the White Queen thought possible—be able to remember the future.

PROBLEMS IN NONTEMPORALISM

I turn now to an examination of problems in nontemporalism, beginning with the form just discussed, according to which time is the result of entropy.

The main problem in this doctrine is the very fact that it does imply that the direction of time could conceivably be reversed. This implication can arguably be considered a *reductio ad absurdum*. For example, P. J. Zwart, who considers it absurd to think the temporal order to be based on the entropic order, has said in an essay entitled "The Flow of Time":

> One thing is quite inconceivable: that we could perceive a later event before an earlier one.... This kind of proposition is self-contradictory, that is to say, time reversal in this sense is *logically* impossible. Reversal of the entropic ordering is not logically impossible, however, though highly unlikely. But even if it occurred, we should only have to adjust our laws, not our *concepts*.[24]

Zwart's point is that, if entropic reversal occurred, we would simply have to change our assumptions about what can and cannot occur. We would *not* need to change our very concepts of 'past,' 'present,' and 'future,' saying that we had hitherto been wrong to think that events in our past always occur prior to events in our future. The fact that the first change would not lead to the second one shows that, while our concepts of past, present, and future may *correlate* with the direction of the entropic process, they are not *based* upon it.

A similar argument is made by Denbigh in *An Inventive Universe*: "Mental processes display irreversibility of a kind not shown by physical processes—that is, in the sense that it is *not conceivable* that they could ever occur in the reverse temporal sequence."[25] Denbigh points out that, if we had settled upon some physical process as a standard for deciding the before-after relationship (for example, an apple falling from a tree to the ground) and then found that the event sequence went in reverse order, we would simply decide that the "standard" was fallacious. "In other words, is it not the case that *what we really mean* by the *before-after* relation is the relation as it is offered by consciousness?"[26]

The criticisms by Zwart and Denbigh agree with that of G. J. Whitrow, who says in *The Natural Philosophy of Time*: "The basic objection to attempts to deduce the unidirectional nature of time from concepts such as entropy is that they are attempts to reduce a more fundamental concept to a less fundamental one."[27] This attempt is especially problematic, all three authors point out, because the less fundamental concept does not have most of the characteristics of the more fundamental one.

These criticisms of the thermodynamic concept of time show that it is not time as known in human experience. While apparently less extreme than the first type of nontemporalism, accordingly, this second view—that time is real insofar as it is grounded in the entropic process of the universe—is still a form of nontemporalism, saying that time as known in human experience is illusory. Davies, for example, speaks of "the apparently illusory forward flow of psychological time."[28]

Having made this point, I now offer four arguments against nontemporalism, the first being the conceivability argument: if time is an illusion, how is it conceivable that this illusion could have arisen?

The Conceivability Argument

Like transcendental nontemporalism, which must explain how the illusion of time was generated in a universe that is identical with a transcendent Ultimate Reality for which time does not exist, reductionistic nontemporalism must explain how the illusion of time was generated in a universe ultimately consisting of elementary bits of matter (or matter-energy) for which time does not exist. This doctrine holds that we human beings, along with all other complex things, are simply aggregations of these timeless particles. The human mind is not some qualitatively different type of actuality with the power to come up with false notions.

In earlier times, the dominant form of reductionism was "epiphenomenalism," according to which the mind, while distinct from the brain, is a noneffica-cious byproduct of the brain's activity. By regarding the mind as distinct from the brain, epiphenomenalism tries to do justice to the fact that we do have experiences, which, epiphenomenalists see, can hardly be considered properties of the brain itself, understood to be an aggregation of billions of insentient bits of matter. In defining the mind as a *nonefficacious* byproduct, however, epiphenomenalism insists that the mind has no power of its own to originate anything. It is totally an effect, not at all a cause. Epiphenomenalism, therefore, cannot explain how the mind, being nothing but a shadow cast up by the nontemporal stuff of the brain, comes up with the idea of time.

More recently, the dominant position has been some form of materialistic "identism," according to which the mind is somehow identical with the brain. In older forms of identism, the mind was said to be identical with the grey matter of the brain. In the presently fashionable form, called "functionalism," what the brain is made of is said to be irrelevant. All that is important is the brain's "program": The relation of the mind to the grey matter is said to be analogous to that between a computer's software and its hardware.

Regardless of which version of materialism is held, however, the mind is not in any sense a distinct actuality with any power of its own. The puzzle remains: If the mind is somehow reducible to the brain, and if the brain is composed exhaustively of things to which time—in the sense of asymmetry, constant becoming, and irreversibility in principle—does not apply, then why does time in this threefold sense seem real to the mind? The answer, as we have seen, cannot lie simply in the fact that the brain, like other complex systems, is subject to entropy, because entropy does not provide time in this threefold sense.

A widespread claim is that time as we experience it arises from the brain's enormous complexity. The human brain is far more complex than any other known object in the universe. But the fact that the brain consists of at least 100 billion neurons cannot answer the question, if the neurons are themselves considered timeless: 100 billion times nothing is still nothing.

Of course, the brain's enormous complexity involves not merely its huge number of neurons but also the fact that each neuron is connected to perhaps 100,000 synapses, so that the brain has the capacity for trillions of configurations. Even this point, however, provides no answer as to how the experience and idea of time could arise. Even though there are some cases in which quantitative changes give rise to a qualitative difference, how is that conceivable in this case? How can things for which the distinction between past and future is not relevant in the slightest give rise to something—our experience—for which this distinction is fundamental?

The fact that reductionistic nontemporalism cannot explain the experience of time is one reason for doubting its truth. I turn now to a second.

The Commonsense Argument

In the reductionistic form of nontemporalism, like the transcendental form, an illusion is said to give rise to an illusion: The human mind is not real but has the power to create the illusion that time is real—an illusion so powerful that we cannot help thinking in terms of it. Einstein called it a "stubborn" illusion.

The stubbornness of this alleged illusion provides, surely, a strong reason for doubting that it is an illusion. As Whitehead said, in agreement with William James, the "stubborn facts"—the ones that will not go away, no matter what— should be taken as the most fundamental facts to which a theory must be adequate. If time or temporality is one of those stubborn facts, then nontemporalism would, precisely by denying the reality of time, show itself to be inadequate.

Nontemporalism is intended, to be sure, to be based upon stubborn facts. Its proponents appeal partly to the negative claim that physics does not provide any basis for speaking of time as known in human experience, partly to the positive claim that some physical theories, such as special relativity theory and quantum theory, actually imply, at least under some interpretations, that time is unreal. It is from these "facts" that the conclusion is drawn that the time of our lives is an illusion.

We have to ask, however, just how fundamental or stubborn the "facts" in question really are. In the first place, as the terms *special relativity theory* and *quantum theory* indicate, these two bodies of thought are themselves not facts but theories—intended to account for various facts. In the second place, the nontemporalist implications are drawn not from special relativity theory as such or quantum theory as such but only from certain interpretations of these theories. We are, accordingly, at least twice removed from any stubborn facts. In the third place, the nontemporal syllogism contains, between the first premise and the conclusion, two other premises (2 and 4), both of which involve complex philosophical issues. The nontemporalist conclusion is, accordingly, based not on any direct inference from indubitable facts, but on a chain of scientific and philosophical reasoning that is dubious at many points. The reality of time is a more fundamental and stubborn fact than the alleged facts on which its denial is based.

This argument stands in the "commonsense" philosophical tradition, which has been characterized by Roderick Chisholm as the view "that we should be guided in philosophy by those propositions we all do presuppose in our ordinary activity.... Any philosophical theory which is inconsistent with any of these data is *prima facie* suspect."[29]

In previous chapters, explaining the sense in which Whitehead stood in this tradition, I called these presuppositions "hard-core commonsense notions." They are common in the sense of being common to all humanity. This does not mean that they are explicitly affirmed by all people; far from it. They are often explicitly denied. But they are common in the sense that all people *in practice* presuppose them, even if they deny them in their theories. Because they would be implicitly presupposed in the very act of explicitly denying them, these hard-core commonsense notions must be taken as the ultimate criteria for our theories, in order to avoid self-contradiction.[30]

This argument will count against nontemporalism, of course, only if the reality of time is a hard-core commonsense notion so that we inevitably presuppose it in thinking about anything. But few if any would deny this, and many have explicitly affirmed it. For example, in *The Language of Time*, Richard Gale says:

> [M]any of our fundamental concepts, such as causality, action, deliberation, choice, intention, memory, knowledge, truth, possibility and identification, logically presuppose an asymmetry between the past and future.... These logical asymmetries interlock ... such that one of them cannot be jettisoned without giving up the others as well. Together these asymmetries form the basis of our common-sense conceptual system.[31]

Although Gale does not explicitly distinguish hard-core common sense from the soft-core type and then specify that the reality of time is of the former type, the fact that he means this is clear from his statement that "temporal notions are implicitly involved in all of the basic concepts by means of which we think and talk about the world."[32]

Gale is surely correct. The very act of living, including the activity of articulating and defending scientific, philosophical, or theological ideas, necessarily presupposes the threefold nature of time discussed earlier: (1) that the present is asymmetrically related to the future and the past, which means that we can affect the future but not the past; (2) that—however inadequately this formulation puts it—the present "now" constantly moves; and (3) that there is an irreversible directionality to reality. The reality of time in this sense is inevitably presupposed in practice. Any theory that denies it is ipso facto inadequate because self-contradictory. Nontemporalism, accordingly, must be rejected.

The importance of the distinction between hard-core and soft-core common sense for this conclusion can be illustrated by returning to Larry Dossey's discussion of this issue. Having quoted Weyl's statement that time does not really exist, Dossey said: "This view is an affront to common sense.... [But we] must assimilate it," for "we cannot ignore what modern physical science has revealed to us about the nature of time." Dossey then justifies this rejection of common sense in the name of science by a reference to Einstein's famous statement that common sense is merely the deposit of prejudices laid down in the human mind before the age of eighteen.[33]

That statement may well apply to common sense in the soft-core sense of the term. Once we clearly see, however, that common sense of this type is different in kind from common sense in the true, hard-core sense of the term, Einstein's statement provides no justification for rejecting the reality of time. We can, with relative degrees of success, overcome many of the ideas we accepted when we were eighteen. Within this set of "prejudices," however, there is a subset that we cannot even begin to eradicate: those beliefs that constitute universal common sense. In referring to time as a "stubborn illusion," Einstein himself implicitly acknowledged that time belongs to this subset. The commonsense argument is that we should, accordingly, have more confidence in the reality of time than we do in any alleged facts from which the unreality of time could be deduced.

The Argument from Abstractness

The commonsense argument presupposes that the alleged facts from which the unreality of time is deduced are not themselves hard-core commonsense notions. And they are not. Far from being directly given facts, they are complex interpretations thereof.

The idea that physics implies the unreality of time is based upon one form of the fallacy of misplaced concreteness: forgetting the abstractness of the "time" in the abstract space-time of physical theory, nontemporalist philosophers and scientists assume that this "time" (symbolized by t) can be equated with the temporal structure of reality itself. As Whitehead says, "an abstraction is nothing else than the omission of part of the truth" (MT 138). The abstraction, accordingly, cannot be equated with that from which it is abstracted, because that part of the truth that is omitted may be crucial to the issue at hand.

This point was seen clearly by Mary F. Cleugh in her 1937 book, *Time and Its Importance in Modern Thought,* which is still one of the best books on the topic. She asked the crucial question: "A fundamental feature of time as experienced is its irreversibility: is this really so, or is it merely an anthropomorphic prejudice, and is physics right in abstracting from it?"[34] Saying that we need to distinguish between *legitimate* and *falsifying* abstractions, she said that the physicist's abstraction from time's irreversibility becomes a falsifying abstraction when it is taken to be a metaphysical truth: "It cannot be too often emphasized that physics is concerned with the measurement of time, rather than with the essentially metaphysical question as to its nature.... We must not believe that physical theories can ultimately solve the metaphysical problems that time raises, or that they have any *special* relevance to these problems."[35] In support of the abstractness of the physicist's time, she quoted A. A. Merrill's statement, in an essay called "The *t* of Physics," that "*t*, while created originally from our direct experience with real time, is subsequently handled in a way that has no relation to real time at all."[36] She then concluded: "If it is claimed, whether openly or by implication, that the characteristics of '*t*' give a finally satisfactory account of time, that claim is unfounded.... The pliable, reversible '*t*' may be very useful and important in its own sphere, but its sphere is not that of metaphysics."[37]

Some scientists may be tempted to say that her point is irrelevant to them, because they are not interested in metaphysics. However, any attempt to state something about the true nature of time is "metaphysics," as she used the term. Nontemporalism, which denies the ultimate reality of time, is a metaphysical doctrine. Her point was that nontemporalism involves an illegitimate jump from a purely physical, nonmetaphysical notion of time, symbolized by *t*, to a metaphysical conclusion.[38]

In the same vein was the thought of physicist Arthur Eddington, who pointed out that the abstractness of time in physics is not unique to it: "Physics has no concern with the feeling of 'becoming' which we regard as inherently belonging to the nature of time, and it treats time merely as a symbol; but equally matter and all else in the physical world have been reduced to a shadowy symbolism."[39]

Like Whitehead, Eddington was warning people not to equate these shadowy symbols, these abstractions, with the concrete realities of the world. With reference to special relativity theory in particular, Eddington said: "Those who suspect that Einstein's theory is playing unjustifiable tricks with time should realize that it leaves entirely untouched that time succession of which we have intuitive knowledge, and confines itself to overhauling the artificial scheme of time which Romer first introduced into physics."[40]

Rebuttal of the Spatialization of Time

One of the nontemporalistic claims made by many proponents of relativity theory is that in this theory time is reduced to a dimension of space. At the outset of this chapter, for example, the following statement about relativity physics by Fritjof Capra was quoted: "Space and time are fully equivalent.... To get the right feeling for the relativistic world of particles, we must 'forget the lapse of time."[41] We have here a clear example of "the spatialization of time," of which Bergson complained: time and space are first said to be equivalent; and then this equivalence is taken to entail the elimination of time (even though the elimination of space would seem to be an equally valid conclusion).

A fourth argument against nontemporalism consists simply of a rebuttal of this spatializing elimination of time. Emile Meyerson long ago criticized this move: "The tendency toward assimilation of time and space—which is really...a transformation of time into space—...exceeds the authority of the most clearly established facts and the most basic foundations of science."[42]

The equally clear-thinking Mary Cleugh also commented upon the widespread idea that relativity physics reduced time to a dimension of space: "In the new physics, when it is said that the dimensions of 'space-time' are at right angles to each other, that does not mean...that time is somehow reduced to a dimension of space. It means precisely the contrary."[43]

For support, she cited Einstein himself, who had said: "The non-divisibility of the four-dimensional continuum of events does not at all, however, involve the equivalence of the space co-ordinates with the time co-ordinate. On the contrary, we must remember that the time co-ordinate is defined wholly differently from the space co-ordinates."[44]

With regard to Einstein's views, many of his statements can certainly be used to support the spatialization of time. He said, for example: "It is a characteristic of thought in physics...that it endeavours in principle to make do with 'space-like' concepts alone." And even less noncommittal statements can be quoted. When the topic was specifically raised by Meyerson, however, Einstein rejected the tendency to transform time into space:

> Meyerson rightly insists on the error of many expositions of Relativity which refer to the "spatialization of time."...The tendency he denounces, although often latent, is nonetheless real and profound in the mind of the physicist, as is unequivocally shown by the extravagances of the vulgarizers and even of many scientists in their expositions of Relativity.[45]

Phillip Frank also pointed out that the metaphysical "extravagances" regarding relativity physics are due not only to the "vulgarizers" but "have their origin in the insufficiently clear formulations which can be found in the treatises of physics themselves."[46] Frank targeted—in an article titled "Is the Future Already Here?"—the attempt to use relativity theory to justify the metaphysical view "that everything that happens is determined from all eternity, and that there is no development and nothing really new in the world." As an example of an extravagant metaphysical claim based upon confusion, he cited a statement by James Jeans: "It is meaningless to speak of the facts which are apt to come…and it is futile to speak of trying to alter them, because, although they may be yet to come for us, they may already have come for others."[47]

This widespread but false idea was extensively discussed by Milič Čapek. He rejected as confused those inferences from relativity theory according to which the relativization of simultaneity destroys the objectivity of temporal order so that events succeeding each other in one inertial system could appear in reverse order in another system.[48] The truth, he argued, is that there is much absoluteness in relativity theory:

> The irreversibility of the world lines has an *absolute* significance, independent of conventional choice of the system of reference….Since the universe consists of the dynamic network of the irreversible causal lines, their irreversibility which remains absolute in relativity theory is conferred to the universe as a whole….Since (the causal) "before-after" relation is invariant in *all* systems, it follows that *in no frame of reference can my particular "here-now" appear simultaneous with any event of my causal future or with any event in my causal past.*[49]

Having made these points, Čapek then rejected categorically the idea expressed in the above quotation from Jeans:

> No event of my causal future can ever be contained in the causal past of any conceivably real observer….*No event which has not yet happened in my present "here-now" system could possibly have happened in any other system.*…[T]he virtualities of our future history which our earthly "now" separates from our causal past *remain potentialities for all contemporary observers in the universe.* Something which did not yet happen for us could not have happened "elsewhere" in the universe.[50]

There is no good reason, in sum, to think that the inseparability of space and time implies the spatialization of time. In fact, Ilya Prigogine and Isabelle Stengers endorsed the view, long advocated by Bergson and Čapek, that it would be more accurate to speak of the "temporalization of space."[51]

One example of the spatialization of time is the idea that, just as particles can move either left or right and either up or down in space, they can also move backward as well as forward in time. This notion came into circulation largely through the influence of Richard Feynman's diagrams and suggestions. Feynman suggested that, rather than interpreting certain interactions as the production and annihilation of particles, it is simpler and preferable to speak of some of the particles as going backward in time. P. J. Zwart, however, has argued convincingly in *About Time* that the original interpretation in terms of pair production and pair annihilation is much less problematic.[52] One reason that the idea of the production and annihilation of particles is thought by some to be problematic is the view that it suggests creation out of nothing. In response, Čapek has said: "It is not true that the process...involves 'creation from nothing' and 'vanishing into nothing'; the pair of particles arises from electromagnetic radiation, into which it can be reconverted."[53]

TEMPORAL-NONTEMPORAL DUALISM

The argument of the previous section was that there is no good reason to accept, and many reasons to reject, the view that physics reveals time to be illusory. The conclusion of the nontemporalist syllogism is to be rejected. The conceivability and commonsense arguments allow us to make this decision even before deciding which premises to reject. Coming up with a more plausible account, however, requires that this second decision be made. To consider this question, it will be helpful to look again at the nontemporalist syllogism.

1. Physics does not reveal time in atomic and subatomic particles.
2. Physics deals with the full, concrete reality of atomic and subatomic particles. Or at least it does not abstract from anything about them that would make time (in the threefold sense of temporal asymmetry, constant becoming, and irreversibility in principle) real for them.
3. Time, therefore, does not exist for subatomic particles.
4. What does not exist for atomic and subatomic particles does not exist, period.
5. Time as experienced by humans and (evidently) other animals is, therefore, an illusion.

The pantemporalist rejects the second premise and thereby the third. This solution, which is advocated here, was already suggested above by the argument from abstractness and the argument against spatialization. Those arguments, however, are also consistent with the position of temporal-nontemporal dualism, which bases its rejection of the syllogism solely on its rejection of the fourth premise. In comparison with pantemporalism, this dualistic position is more in accord with modern soft-core common sense, requiring thereby a less radical readjustment of conventional thought. It will be good, accordingly, to consider it first, to see why the more radical readjustment involved in pantemporalism is necessary.

Most philosophers of time assume—rightly, I hold—that the existence of time requires the existence of temporal actualities. To accept this assumption is to accept the relational, as distinct from the absolute, view of time. According to this relational view, time does not exist independently of temporal processes, as a preexistent container. It exists only as a relation involving such processes.

This relational view has been widely held. It was presupposed by traditional, nontemporal theists, who held that time did not exist prior to God's creation of the world (thereby giving rise to paradoxes as to what God was doing "before" this creative act). This relational view is also held by contemporary cosmologists who think of our universe as having originated in a big bang understood as a "singularity" in which time as well as space first arose (thereby giving rise to paradoxes as to what occurred "before" the big bang to make it possible).

This relational view was even held by Newton. Although the conventional view about Newton is that he held to the absolute view of time, as if time existed apart from any temporal processes, his position must be understood within the context of his temporalistic theism. His "absolute time," as Čapek pointed out, was related to successive states of the divine experience.[54]

The relational view is also held by contemporary nontemporalists. Believing that the ultimate actualities of nature are nontemporal, believing that no temporal actualities have emerged out of them, and not believing in a temporal deity, they believe that time is an illusion.

In any case, given the relational view of time, the question of the ultimate reality of time as known in human experience depends upon the status of temporal processes in the nature of things.

Dualists believe that it is obvious that time is real and that, therefore, temporal actualities exist. They also believe that it is equally obvious, or at least well-grounded, that actual things exist for which time (in the threefold sense at issue here) does *not* exist.

There are at least three forms of dualism with regard to time. According to *everlasting dualism*, temporal and nontemporal actualities have existed from all eternity. According to *created dualism*, affirmed by Descartes and Newton, a divine being created both temporal and nontemporal finite actualities ex nihilo at the outset of the world.[55] A third form is *emergent dualism*, according to which temporal finite actualities emerged out of nontemporal finite actualities, which existed first (whether everlastingly or as created).

Nowadays, given the evolutionary perspective on the origin of our world, this emergent dualism is the prevalent form. Even most dualists who think of the world as divinely created assume that God created temporal actualities long after creating nontemporal ones. We will, accordingly, focus on this emergent form of temporal-nontemporal dualism.

THE EMERGENT DUALISM OF J. T. FRASER

The most extensive defense of emergent dualism has been given by J. T. Fraser, who has probably—along with Čapek—read, thought, and written more about time than anyone else in history. Although my examination of Fraser's position will conclude that it is too problematic to be accepted, I will begin by listing nine points on which Fraser's position is at one with my Whiteheadian pantemporalism.

> 1 & 2. He says, first, that creativity is to be prized and that prizing
> creativity requires, second, a positive appraisal of temporality.[56]
> Fraser is critical of any view, such as the Platonic view of time-
> less forms and their temporal imitations, that suggests "the
> negation of the idea of creativity in nature in general, and in
> the worlds of life, mind, and society in particular."[57] He would,
> for example, think Dossey's attempt to combine nontemporal-
> ism with a positive appraisal of creativity self-defeating. He
> means his position to support creativity by showing temporality
> to be both real and important.
>
> 3. Fraser holds a hierarchical view of reality, rejecting all reduc-
> tionistic views according to which, unless something is in
> physics and its objects, it is not real.
>
> 4. He agrees that in these post-Darwinian times we cannot have a
> worldview that "sees the world as divided into the temporal and
> the timeless."[58]
>
> 5. He also agrees that our world was not created out of absolute
> nothingness but emerged out of a primordial chaos.
>
> 6. Fraser accepts the relational view of time, according to which
> the reality of time presupposes the reality of temporal things,
> with time depending upon the transitions from thing to thing.
>
> 7. Fraser agrees that time involves irreversibility in principle, which
> means that the idea of time's going in the reverse direction is
> meaningless.[59]
>
> 8. Fraser agrees that there can be no asymmetry and irreversibility
> in principle without a "now."
>
> 9. Fraser holds that self-contradictory positions are to be rejected.[60]

However, although Fraser endorses all these ideas, he does not put them together in an intelligible way.

Fraser's entire enterprise is predicated on the assumption that lies at the root of nontemporalism: that time as we experience it, with its asymmetry, constant becoming, and irreversibility in principle, is not real either for physical theory or for the objects it studies. Fraser rejects nontemporalism, however, by holding time to be an emergent reality. I have, accordingly, classified Fraser's position as emergent dualism. Fraser himself prefers to call his position "pluralistic," on the basis that it affirms, instead of a stark contrast between nontemporal and temporal actualities, a variety of intermediary actualities with degrees of temporality. It can, nevertheless, be called "dualistic," insofar as it does affirm the existence of both temporal and nontemporal actualities. Moreover, as we will see, it is even dualistic in the stronger sense. Fraser's actual world does consist, after all, exclusively of actualities that are either temporal or nontemporal.

In what Fraser calls his "pluralistic" view, there is a hierarchy of temporalities with six levels, differing in terms of the kind of causal connectedness that obtains. The first three levels exist below the level of life. The world of quantum physics, the realm of *prototemporality,* is the second level of existence. Below it is an *atemporal* chaos, consisting of "atemporal processes" with no causal connectedness.[61] Above the prototemporal world of quantum physics is the *eotemporal* realm, in which there is still no "now" and therefore no asymmetry of past and future. There is only pure succession.[62] Fraser's belief seems to be that the reason there is no "now" at this level is that there is no experience.

A "now" first arises in the next level, the *biotemporal.* The unique kind of connectedness among events that arises at this level is final causation, or goal directedness, which provides the basis for a "now" dividing past and future.[63] Final causation with its "now" is said to arise at this level because, I assume, experience is thought to arise here.

The fifth level is the realm of the *nootemporal,* constituted by human beings. The new element here is mentality, or at least a qualitatively different form of mentality. Fraser sometimes seems to deny mentality to nonhuman animals altogether, speaking of a pure "physiological present" and of a "perceptual and cognitive set but without mental content."[64] Elsewhere, however, he speaks of "the difference in mental capacity between man and the higher apes." In any case, what is unique about our species is "long-term expectation and memory"; other animals have only "some limited foresight and memory."[65]

The sixth and final realm, the *sociotemporal,* need not concern us here.

PROBLEMS IN FRASER'S EMERGENT DUALISM

Fraser's account, while obviously containing much truth, also contains many problems. One problem is that, although Fraser has said that we should not speak of the world as "divided into the temporal and the timeless,"[66] he in effect does just that.

In the first place, it is not clear how the atemporal realm differs, except verbally, from the strictly nontemporal realm. If whatever "processes" occur at that level are atemporal, involving no causal connectedness, so that there is no transition from cause to effect, then the realm would seem to be strictly timeless.

In the second place, the truly crucial emergence in Fraser's scheme is that from the eotemporal to the biotemporal. It is only in the biotemporal realm that time as we experience it, with a "now" separating a past and a future, arises.

So, although there are said to be six levels, we in essence have a dualism between the top three levels, which are timely, and the bottom three levels, which are timeless. This problem, however, could be easily overcome: Fraser could simply retract his statement about not dividing the world into the temporal and the timeless.

Problems Involving Self-Contradictions

A more serious set of problems arises from Fraser's statement that self-contradictory positions are untenable, which he makes in the context of discussing the type of time called the "B-series" by J. M. E. McTaggart. Whereas the A-series is time involving pastness, presentness, and futurity (which McTaggart considered illusory), the B-series (which McTaggart thought to reflect the real nature of time) contains no "now" but only the distinction between earlier and later.

In response, Fraser says, rightly, that "the concept of the B-series—a condition of earlier-later but without a now—is self-contradictory. For that reason, it must be rejected."[67] But if ideas that are self-contradictory are to be rejected, then some of Fraser's own ideas are in trouble.

For one thing, Fraser says that the eotemporal realm involves succession but no "now." The idea of "succession," however, is in the same boat as that of "earlier and later." The relevant dictionary meaning of succeed is "to follow in time, to come after." If the notion of earlier and later requires a "now," then so does the idea of succession.

A second example involves a statement that is self-contradictory by Fraser's own admission. He holds that "time itself has developed along evolutionary steps." But this idea leads to a serious difficulty, he admits, because "there is no noncontradictory way in which to state that time evolved in time."[68] Fraser seeks to mitigate this difficulty by blaming limitations of language, referring to "prevailing linguistic customs." Language is indeed limited and limiting. But the difficulty here runs deeper. The very concept of time itself as having evolved in time is self-contradictory, because the notion of evolution itself presupposes time. We can no more ask how time evolved than we can ask what caused causality to emerge (which makes problematic Fraser's notion that the first realm, the atemporal, has no causal processes). Some things must simply be, eternally, and time—along with causality, which it presupposes and is presupposed by—must be among them.

Fraser's contrary idea, that time has not always been but began and then evolved (his main book on the subject is *The Genesis and Evolution of Time*) creates more problems of self-consistency. Although Fraser says that the "atemporal chaos…preceded Creation," he recognizes that this way of speaking does not really make sense, because "[w]e thus imagine biotemporal ordering where there can be none." We have to speak this way, even though it is inaccurate, he says, because we human beings, living as we do in the nootemporal realm, "are able to give descriptions only in terms of space and time." Besides, he suggests, the only alternative would be equally bad: "Discussing the dynamics of Creation in tenseless language is awkward and would be just as inaccurate as speaking about chaos having preceded Creation."[69] Given Fraser's starting point, either of the available positions leads to self-contradiction. Fraser himself holds, as we have seen, that self-contradiction cannot be tolerated. It would seem, then, that his starting point should be rejected, which would mean accepting pantemporalism, according to which time has had no beginning.

The paradoxical nature of Fraser's position does not stop there. He says: "Creation was neither followed nor preceded by other instants, because the relationship future-past-present had no meaning in the atemporal, or even in the proto- or eotemporal worlds." Accordingly, because there could be no "relations among events corresponding to the notion of before and after," Fraser says, we must say that those events were "contiguous with the instant of Creation."[70] Fraser adds that we are free to describe these early periods *as if* they were temporal intervals, provided we realize that the description is only a convenient way of speaking. In other words, although it is customary to say that there were several billion years of cosmic evolution prior to the rise of life (on our planet at least), *we cannot really say that any time passed at all*, because prior to life the relation of before and after could not occur. Surely this paradox is intolerable.

A final paradox: The beginning and the end of the universe become the same event. The reason is that humans and in fact all life will have disappeared, so that the biotemporal and nootemporal worlds will be no longer. The most complex world will then again be at the eotemporal level, for which the distinction of past and future makes no sense. Accordingly, although from our nootemporal perspective the beginning is in the past and the end in the future, "from the point of view of the universe itself" the beginning and the end will be indistinguishable. Accordingly, "by the identity of indistinguishables we are compelled to conclude that we have been contemplating only one single event."[71]

Besides the fact that the conclusions to which Fraser is led are self-contradictory, these conclusions tend to undermine his deepest concerns. He wants, as we saw, to support the notion that novelty and creativity are important in the nature of things, which presupposes that temporality is real and important. And yet he says that "the primordial stratum of the universe" is constituted by atemporal processes and that the worlds with real time—the biotemporal and nootemporal worlds—are merely passing fancies.[72] The eotemporal "perspective," in which there is no past, present, or future, is "the point of view of the universe itself." Can we take time, creativity, and novelty seriously while believing that they are, from the ultimate perspective, passing fancies?

The Relation between the Temporal and Nontemporal Realms

As serious as the previous problems are, the most serious problem is that of the relation between the temporal and the nontemporal. Fraser has sought to mitigate this problem by two moves: denying that there is any strictly nontemporal or timeless realm and then having a plurality of temporalities, rather than a stark dualism between the nontemporal and the temporal.

As we have seen, however, Fraser's denial of a realm of timeless actuality seems to be more verbal than real: the atemporal cannot be distinguished from the strictly nontemporal or timeless. And, although Fraser speaks of six realms rather than only two, hence apparently endorsing a plurality rather than simply a dualism, the crucial transition occurs between the third and fourth levels, the eotemporal and the biotemporal. Time as we know it—with its "now," its asymmetry between past and future, and its irreversibility in principle—arises only in the biotemporal realm.

Although the prototemporal realm and especially the eotemporal realm, with its anisotropic succession, are together posited as a buffer zone—an intermediary between the atemporal and the genuinely temporal—the problem is not really mitigated. It is still the case that with the emergence of life, at least animal life, we have the one truly qualitative emergence in the system.

Although the move from the biotemporal to the nootemporal is called a "qualitative" difference, it is really a difference in degree, not kind: memory and expectation become greater.

The move from the prototemporal to the eotemporal is also called a "qualitative change," but it is not really: in neither realm is there any "now," any distinctions between past, present, and future.

The one truly qualitative change is from the eotemporal to the biotemporal. In Fraser's view, it is with life that time as we know it emerges, evidently because Fraser believes that it is when life emerges that experience emerges.

This emergence is not understandable. The distinctive feature of the biotemporal realm is said to be final causation. We cannot understand how final causation—action directed toward a goal—could have emerged out of things that interact solely by means of efficient causation.

Fraser believes that "the qualitative differences among the temporalities of the stable integrative levels of nature derive from the radically different complexities of those levels."[73] In the shift from the eotemporal to the biotemporal levels, however, he is positing a miraculous transmutation that no complexity, no matter how complex, could in principle explain. Again, billions of times nothing is still nothing. If the primordial elements contain no experience, therefore no final causation, therefore no "now," therefore no asymmetry and irreversibility, then even a complexity greater than which none can be thought will be a complexity devoid of all experience, final causation, asymmetry, and irreversibility.

The Experience-Dependent Nature of Time

With my summary and critique, I am emphasizing a point that is more implicit than explicit in Fraser—the point that time in the usual sense presupposes experience. One philosopher of time who has made this point explicitly is Adolf Grünbaum, who has spent much of his life arguing that time in the sense of becoming is a mind-dependent property, from which he concludes that time does not exist in the physical universe. He sometimes speaks of time as "anthropocentric," as if, like Descartes, he attributed mind, and therefore time, only to human beings. In more careful formulations, however, Grünbaum makes clear that he generalizes the kind of mind presupposed by time in the normal sense to other animals. Where exactly he would draw the dualistic line between some mind and none at all is unclear, but it seems to be at about the level of cockroaches, regarding which Grünbaum is agnostic.[74]

But wherever this line be drawn, the point is the same: a dualism between experiencing and nonexperiencing actualities means we must speak of time in the usual sense as something that does not exist prior to the emergence of mind. I am using the term *mind* here in the most generalized sense, as does Grünbaum, to indicate the presence of experience, however minimal, not in that more restricted sense that Fraser has in view when he sometimes limits mentality to human beings. A better way to express the point is, therefore, to say that time in the usual sense is an *experience-dependent* feature.

The great service of Grünbaum and Fraser, especially when taken together (because of Grünbaum's more explicit focus on the experience-dependent nature of time), is that they bring out the paradoxical, even self-contradictory, implications for time that follow from any dualistic view of reality (taking *dualism* to mean that the actual world is composed of both experiencing and nonexperiencing actualities).

This message will be an uncomfortable one for most intellectuals in our culture, insofar as they, on the one hand, are dualists, and yet they, on the other hand, presuppose that time has always existed—at least as long as our universe has existed. They assume that it makes sense to debate whether the universe is, say, 15 or only 14 billion years old, to try to figure out what happened during the first billion years of cosmic evolution, to try to understand the nature and order of the developments on our planet that led to the emergence of life, and so on. And they assume that time in the usual sense—with its distinctions between past, present, and future and its irreversibility—was real all along so that when we try to reconstruct the cosmic past, our intention is to speak about the order in which things really happened, not simply to tell an "as if" story because we as temporal beings can do no other.

Most people assume, in other words, that time as we know it did not suddenly come into existence with the rise of human beings, or even with the rise of animals or life itself. They believe, of course, that the *experience* of time emerged only when beings with experience arose. But they assume that this is an experience of something that had preexisted it, that the experience did not create its own object. They do *not* assume that all the events prior to this emergence of experiencing things were contiguous with the first moment of creation, as if no real time passed between, say, the formation of the Milky Way and the rise of amino acids on the earth. The suggestion that events that are described in our science books as occurring 10 billion years ago and those that are described as occurring 4 billion years ago were, in reality, simultaneous with each other, because both of them were contiguous with the moment of creation, would strike them as absurd, even unthinkable.

And yet Fraser and Grünbaum are right: time in the usual sense cannot be thought to exist without experience. It follows that if experience is a contingent feature of the universe, arising only with the emergence of some particular species of being, then time is likewise emergent. Of course, it is, as Fraser admits, hard to enunciate this position without self-contradictory expressions. One can hardly help saying that "experience first arose at a particular time" and therefore that "time first arose at a particular time." But if the widely held dualistic assumption is maintained, no alternative is possible. The great merit of Fraser's work is that it brings out and forces us to face the various paradoxes about time that must be swallowed if dualism is assumed.

We are confronted, therefore, by a clash between two intuitions that probably seem equally fundamental to most people. The one is the reality of time, back at least to the beginning of our universe; the other is the truth of dualism, in the sense of a division in the world between experiencing and nonexperiencing actualities.

Many thinkers who are dualists, given this definition, refer to themselves, to be sure, not as dualists but as materialists. Being reductionists, they deny that 'mind' refers to a type of actuality, entity, or substance that has equal onto-logical status with nonexperiencing matter. But such thinkers are, in fact, *cryp-todualists*. Regardless of how much they may loathe the idea of dualism, they are dualists in terms of the above definition, because they think of the world as divided between actual things with experience and actual things wholly devoid of experience.

The difference between self-confessed and closet dualists in respect to time is that the self-confessed dualist will speak of time as a real emergent, whereas the cryptodualist is more likely to say that time as we experience it is an illusion. But both must say, if they think as clearly about it as do Fraser and Grünbaum, that time as we know it cannot be attributed to the "history" of the universe "prior to" the rise of experiencing beings. Both types of dualists are, as the words in scare quotes indicate, forced into paradoxical expressions.

The question, then, is what to do about this clash between two seemingly fundamental intuitions. One possibility is simply to make the best of it, as Fraser seeks to do. A second option is to try to overcome the tension by rejecting dual-ism in favor of materialism with its attendant nontemporalism. But this, we have seen, provides only a pseudosolution. As Hartshorne pointed out, people, as examples of beings with experience, cannot really deny the existence of such, so the result is a cryptodualism with all the same problems.[75] The only other possi-bility is to reject dualism from the opposite direction, by denying the existence of nonexperiencing actualities.

PANEXPERIENTIALIST PANTEMPORALISM

Having tried in previous chapters, and more fully in my book *Unsnarling the World-Knot,* to lay out Whiteheadian panexperientialism completely enough to make it intelligible and convincing, I will here focus simply on why Whiteheadian panexperientialism leads to the pantemporalist conclusion that time has always existed. The points needed for this explanation that have been discussed in previous chapters will be stated here very briefly, while new ideas will be discussed more fully.

Actual Entities as Actual Occasions

The first basic idea is that all actual things are momentary events. Whitehead called them "actual occasions" to emphasize their spatiotemporal extensiveness. These events or occasions can be more or less brief. Whereas there may be over a billion such events occurring in each second at the subatomic level, events at the level of the human mind may occur at a rate of about a dozen per second.

Enduring individuals that move through space, such as protons and photons, are not the finally real things. The fully actual entities, which are the momentary events, do not move through space. These actual occasions happen when and where they happen, constituting and filling a particular spatiotemporal locus. What we call "locomotion," or motion through space, is a result of the different spatiotemporal loci of successive occasions within an enduring individual.

Actual Occasions as Occasions of Experience

The other crucial feature of these actual occasions is that each is an "occasion of experience." And just as the spatiotemporal extensiveness of the occasions of experience can vary enormously, so can the complexity and sophistication of the experience. The experience of most actual occasions does not rise to consciousness.

Beyond this negative assertion, it is difficult to find a word to suggest positively the nature of the experience enjoyed by low-grade actual occasions. Here what Fraser says about the limitations of our inherited language is particularly germane, because our language has been heavily shaped by dualistic assumptions. But Whitehead considered the terms *feeling*, *emotion*, and *appetite*, taken in the most general conceivable sense, to be among the least misleading. He said, for example, that "the emotional appetitive elements in our conscious experience are those which most closely resemble the basic elements of all physical experience" (PR 163).

Memory and Anticipation

In explicating this idea, Whitehead said something that moves us toward the issue of time: "The primitive form of physical experience is emotion—blind emotion—received as felt elsewhere in another occasion and conformally appropriated as a subjective passion" (PR 62). This statement expresses Whitehead's notion of prehension, which is his more technical term for "feeling." (To be more precise, a feeling is a *positive* prehension, as distinct from *negative* prehensions, which "eliminate from feeling" [PR 23]. But I will henceforth ignore this distinction, using "prehension" always to mean "feeling" or "positive prehension.") A physical prehension grasps a prior occasion of experience, taking some of its feelings into itself.

The word *appetite*, used above, indicates that the appropriation is not simply for itself in a narrow sense but that there is also an orientation toward the future. Each occasion of experience actualizes itself in such a way as to pass on experiential energy to subsequent occasions. This idea results, of course, from generalizing a ubiquitous feature of our own experience all the way down. This general structure of experience means that there is something analogous to both memory and anticipation in all occasions of experience.

The implications for the question of time are obvious. As Fraser and Grünbaum have rightly seen, time as we know it is unthinkable apart from an experienced "now" that distinguishes between past and future. Our words for this twofold experience are *memory* and *anticipation*. Fraser and Grünbaum conclude, given their dualistic assumptions, that time is therefore unreal in the physical world. But if we can talk with Whitehead about "physical experience," about the presence of at least some iota of experience at even the most elementary level of nature, then we can say that time is real there, too.

Irreversibility

The notion that each event prehends antecedent events—and this feature, that physical prehension is always of *antecedent* events, is fundamental—gives us not only time's asymmetry but also its irreversibility. A prehension should not be thought to be simply a primitive form of sensory perception, at least if sensory perception is thought to involve merely a *representation* of an external thing. Rather, prehension involves an actual grasping of the prehended object so that some aspect of that object is included within the prehending experience. This means that, insofar as we speak of the prior, prehended event as the cause and the prehending experience as the effect, the cause has literally (if only partially) entered into the effect. And it is this that gives time its in-principle irreversibility. In Whitehead's words: "This passage of the cause into the effect is the cumulative character of time. The irreversibility of time depends on this character" (PR 237).

As Fraser has seen, time as mere succession, which he assigns to the eotemporal realm, does not give irreversibility. But this does not mean, according to the panexperientialist view, that we should say that "once upon a time" time had this character of mere succession. Rather, pure succession is merely an abstraction from the full nature of time. In Whitehead's words: "Time in the concrete is the conformation of state to state, the later to the earlier: ... pure succession is an abstraction of the second order, a generic abstraction omitting the temporal character of time" (S 36).

Materialism and the Conventional View

Two unique elements of this Whiteheadian view—the idea that enduring things are really temporally ordered societies of momentary events and that each event is an experience with memory and anticipation—make it possible for us to reject the conventional view that time even in the limited sense of anisotropy does not exist for single atoms—-that is, the view that time in this limited sense would first come into existence with aggregations of atoms complex enough to suffer entropy increase (that is, a decrease in order).

That conventional view assumes a materialistic-substantialist notion of an atom. The atom is assumed to be simply a bit of matter (or matter- energy) that endures as a numerically self-identical individual through space and (what from our perspective is) time. If time is not something that exists absolutely in itself, but only as a result of temporal relations, then time can only exist when truly temporal relations occur. But atoms conceived as material substances buzzing through space do not provide the types of relations needed for true time, because their only changes are locomotive.

In such a universe, there would be nothing to designate one configuration of atoms as having been in the past of another configuration. Even something as remotely analogous to time in our sense as mere anisotropy could arise only with complex aggregations of atoms that could become increasingly less ordered. The direction of this change is usually said to establish time of a sort, since this direction coincides with our own sense of time.

This coincidence is said, however, to be purely fortuitous. And that conclusion follows, given the materialistic substantialist view of atoms, because there is no reason in principle why the processes that have happened in, say, the past ten thousand years could not reverse themselves. The teacup that was broken this morning could spontaneously reassemble itself; the photons arriving from the sun could reverse direction; and so on. Such an eventuality is said to be extremely unlikely, of course, but it is not ruled out in principle. Entropy increase does not give us irreversibility *in principle*.

Panexperientialism and Atomic Time

However, if an atom is not an insentient piece of matter that remains numerically one through (what to us is) time, but a series of occasions of experience, each of which includes its predecessors in itself and projects itself into its successors, then *time in the full-fledged sense exists already for a single atom*. Each atomic event has temporal relations with its predecessors and its successors constituting the enduring atom (as well as with other events). Asymmetry, irreversibility, and constant becoming are already there, with anisotropy being simply an abstraction therefrom.

We do not, therefore, have to say that time emerged sometime within the creation and then try to figure out when and how this occurred. Nor do we have to swallow the paradox involved in saying that this emergence did occur. There has been time as long as atoms, or even subatomic enduring individuals such as photons and quarks, have existed. The idea that time exists wherever such entities exist is built into Whitehead's description of them as "temporally ordered societies." Time exists with such entities because of the temporal relations among the momentary events constituting these enduring individuals.

Chaotic Time

If we had to stop there, however, we would still have the paradox involved in saying that time arose once upon a time. And this paradox would be just as serious whether we located it 1 million, 1 billion, or 15 billion years ago. And it would be equally serious whether we said that a nontemporal God created temporal things and thereby time or that temporal things evolved out of a wholly nontemporal chaos.

The panexperientialist view says, by contrast, that our world did indeed evolve out of a chaos of processes or events (rather than having been created out of absolute nothingness, whether by God or spontaneously), but that *there were temporal relations even in that chaos.*

To call that precreation situation a "chaos" means that it had no enduring individuals, even ones as primitive as photons or quarks. Rather, all the events (by hypothesis) occurred randomly, with none of them organized into temporally ordered societies in which each event largely repeats the form embodied in its predecessor. But even in this chaotic state (which, by hypothesis, is the nature of so-called empty space today), temporal relations occurred. Each event prehended, and thereby was causally affected by, prior events, meaning events that had already enjoyed their "now"; and each event causally influenced, and thereby was prehended by, later events. (Events are contemporaneous with each other when neither causally affects the other.)

Given this view of what actual entities are, therefore, we need not, with Fraser, suppose that the precreation chaos was comprised of processes that are acausal and thereby atemporal. We can assume that time, with its asymmetry, irreversibility, and constant becoming, existed even in this chaos.

Pantemporalism Implies Panexperientialism

This form of panexperientialism thereby implies pantemporalism. And the opposite, which is the main point of this chapter, is equally true, namely, that pantemporalism implies panexperientialism. I have suggested that any position that denies pantemporalism, the view that time has always existed, inevitably runs into paradoxes, the less polite word for which is *self-contradictions.* We can avoid these self-contradictions, if we carry out the logical implications of our premises, only by affirming pantemporalism. And we can do this, once we realize the connection between time and experience, only by affirming panexperientialism.

This postmodern doctrine of panexperientialism, in spite of the fact that it initially seems so counterintuitive to modern minds, turns out to be the key to *protecting* our basic intuitions about time. We should take this route because the two sets of intuitions are not really on the same level. The reasons for initially considering panexperientialism counterintuitive turn out to be defeasible, merely soft-core commonsense intuitions, whereas our intuitions about time are hard-core commonsense notions, which are indefeasible, because we cannot deny them without self-contradiction.

CONCLUSION

The topic of the relation of physics to time as directly experienced is of immense interest in itself. It is also, as discussed at the outset of this chapter, of immense importance for the relation of science to moral and religious thought. The idea that physics shows time to be ultimately unreal would put physics at odds not only with the basic presupposition of the view of reality held by all the Abrahamic religions—Judaism, Christianity, and Islam—and many others besides. It would also put it in contradiction with our hard-core convictions about freedom, creativity, and moral values, all of which are presupposed in religious life.

The truth, however, is that physics itself does not entail the unreality of time. That interpretation results only from a materialistic view of the entities studied by physics, a view that is based on the fallacy of misplaced concreteness.

While this negative conclusion is sufficient to overcome the apparent clash between science, on the one hand, and religion, morality, and hard-core common sense, on the other, the critique of misplaced concreteness also points to an alternative vision: a pantemporalism that both implies and is implied by panexperientialism. The fact that each of these doctrines can be defended in itself while also implying the other provides additional reason to accept them as the best framework for interpreting science, both as an activity and as a body of results.

7

Whitehead and the Crisis in Moral Theory: Theistic Ethics without Heteronomy

There can be little doubt that modern moral theory is in crisis. The only real solution to this crisis, a number of thinkers have argued from a variety of perspectives, is to reject the late modern conviction that ethics, in the sense of moral theory, must be autonomous from religious beliefs, especially any type of theism. In this chapter, I provide a version of this argument, claiming that Whitehead's postmodern theism can overcome the two major weaknesses of late modern moral theory: its inability to defend moral realism and its inability to provide a basis for moral motivation. I point out, furthermore, that it can overcome these weaknesses without returning to the heteronomy of traditional theistic ethics to which the call for complete autonomy from theism was a reaction.

I have found, incidentally, that the first claim of this chapter—that an adequate moral theory finally requires a version of theism—encounters tremendous resistance from fellow liberals, with whom I agree on most moral issues. The reason seems to be that they are strongly committed to the existence of universally valid moral norms, on the one hand, and to the nonnecessity of "belief in God" in order to live a satisfactory life, on the other. This combination of commitments creates a powerful predisposition to reject any contention, whether made by atheists or theists, that apart from theism the idea of universally valid moral norms cannot be rationally defended. This predisposition is even stronger insofar as the conviction that "belief in God is unnecessary for a satisfactory life" is based, at least in part, on the conviction that theism is not rationally defensible. People who have built their lives on the assumption that universally moral norms exist are naturally loathe to accept any claim that would imply that they could not defend the existence of such norms, at least without changing their entire worldview.

Nevertheless, while recognizing that this claim—that only a theistic moral theory can be adequate—is today highly unpopular in liberal circles, I believe that it is true. I here try to explain, as clearly as possible within the confines of a single chapter, why it is true and hence one of the main reasons why Whitehead's postmodern recovery of a theistic worldview is important.

THE MODERN COMMITMENT AND AUTONOMOUS ETHICS

Most premodern and early modern moral theory was theistic. Although different schools of thought had different ideas about various details, most thinkers agreed that morality was divinely sanctioned so that moral principles were—in the phrase made famous by John Mackie—"part of the fabric of the world." Insofar as this theistic framework was taken for granted, all sorts of questions typical of recent ethical reflection—whether moral statements can be true, whether they are even cognitively meaningful, whether philosophers can provide justification and motivation for the moral life—did not arise.

For various reasons, nevertheless, much enlightenment thought decided that ethics needed to become autonomous, weaning itself from all dependence on theistic presuppositions. Although various considerations fed into this conclusion, a crucial one—famously stated in Kant's dictum that *enlightenment* means thinking for oneself—was the insistence that human thought is to reject heteronomy in favor of autonomy, which means that it must break free of all authoritarianism. As we saw earlier, Franklin Gamwell, calling the insistence on autonomy in this formal sense "the modern commitment," says that "modernity is distinguished by the increasing affirmation that our understandings of reality and ourselves in relation to it cannot be validated or redeemed by appeals to some authoritative expression or tradition or institution" but "only by appeal in some sense to human experience and reason as such."[1]

This modern commitment did not by itself, it is important to note, dictate that ethics had to become autonomous from theism. It declared only that moral thought had to be autonomous in the purely formal sense of basing its conclusions on experience and reason. There were many enlightenment thinkers, including Francis Hutcheson, Adam Ferguson, and Thomas Jefferson, who believed that this modern approach, with its rejection of heteronomy, supported a view of divine existence that in turn supported morality.

The idea that the *autonomy of thought from authority* entailed the *autonomy of ethics from theism* followed only when it was concluded, by thinkers such as Hume and Kant, that theism—including the "deism" of thinkers such as Hutcheson, Ferguson, and Jefferson—could not be justified in terms of experience and reason alone. It was the spread of this conviction—which entailed that, in Gamwell's words, "theistic claims are, at least by implication, incurably authoritarian in character"—that provided the link between the autonomy of thought in the purely formal sense and the late modern consensus that moral claims must be justified independently of theistic affirmations.[2] If theism could be supported only by an appeal to authority, then theism necessarily involved heteronomy.

The demand for independence was not unique to ethics. The dominant consensus with regard to ethics is simply one aspect of late modern thought's consensus that *all* areas of thought must and can be worked out independently of any theistic beliefs. Charles Larmore, for example, says that "modernity requires [a] purely naturalistic explanation of nature as well as a purely human understanding of morality." In this statement, "naturalistic," like "purely human," is taken to mean "nontheistic." Besides holding that these nontheistic explanations are required by modernity, Larmore also endorses the conviction that such explanations can be adequate, saying: "We no longer need God to explain the world and to ground the rules of our common life."[3]

After two centuries of the attempt to develop a moral theory that is autonomous in the sense of nontheistic, however, this tradition is in crisis. For a moral theory to succeed, it must provide at least two things. First, it must provide a credible defense of moral objectivity, meaning that some basic moral principles, such as, We should not inflict pain on others simply for fun, constitute genuine knowledge. It might be claimed, of course, that this is not a requirement of an adequate philosophical theory, because it may well be that there *are no* objective moral principles, so that a philosophical account of morality that denied the existence of such principles could be adequate.

The problem with this approach, however, is that we cannot help believing in the objectivity of moral (and other normative) principles. The presupposition that there are such principles is one of our inevitable presuppositions, which I have called our "hard-core commonsense" notions. Whitehead, saying that "the impact of . . . moral notions is inescapable," included among our moral judgments "the ultimate notions of 'better' and 'worse'" (MT 19; ESP 80). These notions are ultimate because we cannot help but believe that some decisions, motives, attitudes, actions, and consequences are better or worse than others and that people are at least partially responsible for their behavior and hence either praiseworthy or blameworthy in a moral sense. Because we cannot help presupposing moral objectivity in this sense, philosophers who deny this objectivity contradict themselves, because they are simultaneously denying (explicitly) and affirming (implicitly) one and the same idea.

Accordingly, a philosophy of morality, to be adequate, and even to be self-consistent, must be able to affirm that our best moral beliefs constitute genuine knowledge, in the traditional sense of "justified true belief." This means that the task of defending moral realism has both ontological and epistemological dimensions. We need an explanation of not only how moral principles can exist but also how, assuming such principles do exist, we can know them.

The second element a moral philosophy needs to supply is some motivation to adopt a moral way of life. Many secular philosophers, to be sure, have said that this task is not an essential part of the philosopher's task. This task, they claim, is limited to explicating the moral point of view—explaining what it is.

To regard the philosopher's task as thus limited, however, is to forget the original claim behind the attempt to provide a purely philosophical, secular account of morality. This claim was that although we can no longer accept a religious-based morality, this is no cause for anxiety, because morality should and could be fully independent from religious beliefs. For nonreligious philosophers now to say that they need not provide any basis for motivation is to announce that the original program has failed, that morality cannot, in fact, be independent of religious beliefs. Moreover, it is simply the case that a system of moral thought is not very helpful if it cannot point to anything that will provide motivation to be moral. It is certainly true that people need help in understanding what "the moral point of view" is and what it implies in particular situations. For a philosophy to provide only this, however, is for it to perform only a part of the task.

Modern moral theory has failed with regard to both moral realism and moral motivation, and this twofold failure is intimately connected with its eschewal of a theistic worldview. I will illustrate this claim first with regard to moral realism, then with regard to the issue of motivation. I will then discuss obstacles to a return to some form of theistic ethics, one of which is the assumption that theism necessarily involves heteronomy. In the final section, I will show how Whitehead's theistic philosophy, besides overcoming these obstacles, can provide a basis for moral motivation as well as an account of how genuine moral knowledge is possible.

MODERN PHILOSOPHY'S FAILURE TO PROVIDE MORAL OBJECTIVITY

In light of Western thought's traditional way of explaining the objectivity of moral principles, the failure of late modern thought is no cause for surprise. This objectivity was based on *moral realism*, according to which normative moral values exist in the nature of things. Because this view was formulated paradigmatically by Plato, as part of his more general affirmation of the existence of ideal forms, it is often called "Platonic realism."

The Platonic Problem

This affirmation raised, however, what can be called "the Platonic problem"—namely, the question of *how* and *where* such forms exist. Plato himself seemed to imply that the ideal forms somehow existed on their own (in the void, as it were), a view that Aristotle and other critics found unintelligible, holding instead that abstract, ideal entities can exist only in concrete, actual entities. Middle Platonism solved this problem with the doctrine that the forms exist in "the mind of God," a thesis that was adopted in most medieval philosophy.

The Benacerraf Problem

This doctrine also solved, in advance, what can be called "the Benacerraf problem." Paul Benacerraf has argued (rightly) that true beliefs can be considered *knowledge* only if that which makes the belief true is somehow *causally* responsible for the belief.[4] For example, my true beliefs about a tree in my garden can be considered knowledge only if the tree's causation is partly responsible for my beliefs.

Benacerraf was concerned with the question of mathematical knowledge, asking how numbers could be causally responsible for mathematical beliefs. But his argument applies equally to the issue of moral knowledge. Moral beliefs cannot be considered knowledge unless, besides being true, they are somehow causally derivative from whatever it is—such as a set of normative values inherent in the fabric of the universe—that makes the beliefs true. The Benacerraf problem for the philosophy of mathematics and the philosophy of morality is how numbers and moral norms, being merely ideal entities, can exert causal efficacy, thereby bringing about mathematical and moral knowledge. The doctrine that mathematical and moral forms are in God had long provided the answer that these ideal entities are given causal efficacy by divine agency.

However, the decision that moral theory must be autonomous from all forms of theism, including the philosophical theism of thinkers such as Aquinas, Berkeley, and Leibniz, meant that the Platonic and Benacerraf problems had lost their long-standing answer. Part of the recent crisis in ethics is due to the resulting loss of faith in moral realism.

The Gödel Problem

There are two sides to the problem of how we can perceive ideal entities, such as numbers and moral norms. In addition to the Benacerraf problem as to how such entities could exert agency, there is the problem of how, even if they do, we could perceive them. We certainly cannot perceive them through our physical sense organs, yet modern thought, as we saw in chapters 1 and 2, has insisted that sensory perception is the only mode of perception we have. Therefore, even if the Benacerraf problem is solved by saying that ideal entities are given agency by a divine actuality, we still, according to modern philosophy, cannot perceive them. As we saw, Kant, one of the founders of modern epistemology, called the idea that we can perceive a divine being a "fanatical religious illusion."[5]

We can name this problem the Gödel problem in honor of the famous mathematician and logician Kurt Gödel, who suggested that our knowledge of mathematical objects comes through a nonsensory type of perception, which we call "mathematical intuition."[6] Although Gödel, rather than simply stating the problem, thereby offered a solution to it, it has not functioned as a solution, because it has been widely and emphatically rejected. For example, Hilary Putnam, insisting that "we think with our brains, and not with immaterial souls," declared: "We cannot envisage *any* kind of neural process that could even correspond to the 'perception of a mathematical object.'"[7] Charles Chihara gave an even more hostile response to Gödel's suggestion, asking, rhetorically: "What empirical scientist would be impressed by an explanation this flabby?"[8]

These three problems have led late modern moral philosophers to the twofold conclusion that moral realism is false, because there is no conceivable way in which moral principles could belong to the nature of the universe, and that even if such principles did exist, there would be no way for us to know about them. These three problems have thereby combined to lead late modern philosophers to reject the idea that any beliefs we have about moral principles could count as knowledge. For illustrations of the role of these three problems in leading to this conclusion, we can look at the writings of John Mackie, Gilbert Harman, and Bernard Williams.

John Mackie

John Mackie, in his well-known book *Ethics*, implied his rejection of moral realism in his subtitle, *Inventing Right and Wrong*. He made this rejection explicit in his denial that values are "part of the fabric of the world."[9] Moreover, referring to social requirements, such as "if someone is writhing in agony before your eyes" you should "do something about it if you can," Mackie denied that they are "objective, intrinsic, requirements of the nature of things."[10] In explaining the basis for this denial, he said: "The difficulty of seeing how values could be objective is a fairly strong reason for thinking that they are not."[11]

The difficulty in question involved what Mackie called "the argument from queerness," which has a metaphysical and an epistemological dimension. Referring to the metaphysical dimension, he said that objective values "would be entities or qualities or relations of a very strange sort, utterly different from anything else in the universe." They would be so odd because they would have *prescriptivity* built into them, as do some Platonic Forms. The Form of the Good, for example, "has to-be-pursuedness somehow built into it."[12]

Mackie explicitly admitted that this metaphysical argument from queerness depended upon the presumption of atheism. Describing his book as "a discussion of what we can make of morality without recourse to God," he added: "I concede that if the requisite theological doctrine could be defended, a kind of objective ethical prescriptivity could be defended."[13] Mackie, however, did not believe that the "requisite theological doctrine" could be defended.

The epistemological part of Mackie's argument from queerness says that, if we were aware of objective moral values, "it would have to be by some special faculty of moral perception or intuition, utterly different from our ordinary ways of knowing everything else." These ordinary ways are said to be limited to "sensory perception or introspection."[14] In other words, Mackie was saying, aside from what we know about our own experience from introspection, everything we know about the world originates in sensory perception. Therefore, the idea that moral principles alone are known by some special faculty should, as a purely ad hoc hypothesis, be rejected.

Although some philosophers who reject moral realism have tried to maintain that this rejection is supported by ordinary language and hence ordinary moral thinking, Mackie did not. He fully admitted that his view, according to which "[t]here are no objective values,"[15] contradicts ordinary moral thought, because "most people in making moral judgments implicitly claim, among other things, to be pointing to something objectively prescriptive." Mackie, frankly asserting that "these claims are all false," thereby affirmed an "error theory" of ordinary moral thought.[16] In short, none of our moral beliefs constitutes knowledge.

Gilbert Harman summarized Mackie's arguments against belief in the existence of objective moral principles as saying that "our scientific conception of the world has no place for entities of this sort, and...there is no way in which we could become aware of such entities."[17] This summary nicely brings out the fact that Mackie's rejection of moral realism rests on our three problems: the Platonic problem as to where values could exist in a godless world; the Gödel problem of how we could perceive such values even if they somehow exited; and the Benacerraf problem of how, even if we had some means for perceiving nonphysical entities, values could be impressed upon us so as to have prescriptivity built into them.

Gilbert Harman

Harman's summary of Mackie's position also summarizes his own position. To be sure, he begins his book on the subject, entitled *The Nature of Morality*, by suggesting that he will do more justice to ordinary moral thinking than did Mackie. "[I]f a philosophical theory conflicts with ordinary ways of thinking and speaking," says

Harman, "something has probably gone wrong.[18] Indeed, having defined nihilism as "the doctrine that there are no moral facts, no moral truths, and no moral knowledge," Harman early in the book promises to retain "our ordinary views and [avoid] endorsing some form of nihilism."[19]

By the end of the book, however, we learn that "there are no absolute facts of right or wrong, apart from one or another set of conventions," but only "relative facts about what is right or wrong"—relative, that is, to some set of conventions adopted by a particular society.[20] But that is simply a restatement of the nihilistic position. Accordingly, in spite of Harman's early statement that something has probably gone wrong "if a philosophical theory conflicts with ordinary ways of thinking and speaking," he later concludes that "[w]e cannot have morality as it is ordinarily conceived."[21]

This conclusion depends partly on the Platonic problem. We should, Harman says, approach moral theory from a scientific viewpoint, and this means that we should "concentrate on *finding the place* of value and obligation in the world of facts as revealed by science." The upshot of this search, he then reports, is that "our scientific conception of the world *has no place* for entities of this sort."[22]

This conclusion follows from Harman's assertion that science entails naturalism, with naturalism understood to be what Harman (tendentiously) calls "the sensible thesis that *all* facts are facts of nature."[23] This is the doctrine that I, in chapter 2, called "naturalism$_{nati}$," with "nati" meaning "nature is all there is" and with "nature" in this phrase understood to mean the totality of finite things. Naturalism thus defined explicitly rules out the existence of a divine actuality. Harman, believing that science as such implies naturalism of this type, asserts that science implies atheism, saying: "Our scientific conception of the world has no place for gods."[24] The implication of Harman's discussion is that because "nature" neither includes, nor is included in, nor is the product of, a divine being, there is no "place" for normative values. The Platonic problem rules out moral realism.

Harman's conclusion that ordinary morality, with its belief in objective values, cannot be affirmed is based equally on a combination of the Benacerraf and Gödel problems.

At the heart of Harman's argument against the idea that moral beliefs can count as knowledge is his claim that whereas scientific assertions are based on observations of facts, moral assertions are *not*. He says, for example: "Facts about protons can affect what you observe, since a proton passing through the cloud chamber can cause a vapor trail that reflects light to your eye.... But there does not seem to be any way in which the actual rightness or wrongness of a given situation can have any effect on your perceptual apparatus."[25] Accordingly, he says, if there were such a thing as moral knowledge, it "would have to be a kind of knowledge that can be acquired other than by observation."[26]

The primary basis for this claim seems to be the Gödel problem, created by Harman's acceptance of the sensationist doctrine of perception. But the Benacerraf problem of causation also plays a role. With an allusion to Benacerraf's famous essay, Harman faces the embarrassing fact that mathematics is also not based on observation: "We do not and cannot perceive numbers," Harman says, "since we cannot be in causal contact with them." Explicitly pointing out that ethics and mathematics are in the same boat, he adds: "Relations among numbers cannot have any more of an effect on our perceptual apparatus than moral facts can."[27]

This parallel is embarrassing because Harman, believing that his naturalism is vouchsafed by natural science, would be loath to admit that his epistemology is inadequate for mathematical physics, which is generally regarded as the pre-eminent natural science. How can he argue that because ethical beliefs are not based on observation, they cannot be considered knowledge, while recognizing that mathematical truths are also not based on observation?

Harman handles this problem by saying that we can speak of mathematical knowledge because mathematics has "indirect observational evidence."[28] This is clearly special pleading, because one could make exactly the same claim about moral principles (as does Charles Larmore, discussed later). Whether justifiably or not, in any case, Harman, like many other modern philosophers, uses the Platonic, Benacerraf, and Gödel problems to rule out moral knowledge without employing them against mathematical knowledge.

Bernard Williams

A similar contrast between science and ethics is central to the denial of an objectivist view of ethics articulated by Bernard Williams in his major book on the issue, which he entitled *Ethics and the Limits of Philosophy*. In scientific inquiry, says Williams, we expect convergence of opinion, with the convergence explained by the fact that the thinking of the scientists is guided by the way the world really is. But in ethical thinking, Williams claims, there is no basis for expecting convergence. Because we cannot perceive moral norms, there is no way for the world to guide the thinking of moral philosophers.[29]

We cannot, therefore, speak of "knowledge" in ethics, says Williams, because knowledge requires not only that a proposition believed by a person be true but also that the truth and the belief be "nonaccidentally linked." In science, this link is provided by perception of the physical world, but ethical beliefs, Williams holds, are not based on perception.[30] Although he recognizes that some philosophers have claimed that "something like perception," sometimes called "moral intuition," accounts for our ethical concepts, Williams believes that "the appeal to intuition as a faculty...seemed to say that these truths were known, but there was no way in which they were known."[31]

As these statements show, Williams' denial that moral beliefs could be considered knowledge was based heavily on the Gödel problem. He evidently found the idea that we could know things through nonsensory perception simply inconceivable. While aware that some philosophers have claimed an analogy with mathematical knowledge, Williams, like Harman, quickly dismissed this analogy, concluding that "[w]e must reject the objectivist view of ethical life as...a pursuit of ethical truth."[32]

As with Mackie and Harman, however, this conclusion also rested on the presumption of atheism. Part and parcel of the loss of belief in God, Williams points out, was the collapse of teleological assumptions. Those assumptions, by allowing people to believe that they lived in a "teleologically significant world," had allowed them to regard their purposes as linked with purposes of the universe.[33] By way of indicating the crucial importance of this collapse, in his estimation, he added: "No one has yet found a good way of doing without those assumptions."[34]

One way in which the loss of those assumptions was a watershed event is that it led to the conclusion that "our values are not 'in the world.'" This conclusion, which Williams considered a "discovery," led in turn to the conviction that it is a fallacy—the *naturalistic* fallacy—to think that value could somehow be derived from fact, so that *ought* could somehow be derived from *is*.[35] We see here another way of putting Mackie's point that in an atheistic universe, we cannot understand how any principles about ways of thinking, acting, and feeling could have prescriptivity built into them.

Williams, in fact, comments on the phrase made famous by Mackie, asking "what it could mean to say that a requirement or demand was 'part of the fabric of the world.'" Williams points out that it "might possibly mean that some agency which made the demand or imposed the requirement was part of the fabric."[36] Williams, of course, did not believe in any such agency any more than did Mackie. The important point for our purposes, however, is the fact that Williams explicitly pointed out that it is the presumption of atheism that makes the Platonic and Benacerraf problems insoluble. Given this recognition on his part, Williams perhaps should have given his book the somewhat more modest title, "Ethics and the Limits of Atheistic Philosophy."

In any case, Williams, having been led by the Platonic and Benacerraf problems (along with, as discussed earlier, the Gödel problem) to reject a realist or objectivist view of ethical beliefs, he summarizes his view pithily by concluding that although the moral law may seem to come "from outside," it really comes from "deeply inside."[37] By this he means that "our values are not 'in the world'" but are instead "projected on to our surroundings."[38]

❧

The views of Williams, Mackie, and Harman cannot be dismissed as those of minor or unrepresentative figures. They have all been major figures in moral philosophy, teaching in major universities (Cambridge, Oxford, and Princeton, respectively). The commonplace nature of their views among moral philosophers is illustrated, furthermore, by the fact that in a symposium on Mackie's moral thought, R. M. Hare said, nonchalantly: "It was John Mackie's great contribution to ethics to display clearly the absurdity of realism."[39]

The fact that Mackie, Harman, and Williams can be employed as representative can be seen, moreover, from the fact that their position on moral facts is not essentially different from that of John Rawls, widely considered the leading moral philosopher of recent decades. In 1980, for example, Rawls wrote:

> What justifies a conception of justice is not its being true to an order antecedent to and given to us, but its congruence with our deeper understanding of ourselves and our aspirations, and our realization that, given our history and the traditions embedded in our public life, it is the most reasonable doctrine for us. . . . Kantian constructivism holds that moral objectivity is to be understood in terms of a suitably constructed social point of view that all can accept. *Apart from the procedure of constructing the principles of justice, there are no moral facts.*[40]

In his later thought, although Rawls sought to replace his earlier "substantive" conception of justice, based on Kantianism, with a purely "political" conception, he continued to affirm "a constructivist view" in distinction from an "order of moral values, or the dictates of what some regard as natural law."[41]

Late modern moral philosophy is in crisis partly because this view—according to which our moral convictions are not reflections of anything in the fabric of the universe—is widespread.

Another reason, however, is that late modern moral philosophy, with its insistence on autonomy from all religious beliefs, cannot provide motivation to be moral.

THE FAILURE TO PROVIDE MORAL MOTIVATION

In light of the basis for motivation provided by traditional thought, it should be no surprise that late modern moral theory, with its autonomy from religious belief, has also failed in this respect.

The Religious Perspective

That traditional basis was what Clifford Geertz calls the "religious perspective," which involves "the conviction that the values one holds are grounded in the inherent structure of reality, that between the way one ought to live and the way things really are there is an unbreakable inner connection."[42] This feature of the religious perspective accounts for religion's moral vitality: "The powerfully coercive 'ought' is felt to grow out of a comprehensive factual 'is.' . . . [The power of sacred symbols] comes from their presumed ability to identify fact with value at the most fundamental level."[43]

Geertz's characterization of a "comprehensive factual 'is,'" in which "fact and value [are identified] at the most fundamental level," is a characterization of the Holy—of something that is intrinsically good in an ultimate, nonderivative sense. In traditional cultures, the ultimate motivation for the moral life could be provided by some such idea because the Holy Reality is a fact—an "is"—that generates a powerful "ought."

The way in which a moral "ought" is uniquely generated from a Holy "is" can be called "the logic of the Holy." This logical argument, usually only implicit, can be explicated thus:

1. To be in harmony with the Holy Reality requires that we X.
2. We want to be in harmony with the Holy Reality (because it is that which is good in an ultimate, nonderivative way).
3. Therefore we ought to X.

When Hume famously argued that an "ought" cannot be deduced from an "is," he failed to reflect on the exceptional nature of an "is" that is *Holy*. If we ignore this exception, however, Hume's argument is entirely correct. It would seem likely, therefore, that ethics, once disconnected from any belief in a Holy Reality, would be unable to provide justification and motivation for a moral life. This is indeed what we find.

The Argument of Bernard Williams

Bernard Williams, in referring to philosophy's "limits" in relation to ethics, meant that morality "can[not] be justified by philosophy."[44] Closely related was his argument that philosophy also could not provide motivation to be moral. The presumption of atheism is also central to this part of his argument.

This centrality can be seen in his reflections on the fact that we seem to have an inescapable sense that some things are *important*—and not merely important for some people but "important *überhaupt*." Puzzling over what this might mean, Williams was certain only about what it does *not* mean: "It does not mean that it is important to the universe; in that sense, nothing is important."[45]

Williams, of course, must hold this because to affirm that something is important to the universe would be to express the theistic idea that the universe itself has a perspective on things. It would be to say that, beyond all our finite perspectives, there is an ultimate, divine perspective. Denying the existence of a divine perspective is a way of denying that there is anything holy—any comprehensive "is" from which an "ought" could be generated. Given this denial, Williams sees no way in which philosophy can say anything that could motivate people to take the moral, meaning the impartial, point of view.

Williams' critique on this point is especially directed at Kantians, who believe that the moral point of view can be justified without moral realism, because it can be justified on the basis of reason alone. In opposition to this view, Williams argues that "there is no route to the impartial standpoint from rational deliberation alone." Why? Because: "The *I* that stands back in rational reflection from my desires is still the *I* that has those desires and will, empirically and concretely, act; and it is not, simply by standing in reflection, converted into a being whose fundamental interest lies in the harmony of all interests. It cannot, just by taking this step, acquire the motivations of justice."[46] The message of Williams' book is that such motivations could be provided only by a view of our place in the universe that, with the decline of theistically rooted teleology, is no longer possible.

The Example of Jürgen Habermas

Jürgen Habermas is a Kantian philosopher who would at first glance seem to differ with Williams. Emphasizing the nontheistic context of contemporary ethical philosophy, Habermas says that we need "a posttraditional" or "postmetaphysical" morality, meaning one that has "detached itself from the religious and metaphysical context from which it arose."[47] Such a position, he claims, "can explicate the moral point of view," which means the impartial point of view.[48] Habermas might thereby seem to be claiming to do what Williams said cannot be done.

Habermas, however, concedes that his position cannot provide motivation. It cannot do this primarily because one cannot "salvage an unconditional meaning without God." Accordingly, he, as a postmetaphysical philosopher, cannot say that in our moral life "something incomparably important is involved." He concedes, therefore, that he cannot "provide a motivating response to the question of . . . why we should be moral at all."[49]

For motivation, Habermas says, we must rely on socialization, especially from religion.[50] But Habermas as philosopher cannot give any rational support for taking religious beliefs seriously. His position, in fact, includes the conviction that the world has become irreversibly disenchanted.[51] According to Habermas, therefore, moral philosophy will forevermore be unable to appeal to a religious worldview for motivation.

Although Habermas, unlike Williams, emphasizes what autonomous reason *can* do, rather than what it *cannot* do, he agrees that because philosophy cannot speak of something incomparably important—of something holy—it can provide no motivation to take the moral point of view.

A GROWING CONSENSUS

On the basis of the above and similar writings, a consensus has been growing that autonomous moral theory has failed.

One example of this growing consensus is provided by Alasdair MacIntyre. Referring to the modern idea of "rights attaching to human beings simply *qua* human beings," MacIntyre contends that "there are no such rights, and belief in them is one with belief in witches and unicorns." The best reason for asserting that there are no rights, continues MacIntyre, is "of precisely the same type as the best reason which we possess for asserting that there are no witches and...no unicorns: every attempt to give good reasons for believing that there *are* such rights has failed."[52]

By "every attempt," MacIntyre means every attempt *within* what he calls "the Enlightenment project" of providing "a secular, rational justification for [one's] moral allegiances."[53] MacIntyre is saying, in other words, that the project of autonomous ethics has failed.

A commentator who agrees is J. D. Goldsworthy, who has written an essay titled "God or Mackie? The Dilemma of Secular Moral Philosophy." After reviewing the work of various Kantian theorists as well as Mackie and MacIntyre, Goldsworthy says that "moral philosophers have conspicuously failed to find any plausible foundation for the supposed authority of moral precepts." His title—"God or Mackie?"—is meant to suggest that only a theistic ethic could provide the needed foundation. "It seems doubtful," Goldsworthy concludes, "that any secular philosophy can carry ethics to higher ground."[54]

Jeffrie Murphy, who had previously believed that morality did not require theism, provides yet another example of this growing consensus. Reflecting on the fact that recent moral and legal philosophers have found it difficult to provide a basis for affirming universal human rights, Murphy writes:

> [W]e at present live in a time when it is widely believed—under the impact of work by such writers in the "analytic" tradition as Gilbert Harman and John Mackie and such writers in the "pluralist" tradition as Richard Rorty and Alasdair MacIntyre—that all...attempts rationally to demonstrate the objective correctness of certain moral claims are doomed to failure.[55]

Finding it especially disturbing that such philosophers cannot explain "why anyone is morally required to *care* whether or not another's situation is worsened,"[56] Murphy connects this failure with the divorce of ethics from theism.

Murphy's analysis is especially significant in light of the fact that he had previously argued that Nietzsche's proclamation that "God is dead" was no "big deal" because morality does not depend on belief in God.[57] Having in the meantime concluded that the idea of human rights presupposes the notion that human beings are somehow sacred, Murphy now asks, rhetorically: "How can one expect to dump God and a religious vision of the universe and yet retain a strong concept of the *sacredness* of anything?"[58]

For a final example of the growing consensus, we can turn to the argument of Basil Mitchell in a book titled *Morality: Religious and Secular: The Dilemma of the Traditional Conscience.* In speaking of the "traditional conscience," Mitchell refers to people who still hold that we should obey our traditional moral intuitions even though they have given up the religious basis for morality and hence the idea that morality "was based on a purpose written in the nature of things."[59] The "dilemma" faced by such people is due to the fact that the various forms of secular humanism have failed "to provide a rationale for morality as traditionally conceived." These people hence face the dilemma of either modifying their conscience or questioning their secular assumptions.[60] Mitchell's book is an argument for the second option and hence for a return to religious morality, grounded in theism.

IS A RETURN TO THEISTIC ETHICS POSSIBLE?

Mitchell's book is only one of many recent writings that, reflecting on the failure of secular moral theory, call for a return to theistic ethics. Most of these writings, however, fail to address the fact that such a return is, for most thinkers who have rejected theism, simply inconceivable. The dilemma faced by those who have recognized the instability of a purely secular humanism is, therefore, even worse than Mitchell says. Their dilemma is that although they recognize the need for a justification of basic moral principles that a nonreligious ethic cannot provide, they also find themselves unable to return to the kind of religious worldview evidently required.

For example, Jeffrie Murphy, having argued that "the liberal theory of rights requires a doctrine of human dignity, preciousness and sacredness that cannot be utterly detached from a belief in God or at least from a world view that could be properly called religious in some metaphysically profound sense," adds: "For those, such as I, who find it very difficult—perhaps impossible—to embrace religious convictions, the idea that fundamental moral values may require such convictions is not one to be welcomed with joy. This idea generates tensions and appears to force choices that some of us would prefer not to make."[61]

As Murphy illustrates, the mere fact that people see a "need" for religious belief does not settle anything, because this perceived need may be outweighed by the conviction that holding a religious worldview, especially a theistic one, is no longer rationally impossible. I suggest that to be credible, an argument for returning to theistic moral theory would need to include at least the following ingredients.

The argument, for starters, must recognize that the original rejection of theism was not made lightly or without many good reasons. This rejection, which involved one of the greatest cultural upheavals in the history of Western civilization, involved much soul searching on the part of thousands of highly intelligent and sensitive individuals. Many of these individuals realized that the effects—both religious and moral, both personal and institutional—would be catastrophic. They concluded, nonetheless, that the received idea of God was both intellectually incredible and morally perverse—recall Stendahl's quip that God's only excuse is that he does not exist! The reasons for rejecting this idea of God were at least as persuasive as the present reasons for holding that nonreligious moral theory is inadequate. The idea of a "return to theism" cannot, therefore, be equated with a return to *traditional* theism. It must be a "return forward," to something quite different.

The argument for such a new form of theism must show that it, besides grounding traditional moral principles at least as well as traditional theism, overcomes its many problems. One problem was the fact that, in spite of all the arguments made on its behalf, traditional theism could not really be rationally justified, so its acceptance finally rested on authority. This fact about traditional theism is widely applied to theism as such. Habermas, for example, dismisses the possibility of a theistic grounding for morality because theism cannot be "vindicated before the tribunal of justificatory discourse."[62]

A distinction crucially needed here is that between genus and species. If a genus has more than one species, it is a logical error to dismiss the genus on the basis of only one of its species. Traditional theism, held by Augustine, Thomas, Calvin, Luther, Descartes, Newton, and Paley, has certainly been the best-known species of theism in the West. But it is far from the only one. Philosophers cannot justifiably infer from its defects that similar defects would necessarily infect all other species of theism worthy of the name.

The importance of this elementary logical point can be seen by reflection on Mackie's admission that "if the requisite theological doctrine could be defended, a kind of objective ethical prescriptivity could be defended." In spite of making this admission, Mackie quickly dismissed this possibility on the grounds that the existence of God is highly improbable, especially in light of the problem of evil.

Mackie argued for this conclusion in a subsequent book, which he titled *The Miracle of Theism: Arguments for and against the Existence of God*. An examination of this book, however, reveals that it does not deal with theism as such but only with *traditional* theism, according to which one of God's attributes is "able to do everything (i.e. omnipotent)."[63] Mackie's conclusions that the world's evil renders *this* being's existence highly unlikely is widely accepted, even by many theists—namely, those who defend nontraditional versions of theism. Mackie himself, in fact, pointed out that his argument would cause no difficulty for forms of theism that do not accept the traditional view of divine power.[64] Mackie, however, did not highlight this crucial admission. As a result, his book has been widely accepted as an argument—as the title suggests—against theism as such and hence as an argument for the probable truth of atheism—the conclusion that Mackie had presupposed in his book on ethics.

Once we clearly make the genus-species distinction between theism as such and traditional theism, we can see that Mackie's book says nothing about whether one of the forms of theism that he did not examine might be rationally defensible. Nothing in Mackie's argument, in fact, rules out the possibility that some form of nontraditional theism might even seem more probable than atheism.

A similar point can be made about Habermas. Although Habermas's whole program rests on the assumption that theological discourse is cognitively inadequate, he for the most part simply repeats Kant's conclusions about traditional theism. One will look in vain in the writings of Habermas for any examination of the many varieties of theism that have arisen since the time of Kant. Insofar as Habermas, Mackie, and other nontheistic thinkers have not even examined these other forms of theism, there is certainly no reason to take them as authorities about the rational defensibility of these other doctrines. And, insofar as we consider these philosophers' views about morality inadequate, we have every reason to examine these other forms of theism, to see if they can fill the bill.

I myself have argued for the rational defensibility of a version of the process theism suggested by Alfred North Whitehead, with my defense having both negative and positive dimensions. The negative dimension involves showing that the problems that counted against traditional theism do not count against theism of this sort. The positive dimension is more ambitious, seeking to show this form of theism to be more probable than atheism.[65]

The enterprise of engaging in "arguments for the existence of God" has been, to put it mildly, out of favor. Arguments of this kind, it is widely assumed, can easily be shown to be worthless. But it is precisely in relation to this question that it is most important to take seriously the genus-species distinction. Almost all "arguments for the existence of God" have been offered on behalf of traditional theism's idea of God. Virtually all criticisms of the arguments, therefore, have been criticisms of arguments purporting to support the existence of God thus conceived—Kant's demonstration, for example, that the design argument does not prove the existence of a deity who created the world ex nihilo. Such critiques say nothing about the persuasiveness of arguments for the kind of creator envisaged by process theism, who created our world out of chaos. I have argued, in fact, that implicit in Whitehead's system are thirteen arguments for the existence of the divine being of which he speaks. With so many considerations counting in favor of the existence of this deity and none counting against it, the truth of something like process philosophy's theism is, I argue, "overwhelmingly more probable than the truth of atheism."[66]

Insofar as this conclusion is accepted, the connection between theism and heteronomy is broken. Belief in God no longer needs to be seen to rest on an appeal to authority. It can instead be regarded as part of the most plausible account of the nature of reality.

At the center of the cultural transition from theism to atheism has been the assumption that this transition is supported by the natural sciences. The most effective way to argue the need to return to a theistic worldview, therefore, would be to show that science, far from implying atheism, cannot be made intelligible apart from a theistic framework. I will illustrate this approach in terms of one of the thirteen arguments implicit in Whitehead's philosophy, the argument from mathematical forms—then point to its similarity to the argument from moral norms.

CAN THE PHILOSOPHY OF MATHEMATICS BE AUTONOMOUS?

The project of making all disciplines independent from theology meant that the philosophy of mathematics had to become autonomous. As we have seen, however, it, like moral philosophy, is plagued by the Platonic, Benacerraf, and Gödel problems. In this section, we will look more closely at the implications of these problems for the question of returning to a theistic framework.

The Platonic Problem

The Platonic problem faced by the philosophy of mathematics has been well brought out by Reuben Hersh, who wrote:

> An inarticulate, half-conscious Platonism is nearly universal among mathematicians.... Yet most of this Platonism is half-hearted, shamefaced. We don't ask, How does this immaterial realm relate to material reality? How does it make contact with flesh and blood mathematicians? We refuse to face this embarrassment: Ideal entities independent of human consciousness violate the empiricism of modern science.

Pointing to the background of this problem, Hersh continues:

> For Leibniz and Berkeley, abstractions like numbers are thoughts in the mind of God.... [But] the Mind of God [is] no longer heard of in academic discourse. Yet most mathematicians and philosophers of mathematics continue to believe in an independent, immaterial abstract world—a remnant of Plato's Heaven..., with all entities but the mathematical expelled. Platonism without God is like the grin on Lewis Carroll's Cheshire cat.... The grin remained without the cat.[67]

The situation to which Hersh refers can be illustrated in terms of the "physicalism" of Willard Quine. Although many writers equate physicalism with materialism, Quine defined physicalism not in ontological terms but as the purely formal doctrine that our ontology should be settled by the discipline of physics. Physicalism, in other words, means that physics becomes the arbiter of what does and does not exist. If physics needs Xs, then Xs exist; if physics does not require Ys, then Ys do not exist.

One idea that is indispensable to physics, Quine pointed out, is the existence of numbers as existing independently of us. Quine thereby felt compelled, on the basis of this "indispensability argument," to affirm the existence of mathematical objects.

This affirmation, however, was at odds with one of Quine's other major points—his emphatic and oft-repeated contention that nothing should be allowed into our ontology that cannot pass the "tribunal of sense experience."[68] Since sensory perception is activated only by material objects, this criterion of existence should have led Quine to a completely materialistic ontology. Like Gilbert Harman, to be sure, he did employ this criterion to deny the objective reality of moral norms.[69] But he inconsistently, on the basis of his indispensability argument, allowed mathematical objects to sneak past his "tribunal of sense experience." As a result, his ontology, according to his own statement, "is materialism, bluntly monistic except for the abstract objects of mathematics."[70]

This exception, however, raises a serious problem. How is it conceivable that, as Quine put it, these abstract mathematical objects, which are not located anywhere in space or time, somehow exist, in Quine's words, "over and above the physical objects"?[71] *How* and *where* would they exist in an otherwise materialistic universe? This is, of course, the Platonic problem, but Quine failed to address it.

The Benacerraf and Gödel Problems

The Banacerraf problem, how abstract entities can exert causal agency, and the Gödel problem, how they can be perceived, can be regarded as a single problem: how can we be affected by them? One way to respond to this problem is to ignore it. For example, Willard Quine simply "ignore[d] the problem," said his Harvard colleague Hilary Putnam, "as to how we can know that abstract entities exist unless we can interact with them in some way."[72]

Other philosophers of mathematics have argued that these two problems, as well as the Platonic problem, cannot be ignored. Penelope Maddy, for example, puts the Benacerraf problem thus: "[H]ow can entities that don't even inhabit the physical universe take part in any causal interaction whatsoever? Surely to be abstract is to be causally inert. Thus if Platonism is true, we can have no mathematical knowledge."[73]

William Lycan, likewise, admits that his own appeal to mathematical sets "is indeed an embarrassment to physicalism, since sets et al. are nonspatiotemporal, acausal items." Accordingly, Lycan says, he must either naturalize mathematical sets or entirely reject set theory.[74]

To reject set theory would be to reject the existence of numbers. This extreme solution has, in fact, been advocated by several philosophers of mathematics, as illustrated by book titles such as *Science without Numbers* and *Mathematics without Numbers*.[75] However, this "nonrealist" or "formalist" solution, most commentators agree, suffers from a fatal problem: it is wholly inadequate to the presuppositions of mathematicians themselves. As Y. N. Moschovakis put it, in a representative statement,[76] this solution violates "the instinctive certainty of most everybody who has ever tried to solve a [mathematical] problem that he is thinking about 'real objects.'"[77]

The other remaining option suggested by Lycan, to "naturalize" the objects of mathematics by redefining them as aspects of material things, has been developed in Penelope Maddy's *Realism in Mathematics*, which seeks to develop a materialistic version of the Platonic or realist view. We can overcome the problem of "unobservable Platonic entities," she suggests, by "bringing [mathematical] sets into the physical world" so that they are no longer "abstract" but have "spatio-temporal location."[78]

This solution, however, is clearly desperate. What could it mean to say that the entire realm of mathematics is embodied in the physical world in such a way as to be observable? The problems of this move become even clearer when we reflect on the fact that only a small portion of the realm explored by pure mathematicians is exemplified in our world.

Philosophers have, as this discussion illustrates, been unable to come up with an adequate alternative to the traditional view, which explained both the locus and the efficacy of mathematical objects by placing them in an all-inclusive actuality. This fact suggests that science, insofar as it requires an intelligible worldview, will need to posit such an actuality. This conclusion will be stronger, of course, to the degree that it is supported by other considerations.

Larmore's Indispensability Argument for Moral Realism

One of these considerations is the fact that Quine's indispensability argument for realism about mathematical objects is paralleled by an indispensability argument for realism about moral norms. Charles Larmore argues that we cannot do justice to human experience unless we say, with Plato, that the world contains not only actual things but also a realm of values.[79] This affirmation, says Larmore, is necessary to do justice to our moral experience, which assumes—as even Mackie and Harman have admitted—that ordinary moral judgments presuppose moral truths that exist independently of our preferences.[80]

Moreover, adds Larmore, the affirmation of a realm of values is necessary in order to do justice not only to our moral values but also to our other normative values, including cognitive values about "the way we ought to think." For example, Larmore argues, Harman's denial of a normative realm makes it self-contradictory for him to argue that naturalism, understood as a worldview that denies the existence of normative values, should be accepted.[81]

In other words, the normal reasons for denying the reality of objective moral values cannot be defended without self-contradiction, because the reasons for doubting that moral values exist—such as Mackie's charge that they would be metaphysically "queer"—apply equally to *cognitive* values. But to deny that any objective cognitive values exist would mean that the idea that we ought to avoid self-contradiction is merely a preference, with no inherent authority.[82] And such a conclusion, Larmore points out, constitutes a *reductio ad absurdum*.

> Imagine thinking that even so basic a rule of reasoning as the avoidance of contradiction has no more authority than what we choose to give it. Imagine thinking that we could just as well have willed the opposite, seeking out contradictions and believing each and every one. Has anyone the slightest idea of what it would be like really to believe this?[83]

Larmore's overall point is that anti-Platonic naturalism, if carried through consistently, "would destroy the very idea of rationality." The affirmation of a normative realm, therefore, is implied by reason as such and hence by scientific reason in particular.[84]

In spite of the cogency of this argument, however, Larmore fails to develop his Platonism into an intelligible worldview. This failure is due partly to the fact that, as we saw earlier, Larmore insists that modernity requires that our explanations of both nature and morality be entirely nontheistic.[85] As a result, his position is weakened by his failure to answer the Platonic and the Benacerraf problems.

Larmore does at least acknowledge the Benacerraf problem, pointing out that some thinkers have rejected the existence of moral facts because they could not understand how such facts could be causally responsible for beliefs about them.[86] Larmore seeks to handle this problem by arguing that, besides causal explanations, there are also normative explanations, with normative truths being known not through perception—the reverse side of which would be causation—but through reflection.[87] As Larmore himself admits, however, there are "great difficulties" in this conception of normative knowledge.[88] Larmore fails, furthermore, even to acknowledge the Platonic problem.

Larmore's position is further weakened by the Gödel problem, because in spite of his Platonism, he does not challenge the modern consensus that perception is to be entirely equated with sensory perception. Larmore repeatedly says, in fact, that his position does not involve "some obscure faculty of 'intuition'"; and he rejects any analogy with mathematical knowledge.[89] He says, accordingly, that if all knowledge had to be based on perceptual experience, moral knowledge would be impossible.[90] But then, after proposing that the "organ" or "faculty" of moral knowledge is reason or reflection,[91] he rejects the Kantian idea that reason can "take over the function of grounding morality, now that God has been dispensed from the task."[92] As a result, his Platonic affirmation of ideal norms does not save him from a purely relativistic moral stance, in which our conscience is the voice not of eternity but merely of "our form of life."[93]

Larmore, in sum, makes an important contribution by pointing out that belief in an objective realm of normative values is as indispensable to our thought as is belief in an objective realm of mathematical truths. He does not provide a position that could overcome the modern crisis in moral theory, however, because of his endorsements of the sensationism and atheism of the late modern worldview.

The upshot of this discussion is that, late modern dogma notwithstanding, neither the philosophy of mathematics nor the philosophy of morals can be autonomous in the sense of being independent from theism. They can be made intelligible only within the framework of a theistic worldview (one component of which is a nonsensationist doctrine of perception). This was the position that Whitehead—who had spent much of his professional life dealing with mathematical principles—adopted in the last period of his life. Insofar as we see that even making sense of mathematics finally requires reference to theism, we can see that the return to theistic morality does not involve a return to heteronomy. I turn now to the way in which Whitehead's turn to a form of theism allowed him to overcome the problems in moral theory with which we have dealt.

WHITEHEAD ON GOD AND MORAL IDEALS

The Platonic and Benacerraf Problems

The point behind Hersh's metaphor of the grin needing the cat was made by Whitehead in terms of what he called the "ontological principle," one formulation of which is: "Everything must be somewhere; and here 'somewhere' means 'some actual entity.' Accordingly the general potentiality of the universe must be somewhere. . . . The notion of 'subsistence' is merely the notion of how eternal objects [Whitehead's term for Platonic forms] can be components of the primordial nature of God" (PR 46). Whitehead's ontological principle was hence explicitly intended as an answer to the Platonic problem as to where ideal entities (eternal objects) could exist.

The ontological principle also explicitly addresses the Benacerraf question about the source of the efficacy of ideal entities, saying, in another formulation, that "apart from things that are actual, there is nothing—nothing either in fact or in efficacy" (PR 40). Whitehead's answer to the Benacerraf problem, provided in advance, is that the eternal objects can be effective, in spite of having merely ideal existence, because the "primordial nature of God," which Whitehead also called "the Eros of the Universe," is "the active entertainment of all ideals, with the urge to their finite realization, each in its due season" (AI 11, 277).

Whitehead came to this view only late in life, after he began constructing a systematic metaphysics. Given his long involvement with mathematics and logic, he was aware that a metaphysical position would need to explain how the ideal entities studied by these disciplines could exist and be effective in the world. He also became convinced that his metaphysics needed to do justice to the fact that "the impact of aesthetic, religious and moral notions is inescapable" (MT 19). He realized, therefore, that his metaphysics had to have room not only for "mathematical Platonic forms," which he called "eternal objects of the objective species," but also for "eternal objects of the subjective species," which include normative values (PR 291).

Whitehead at first thought that an "envisagement" of the eternal objects, through which they could be effective in the world, could be attributed to what he in his first metaphysical book called the "underlying eternal energy" (SMW 105),[94] which he later called "creativity." He quickly realized, however, that he could not attribute any kind of activity, even "envisagement," to energy or creativity, because to do so would violate the ontological principle, which says that only *actualities* can act.

Whitehead's resulting conviction was that "the agency whereby ideas obtain efficiency in the creative advance" is "a basic Psyche whose active grasp of ideas conditions impartially the whole process of the Universe." Whitehead's formulation of this idea was an attempt, he said, at "understanding how the Ideals in God's nature, by reason of their status in his nature, are thereby persuasive elements in the creative advance" (AI 147, 168).

Given this conviction—that ideal entities, including moral and aesthetic ideals, can be effective in the world in general, and therefore in human experience in particular, only by virtue of being actively envisaged by an omnipresent actuality—our experience of ideals became evidence for the existence of such an actuality. In Whitehead's words: "There are experiences of ideals—of ideals entertained, of ideals aimed at, of ideals achieved, of ideals defaced. This is the experience of the deity of the universe.... The universe is thus understood as including a source of ideals. The effective aspect of this source is deity as immanent in the present experience" (MT 103). To give an accurate account of our moral experience, therefore, a moral philosopher needs to speak of God.

The Gödel Problem

Whitehead also provided an answer to the Gödel problem as to how we can perceive ideals even if they are presented to us energetically through the causal efficacy of a divine actuality. This answer is contained in his nonsensationist doctrine of perception, according to which we can have a direct perception (prehension) of the divine actuality (analogously to the way in which people's brain cells can prehend their psyches, as discussed in chapter 3).

In giving this answer to the Gödel problem, Whitehead was giving the same kind of answer that Gödel himself gave. This answer has, as we have seen, been widely rejected. This rejection has been due in part, of course, to the widespread prejudice against the idea of nonsensory perception that has obtained ever since the sensationist doctrine of perception acquired paradigmatic status as one of the key doctrines of the worldview that emerged victorious in the seventeenth-century battle of the worldviews (as described in chapter 2).

But there was also a second reason behind the fact that Gödel's suggestion was not taken seriously. His suggestion had the appearance of an ad hoc hypothesis, intended to explain only how we can know mathematical and logical truths. Whitehead's version of this suggestion, by contrast, is presented as part of his nonsensationist, prehensive doctrine of perception, which can be seen to be a natural implication of his panexperientialist worldview. This nonsensationist doctrine of perception can also be seen, as discussed in the first two chapters, to be necessary to explain the basis for a number of our hard-core commonsense ideas, such as the existence of causation, an actual world, the past, and time, in addition to our beliefs in normative values and in mathematical and logical truths.

The importance of this difference can be seen by recalling that one of John Mackie's main arguments against a direct perception of moral norms was that such a perception would be epistemologically queer, because "it would have to be by some special faculty of moral perception or intuition, utterly different from our ordinary ways of knowing everything else." It was because he assumed that moral intuition would presuppose some special faculty that Mackie overrode his own point, made against Kantians, that "'[m]oral sense' or 'intuition' is an ini-tially more plausible description of what supplies many of our basic moral judge-ments than 'reason.'"[95] As we also saw, Charles Larmore and Bernard Williams rejected the idea that we could have a direct perception of moral truths on the assumption that this idea required "some obscure faculty of 'intuition'" and that it amounted to no more than saying that "these truths were known, but there was no way in which they were known."[96] Whitehead's philosophy avoids these objections by showing that the perception of moral norms does not require an ad hoc postulation of some special "moral faculty" or "moral sense." Rather, we can perceive moral norms through a mode of perception that we share with other creatures and through which we know about the external world, causation, the past, time, and mathematical and logical forms.

The fact that Whitehead's response to the crisis in moral philosophy depends upon his doctrine of perception as well as this theism illustrates the point, made in chapter 2, "that process philosophy's naturalistic theism, or panentheism, is not a doctrine that can intelligibly be affirmed in isolation. It is instead an integral part of a new, overall worldview [naturalism$_{ppp}$]."[97] This point is further illustrated by the fact that a complete Whiteheadian response to the current crisis in moral theory would require a defense of human freedom of the type sketched in chapter 3, which depends upon the doctrine of panexperi-entialism. A complete response, in other words, would require all three dimen-sions of naturalism$_{ppp}$—its prehensive doctrine of perception and its panexperientialism, as well as its panentheism. The main emphasis of the pres-ent chapter, however, is that the panentheism *is* needed in order to respond to the Platonic and Benacerraf problems.

Moral Motivation

Whitehead also came to hold that theistic belief on the part of ordinary persons is necessary to sustain the moral point of view, especially in light of the fact that natural sympathy, on which Hume rested morality, does not extend, as Hume recognized, much beyond a rather limited circle (AI 36). Having pointed out that modern thought, from Hume to Darwin, has eroded the basis for the humanitarian ideal, which involves respect for human beings qua human beings, Whitehead suggested that we need "a reconstructed justification" for the cultivation of this respect (AI 28–38). In his own outline of such a justification, Whitehead ended by speaking of a "bond of sympathy" that can extend to all humanity. "This bond is the growth of reverence for that power in virtue of which nature harbours ideal ends, and produces individual beings capable of conscious discrimination of such ends. This reverence is the foundation of respect for man as man" (AI 86).

More and more philosophers, as we have seen, have come to the conclusion that motivation to live in terms of the moral point of view can finally be nourished only by a religious vision. Whitehead, besides coming to this conclusion many decades ago, also suggested, and provided a rational defense for, a new religious vision that does this while overcoming those aspects of traditional theism that have rightly caused offense.[98]

CONCLUSION

As pointed out in chapter 1, we can capture the nature of Whitehead's version of postmodernism better if we call it "postmodern modernism." In this phrase, "modernism" refers primarily to two formal commitments: the commitment to universal liberation, emphasized by Habermas, and the "modern commitment," so named by Gamwell, to base all truth claims on experience and reason rather than an appeal to authority. Thus far the results of these formal commitments have been highly ambiguous, in part because they were intertwined with various formal and substantive modern tendencies that undermined them.

To refer to Whitehead's position as "postmodern" modernism is to emphasize the fact that it has overcome at least some of those problematic tendencies. In previous chapters, I have shown how Whitehead overcame the materialistic view of nature (common to both dualism and materialism), the sensationist doctrine of perception, and the contentment with a divorce between theory and (some inevitable presuppositions of) practice. In the present chapter, I have shown how he also overcame, in part by replacing early modern theism and late modern atheism with a new conception of deity, the assumption that the rejection of heteronomy requires the rejection of theism of all sorts.

Part 3. The Coherence of Whiteheadian Theism

8

Relativity Physics and Whiteheadian Theism: Overcoming the Apparent Conflicts

The fact that Whitehead's version of postmodern philosophy involves a form of theism, best called "panentheism," has already been pointed out, especially in chapters 2, 4, 5, and 7, in which I have shown how it serves to overcome various problems. Some philosophers, however, have suggested that this form of theism is itself problematic. In this final part of the book we will examine two forms of this contention. In the present chapter, I argue against the common claim that relativity physics is incompatible with the temporalistic type of theism affirmed by Whiteheadian process philosophy. In the final chapter, I will examine Robert Neville's claim that Whitehead's process cosmology would be more adequate and coherent if its process theism were replaced by a radically different doctrine of God.

As just indicated, the doctrines of God articulated by Alfred North Whitehead and Charles Hartshorne are examples of what is more generally called "temporalistic" theism. Unlike classical theism, according to which God exists "outside of" or "above" time, temporalistic theism holds that time is real for God, in the sense that the distinctions between past, present, and future exist for God as well as for us. This means that God does not know the future—except insofar as certain abstract features of the future are already rendered certain by present facts—because "future events" do not yet exist to be known.

In the most consistent versions of temporalistic theism, such as those of Whitehead, Hartshorne, and other process theists, time is real for God because it belongs to the ultimate nature of reality. Time or temporal process, in other words, is not a contingent feature of reality, which was freely created by God, as classical theists say. Rather, it exists necessarily and hence eternally, in the sense that there have always been finite events that were influenced by antecedent

events and that influence subsequent events. Some temporalistic theists, however, believe that God freely created temporal processes, and thereby time, but
hold that, now that time exists, it is real even for God, so that God does not
know the details of the future (perhaps because of a voluntary self-limitation
upon divine omniscience). All temporalistic theists, in any case, say that the distinctions between past, present, and future obtain for God, so that God's present
experience divides events into those that have already happened, those that are
happening now, and those that have not yet happened.

One criticism of temporalistic theism has been that it, by implying that
there is an unambiguous cosmic "now," is contradicted by special relativity
physics. This issue has been discussed in relation to temporalistic theism in general[1] as well as in relation to process theism in particular. In the present chapter,
I deal with the issue in relation to the Whiteheadian-Hartshornean version of
process theism. At least most of this discussion, however, is relevant to other
versions of temporalistic theism.

HARTSHORNE'S QUANDRY

Hartshorne himself was unable to settle on a solution. He rested the case for his
philosophy on its coherence and its adequacy to the facts of experience, including the well-established teachings of the physical sciences. And yet he admitted
over the years that he had not reconciled his philosophy with this aspect of
physical theory. For example, in his response to William Reese in the 1991
Library of Living Philosophers volume, *The Philosophy of Charles Hartshorne*, he
said that Reese had raised "a problem, even *the* problem, for me: how God as
prehending, caring for, sensitive to, the creatures is to be conceived, given the
current non-Newtonian idea of physical relativity, according to which there is
apparently no unique cosmic present or unambiguous simultaneity."[2] Hartshorne
said, further, "that relating the divine becoming to the problem of simultaneity
in physics exceeds my capacity.... I feel incapable of solving the problem, and it
seems clear that Whitehead did not solve it."[3]

The failure to find a solution was not for want of trying. As Frederick Fost
helpfully documented in 1973,[4] Hartshorne had been perplexed by this difficulty
from the earliest period of his writing. And several other writers joined the
effort, including John T. Wilcox in 1961, Lewis Ford in 1968, and Paul Fitzgerald
in 1972.[5]

The admission by the world's preeminent process theist that he could not
reconcile his doctrine of God with relativity physics, especially after considerable attention had been devoted to the problem by him as well as several other
thinkers, constitutes a serious difficulty for process theism. Given Whitehead's
background in the physical sciences, process philosophy has been especially

concerned to be adequate to and illuminating of those "facts" that are considered to be well established by the physical sciences. To be incompatible with the special theory of relativity would seem to be a serious failure. Indeed, one critic, Royce Gruenler, has lifted up this incompatibility as a principal reason to reject process thought.[6]

Hartshorne, to be sure, was right to say that process philosophy need not solve every problem in order to have provided the best cosmology conceived thus far; it need only be superior to all the known alternatives.[7] Nevertheless, the idea that God temporally experiences the temporal world is so central to theistic process philosophy that advocates cannot rest content with an unresolved tension between this idea and relativity physics, so long as relativity physics itself is accepted. The same would be true, of course, of an apparent contradiction between process philosophy and any other apparently well-established result of the sciences. But Hartshorne's testimony that the tension between relativity physics and his theism had been *the* problem for him is reason to consider this tension as at least one of the most serious theoretical problems now facing process theist and, as Wilcox pointed out,[8] all temporalistic theists.

THE PROBLEM

The problem arises from the fact that process theism, like other forms of temporalistic theism, seems to presuppose a cosmic "now," while the special theory of relativity has seemed, at least to most interpreters who have discussed the issue, to entail that no such "now" exists.

To begin with relativity physics: I will not repeat here the detailed explanations, which can be found in the articles by Wilcox, Ford, and Fitzgerald, as to why, according to special relativity theory, a cosmic "now" apparently does not exist. The main point is summarized nicely by Fitzgerald:

> [A]ccording to relativity theory there is no such thing as absolute simultaneity for spatially separated events. Certain pairs of events A and B are such that whether A is to be regarded as occurring before B, simultaneously with B, or after B, depends on the coordinate-system with respect to which one judges. These event pairs, which Whitehead calls "contemporaries" of one another, are picked out by the fact that no light signal traveling even *in vacuo* from either could reach the other. This entails that what counts as "the past" or "the future" is also relative to coordinate-systems.[9]

As Fitzgerald's statement makes clear, the problem exists only with regard to spatially separated events, meaning ones that are *contemporaneous with each other in the sense that they cannot be connected by a light signal.* Every given event has an absolute past, which affects it, and an absolute future, which it affects. But an indefinite number of events are contemporary with the given event. Of these contemporaneous events, finite observer A will calculate that one set of them will be strictly simultaneous with the given event; observer B, operating with a different coordinate system, will calculate another set of events as being strictly simultaneous; observer C, operating with yet another coordinate system, will provide yet another answer; and so on. Wilcox summarizes the main point by saying: "There is physically no unique meaning for simultaneity in the case of causally separate events."[10]

Process theism, by contrast, seems to require the existence of a universe-wide "now." Hartshorne, for example, said: "I suppose God to have this cosmic *now* as his psychological simultaneity."[11] The reason for this requirement is the idea that God prehends only actual occasions that have, by completing their concrescences, achieved "satisfaction." God does not prehend future actual occasions, because there are none to prehend (they exist at most as anticipated probabilities). And God does not prehend actual occasions that are presently concrescing because they, not yet being "beings," have no determinate satisfaction to be prehended.

The divine experience, accordingly, divides the universe, or knows the universe to be divided, into the *past* universe, which causally influences the present divine experience, the *future* universe, which the present divine experience will influence, and the *present* universe—the cosmic "now"—which the present divine experience neither influences nor is influenced by. ("Universe" here is taken to mean the totality of finite occasions of experience, even though in abstraction from God's all-inclusive experience it would be more a multiverse than a universe.) Fitzgerald sums up the resulting problem: "[Relativity theory's] teaching that the world lacks a unique cosmic advance of time makes it hard to see why a cosmic being like God should experience a unique one."[12]

Hartshorne's form of process theism, according to which God is a personally ordered society of divine occasions of experience, makes even clearer than Whitehead's that a cosmic "now" is presupposed. In Whitehead's view, according to which God is one everlasting actual entity, God is in "unison of becoming" with all worldly occasions and yet somehow prehends and is prehended by them. By thereby suggesting that God and contemporary occasions could prehend each other, Whitehead's position does not make so acute the question of whether unambiguous distinctions between past, present, and future occasions could exist.

One difficulty with Whitehead's position, however, is that it renders problematic the interaction between God and the world. Whitehead had said that God should not be made an exception to general metaphysical principles (PR 343). Yet the causal independence of contemporaries seems to be a metaphysical principle of his system. This principle is not arbitrary but rests on the fact that an occasion while in the process of concrescence is still becoming determinate so that, before reaching satisfaction, it has nothing determinate to offer. What is particularly hard to understand is how God, if always a becoming subject, could be prehended by worldly occasions. A. H. Johnson reports having asked Whitehead: "If God never 'perishes,' how can he provide data for other actual entities? Data are only available after the 'internal existence' of the actual entity 'has evaporated'" (citing PR 220). In response, Whitehead reportedly said: "This is a genuine problem. I have not attempted to solve it."[13] It was partly to solve this problem that Hartshorne redefined God as a *personally ordered society* of divine occasions, so that God perpetually oscillates between being subject and object. But in solving this problem, Hartshorne rendered more acute the problem of the compatibility of process theism with relativity physics.

Some critics of the Hartshornean societal view of God believe, in fact, that it not only renders the incompatibility between God and relativity physics more acute but actually first creates this incompatibility. Lewis Ford, for example, argued in 1968 that if Hartshorne's view is that "each divine occasion constitutes one particular duration of simultaneity, then God's experience defines a privileged inertial system contrary to relativistic principles" and that Hartshorne's attempts to avoid this conclusion result in a position lacking simplicity and elegance.[14]

Ford then suggested a solution based on Whitehead's view of God as a single actual entity. Subsequently, however, Ford decided that that solution is untenable, in part because the attempt to return to Whitehead's view of God involves "insuperable difficulties."[15] The chief of these is the one I discussed earlier. In Ford's words: "Despite some very ingenious efforts to resolve or to avoid the problem, the central difficulty remains: in Whitehead's philosophy two concurrent concrescences cannot prehend each other. If God is an everlasting concrescence, it is difficult to see how it could influence present concrescences."[16] Nevertheless, while no longer using the clash between Hartshorne's idea of God and relativity physics as a reason simply to return to Whitehead's idea of God (rather than modifying it), Ford has continued to cite this clash as the chief problem with Hartshorne's theism, saying that each Hartshornean divine occasion "defines a privileged meaning of simultaneity contrary to relativity physics."[17]

The extent to which Hartshorne himself felt the problem is shown by the fact that he was sometimes tempted to try to solve it by giving up, or at least severely modifying, the notion of the divine individuality. Instead of speaking simply of "God," Hartshorne once suggested, we would speak of "God here now." That this would be a drastic move was seen by Hartshorne: "If *God here now* is not the same concrete unit of reality as God somewhere else 'now,' then the simple analogy with human consciousness as a single linear succession of states collapses."[18] Given Hartshorne's earlier insistence that "the unity of our experience is the unity in which everything is initially found, and only by abstraction from or analogy with this unity can we understand any concrete unity,"[19] this move, as Fost has pointed out,[20] would be no minor modification on Hartshorne's part. Although Fitzgerald has opined that, of the various views he has considered, a version of this view, which he calls the "God of Infinitely Interlaced Personalities," "does the least violence to relativity theory and process philosophy together,"[21] most process theists would surely prefer another solution, if such is available.

A POSSIBLE SOLUTION

It is important to realize that almost all the published discussions of process theism and relativity physics, including all the possible solutions surveyed by Fitzgerald, have assumed that relativity theory gives us the best clue currently available to the nature of time. Fitzgerald, for example, says: "If we assume that relativity theory is giving us something close to the truth about space-time, at least in our present cosmic epoch, and is not simply a computational device with no ontological significance, then we must be sure that any form of process theology which we are to accept is tuned to harmonize with it."[22] Given this assumption, which Hartshorne himself generally accepted, the issue is how to make our idea of God compatible with the fact that physical interaction among worldly events provides no unambiguous meaning for past, present, and future.

Another way to solve the problem, however, would be to say, as suggested in chapter 6, that Einsteinian special relativity physics does not provide the metaphysical truth, or even the ultimate cosmological truth, about time. Hartshorne himself once made this suggestion, saying that "there is the haunting question, can physics, judging reality from the standpoint of localized observers, give us the deep truth about time as it would appear to a non-localized observer?"[23]

Hartshorne's way of putting the question suggests that the deeper truth about time might be discernible only by God, and this is likely true. But the question before us is whether we, from our standpoint as localized observers, can see some way in which a nonlocalized omniscient observer, knowing the universe truly, would know it to have a universal "now." If so, we could challenge the assumption that time as defined by relativity physics should be accepted as the ultimate truth about time, even in our cosmic epoch.

A crucial fact about the special theory of relativity, at least as usually interpreted, is that it assumes, in Fitzgerald's words, "that no causal influence can be transmitted faster than the speed of light *in vacuo*."[24] This assumption lies behind standard interpretations of the "light cone," which contains an indefinite number of events that are "contemporaries" with any given event. For example, it takes over eight minutes for the light from the sun to reach the earth, and the same amount of time for light released from the earth to reach the sun. Accordingly, all the events in the sun's life for over sixteen minutes are said to be contemporaneous with the present moment of my experience, because those events can neither influence that experience nor be influenced by it—assuming that no supraluminal influences occur.

Relativity physics can also be interpreted, however, as simply not speaking to the issue of whether or not supraluminal influences occur. On this interpretation, if some such influence *does* occur, it would not necessarily contradict relativity physics. As John Lucas says, "Einstein's principle of relativity is concerned only with electromagnetic phenomena, and tells us that, *so far as those phenomena are concerned*, all inertial frames of reference are equivalent."[25] In James Devlin's words, "relativity physics is concerned with influence as limited by maximum signal speed, that of light."[26] "Supraluminal" influence might not involve faster-than-light signals; the influence might be different in kind from that involved in "signals."

Whitehead suggested that some such influence occurs. He did, to be sure, announce his adoption of "the 'relativity' view of time," which entails, contrary to "the classical 'uniquely serial' view of time," that "no two actual entities define the same actual world" (PR 65–66). In one place, Whitehead suggested that his adoption of the relativity view in place of the classical view was partly "because it seems better to accord with the general philosophical doctrine of relativity which is presupposed in the philosophy of organism" (PR 66). In another place, however, he said that this adoption "is based on scientific examination of our cosmic epoch, and not on any more general metaphysical principle" (PR 125).

I believe that Whitehead's second statement more correctly portrays his position. To explain: he rejected the classical view, he said in one place, because "its consequences, taken in conjunction with other scientific principles, seem to be false" (PR 66). The "other scientific principles" here would seem to include the limitation of causal influence to the speed of light. Elsewhere, however, Whitehead spoke of a kind of causal influence that would seem not to be thus limited. With light signals and other forms of radiation, the influence between remote loci is transmitted (in Whitehead's cosmology) through a series of contiguous occasions. The speed of light evidently indicates an upper limit on the speed by which such causal influence can be transmitted. But Whitehead in places also referred to a kind of influence between remote occasions that is not transmitted through contiguous occasions.[27]

Such direct causal influence between noncontiguous events is implied in Whitehead's discussion of the world as a transmitting medium.

> Any actual entity, which we will name A, feels other actual entities, which we will name B, C, and D. Thus B, C, and D all lie in the actual

world of A. But C and D may lie in the actual world of B, and are then felt by it; also D may lie in the actual world of C and be felt by it.... Now B, as an initial datum for A's feeling, also presents C and D for A to feel through its mediation. Also C, as an initial datum for A's feeling, also presents D for A to feel through its mediation. Thus, in this artificially simplified example, A has D presented for feeling through three distinct sources: (i) directly as a crude datum, (ii) by the mediation of B, and (iii) by the mediation of C.... There are thus three sources of feeling, D direct, D in its nexus with C, and D in its nexus with B. (PR 226)

Whitehead's focus in this passage is on the way in which the remote actual occasions are felt through the mediation of occasions that are contiguous with the prehending subject; and yet in passing he mentions that this subject also prehends the remote occasions *directly*. There is, accordingly, causal influence at a distance. And, with regard to spatial distance, there would be no reason to suppose that this direct influence at a distance would require the same time as that needed for influence transmitted through a sequence of contiguous occasions. The influence might, in fact, be instantaneous. By *instantaneous*, I mean that, as soon as the occasion had completed its concrescence, achieving satisfaction, it would exert a type of influence upon all prehending occasions, regardless of their spatial location.

Whitehead discussed this issue more explicitly in another passage, in which the topic was the notion in science of 'continuous transmission.' This notion, he said, must be understood in terms of "the notion of immediate transmission through a route of successive quanta of extensiveness." "Immediate" refers, he had explained, to the (direct) objectification of contiguous occasions, in contrast with the (indirect) objectifications of the more distant past, which he calls "mediate." The "successive quanta of extensiveness," he explained, are the "basic regions of successive contiguous occasions" (PR 307).

Thus far, in speaking of causal influence as transmitted through series of contiguous events, Whitehead seemed to be endorsing the dominant modern view, which is that there is no causal influence at a distance.[28] But he then added: "It is not necessary for the philosophy of organism entirely to deny that there is direct objectification of one occasion in a later occasion which is not contiguous to it. Indeed, the contrary opinion would seem the more natural for this doctrine" (PR 307–08).

Having affirmed a type of causal influence at a distance, Whitehead then quickly added two qualifications perhaps designed to assure the reader that this idea, while metaphysically heretical, should not be threatening to cosmologists. Here is the first qualification: "Provided that physical science maintains its denial of 'action at a distance,' the safer guess is that direct objectification is practically negligible except for contiguous occasions; but that this practical negligibility is a characteristic of the present cosmic epoch, without any metaphysical generality" (PR 308).

This qualification suggests that the implications of this idea of influence at a distance are almost entirely metaphysical, having little if any significance for science. Because this type of influence is probably "practically negligible" in our cosmic epoch—assuming, of course, that physical science continues to find no evidence of it—it can, Whitehead suggested, be ignored by scientific cosmologists.

The second qualification involves a distinction between two species of physical prehensions: pure and hybrid.

> A pure physical prehension is a prehension whose datum is an antecedent occasion objectified in respect to one of its own *physical* prehensions. A hybrid [physical] prehension has as its datum an antecedent occasion objectified in respect to a *conceptual* prehension. Thus a pure physical prehension is the transmission of physical feeling, while hybrid prehension is the transmission of mental feeling. (PR 308)

This distinction allowed Whitehead to endorse the widespread scientific assumption that no causal influence at a distance occurs with regard to the causal relations studied by physicists, which Whitehead called "pure physical prehensions," while still allowing for a type of influence at a distance: "There is no reason to assimilate the conditions for hybrid prehensions to those for pure physical prehensions. . . . [T]he doctrine of immediate objectification for the mental poles and of mediate objectification for the physical poles seems most consonant to the philosophy of organism in its application to the present cosmic epoch." The lack of revolutionary implications for physical cosmologists is further suggested by the illustrations of influence at a distance offered by Whitehead: "This conclusion has some empirical support, both from the evidence for peculiar instances of telepathy, and from the instinctive apprehension of a tone of feeling in ordinary social intercourse" (PR 308). Because the only illustrations of hybrid physical prehensions offered by Whitehead involve human minds, it would be easy for the reader to conclude, given the usual dualistic assumptions, that influence at a distance has no implications whatsoever for physical cosmology.

Whitehead failed explicitly to bring out here the fact that this idea might have at least one implication for physical cosmology. More precisely, whereas it might not have any direct implications for physical cosmology as such (at least if physical cosmology is understood to deal only with those types of causal influences that Whitehead calls "pure" physical prehensions, and if these are indeed effective only between contiguous occasions), this idea of causal influence at a distance could have implications for the status of physical cosmology insofar as it embodies the special theory of relativity. This implication would be that this physical cosmology with its understanding of time would not be assumed to be definitive for the ultimate nature of time.

We could, therefore, affirm the existence of a preferred frame of reference, as John Lucas has pointed out. Earlier I quoted the observation by Lucas that "Einstein's principle of relativity is *concerned only with electromagnetic phenomena*, and tells us that, so far as those phenomena are concerned, all inertial frames of reference are equivalent." Just prior to that statement, Lucas had said: "Contrary to much recent thinking, there is nothing wrong with preferred frames.... [If telepathy were accepted as] a mode of instantaneous transmission of messages..., we should have both Absolute Simultaneity and Absolute Space. There is nothing wrong with these concepts."[29] Lucas later adds that although the idea of events known by God to be "really simultaneous" plays no part in the special theory of relativity, it also is not inconsistent with it.[30]

From this perspective, the scientific theory known as the special theory of relativity would not be assumed to have settled the metaphysical (or even the ultimate cosmological) truth about time. The assumption that it has, of course, is what has generated the apparent conflict between temporalistic theism and relativity theory. To cite Wilcox's statement again: "There is physically no unique meaning for simultaneity in the case of causally separate events."[31] The conflict is generated by the assumption that because there is *physically* no such meaning for events that are causally separate (with "causality" defined in terms of light signals), there is *metaphysically* no such meaning.

This assumption can be seen to depend on what Whitehead has criticized as the "fallacy of misplaced concreteness." The main form of this fallacy, as we saw in chapter 6, is that of taking the abstractions about some actuality that are focused on by some particular science, due to its limited interests, to be a complete description of the actuality in its concreteness. We explored in that chapter the way in which physical science, by abstracting from the fact that individual events prehend the past and anticipate the future, has difficulty affirming the reality of time in the "physical world." We also saw how Whitehead's position, by overcoming the fallacy of misplaced concreteness, can affirm that asymmetrical, irreversible time exists for individual atoms and electrons. By following Whitehead's analysis of actual entities, accordingly, we need not try to figure out how God as temporal could have interacted with a world that was nontemporal for billions of years (let alone trying to figure out what that might mean). A similar situation exists, I suggest, with respect to the relativity view of time.

The relativity view of time could be said to follow from that form of misplaced concreteness that involves equating, at least implicitly, an actual entity's entire causal influence with that aspect of its causal influence that results from its physical pole and thus with what can be called—by extrapolation from "pure physical prehension"—its "pure physical causation." On the basis of that assumption (combined with the correlative assumptions that all pure physical causation occurs between contiguous events and that the speed of light *in vacuo* is the fastest that such causal influence can be transmitted), it would follow that there is no causal relation of any kind that occurs more quickly than those relations limited to the speed of light. The physical theory would then also state a metaphysical truth, or at least an ultimate cosmological truth.

Whitehead's more complete account of actual entities in their concreteness, however, suggests that this would not be the case. All actual entities have mental poles as well as physical poles. On the basis of this distinction, he suggested that there must be two kinds of causal influence between actual entities: (what I am calling) "hybrid" physical causation as well as (what I am calling) "pure" physical causation. He then added that, assuming that the pure kind of physical causation occurs only between contiguous events, there is no reason to assume the hybrid form to be thus limited. And, although Whitehead did not spell this out, the implication would seem to be that this direct causal influence at a distance, not being transmitted through a chain of contiguous events, would "arrive" faster than the speed of light. Whitehead would thereby have seemingly affirmed supraluminal causal influence, so that events that are considered "spacelike separated" in physical relativity theory would not necessarily be causally separated in every sense. The ultimate truth about time, even in our cosmic epoch, would thus not be provided by special relativity theory. Whiteheadian relativity would include, but not be limited to, Einsteinian relativity.

If this *is* the implication of Whitehead's allowance for direct prehension of noncontiguous events, why he evidently did not see it is a puzzle. Perhaps it was because he came to the distinction between pure and hybrid physical prehensions late, while he was hurriedly finishing up *Process and Reality*. If that is the explanation, one might still think that he would, while reading proofs, have reversed or at least qualified his adoption of the relativity view of time. But Whitehead was not a careful proofreader; and Lewis Ford's reconstruction of the composition of *Process and Reality* suggests that Whitehead quite often let passages stand after he had developed a new doctrine.[32] However, even if such considerations can account for Whitehead's failure to qualify his adoption of the relativity theory of time in *Process and Reality*, we could reasonably expect that some such recognition would appear in later writings. He does indeed, in *Adventures of Ideas*, reaffirm his belief in what he had earlier called "hybrid" physical feelings.

> Perhaps . . . although the antecedence and the consequence,—the past, the present and the future—still hold equally for physical and mental poles, yet the relations of the mental poles to each other are not subject to the same laws of perspective as are those of the physical poles.

> Measurable time and measurable space are then irrelevant to their mutual connections. Thus in respect to some types of Appearance there may be an element of immediacy in its relations to the mental side of the contemporary world. (AI 248)

Whitehead does not in this passage say that his doctrine undermines the assumption that special relativity theory gives us something like the truth about the relations between past, present, and future. He does, however, make explicit one point that was left implicit in *Process and Reality*: the fact that "measurable time" is irrelevant seems to mean that the direct prehension of a remote event would involve a supraluminal influence, which would implicitly undermine that assumption.

If supraluminal influences occur, the next question would be: how "supra" are they? Do they occur at a supraluminal but still finite speed? Or are they instantaneous? The passage does not speak directly to this issue—unless the reference to "immediacy" suggests an instantaneous relation. In any case, this would be a natural assumption to make. If the present subject *directly* prehends remote as well as contiguous events, then the influence from the remote and the contiguous events would be exerted on the prehending subject simultaneously.

To refer to an instantaneous causal relation between noncontiguous events would *not*, of course, be to speak of a causal prehension of "contemporaries" in the strictest sense, meaning occasions that are in "unison of becoming" with each other. The instantaneous influence at a distance would occur, as with any causal influence, only after the occasion's concrescence had resulted in satisfaction. The "elbow-room" within the universe (AI 195) would still be preserved.

This instantaneous influence *would* mean, however, that most of those remote events that are considered contemporaries within special relativity theory would be connected by causal relations (of the hybrid physical sort) going in one direction or the other. For example, my present experience would be affected, even if negligibly, by all the events occurring on the sun from about eight minutes ago up to a fraction of a second ago; and my present experience would exert causal efficacy—surely of the most negligible sort—upon events occurring on the sun over the next eight minutes (as well as beyond). Furthermore, if the influence is truly instantaneous, having no travel time, then the effect upon a location a million light-years away would occur simultaneously with that upon a location an inch away. This is a staggering thought, of course; but it would seem to follow, if there truly is some kind of instantaneous influence.

To adopt this view would not mean a simple return to a prerelativistic universe, for the reason indicated in the next paragraph. It would, however, give us what could be called a "postrelativistic" universe, in which all events are unambiguously either in the past of, or in the future of, or contemporary with, all other events. There would be, accordingly, a cosmic "now," dividing all events into either the past, the future, or the present, with the present being comprised exhaustively of events in unison of becoming. The assumption behind all this is that, with regard to the kind of causality that is exerted instantaneously rather than with merely the speed of light, different inertial systems would not lead to different assessments of simultaneity. For example, three perceivers in three different parts of the universe and in motion with respect to each other would all agree, insofar as they could detect the subtle kind of influence in question, as to what set of events in the universe had just occurred.

If these assumptions and conclusions are valid, there would then be no conflict between Einsteinian physical cosmology and temporalistic theism. Special relativity theory could be retained as a theory with great significance, but with limited scope. That is, it would be seen as specifying the implications of taking into consideration only that form of causal influence that is generally most powerful, namely, pure physical causation. But it would not be thought to carry the additional weight of indicating an ultimate metaphysical truth about the nature of time. We would come to understand it as a theory only about causality—namely, the kind of efficient causality that does not (at least usually) occur at a distance and is by far the most powerful kind of efficient causality[33]—rather than as also a theory about time. This new interpretation would not, however, break the connection between time and causality altogether. The past would still be defined in terms of all those events that causally influence the present. The difference is that now it would be the instantaneous hybrid physical causation, rather than the (at least usually) slow-as-light pure physical causation, that would have the privileged position of defining the past, the future, and the present.

One would not, accordingly, need to revise temporalistic theism to make it compatible with cosmology by, perhaps, thinking of God as the chief exemplification of the multiple personality syndrome, or by putting God as a whole back outside of time, or by positing that God creates a cosmic "now" that would not otherwise exist, or by any other stratagem. One could assume, instead, that God knows a cosmic "now" simply by knowing reality as it is. That is, although God, as the all-inclusive perceiver, would be the only being who *knows* the cosmic "now," this cosmic "now" would not first result from God's perception and/or activity.

I should add that, to overcome the charge that special relativity theory rules out the possible coherence of temporalistic theism, one need not prove the reality of an instantaneous influence that produces a cosmic "now." After all, no one has any proof that such an influence does not occur, and only with such a proof could one argue definitively that special relativity physics provides metaphysical, or even ultimate cosmological, truth. The intelligibility of temporalistic theism with regard to this issue is defended if the idea of a cosmic "now" grounded in instantaneous influences can be made plausible.

The idea of instantaneous action at a distance is, to be sure, one that makes many intellectuals nervous. One of the chief aims of modern ideology has been to discredit this idea and anyone publicly admitting to accepting it, and this ide-ology has performed its task well. Nevertheless, things are changing rapidly with regard to this issue, especially in the physics community. Physical theories based on the notion of instantaneous action at a distance have, for example, been developed by both David Bohm and Henry Stapp, and they have both expressed essential agreement with the proposal made above. In a letter to me of April 16, 1992, Stapp wrote:

> I agree essentially with your views.... Physicists have never showed, or claimed to show, that there *could not be* a sequence of preferred global 'nows' that define absolute simultaneity. They simply abandoned the idea for practical reasons (abetted by a positivistic philosophy that is now in disrepute). If the laws of nature exhibit Lorentz invariance, as they currently appear to do, then it turns out to be impossible to ascer-tain the forms of these preferred global 'nows' from the empirical data available to physicists. Thus there was no compelling reason within physics to hang onto the concept of global 'nows,' and a good practical reason for dropping it: the elimination of the concept made it techni-cally easier to exploit the property of the Lorentz invariance of the laws of physics.
>
> Few if any physicists of today would claim that any deep metaphys-ical ontological conclusions could be deduced (with any high degree of confidence) from those practical considerations. For one thing, we are now aware of the 2.7 blackbody background radiation, which appears to define a preferred reference frame within which massive objects tend to move 'slowly.' For another thing, Kurt Gödel has noted that there are preferred definitions of global 'nows' in all the models in general rela-tivity (see *Albert Einstein: Philosopher/Scientist*, ed. A. Schilpp, Tudor). Furthermore, the idea that there is no preferred sequence of global 'nows' seems to entail that the whole spacetime universe already exists, in some absolute sense. That conclusion is hard to reconcile with our psychological feeling of the unfolding of nature, and with the quantum mechanical idea of indeterminism, which says that things are *not* already all laid out.
>
> The simplest picture of nature compatible with quantum theory is the model of David Bohm. It explains all of the empirical facts of a rel-ativistic quantum theory, including, in particular, the impossibility of transmitting 'signals' (i.e., controlled messages) faster than light. In spite of this complete agreement with relativistic quantum theory at the level of observed phenomena, and the strict prohibition of all observable faster-than-light effects, Bohm's model is based explicitly on the postulated existence of an advancing sequence of preferred global

'nows,' which single out a preferred reference frame for defining absolute simultaneity. In this frame there is an instantaneous action-at-a distance, which, however, does not disrupt the relativistic invariance at the level of observed phenomena. Bohm's model provides physicists with the simplest way of understanding all of the puzzling features of quantum phenomena in a completely clear way, provided one is willing to accept preferred global 'nows' at the fundamental level.

One of the most popular quantum ontologies of today is the model of Ghirardi, Rimini and Weber. This GRW model, like Bohm's model, is based on an advancing sequence of global 'nows.' It features a *well-ordered sequence of Heisenberg-type actual events*, each of which induces a large instantaneous action at a distance. Heisenberg-type actual events are the counterparts in modern science of Whitehead's actual occasions.

These remarks show that your proposals to accept, at the fundamental level, the concept of absolute simultaneity is very much in line with certain contemporary developments in physics. These developments have grown out of the need to extend quantum theory, in a rationally coherent way, beyond the domain of atomic physics. Hartshorne was, I believe, completely correct in recognizing the importance of this break with the positivistically inspired philosophical ideas of the past. Of course, some physicists remain wedded to the older idea, but the influence of positivism is on the wane: there is a growing feeling among physicists that it was wrong to dismiss the idea that science should provide, among other things, also 'understanding.'

David Bohm, in a letter of May 17, 1992, responded to my proposal in these terms:

I think we are in basic agreement about relativity. However, I would go further and suggest that at a deeper level, relativity doesn't hold *even physically*. More precisely, the idea is that relativity doesn't hold for *individual* quantum processes, but is valid only statistically. (The validity would include the classical limit, which arises when there is a large number of quantum processes, as the movement of grains of sand approximates a continuous movement that is determined by a simple law of flow.) For individual quantum processes, there would be a unique space-time frame, in terms of which "simultaneous contact" would be specified. The latter frame would be determined by the line connecting any given point to the presumed origin of the universe. Empirically, this should be close to the frame in which the mean velocity of the 3 K radiation background in space is zero.

This means that matter and mind share nonlocality, and have a common frame determining simultaneity. So matter and mind both share in one universal process of becoming.

These responses by Stapp and Bohm seem to show that, at the very least, my proposal cannot be rejected on the grounds that it is incompatible with physics.

GOD-WORLD SYNCHRONIZATION

Another point to make about this proposal is that it is not necessarily burdened with an assumption that has generally been thought to be part and parcel of the Hartshornean view of God as a personally ordered society: the assumption that the divine occasions must be extremely thin temporally. This assumption is sometimes used as a basis for rejecting the Hartshornean view. For example, Marjorie Suchocki has written that "the societal view... entails the problem that the number of unifications required in a series in order to match every single finite concrescence whatsoever defy probability."[34]

Hartshorne himself is the source of this problematic assumption. In 1941, after having stated his view that the divine present would be "an 'epochal' affair, not a mathematical instant," he continued:

> What will be the length of this epoch? I should suppose it would be identical with that of the shortest creaturely unit or specious present, since the perfect perception (physical prehension) will make whatever discriminations are necessary to follow the distinctions in the things perceived, no more and no less. The longer units will then be experienced by God as overlapping several of the shorter. But this involves problems of synchronization that inevitably baffle my lay mind.[35]

This assumption was reiterated by Hartshorne in 1964 in a statement that was only partially quoted earlier: "[T]he notion of a 'creative advance of nature' seems to imply a cosmic 'front' of simultaneity as short as the shortest specious present. I suppose God to have this cosmic *now* as his psychological simultaneity."[36]

The last sentence of the indented quotation above reveals Hartshorne's awareness that difficulties are created by his reasoning. A 1965 statement by John Cobb brings out the extent of the difficulties even more clearly while reinforcing the assumptions behind them:

> [W]e must ask how many occasions of experience would occur for God in a second. The answer is that it must be a very large number, incredibly large to our limited imaginations. The number of successive electronic occasions in a second staggers the imagination. God's self-actualizations must be at least equally numerous if he is to function separately in relation to each individual in this series. Since electronic

occasions are presumably not in phase with each other or with other types of actual occasions, still further complications are involved.[37]

One problem with this Hartshorne-Cobb assumption, especially in the light of the Bergsonian background of the Whiteheadian-Hartshornean ontology, is that it involves a reversal of what would otherwise seem to be a universal correlation. Henri Bergson, who anticipated Whitehead's idea of matter as consisting of repetitions of events with finite durations,[38] stressed that in different types of organisms the durations are different. In living organisms the durations are longer than those in subatomic individuals, and in human experience the durations are longer yet.[39] Bergson, to my knowledge, never explicitly said that there is a correlation between duration and spatial extensiveness, but the idea seems implicit. He suggested, for example, that photonic durations are to human durations as the latter are to the divine.[40]

Whitehead and Hartshorne seemed to presuppose the twofold idea that different levels of organisms have vastly different rhythms and that a positive correlation obtains between spatial and temporal extensiveness. The latter idea seemed even more clearly presupposed in Hartshorne, in that he explicitly stated that events of greater complexity occupy a more extensive spatial standpoint. The region of the living occasions of the cell, he said, includes the regions of all the subordinate constituents of the cell, and a human occasion of experience is coextensive with the entire brain, perhaps even the entire nervous system.[41]

It is odd, therefore, that Hartshorne would have considered the divine occasions, which are spatially far more extensive than all worldly occasions, to be temporally as thin as, or even thinner than, the briefest worldly occasions. One would, with Bergson, expect that the divine occasions, being coextensive with the entire universe, would be of greater duration than any other events. Why was that normal expectation reversed?

The reasons, which are suggested in the above quotations from Hartshorne and Cobb, are brought out more explicitly by John Robert Baker, in an article devoted to showing that the question of the divine present's temporal span is problematic for a Hartshornean conception of God. Baker reconstructs the Hartshorne-Cobb argument thus:

> God must be able to prehend the satisfaction of every actual entity of the temporal process. God's omniscience requires this. Furthermore, the satisfaction of a divine occasion must be able to be prehended by every incipient actual entity. God's creative role in the world requires this. It follows then that God's successive experiences must coincide with the inception and satisfaction of every actual entity, lest there be an actual entity for whom God is not available as an initial datum, or

an actual entity whose satisfaction is not prehended by God.... The frequency of the cosmic present, or the divine "psychological simultaneity," is such that no actual entity fails to be creatively related to God. God's life must be synchronized with the lives of every actual entity. What then is the temporal length of a divine occasion? God's successive experiences must be as rapid as those of any in creation, lest God's knowledge and creativity be diminished.[42]

Baker goes on to argue that, because—as the quotation from Cobb mentioned—the actual occasions of the world are surely not in phase, the divine occasions of experience must be temporally even thinner than those of subatomic entities.

Now that the assumptions are before us, they can be questioned. One of the assumptions is that, for God to be prehendable for each occasion of an experience in a personally ordered society, such as an electron, there would have to be a divine occasion that occurred after one electronic occasion (call it A) had achieved satisfaction and before the next occasion (B) began. God would prehend A and then, on the basis of this knowledge of A, provide an initial aim for B. It is this assumption (combined with the perfectly reasonable presupposition that the trillions of subatomic enduring individuals in the universe are not in phase with each other) that generates the conclusion that the divine occasions must be vanishingly thin. But why accept this assumption?

One reason to accept it would be the view of some—held as the correct reading of Whitehead and/or as ontological truth—that only contiguous occasions can be prehended. Accordingly, a divine occasion would have to be temporally (as well as spatially) contiguous with electronic occasion B for that occasion to prehend it; and that divine occasion would have had to be temporally contiguous with occasion A to prehend *it*. But if that view is rejected, both ontologically and as a reading of Whitehead, then one need not suppose that a divine occasion occurs between every pair of events in the world. One would then be free to adopt what I above called the "more natural" position.

According to that position, the divine occasions of experience, being more extensive spatially than other occasions, would also be more extensive temporally. Let us arbitrarily suppose, for the sake of discussion, that a divine occasion occurs every second. This would mean, assuming (for the sake of discussion) that there are ten human occasions of experience every second, that after God has responded to me in one moment, I would have ten occasions of experience prior to God's next response. In that response, God would become aware of those ten new occasions, then provide aims that would have to serve for my next ten occasions. With regard to electrons, of course, the lag would be much greater. A billion some electronic occasions would occur between divine responses.

One reaction to this suggestion might be that it would make God's guidance of the universe impossible. But an analogous situation exists, by hypothesis, in the mind-body relation. If every second there are, say, ten dominant occasions of experience and, say, one hundred living occasions in each brain cell, there would be ten cellular occasions between every dominant occasion. And yet the mind is able to provide tolerable guidance for the body.

A Hartshornean response to this suggestion of lengthier divine durations might be that it does not do justice to the idea of divine perfection, because it fails to portray God as the greatest conceivable being. Compared with a God who responds immediately to every new state of the world, Hartshorne might have said, a God who allows ten human occasions of experience, and a billion some subatomic experiences, to go by before responding knows the world less perfectly and provides less intimate guidance for the world. Although what I am calling the "more natural" view might be more *imaginable*—I am supposing the Hartshornean reply to be—the other view is logically possible and therefore *conceivable*. This other view must be maintained, therefore, if God is to be portrayed as a being greater than which none is conceivable, and hence as *God*.

The connection between divine perfection and extremely brief divine durations is found, incidentally, in the extract from Hartshorne at the outset of this section, which speaks of "perfect perception," and in the closing line of the quotation from Baker.

This connection, however, can be questioned, even on Hartshornean principles. Classical theists have long criticized process theism's God as imperfect because not capable of knowing the future and controlling the present. Hartshorne and his followers have long replied that "failure" to do the metaphysically impossible betokens no imperfection and that, because of the creativity inherent in the creatures, no conceivable being could (completely) control the present or (infallibly) know the future. Likewise, one dimension of the problem of evil is the question as to why God did not make human beings less dangerous. The Whiteheadian-Hartshornean reply, which I have developed,[43] is that a correlation between value and power is inherent in the metaphysical structure of reality so that any creatures with our high-level capacity for the realization of values would necessarily have power comparable to ours, including our power to deviate radically from the divine will and to inflict suffering upon others. Because this correlation between value and power is part of the metaphysical essence of reality, the fact that God did not create a world with less dangerous human-like beings betokens no divine imperfection.

In the same way, we can suppose, the normal correlation between spatial and temporal extensiveness is metaphysical. Accordingly, if God is the chief exemplification of the metaphysical principles, rather than an exception to them, the divine occasions would necessarily have a longer duration than any worldly occasions. No imperfection is entailed, therefore, by the fact that God neither knows each occasion as soon as it has occurred nor provides a fresh creative influence between every pair of occasions.

CONCLUSION

The idea that the special theory of relativity creates problems for temporalistic theisms, such as those of Whitehead and especially Hartshorne, arises from a combination of a fact and an assumption. The fact is that this theory does not provide the basis for a cosmic "now." The assumption is that this theory has ontological implications for the truth about time. Combining the fact and the assumption creates the idea that special relativity physics rules out the possibility of a cosmic "now." And that idea, if true, would rule out, or at least render highly problematic, the possible truth of temporalistic theisms in which God and the world interact.

We need not assume, however, that special relativity physics has ontological implications for the nature of time. And it does not have such implications if, as Whitehead's philosophy suggests, there is a mode of causal influence that is instantaneously exerted on noncontiguous events. This proposal receives support from some positions currently proposed by physicists, in which a cosmic "now" based on instantaneous effects is affirmed. The fact that the temporalistic theism of process philosophy implies the existence of a cosmic "now," accordingly, poses no problem for this form of theism.

A final point: this chapter has been based upon the assumption that Einsteinian relativity must provide at least the starting point for any discussion of the existence of a cosmic "now." Recently, however, this assumption has been powerfully challenged by Reginald Cahill, who has developed a "process physics." Although this new approach employs various ideas drawn from Whitehead, it is based, in the first place, on empirical evidence that challenges basic assumptions on which Einstein's theories were based. Cahill shows, in particular, that the standard interpretation of the Michelson-Morley experiment, according to which it revealed no evidence of absolute motion, is false, and that such evidence has been found in several subsequent experiments. For our present purposes, the most important implications of Cahill's approach are that space and time are decoupled, so that in place of the four-dimensional spacetime of Einstein we have three-dimensional space (with time understood as completely different from geometry); this three-space constitutes a "preferred frame of reference"; and the existence of "non-local instantaneous effects" means that there is "universal sychronicity."[44]

The fact that Cahill's cosmology is in harmony with the spirit of Whitehead's is shown by Whitehead's discussion of the notion of "the immediate present condition of the world at some epoch," which was part of "the old 'classical' theory of time." Saying that "the philosophy of organism accepts and defines this notion," he added that [s]ome measure of acceptance is forced upon metaphysics" by the very "obviousness" of its truth (PR 125).

9

Whiteheadian Theism: A Response to Robert Neville's Critique

Robert Cummings Neville has become one of America's leading philosophers, philosophical theologians, and Christian theologians, having produced a body of writing that is impressive both in quantity and quality. As his writings show, Neville likes and adopts—with a few modifications—Whitehead's cosmology, but he does not like Whiteheadian theism. He presents his own system, accordingly, as an alternative to process theology.[1]

Neville rejects process theism on the grounds that it is incoherent, superfluous, and descriptive of an alleged reality that would not be worthy of worship even if it existed. Neville's critique applies not only to Whitehead's own doctrine of God but also to that of Charles Hartshorne and to various other versions of process theism that are derivative from the ideas of one or both of these philosophers. To this extent, Neville endorses Donald Sherburne's call for "Whitehead without God."[2] Unlike Sherburne, however, Neville wants to eliminate the Whiteheadian God to make room for another God that is deemed to be coherent, necessary, and worthy of worship. Neville's twofold thesis, then, is that "Whitehead's conception of God is largely mistaken and that an alternate conception is to be preferred."[3]

In this chapter, I examine Neville's critique of Whiteheadian theism and his alternative concept of 'God.' This latter examination, while it cannot be thorough, is integral to my examination of Neville's claims, because his criticisms of process theism are largely comparative points, made with the superiority of his own idea of God in mind.

Although I agree that some of Neville's criticisms are cogent with respect to some versions of process theism, I will argue that these criticisms are not applicable to all versions of process theism. Interestingly, although Neville says "If theism is true, it is not true in the process form," he acknowledges that he has not examined all the versions of process theism.[4] In any case, I conclude that all his universal criticisms, meant to apply to all forms of process theism, fail. Regarding Neville's own idea of God, I suggest that it is the more appropriate bearer of the three attributes he applies to Whiteheadian theism: incoherent, superfluous, and unworthy of worship.

However, in making this threefold charge, which is as strong as Neville's charge against process theism, I want to stress a couple of Whiteheadian points that I think Neville also affirms: all dogmatism should be avoided in the formulation of theological doctrines, because in these matters we see in a glass very darkly, if at all; and different types of people, with different temperaments and different intuitions, require different formulations. This latter point does not necessarily imply contentment with a complete relativism, in which all mutual criticism is out of place. But my criticisms of Neville's doctrine of God are made less to show that it is wrong than to show that the same criticisms he finds convincing in relation to process theism can be made, by someone having different ultimate intuitions, with at least equal plausibility against his idea of God.

I organize my examination of Neville's critique of process theism in terms of the categories in which he himself summarizes his critique. In the first section, I examine what he calls the "ontological" issue. In the second section, the issue is God's presence and activity in the world. The third section focuses on the issue of the world's bearing on God. The fourth deals with the coherence of the (Hartshornean) societal view of God as a living person. My criticisms of Neville's own idea of God are spread throughout these four sections. I draw primarily, although not exclusively, upon Neville's *Creativity and God*, which he subtitled *A Challenge to Process Theology*.

THE ONTOLOGICAL ISSUE

Neville's Critique

Neville's first, and probably in his own mind most important, criticism of Whiteheadian process theism is that it provides no answer to what Neville calls the "ontological question." Neville, like Heidegger and Tillich, sometimes poses this as the question of why there is anything, rather than nothing at all.[5] But generally, agreeing with Charles Peirce that chaos needs no explanation, he says that the issue is why there is anything ordered, or better, why there is anything "definite," or "determinate," or "complex," or "determinately complex."[6] In application to Whitehead's cosmology, this means: Why are there any actual entities, which are complex unities, at all? Why does the category of the ultimate, in which the many and the one are united through creativity, obtain?[7]

Neville launches an internal criticism with the charge that Whitehead provides no answer to this question and, in fact, does not even raise it, although his own "ontological principle" implies that an answer is necessary. Why so? Because, Neville says, the ontological principle states that "anything complex is the result of decision," that "any complex state of affairs calls for an account by reference to the decisive actions that determine it."[8] The category of the ultimate is a complex unity, says Neville, because the many and the one are united in it through creativity. Whitehead's "ontological principle," therefore, requires that the category of the ultimate be explained by reference to a creative decision.

This ontological question, being unique, requires a unique kind of answer, one that speaks of a unique kind of causation or creativity. What Whitehead calls the "ontological principle," continues Neville, says that every particular effect within the cosmos must be explained in terms of the decision of one or more actual entities. Because this principle presupposes the existence of actual entities as such, it refers to cosmological causation and should, therefore, be called the "cosmological principle." To explain the category of the ultimate and thus the underlying unity of the one and the many through creativity, which makes actual entities possible, we must speak of "ontological creativity," or "ontological causation."[9] This kind of causation must explain, not presuppose, the existence of determinately complex unities and must account for Whitehead's so-called ontological principle itself.[10]

This issue is central to Neville's religious vision. For him, to speak of ontological causation is to speak of "a spiritual or religious dimension to things."[11] Not to raise and answer the ontological issue is to fail to take responsibility for our own existence, to forsake the true center and meaning of existence. It results in idolatry, meaning "the attempt to make some cosmological part of the world play those ontological roles."[12]

In saying this, Neville has implicitly accused Whitehead of idolatry. Elsewhere he is more explicit, saying in opposition to Whitehead's God: "I think nothing short of the ground or principle of the whole of things is supreme enough to be worshiped."[13] Whitehead's God is not worthy of worship, Neville holds, because this God is finite, not the infinite source of everything determinate.

The fatal flaw in Whitehead's theism, in Neville's opinion, is his distinction between God and creativity. It is this distinction that makes Whitehead's God finite, he maintains, preventing this God from providing an answer to the ontological question of why anything complex or determinate exists at all.

Although Neville sometimes says that Whitehead gives no answer to the ontological question, he elsewhere says that Whitehead did, at least implicitly, offer an answer: "The ontological question as to why there exist any cosmological unities," says Neville, "is answered, allegedly, by the category of the ultimate."[14] The question is, "Why does there exist a unification of that manifold of actual entities?" Whitehead's answer is, "Where there is a many, creativity creates a one unifying them."[15] But, Neville says, creativity is for Whitehead merely an empirical generalization, not a normative principle saying that pluralities *must* get unified. Therefore, Neville concludes, "the category of the ultimate does not genuinely address the ontological question."[16]

Although Neville's reason for drawing this conclusion can be questioned (and will be, below), his conclusion as such is correct. Whitehead does not say, or imply, that "creativity creates." That would be to violate his ontological principle, that only actual entities can act and therefore be reasons. Because creativity as such is not an actuality, it cannot be the reason for the existence of actual entities. Although it might be thought that the ontological principle applies only to what Neville calls "cosmological causation," therefore being inapplicable to what Neville calls "ontological causation," that distinction is foreign to Whitehead. He neither explicitly nor implicitly has a category of ontological causation. His principle of coherence forbids it. I will come to that in a moment.

First, however, I must look at Neville's consideration of a second possible answer to his ontological question: that an answer is given by the doctrine that the primordial nature of God is a primordial *decision*. The crucial text is that God's "conceptual actuality at once exemplifies and establishes the categorical conditions" (PR 344).[17]

Neville contends, rightly in my view, that this answer would be untenable, because Whitehead's statement is self-contradictory. If, on the one hand, the principles are already determinate prior to the divine decision, so that it *exemplifies* them, then it does not *establish* them. If, on the other hand, the divine decision really does establish them, then it could not exemplify them. In either case, something determinate and complex is presupposed, either God or the metaphysical principles, so that no answer is given to the existence of determinate complexity as such.[18] More generally, Neville argues that creativity, "being complex, must be the result of some decision," and Whitehead says that the primordial nature of God presupposes creativity.[19] The primordial decision of God cannot, therefore, provide the answer to the ontological question.

This discussion sets the stage for Neville's own doctrine of God. He suggests that we think of God as the ontological creator, who creates the metaphysical principles and everything else that is determinate.[20] His doctrine does not presuppose the prior existence of something determinate because, prior to creating the world, this God is not determinate: "the only determinate character which God has is what he gives himself in creating."[21]

Evaluating Neville's Critique

Although Neville assumes that he has thereby made an advance, making the world more intelligible than Whitehead did, this assumption is questionable.

The main problem is whether this idea of divine creation, according to which that which is absolutely formless and indeterminate gives rise to everything that is formed or determinate, is intelligible. In other words, does "ontological causation" make any sense? I will argue later that it does not, that it is an incoherent idea.

Besides being incoherent, Neville's doctrine is, I claim, superfluous. There is no need to search for a causal explanation of the category of the ultimate and the other metaphysical principles exemplified by them. Neville claims, as we have seen, that this search is necessitated by Whitehead's own ontological principle, but let us look more closely. In a characteristic passage, Neville says that the ontological principle stipulates that "anything definite or complex needs to be explained by reference to the various decision points which determined it to be the way it is."[22] For support, he cites the passage in which Whitehead formulates the eighteenth category of explanation. However, neither in this passage nor in any other formulation of the ontological principle does Whitehead say that everything definite, determinate, or complex must be referred to a decision.[23]

If Neville's formulation is inaccurate, what then is the true scope of the ontological principle? To what type of things does it apply? While recognizing that a few passages (those attributing metaphysical principles to a primordial divine decision) are inconsistent with this view, I have argued that the ontological principle should be understood to apply only to contingent, arbitrary, or merely "given" features of the world, as distinct from metaphysical features, which exist necessarily.

For example, in one of his longer formulations of the ontological principle, Whitehead defines it as "the principle that the reasons for things are always to be found in the composite nature of definite actual entities—in the nature of God for reasons of the highest absoluteness, and in the nature of definite temporal actual entities for reasons which refer to a particular environment."[24] The crucial question here is how to interpret "reasons of the highest absoluteness." This phrase could be taken as a reference to the metaphysical principles. Regardless of what Whitehead had in mind while writing the passage, however, I contend that we should not interpret the ontological principle in this way, for a reason that has support in Whitehead's own writings as well as making sense in itself. I quote here the argument I gave in *God, Power, and Evil* (the pagination for *Process and Reality* has here been changed to that of the corrected edition).

> [T]he notion that the metaphysical principles are rooted in a "decision" is undercut by the distinction between cosmological generalities, which hold true only for a particular cosmic epoch, and the metaphysical principles, which hold true for all cosmic epochs (PR 36, 66, 96, 288). In Whitehead's thought, the forerunner to the primordial nature of God was the "principle of limitation," which was introduced in *Science*

and the Modern World (1926) to account for "those matter-of-fact determinations…which are inherent in the actual course of events, but which present themselves as *arbitrary* in respect to a more abstract possibility" (SMW 232; italics added). As examples of these arbitrary factors he lists "the three dimensions of space, and the four dimensions of the spatiotemporal continuum" (ibid.). These items are described in *Process and Reality*…as "arbitrary, as it were 'given,' elements in the laws of nature" which "warn us that we are in a special cosmic epoch" (PR 91, cf. 91–92). As such they are distinguished from metaphysical principles. Now, metaphysical principles are called "necessary" (PR 3, 4), and are said to be "characteristics so general that we cannot conceive any alternatives" (PR 288). Since they are without conceivable alternative (Whitehead and Hartshorne agree on this formal definition), they are not "given" in the sense of being "arbitrary." Hence, in *Process and Reality*, after the distinction between arbitrary cosmological principles and necessary metaphysical principles has been made, Whitehead should no longer speak as if the latter required grounding in a decision. A "decision" by definition cuts off alternative possibilities and results in that which is "given" in distinction from that which is *not* "given" (PR 42–43). Since the metaphysical principles have no conceivable alternatives, they are not "given," not "arbitrary," and hence should not be thought of as resulting from a volition.[25]

Further evidence that Whitehead's thought was moving in this less voluntaristic direction is found in a later passage, in *Adventures of Ideas*: "Metaphysics requires that the relationships of God to the World should lie beyond the accidents of will and that they be founded upon the necessities of the nature of God and the nature of the World" (AI 168).

An additional reason for contending that this is how *we* should think about this issue is the Aristotelian-Hartshornean position that the eternal and the necessary are equatable. Given this equation, the idea of a "primordial decision" does not make sense (assuming "primordial" means "eternal"; if it simply means "prior to our cosmic epoch," there is no problem). All decisions are temporal.

The ontological principle, then, refers only to contingent features of the universe, as distinct from its necessary features. Neville himself sometimes formulates the ontological principle in a way consistent with this understanding of it. He says that it entails that "for every particular factor there is a decision somewhere that accounts for it"[26] (*particular* factors would be distinguished from the *universal* factors). Neville also says that this principle entails that "nothing enters the universe that is not the product of some actual entity's decision"[27] (those things that *enter* the universe would be distinguished from those things that, being necessary, are always already *here*).

Neville, however, argues against this position. Although he might be persuaded that this is how Whitehead should be read, he has argued that this view is not satisfactory. The possible version of this view that Neville attacks is the simple rejection of the ontological question, the claim that we simply cannot say "why there are creative actual entities."[28]

However, the version of this view that I hold—as a Hartshornean interpretation of Whitehead's position (which fits with most of his statements)—is that there is an answer but that this answer does not involve a decision. A realm of finite actual entities, with their creativity and metaphysical principles, exists necessarily, not contingently, and therefore does not come under the scope of the ontological principle, which applies only to contingent features of reality. No decision is needed. Neville claims that "Whitehead is not entitled to reject the ontological question." My point, however, is that Whitehead (as here interpreted) does not reject this question; he simply gives a different answer from the one that Neville prefers.

Neville to some extent responds to this answer, formulating it in these terms:

> Whitehead's response, here then, would have to be that the ontological principle does not apply to ontological unity in the sense described. There is no decision responsible for the basic togetherness of one and many in creativity. Precisely because the category of the ultimate is the universal of universals there can be nothing "responsible" for it. Creativity must simply be accepted as something given.[29]

Neville argues that to accept this position would be to accept "the irrationality of the category of the ultimate" and thereby to succumb to "a betrayal of rational faith."[30] But this formulation misstates the case, if the closing word "given" means being present contingently rather than necessarily. And this is indeed what Neville means, saying that "Whitehead was right to see that any complex unity is contingent and needs an account."[31] But this statement, exegetically, reflects the misreading of Whitehead's ontological principle with which I dealt above.

This statement also, philosophically, begs the question, by assuming that "any complex unity is contingent" or, more precisely, by assuming the scope given by Neville to the notion of "complex unities." If by "any complex unity" one means *any actual entity*, then Whitehead and Hartshorne would agree with Neville: even the divine actual entity, for Whitehead, and the divine actual occasions, for Hartshorne, are contingent, in that they contain contingent elements. (The divine existence and essence, to use Hartshorne's terminology, are necessary, while the divine actuality, which also includes the past world and responses thereto, is always contingent.) Neville, however, gives "complex unity" virtually unlimited scope, applying it also to the category of the ultimate, to the metaphysical principles in general, and to the realm of eternal objects.

The idea that all of these realities are contingent goes directly counter to Whitehead's ideal of coherence. Whitehead says, for example: "[God] does not create eternal objects; for his nature requires them in the same degree that they require him. This is an exemplification of the coherence of the categoreal types of existence" (PR 257). Coherence is "the ideal of speculative philosophy that its fundamental notions shall not seem capable of abstraction from each other" (PR 3). In a more complex illustration of this principle, Whitehead says: "there is no meaning to 'creativity' apart from its 'creatures,' and no meaning to 'God' apart from the 'creativity' and the 'temporal creatures,' and no meaning to the 'temporal creatures' apart from 'creativity' and 'God'" (PR 225). If eternal objects, creativity, divine existence, and finite existence are tendentiously to be called "complex unities," then Whitehead emphatically did not think that "any complex unity is contingent."

While Neville, like many other defenders of the doctrine of creatio ex nihilo, believes that "rational faith" requires the existence of everything except God to be rooted in God's creative act, Whitehead holds just the opposite, saying: "The requirement of coherence is the great preservative of rationalistic sanity" (PR 6).

As Neville sees, we have here two differing intuitions as to what constitutes an ultimately satisfying explanation. At this stage of the argument, interestingly, Neville no longer tries to justify his position as the more "rational" one but instead distinguishes between a "rationalist sensibility," which Whitehead approached and Hartshorne fully exemplified, and an "empiricist sensibility," which Neville himself reflects. The rationalist view is that "an ultimately satisfying explanation is a reduction of things to [determinate] first principles." These determinate first principles themselves "do not need to be accounted for if indeed they are 'first'—the ultimate and primordial explanatory principles."[32] The so-called empiricist view is that "an ultimately satisfying explanation consists in locating the decisive actions from which things take their form." From this viewpoint, "even the first principles, being determinate, need an account."[33]

Thus phrased, the difference between the two views on the ontological question seems to be relativized to a standoff between two confessional stances. Neville says:

> The difficulty alleged against the empiricist sensibility is that there is nothing in the character of the ontologically creative act that accounts for the product of the act (as indeed there cannot be if everything determinate must be within the product); therefore, explanation by reference to a decisive action is not an explanation at all, but merely a pointing at what needs explanation. But then, this objection begs the

question in favor of the rationalist sensibility, since only a rationalist would want something determinate in the *character* of the explanatory principle that would explain. Being of the empiricist sort, I can only confess that the rationalist approach cannot account for existence.... Only the empiricist approach can address the problem of accounting for the reality of things.[34]

Neville, however, does not really rest with a relativism of equally valid sensibilities. He argues that his so-called empiricist sensibility is superior, because "the explanation of a state of affairs in terms of first principles is not as penetrating as the explanation of the first principles themselves."[35]

I likewise do not consider the two approaches to be equal, but I come down on the other side. This is not, however, because of a preference for rationalism over empiricism. Just as I earlier refused Neville's claim to represent Whitehead's "rationalist faith" more consistently than did Whitehead himself, I also reject his claim to be more of an empiricist than Whitehead or Hartshorne on this issue.

With regard to *conceptual empiricism*, the doctrine that all meaningful concepts are rooted in immediate experience, Whitehead endorses "Hume's doctrine that nothing is to be received into the philosophical scheme which is not discoverable as an element in subjective experience." Whitehead concludes that "Hume's demand that causation be describable as an element in experience is, on these principles, entirely justifiable" (PR 166–67).

Neville probably thinks that he abides by this conceptual empiricism, but his notion of 'ontological causation' violates it. As Whitehead says, "our notion of causation concerns the relations of states of things within the actual world, and can only be illegitimately extended to a transcendent derivation" (PR 93). In making this point, Whitehead is rejecting the traditional cosmological argument, which had a fully determinate God bringing a wholly contingent world into existence ex nihilo. But this point would apply even more to Neville's doctrine, according to which a wholly indeterminate reality brings determinate things and thereby determinateness itself into existence. There is no analogy between this type of causation and the causation we experience, which always presupposes determinate causes. As Hartshorne says, "formless ground of formed actualities seems to break any analogy available from experience."[36] How then can an empiricist claim that the term *causation* in the phrase *ontological causation* has any shred of meaning? As an empiricist, Neville says that "experience is the final arbiter" and that "all our ideas are suggested by generalizing notions from this world."[37] But his notion of ontological causation violates this conceptual empiricism.

Neville argues against the (possible) view "that 'first principles' call for explanation but no explanation can be given." This view, Neville says, "is contrary to fact, because explanation can be given by reference to a divine creative act which apart from actually creating, would not be determinate or complex."[38] An alleged explanation does not explain, however, if it is not an *intelligible* explanation. From an empiricist standpoint, from which Neville himself means to write, his explanation is not intelligible and is therefore no explanation at all. Although he says that Hartshorne's theory "suffers from its lack of an account for form itself,"[39] his own position gives no such account. He *says*, to be sure, that the formless former gives rise to forms and the formed. But these words, I maintain, do not elicit a meaningful proposition in our minds.

Furthermore, even if they did, would we have a gain in intelligibility? I hold with Whitehead that eternal objects, creativity, God, and some finite actual entities all presuppose each other, that they obtain eternally and therefore necessarily. What exists necessarily is God-and-a-world, along with the embodied creativity and the objective and subjective species of eternal forms. Neville evidently holds that that which is necessary and eternal is simply an indeterminate deity. Each position has to presuppose that *something* is eternal and necessary. Why is it any more explanatory to say that this something is simply God than to say it is God-and-a-world?

Neville's reply is that his "God" is, apart from creating a world, wholly indeterminate and that what needs explanation is that which is determinate, or determinately complex. But that principle is arbitrary. As we saw earlier, it is not identical with, or implied by, Whitehead's ontological principle. And it is not a self-evident intuition.

This intuition may seem self-evident to Neville. But I share the intuition of Aristotle, Hartshorne, and—at least for the most part—Whitehead that what needs explanation is that which is contingent rather than necessary. And the contingent is not equatable with the "determinately complex," at least as Neville conceives it. My intuition, furthermore, is that in spite of Neville and Shankara, the formed cannot be generated out of that which is wholly devoid of form. And this intuition has been widely held, because the phrase *ex nihilo nihil fit* has surely meant "out of nothing [determinate], nothing [determinate] is made." In other words, there could be nothing determinate now unless there had always been something determinate. Neville, then, seems to have nothing to commend his own position except his own intuition, which he cannot call the intuition of the majority.

Whitehead's approach seems both more empirical and more rational. His approach is to try to discern which elements in *our* world—our cosmic epoch—are the most general, ultimate elements, which seem to have no conceivable alternatives, and then to posit that these elements are *metaphysical*, meaning that they exist necessarily and have hence always existed.

Although Neville calls this the method of "empirical generalization,"[40] it is more than that. It begins with the empirical but tries to discern within it that which is more than merely empirical, in the sense of that which might be absent. It tries to discern that which is metaphysical, which could never be absent. Whitehead called it the method of "imaginative" generalization (PR 4–5). But it *is* empirical in that it stays closer to experience than does Neville's approach, in which the philosopher, after noting that a number of elements always are present, selects one of them out and speculates that it is the source of the others. Neville's approach seems to me as arbitrary and counterintuitive as that of Nicholas Rescher. Also believing that an ultimately satisfying explanation must account for the existence of actuality as such, Rescher speculates that only value is primordial, with actuality having been created out of it.[41] Neville's position equally violates the intuition that only that which is actual can act.

Finally, even if these problems were not inherent in Neville's position, it would provide no advance in explanatory power. He says that his doctrine explains why there is a world. But it does not, he admits, provide any hint as to why the world is the kind of world it is. He points out, for example, that "there is no explanation of why this world is created that has process in it rather than one without process."[42] ("God could have created a different kind of world," he claims, "one with no time.")[43] Because Neville thinks that all forms and categories are contingent, so that God's creation of the world "cannot proceed according to any preestablished principles," he has to conceive of philosophy as wholly empirical and hence of the world as one that simply "happens to be one of process."[44]

I have found more illuminating the suggestion of Whitehead and Hartshorne that process or creativity is the ultimate reality, which implies that to be an actuality is necessarily to be a process of creative synthesis, so that any world would of necessity be a world of process. Neville says that his position makes the advance of explaining "how such a world is possible" by saying that "it is ontologically created . . . by a transcendent creator that makes itself creator in the act of creating."[45]

However, in addition to having the aforementioned problem of how the formless could give birth to the formed, Neville's position evidently fails to explain not only why our kind of world exists but also why *any* world actually exists (in distinction from "how there could be any world").[46] Even if it were granted that an unformed former *could* pull off the feat of ontological creation, we would not have any hint as to *why* it would have actually done so. For example, Neville prefers the more voluntaristic, Scotistic position to the more rationalistic, Thomistic position.[47] But he evidently cannot intelligibly say that the world exists because God chose to create it, or, if he could say this, he can give no glimmer of a motive for this divine choice. By contrast, Whitehead, in speaking of the divine appetite for the finite realization of values, provides a motive as to why God would be interested in bringing a richly ordered world out of a relatively chaotic state. Neville's position seems to be a step backward, not forward, in intelligibility.

For Neville, the distinction between these two views is relevant not only to philosophical intelligibility but also to religious worship. Whitehead's creator God is less worthy of worship, he believes, than his own. The Whiteheadian God is finite, he says, and "the real onus of the charge that God should not be finite is the subordinate status a finite God would have relative to any whole including God plus the other ontologically independent beings."[48] Whitehead refers to God plus the world as the "solidarity" of God and world in the creative advance. This raises the crucial question, Neville says, "whether the solidarity of the advance is not more divine, more worshipful, than Whitehead's God."[49] By virtue of the solidarity, "God and the world are mutually dependent" in Whitehead's view, but religious experience, Neville claims, "seems to prefer the relatively more independent," which means "the complete creative advance," which has "a total holiness superior to the dependencies of the divine pole." Neville adds:

> There may be difficulties with the quasipantheism of the claim that the creative advance is most divine.... But pantheism has a solid footing in religious experience, as nearly every religious tradition exemplifies. In essence, I think nothing short of the ground or principle of the whole of things is supreme enough to be worshiped.[50]

This discussion raises several crucial questions. As Neville mentions, but does not flesh out, pantheism has difficulties. One of these is the problem of whether it is more important that the object of our devotion be literally *infinite* and thereby the *whole of* things, in every conceivable sense of those words, or that this object of devotion be unambiguously good. This question becomes the more important to the degree that one believes, as I do, that we tend to mold ourselves in the image of that which we worship. As Neville frankly admits, pantheism means that the divine reality is thoroughly ambiguous—as ambiguous as the world is, because God *is* the world ("the complete creative advance"). God is terrible, as the source of cancer and holocausts, as well as good. Do we want people, especially in this nuclear age, to mold themselves in terms of this notion of holiness?

Pantheism also undermines the distinction between *is* and *ought*, implying that the way things are is the way they ought to be. Morality, at least of the prophetic type supported by the biblically based religions as well as many others, is thus undermined. Neville is right to say that pantheism has a foothold in "nearly every religious tradition." Neville is claiming, however, that this theology is superior to process theology for the Christian tradition (as well as for others). He surely knows that pantheism has had only a tiny foothold, not a solid one, in Christian history, and has generally been excoriated by Christian theologians, not least for the above-mentioned reasons.

Another question raised by Neville's discussion is whether it accurately reflects the position of process theologians on the question of divine dependence and independence. "Dependence" tends to suggest contingency. To say, without further clarification, that God is dependent upon the world suggests that God exists contingently.

But that is not true for Whitehead or Hartshorne, as Neville knows. In their respective versions of dipolar theism, only one pole or aspect of God is dependent on the contingent course of the world. For Hartshorne, who developed this distinction more completely, the *concrete states* of God are dependent upon the world and perfectly so. This is "the divine relativity." But the *existence* of God is fully independent of anything that could happen, as is the divine *essence*. Nothing could prevent God from existing, and nothing could prevent God from being God—from being omniscient, perfect in power, perfectly loving, and everlasting.

Neville would reply that God's existence for Whitehead and Hartshorne does depend upon there being a world—some world or other of finite actualities. That is true, but the existence of some such world is for Whitehead and Hartshorne not a contingent fact but a necessity. We can even say that the world—not this particular world, but some world or other—exists necessarily because God's existence, which is necessary, requires it. Process theism therefore provides all the independence required by religious experience while also providing a basis for the distinction that religious-moral experience usually makes between the demonic and the divine, and hence between what *is* the case and what *ought* to be the case.

GOD'S PRESENCE AND ACTIVITY IN THE WORLD

Neville's second set of criticisms of process theism involves the idea of God's presence and activity in the world. I will argue, again, that his criticisms of process theism misfire and that his own position is more problematic.

Neville's Critique

One of Neville's criticisms is the charge that Whitehead's doctrine of initial aims from God threatens creaturely, especially human, freedom. Although Neville is postmodern in a Whiteheadian sense in some respects, especially in basing his cosmology on value, he is quintessentially modern in his conception of freedom. Freedom is understood as autonomy with respect to one's environment, and if I read Neville correctly, one is less free the more one is influenced by the environment.

From this perspective, he reads Whitehead's doctrine of the initial aim as a limitation on freedom, saying that Whitehead's God is "an external limit on freedom in the same sense that other things limit freedom."[51] Whitehead's doctrine means that "people's choices are hedged in by divinely urged possibilities and values."[52] Insofar as God determines the value that the occasion realizes, "the occasion's own choice is depleted."[53] Neville, believing that divine determination in process theology is virtually complete, says that the occasion's "ability to alter the subjective aim . . . is trivial."[54]

Neville promised in the preface to *Creativity and God* to give a "sympathetic critique of process theology."[55] His language here, however, suggests that he has little sympathy for process theism. (Indeed, he subsequently refers to his "somewhat unfriendly analysis of Whitehead's theory of God" in this book.)[56] He compares God to a "smother-mother, structuring all possibilities and continually insisting on values of her own arbitrary choice." He says that "the *function* of God is . . . to force feed a person's intentions even more powerfully than other things do."[57] If we are to be free, Neville says, our activities must be genuinely our own, and this implies that there can be no "interference" from a divinely rooted initial aim.[58] He asks, rhetorically: "who can be responsible for resisting an infinite Nudge?"[59]

Neville's criticism here seems to be in some tension with his criticism in the first section. There he was complaining that process theology's God was not fully responsible for the existence of all creatures. Here he is complaining that this God is *too* responsible.

Neville, nevertheless, does mean to have a self-consistent position. In stating his own view, he says "that God is the creator and is responsible for everything in one sense, that people are free agents and creative in another sense, and that these two senses are compatible and in fact complementary."[60] This compatibilism, based on a version of the schema of primary and secondary causation, has been central to Neville from the beginning. In a 1968 essay, for example, he argued that we can affirm, without inconsistency, both of the following doctrines (which he held to be necessary implications of the Christian gospel): (1) God is creator of everything finite and contingent, including people and their responses, and (2) people may respond freely to God.[61] Neville thinks of us as wholly dependent upon God *ontologically* but entirely free from God *cosmologically*. That is, God is not at all another determinate being contributing something to our specific character.[62]

Neville considers the Whiteheadian idea of divinely given initial aims to be both superfluous and intuitively implausible.[63] In Neville's view, God accounts for the fact that we exist and for our spontaneous, self-determining features. "God creates the spontaneous features of the moment. . . . God's contributions simply *are* the present decisive acts by which the process exists as something over and above its past conditions."[64]

From this standpoint, according to which we are totally dependent upon God and yet totally free, Neville finds the Whiteheadian God—who does not in any sense fully determine us and yet who does influence us in somewhat the same way as other actual entities do—both too limited and too limiting. Whitehead's God is too limited because, being "a concrete cosmological entity among the other entities of the world," this God had to be made finite to allow room for freedom.[65] But this God is too limiting because it is one more external cause operating upon us. "God's input . . . is an external imposition magnified to divine proportions." This divine input, as described by Whitehead, "hands human freedom a stacked deck, more stacked than experience indicates."[66]

Evaluating Neville's Critique

Having tried to understand the perspective from which Neville's critique is launched, we need to ask if it is just. I think not. In the first place, whereas Neville seems to think of the environment in primarily negative terms, as that which limits our freedom, Whitehead thought—more accurately—of the environment as making positive contributions as well as imposing limitations. Whitehead did stress that "whatever be the freedom of feeling arising in the concrescence, there can be no transgression of the limitations of capacity inherent in the datum." He quickly added, however, that "[t]he datum both limits and supplies" (PR 110). Indeed, his whole picture of the universe, as societies within broader societies within still broader societies, emphasizes the extent to which we can exist only because of multiple levels of societies of actual entities, which not only are permissive of our existence and high level of freedom but also enable this free existence. Within this framework, to suggest that God is, in one sense, *a cause that influences us in somewhat the same way as do other actual entities* does not imply that God is more of a limiter than a supplier of our freedom.

In the second place, it becomes clear that God is firmly on the supply side of Whitehead's cosmology of increasing freedom once we explicate the "somewhat" in that italicized phrase. Neville has described the implications of his own doctrine in these terms: "God makes people free; he does not inhibit their freedom of action. . . . God adds new potentiality to one. But this only increases one's range of responsibility. It does not narrow it. God makes freedom of choice possible, not impossible."[67] No better description of the implications of Whitehead's own position could be wanted.

Whitehead's God, in providing us with an initial aim, does not limit our freedom by depleting our choices but provides the necessary condition for our freedom by increasing our choices beyond what they would be if we, *per impossibile,* existed apart from this ever-present enabling grace. If we could exist apart from this divine grace, we would be condemned to repeat the same old forms that had already been realized in our past. In such a world, of course, we would not exist because no evolutionary progress would have ever occurred. No forms and values beyond those realized in the most trivial chaos possible would have had any doorway into the world. The divinely rooted aims, expressing the divine appetite for increased harmonious intensity, are the source of the increased freedom that has been brought into the world in general and of our own freedom in particular.

Neville's charge that the initial aim virtually determines our subjective aims simply has no support. Whitehead says instead that what the finite occasion receives from God is "that initial aim from which its self-causation starts" (PR 244). He stresses that once the subject is constituted by the character of the creativity it had received from God and the past world, it "is the autonomous master of its own concrescence into subject-superject" (PR 245). And he says that we are not all on the same level in this respect. Very low-grade occasions have "negligible autonomous energy" and thereby trivial capacity to determine their own subjective aims. But there are many grades of actual occasions, and "as soon as individual experience is not negligible, the autonomy of the subject in the modification of its initial subjective aim must be taken into account" (PR 245). Human freedom is the extreme example, on this planet at least, of nonnegligible autonomous energy and therefore of a nontrivial capacity to modify the initial aim. There is no basis for Neville's equation of a nudge from the infinite with an "infinite Nudge."

Whitehead, indeed, is arguably the first philosophical theologian in the West to provide an account that truly reconciles prevenient grace with human freedom. In the light of John Wesley's concern with this issue, one would think that Neville, who is, as he says, a "Methodist from Missouri,"[68] would be more interested in exploring this doctrine than caricaturing it. He was led to caricature it, I suggest, in part because of his desire to replace Whitehead's view of the God-world relation with his own. This raises the question of whether, on this issue in any case, Neville's view is superior, or at least equal, to Whitehead's. Before examining this question, however, we need to consider more of Neville's criticisms of the Whiteheadian view of God's presence and activity in the world.

Neville's second criticism is in effect a reply to my response to his first criticism. Neville says that if process theology does allow human beings to have real freedom vis-à-vis God, "the price of this move is to make the actual course of events *irrelevant* to God's moral character." This conclusion, he says, "goes counter to the religious feeling that God's moral character is *revealed* in events, for better or worse."[69] Neville has here constructed a damned-if-you-do-and-damned-if-you-don't argument. That is, if you say that God is really effective in human experience, you have denied human freedom; if you say that this effectiveness does not preclude human freedom, you have denied divine providence.

But surely, as John Cobb has pointed out in response to Neville, a middle position is possible. God can be regarded as somewhat expressed by all events, and some events can be understood as more revelatory of God than others. Process theology explains how this can be so.[70] Indeed, Cobb himself provided this explanation in some early essays on christology,[71] and I oriented my own first book, A *Process Christology* and several of my early articles around this idea.[72] This is one of several examples of why I do not find that process theology as I understand it is really engaged by Neville's critique. In any case, I do not agree with Neville's view that "religious feeling" holds that God's character is *equally* revealed in all events. With regard to Christian religious feeling, the conviction that Jesus is a *decisive* revelation of God sets a precedent for thinking of different events as expressing the divine character to varying degrees. Jewish and Islamic religious feeling is analogous. Indeed, most theistic religions seem to have some version of this belief.

Another criticism, again apparently in tension with Neville's criticism that God is too determinative of our decisions, is that God's presence in us is not intimate enough. Most religious experience, Neville says, feels that God is "at the depths of one's own being," that God is in fact "that most real part of ourselves," whereas Whitehead's view "allows God only to be felt as other."[73] As Cobb points out in response, however, "one can hardly imagine a doctrine that more fully expresses the intimacy of grace than does Whitehead's—unless, that is, one demands that intimacy be identity."[74]

Cobb's point is on target, because that is what Neville demands. Saying that "most religions exhibit something of the feeling that God is experienced at the center of one's own heart, that Atman is Brahman,"[75] Neville holds that "God is not ontologically distinct from creatures."[76] Rather, God's contributions "simply *are* the present decisive acts by which the process exists as something over and above its past conditions. God is closer to us than we are to ourselves."[77] From this point of view, Neville finds unsatisfying the intimacy portrayed by Whitehead, which is, in Cobb's terms, an intimacy of communion rather than an intimacy of identity.

Perhaps part of the reason Neville finds this account unsatisfying is that he distorts it. He says, for example, that for Whitehead "God is no more at the heart of human subjectivity than any other thing which enters among the initial data of experience."[78] This statement falsely implies that the other things that enter our experience are *not* at the heart of our subjectivity.

As Cobb points out, however, Whitehead's view is that the many *become* one, being thereby constitutive of it, incarnate in it. God is, accordingly, constitutive of our experience, incarnate in the heart of our coming-to-be. Furthermore, this incarnation of God in us is the initial aim from which our subjective aim begins, so we can say that God is even more intimate to our process of self-constitution than any other actuality (except perhaps our own prior occasion of experience). Finally, Cobb's discussion of Jesus' structure of existence shows how the divine presence in Jesus could have been felt less as "other" than as the very seat of Jesus' existence.[79] And there is no reason why other people could not embody God in a similar way.

Neville's reply to Cobb's distinction between the two types of intimacy is that an intimacy of communion between two societies of actualities seems counterintuitive, that it does not reflect his own experience of divinity, that it sounds like a wish projection, and that it would put God in competition with his wife.[80] The crux of the matter seems to be, as before, that Neville has another vision, which he considers superior. It is time to examine this vision, to see if it is indeed superior.

Neville's Alternative Vision of Divine Presence and Activity

Neville's own vision of God's presence and activity in the world, it will be recalled, replaced the Whiteheadian notion of a divinely given initial aim, which he regards as superfluous as well as implausible, with the idea that divine and creaturely causation are on two entirely different levels. I should say at the outset that although most doctrines of primary and secondary causation are incoherent, Neville's is not necessarily so. The difference is that most such doctrines think of God as a determinate being who exerts efficient causation upon us. In Neville's view, in which the word *God* refers to something similar to Whiteheadian "creativity" or Buddhist "emptiness,"[81] no contradiction is necessarily involved. There are not (*per impossibile*) two determinate sufficient causes for each event. The problems lie elsewhere.

One problem is how Neville accounts for the entrance of novelty into the universe. In one passage, for example, Neville is speaking of "the ideals directing the process of unification, the lures for integration." He says that "these are derived from past facts, perhaps."[82] But if all lures for integration are derived from the past finite world, we are in a Nietzschean universe, in which the same forms must be endlessly recycled. That cosmology is not adequate to our evolutionary universe in general, nor to our direct experience of being called forward to actualize novel possibilities in particular.

A second problem is how to account for the order of the universe in this "cosmology of freedom" in which all actual entities embody some degree of spontaneity. My own intuition is that the manifest order of the world, which is not absolute but nonetheless very real, implies the type of cosmic source of order that Whitehead posits but that Neville has excised from his otherwise Whiteheadian universe. These problems of novelty and order suggest that divine initial aims are not, *contra* Neville, superfluous.

A third problem that is solved by the Whiteheadian idea of God, but that is reintroduced by Neville's idea of God, is the problem of evil. To be sure,

Neville's God, not being a determinate efficient cause, cannot be responsible for evil in the same way that, say, Calvin's God is. Nevertheless, because that which Neville calls "God" is said to have unilaterally determined what kind of world this is, to have created all possibilities (such as the possibility of cancer and nuclear weapons), and to be the cause of all the events in the world, including all human decisions, that which is called "God" is the cause of all evil.

Neville, in fact, stresses this aspect of his position, saying that Whitehead was wrong to try to keep God wholly good.[83] The world (including its holocausts) is, Neville says, "the normative expression of the creator" so that "if God is to be judged by moral categories..., the divine character is only as good as experience shows it to be as creator of just this world."[84]

Neville evidently believes that this is a strength, not a weakness, of his position, and that this view of the deity is closer to real religion than that of a wholly good deity. He says, for example, that "the Bible as I read it has God both good and terrible at once."[85] That sentiment is indeed expressed by some passages. But most of that collection of writings portrays God as perfectly good, as perfect love. And this has surely been the dominant sentiment among Christians. If Neville's claim here is partly empirical, I would challenge him to return to his roots and interview his fellow Methodists in Missouri. Most of them would surely reject the notion that God determines all human responses, hence being terrible as well as good, in favor of Charles Wesley's view that God is "pure, unbounded love."

THE WORLD'S BEARING ON GOD

The third set of criticisms Neville levels against process theism involves the world's bearing on God—what Whitehead calls the "consequent nature," and Hartshorne the "consequent states," of God.

Neville's First Criticism

One of Neville's criticisms is that the God of process theology does not "account for the unity of things," does not "unify the particulars of the world."[86] The stated reason is that God's experiences do not contain the creative activity of the world's actual occasions.[87] The basis for this claim is the Whiteheadian doctrine that actual occasions cannot be prehended in principle, and therefore not even by God, until their moment of subjective self-creation is completed. The present in the strictest sense of the word—meaning the occasions that are presently concrescing—are therefore always external to God, in the sense that they are not being prehended by God *while* they are concrescing.

This issue is clearest in relation to Hartshorne's version of process theism, according to which God is a personally ordered society of divine occasions of experience. Each divine occasion is all-inclusive, in that it has an all-inclusive standpoint and includes all past or completed actual occasions within itself. However, those worldly occasions that are strictly contemporaneous with it, being in unison of becoming with it, are not included. They *will be* included in an immediately following divine experience, but they are not included in the contemporary divine occasion. A part of "the world"—the part that is presently happening—is, therefore, external to God. The world in its entirety is not unified by God. Neville believes that this makes process theism inadequate.

Evaluating Neville's First Criticism

Inadequate, however, to *what*? Where is it written that God must unify the world in just this sense? The idea that the divine reality should be omniscient does, it is true, imply that God should know everything that is knowable. Most theists, however, have not insisted that God should be able to do that which is inherently impossible. Thomas Aquinas said that God could not change the past because the past is unchangeable. No one should, by the same token, require that God be able to know that which is in principle unknowable. The reason a concrescing occasion is in principle unknowable is that it is not yet fully determinate. It, therefore, can present nothing definite to be known. Neville, who has thought so much about the distinction between determinateness and indeterminateness, should be more sensitive than most philosophers to this issue.

At first blush, to be sure, the idea that the present is in principle unknowable seems counterintuitive. Most people would think, in fact, that the present is the only thing that *is* directly knowable. But the Whiteheadian analysis of actuality, with its momentary acts of concrescence and its epochal theory of time, is a quite unique, virtually unprecedented, view, at least in Western thought. (Buddhists have had something like it.) When ideas of what omniscience entailed were thought through in previous centuries, therefore, this highly precise, technical sense of "the present" was not in view. In the light of the fact the durations of actual occasions may range from a tenth to less than a billionth of a second, what almost everyone would mean by "the present" *is* included within the divine experience. It seems tendentiously picayune to maintain that process theism is religiously or philosophically inadequate because the cutting edge of the temporal advance, a cutting edge probably constituting at most a tenth of a second, is not yet included in the divine experience.

Neville's own position, furthermore, seems to provide for even less unity than does process theism. As Hartshorne formulates the process view, God includes—or in the immediate future *will* include—everything. But Neville's

God is not a determinate being, distinct from the world, and is therefore not an experiencing subject at all. Neville rejects the consequent (as well as the initial-aim-giving primordial) nature of God. He therefore, as he points out, rejects the notion of the 'totality' implicit in Whitehead's conception of God's consequent nature.[88] It is puzzling, therefore, why he criticizes process theism on this point as if he had some more adequate sense of God's unification of the world. When he alludes to his own theory, he refers to God's presence to the creatures "as their creative ground."[89] That, however, is to return to the previous issue of *God's presence to finite things* rather than to stay with the issue of *how finite things are unified in God*. The idea that a God who is not an individual is somehow ontologically identical with all occasions does little to mitigate their plurality.

Neville's Second Criticism

Neville's criticism on this point is not limited to the philosophical question of cosmic unity. He says that the inability of God to prehend the subjective realities of actual occasions in the process of concrescence is "a disastrous consequence for the religious applicability of the neoclassical concept of God."[90] This allegedly disastrous consequence is that "God cannot prehend [people] in their hearts, in their processes of becoming."[91] The charge that Neville is making, evidently, is that process theism cannot do justice to the biblical idea that "God looks on the heart."

Evaluating Neville's Second Criticism

The validity of this charge depends upon the legitimacy of Neville's equation of the biblical idea of the human "heart" with the Whiteheadian idea of an actual occasion in its process of concrescence, while it is a subject enjoying subjective immediacy—in distinction from the occasion as superject, with objective immortality in subsequent subjects. Neville explicitly makes this equation, saying, "God cannot know us as we are in our hearts, where that means the subjective immediacy of our own concrescence."[92]

That equation, however, is surely strained. On the one hand, to say that God looks upon the heart has always meant that God's knowledge of our inner life is not based solely upon the clues that can be discerned from our outer appearance. God's perceptual knowledge of us is not like human sensory perception, which is restricted to our bodily features and expressions; God sees right through to the soul, which cannot be directly perceived by means of the human senses. The idea that the soul is a temporal society of occasions of experience, and therefore oscillates between subjectivity and objectivity, was surely not in the mind of the biblical writers who expressed this idea. Their distinction was between inner and outer, soul and body, unobservable-by-the-senses and observable-by-the-senses, not between concrescence and transition, subject and superject.

On the other hand, the Whiteheadian idea that an occasion's "subjective immediacy" in the technical sense cannot be known by God does not mean that a person's subjectivity, in the more ordinary sense of the term, cannot be known. In this more ordinary sense, one's subjectivity is one's emotions, attitudes, and thoughts, including unconscious thoughts. These are not forever locked up in the privacy of a concrescence. As Whitehead says, "there is nothing which belongs merely to the privacy of feeling of one individual actuality. All origination is private. But what has been thus originated, publicly pervades the world" (PR 310). In other words, an occasion of experience, in being objectified for others, thereby transcends itself, and "such transcendence is self-revelation" (PR 227).

Accordingly, our emotions, attitudes, and thoughts are known as soon as they are knowable. In relation to other finite experiences, they are revealed most directly and fully to the next occasions of experience of our own soul. They are revealed with equal directness, of course, to our bodily occasions, especially our brain cells, but with much less fullness, due to the lowly nature of these bodily members. Other people, insofar as they know us through their sensory organs, know our thoughts and emotions only very indirectly and fragmentarily. Insofar as they know our souls (or "hearts") directly, meaning telepathically, this knowledge usually remains unconscious. Even when, in rare moments, it becomes conscious, it is very abstract compared with our direct knowledge of our own immediately prior conscious experiences. This immediate "memorizing" knowledge provides our best clue, therefore, to the kind of knowledge of our subjectivity (in the ordinary sense) that is possible. From the perspective of process theism, then, God would know our subjectivity, our "heart," with this much directness and completeness—and more, knowing even our unconscious thoughts and feelings.

Neville's characterization is, therefore, very misleading. The fact that God cannot know the subjective immediacy of an actual occasion while it is in concrescence and therefore still indeterminate, with nothing definite yet to be known, has nothing to do with the question of whether the God of process theism "looks on the heart" in the biblical sense.

The technical issue of the unprehendability of a concrescence also does not, *contra* Neville, imply that God's love is not unbounded. Neville says that for Whitehead, God's love "is bounded by the limits of the objective reality of the things in the world. God cannot love things in their processive subjective reality because *that* cannot be prehended."[93] Is Neville going to claim that the knowledge of the God of St. Thomas was bounded because this God could not know unknowable things such as round squares? Things that in principle cannot yet be loved set no bounds to the divine love. The subjective immediacy of an occasion, which is striving to become something determinate, is not lovable, because it provides nothing determinate to be loved. It is surprising that Neville, who understands the technicalities of process philosophy so well, would make criticisms of this sort.

Neville's criticisms about the knowledge and love of the God of process theism become all the more surprising when it is realized that Neville's own God cannot be said to know or love the world at all, at least not in any non-Pickwickian sense. In the light of this fact, some of his statements are seriously misleading. He says, for example, that in his view "God is not separate from the creatures so as to have a problem knowing them" and that God does "not have to prehend only the objective character of occasions as finished facts."[94] These statements misleadingly imply that Neville's God is one who can prehend and know more fully than can the God of process theism, whereas in reality, not being an individual, it cannot prehend or know anything. Equally misleading is the following passage: "God eternally has the character that in the 14th or 13th century B.C. he raised up Joseph in Egypt, perhaps vaguely aware then that in the 12th century he would have to get the Hebrews out of the country, but probably without any idea that he would have to do so with Moses."[95] If I have correctly understood what Neville means by "God," then the only accurate reflection of his position on divine knowledge in this passage is the statement that God is "without any idea." He cannot legitimately speak of God as being "aware," even vaguely.

Neville's Third Criticism

Another criticism by Neville of process theology's doctrine of God's consequent nature is that it does not, in spite of the claims of its advocates, answer the question of the ultimate significance of life. He claims that Schubert Ogden fails to show "that God's relativity to the world bestows significance."[96] The fact that if process theism is correct, we are not forgotten by God, Neville claims, "is beside the point."[97]

Evaluating Neville's Third Criticism

The apparent flippancy of this comment is surprising, especially in the light of Neville's awareness that this issue is at the heart of the ultimate religious problem for Whitehead as well as Hartshorne. Whitehead says that

> the culminating fact of conscious, rational life refuses to conceive itself as a transient enjoyment, transiently useful.... [T]he higher intellec-

tual feelings are haunted by the vague insistence of another order.... This is the problem which gradually shapes itself as religion reaches its higher phases in civilized communities. The most general formulation of the religious problem is the question whether the process of the temporal world passes into the formation of other actualities, bound together in an order in which novelty does not mean loss. (PR 340)

Neville ordinarily values direct testimony of ultimate religious intuitions. Whitehead has here clearly confessed his deepest religious intuition. And yet Neville has in effect dismissed it, seemingly casually, saying that it is "beside the point." What really makes life significant, Neville insists, is "the pattern of the harmonies of prehensions."[98] Neville here has confused intrinsic value with everlasting significance. He does see the distinction, however, adding that in a Whiteheadian cosmology devoid of a Whiteheadian God, every occasion must be prehended by other occasions, which will be prehended in turn by later occasions, thereby "always having significance in the sense of making a difference."[99]

But for Whitehead, this idea of physical, biological, and social immortality simply raised the ultimate problem. He said: "But objective immortality within the temporal world does not solve the problem set by the penetration of the finer religious intuition. 'Everlastingness' has been lost; and 'everlastingness' is the content of that vision upon which the finer religions are built—the 'many' absorbed everlastingly in the final unity" (PR 347). Neville does acknowledge that this would be a problem in a Whiteheadian world without a Whiteheadian God, as he adds: "True, people would be prehended in ways that do less than the best with them, and this may be a source of concern."[100] However, rather than dwelling on the fact that his position has no way to respond to this concern, Neville tries to relativize it, claiming that for Whitehead, "God's perfect prehension is equally a source of concern, however, in that God by metaphysical necessity must be perfectly just; God cannot forget evil or forgive sins, only make the best of them."[101] Does the idea that God knows us perfectly and with perfect compassion raise concerns "equally" as serious as the idea that, apart from a divine knower, the partiality of all finite prehension means that eventually we will be entirely forgotten, and our effects will be negligible?

One of Neville's convictions reflected in this passage is that some of God's relations to the world, such as those of redeemer and lover, should be thought of as "a matter of grace, not necessity."[102] Neville is right that much traditional theism has wanted to say this. But the idea that God can choose to love some people, hate others, and be indifferent to still others has every sign of being a projection of our finitude and limited sympathies unto God. It also stands in strong tension with the biblical conviction that God *is* love, that love is of the essence of God. To say that the God of process theism cannot "forget evil" is simply to rephrase the divine omniscience, which is surely a perfection. And to say that the God of process theism cannot "forgive sin" is simply wrong; I cannot imagine from which process theologian Neville got that idea.

Neville's voluntaristic criticism should have been, I would think, that the process God *must* forgive sin. As Neville explicates the implication of process theism elsewhere, "God must prehend people exactly as they are, necessarily loving them despite their sins, and always doing the best with them."[103] What is this other than the forgiveness of sins? For us to forgive another is not necessarily to forget what the other did, but to love the other in spite of it, wishing the other well, doing what we can to elicit the best from the other, having compassion for the other's failings and sufferings, and rejoicing with the other's successes and joys. The practical meaning of forgiveness is, in the New Testament and in real life, to return good for evil. This is what God does by nature, according to process theism and according to the intuition that God *is* love. Given our religious inclination to imitate deity, to mold ourselves in accordance with our image or concept of the divine, this view is pragmatically far better than one that portrays the divine love and forgiveness as a matter of will or grace, which we can then imagine to be selective, not granted to those whom we regard with hate or indifference.

Process theology is not, however, so necessitarian as to deny all truth whatsoever to Neville's voluntaristic intuitions. Neville says:

> My own religious intuitions tell me that, if God wipes away the tears, it is out of divine freedom, not because God is metaphysically obliged. The depth of my experience, and that of people through the ages and across all cultures, is slighted by metaphysical resolutions of its ambiguity. If the ambiguity is not the last word, at least its resolution should be by creative free choice and our metaphysics should reflect this possibility.[104]

Taken to extremes, this intuition would simply oppose Whitehead's intuition, quoted earlier, that "the relationships of God to the World should lie beyond the accidents of will," that they should instead "be founded upon the necessities of the nature of God and the nature of the World" (AI 168). I have argued elsewhere that the nature of prehension as sympathetic, together with the nature of God as impartially omniscient, implies that God is necessarily compassionate.[105] God by nature feels our feelings sympathetically and desires our happiness. There is room for freedom, however, with regard to how this compassion is expressed. Any loving parents, by virtue of their nature as loving, will seek to "wipe away the tears" of their child. But there are usually many ways in which they can seek to do this.

To summarize: acknowledging that his position cannot provide a satisfactory answer to what Whitehead called "the most general formulation of the religious problem," Neville has attempted to dismiss this deficiency by claiming that process theism's solution to that problem raises equally serious concerns. This attempt, I have argued, is unconvincing. More generally, with regard to this section as a whole, I have argued that Neville has not raised any decisive objections to process theism's doctrine of God's consequent nature. I have also suggested that Neville's own view of God is less adequate by virtue of having no such doctrine.

THE COHERENCE OF THE SOCIETAL VIEW OF GOD

Many process theologians believe that Whitehead's view of God as a single, everlasting actual entity involves too much incoherence to be retained. On the one hand, Whitehead says that God should not be an exception to metaphysical principles, but their chief exemplification. On the other hand, he says that contemporaries cannot interact; his view of God as a single actual entity implies that God is contemporaneous with all worldly occasions; and yet he says that God and the world interact.

One way out of the seeming contradiction would be to say that the doctrine that contemporaries cannot interact is, like the doctrine that objectification involves abstraction (PR 340), a cosmological truth but not strictly a metaphysical principle. But it certainly seems to be a metaphysical principle. Neville allots considerable space to the difficulty.[106] I have allotted no space to his criticisms because I agree with them.

I have also spent no time on Neville's criticisms of Lewis Ford's efforts to salvage the view of God as a single actual entity, partly because I do not find Ford's efforts successful and partly because I do not think that this view *should* be salvaged.[107] After all, Whitehead himself says that the traditional idea of an enduring substance—"the notion of an actual entity which is characterized by essential qualities, and remains numerically one amidst the changes of accidental relations and of accidental qualities"—is a metaphysical error (PR 79).[108] I have from the first been convinced by Hartshorne's arguments, along with John Cobb's arguments in A *Christian Natural Theology*,[109] that Whiteheadian metaphysics requires that God be conceived not as an everlasting concrescence but as an everlasting personally ordered society of all-inclusive occasions of experience. Only through this modification can process theism be made coherent.

Neville's Critique

Neville, however, believes that this latter view of God is also incoherent. He makes a strong claim, saying that Hartshorne's doctrine of God is "radically incoherent," with difficulties "just as grave" as those it imputes to traditional theism.[110] I have examined most of the arguments supporting this claim above and found them wanting. However, one major argument remains, this one being directed specifically against the idea of God as a personally ordered society of divine occasions of experience.

What Neville attacks is Hartshorne's claim that concrete states of God, which involve contingency, include the abstract essence of God, which is neces-sary. Neville claims that "the conception of God as inclusive of the structures that provide the necessary divine nature cannot be made coherent."[111] The crux of the argument is that "it is difficult to see how a universal can be exhausted in even an infinite set of instantiations."[112] The problem, says Neville, is that the finite cannot include the infinite, the general cannot include the universal: "The universal always transcends the concrete."[113]

Evaluating Neville's Critique

The incoherence Neville believes he has spotted rests on an ambiguity in the word *include* in the question whether the concrete contains the abstract or the abstract the concrete. There is one sense in which the concrete includes the abstract, rather than the opposite. For example, red things, such as a red ball, include redness, whereas redness does not include the red ball, because most of the properties and relations of the ball are not covered by the notion of redness. Likewise, my character, being an abstraction, can be included in each of my con-crete experiences in a sense in which my character cannot include my concrete experiences. For example, if I am a chronically tardy person, each instance of my being tardy includes the abstract element of tardiness. From this abstract feature one can predict that, no matter what I am supposed to do, I will usually be tardy. But one could not deduce the concrete events in which this tardiness will be exemplified. Also, there will be many details in each such event that are not covered by the term *tardiness*. The concrete transcends while including the abstract. This is the point Hartshorne is making. The fact that the concrete states of a person are richer than the person's character allows us to understand how the concrete experiences of God can be contingent even though it is not contingent that experiences embodying the divine essence continue to occur. Because the concrete is greater than the abstract, it can as a whole be contin-gent while including a necessary aspect. (If A is necessary, and B is contingent, AB is contingent.) Inclusion in this sense can be called "actual inclusion."

On the other hand, there is a sense in which the abstract universal includes the concrete rather than the opposite. The abstract quality red includes all red things in the sense that all red things will fall under the universal, while a billion trillion red things will not exhaust red as a universal. Inclusion in this sense can be called "logical inclusion."

Neville's contention that Hartshorne's doctrine of God is incoherent is based on a confusion between these two meanings of inclusion. Neville is thinking of logical and therefore exhaustive inclusion. He quite rightly says that the concrete states of God cannot exhaustively include the divine essence and thereby the divine necessity. The divine essence, with its necessary existence, transcends any and all divine states, in the sense that it could have been exemplified in an infinite number of other divine states.

However, when Hartshorne said that the concrete includes the abstract, he was speaking of actual inclusion, not logical inclusion. He therefore did not mean that the abstract essence of God, with its necessity, is exhaustively contained in each divine state, or even all of them combined. In fact, to say this would move us back to a completely necessary universe, in which alternative possibilities do not really exist. There can be freedom only if the essence and actuality of God are distinct, so that the divine actuality *actually* transcends the divine essence, and this divine essence *logically* transcends the divine actuality. Therefore, Hartshorne could, without contradicting anything he meant, agree with Neville's statement that "the necessity in God must somehow transcend God as such, if God be a society."[114]

This point, however, does not necessarily lead to Neville's conclusion that the status of the transcendent metaphysical principles is a "more interesting prospect for divinity than Hartshorne's candidate."[115] In another formulation of this point, Neville says: "The transcendent normative reality of these requirements for divinity would seem to be more divine than the mere actual enduring individual."[116] This statement seems to illustrate Neville's tendency to take transcendence as a sufficient as well as necessary condition for deity, therefore being content with an extremely abstract deity. To say that we should worship the metaphysical principles constituting the abstract essence of deity, rather than the actual being who (actually) embodies those principles, seems odd to me. I doubt that arguments would be of any avail here. Neville and I probably simply have different ultimate intuitions.

But Neville's claim, if carried through analogically in practice, would have interesting consequences. For example, say that a wealthy woman with similar intuitions was so pleased, upon reading Neville's books, to find these sentiments expressed in the public arena that she gave a million-dollar award. But when Neville went to collect the money, he was told by the executor: "I'm sorry, sir, but what attracted the donor was the abstract essence Nevilleship. The award is for it. She designated nothing for any mere actual enduring individual in which Nevilleship is embodied."

Although this is a silly *reductio ad absurdum*, it drives home the fact that logical inclusion is not always the most important issue. It is the actual individuals, who actually include universals—not the universals, which logically include the actual individuals—who do things, who have intrinsic value, and who contribute value to us. We should settle for something else as a divine reality, I would say, only if we believe that an *actual* deity does not exist.

This belief, of course, lies behind Neville's various criticisms of process theology. The motivation behind these criticisms is perhaps best stated by Neville: "If there are as many difficulties with the process conception of God as 'individual, actual, and knowledgeable' as I have argued, then it is not out-of-hand to prefer another conception."[117] I have argued not only that Neville's alternative conception of God—as nonindividual, nonactual, and unknowing—is very problematic, but also that the difficulties that he alleges with the process conception of God disappear under close examination.

Appendix

Whitehead's Subjectivist Principle: From Descartes to Panexperientialism

This chapter has been relegated to an appendix partly because, although it makes an important contribution to this book, it is not absolutely essential to its argument, and partly because it is far more technical and exegetical than the other chapters. An earlier version—coauthored with Olav Bryant Smith—was published in *Process Studies*,[1] where authors can presuppose that readers know Whitehead's thought and technical terminology. The original purpose of that essay was simply to answer the question, What did Whitehead mean by "the subjectivist principle"?—a question of interest only to a small coterie of Whitehead scholars.

But this piece, in revised form, is included here because of the importance of the answer. This answer suggests that most of modern philosophy has been based on a mistake, because Descartes did not see the ontological implications of his own methodological discovery—a discovery that inaugurated the "subjectivist turn" of modern philosophy. This failure lies not only behind Descartes' dualism, with its insoluble mind-body problem, but also behind the various forms of materialism, idealism, and phenomenalism that have been proposed as alternatives. What Whitehead argues is that Descartes' subjectivist turn implies panexperientialism. If this is true, it is an insight of greatest importance.

The importance of getting clear what Whitehead meant by the "subjectivist principle" is also shown by the fact that he called it "the greatest philosophical discovery since the age of Plato and Aristotle." Unless one understands what Whitehead meant by this principle, one will necessarily have an inadequate understanding of what his philosophy is all about.

I hence offer this chapter, in spite of its exegetical and technical nature, because of the importance of its argument. Some readers, I should add, may want to skip directly from the first section, below, to the fourth section ("Interpretation SG"), so they can see that this chapter is headed toward a conclusion important enough to be worth slogging through the rather difficult intervening sections.

VARIOUS DEFINITIONS OF THE SUBJECTIVIST PRINCIPLE

What exactly does Whitehead mean by "the subjectivist principle" in the chapter with that title in *Process and Reality*? James E. Lindsey Jr. and I have both written essays seeking to answer this question. Neither of our essays, however, could make sense of all the relevant passages. The difficulty of doing so can be approached by examining two definitions given by Whitehead:

> Definition 1: "The subjectivist principle is, that the datum in the act of experience can be adequately analysed purely in terms of universals." (PR 157:25–26)[2]

> Definition 2: "The subjectivist principle is that the whole universe consists of elements disclosed in the analysis of the experiences of subjects." (PR 166: 36–38)

Definition 1, which is more prominent by virtue of being on the first page of Whitehead's chapter entitled "The Subjectivist Principle," is given as half of Whitehead's analysis of Hume's "sensationalist doctrine" (the other half of which is the "sensationalist principle," according to which "the primary activity in the act of experience is the bare subjective entertainment of the datum, devoid of any subjective form of reception" [PR 157:27–29]).

A comparison of Definitions 1 and 2 suggests that Whitehead used "the subjectivist principle" for two radically different principles. Whereas the first one is about the *datum* of experience, the second one is about the nature of *reality*. Also, whereas Whitehead clearly *affirms* the subjectivist principle of Definition 2, he clearly *rejects* the subjectivist principle of Definition 1, saying that it presupposes the 'substance-quality' concept of actuality (which Whitehead rejects) and that it has created great problems for modern philosophy, especially the difficulty of avoiding solipsism (PR 157–58). The reader can wonder, therefore, whether Whitehead intended the chapter title to refer to the principle of the first definition, the second one, or both.

The difficulty of discerning his meaning is increased by the fact that Whitehead, telling us repeatedly that he accepts a "reformed subjectivist principle" (PR 157, 160, 166, 167), defines it, in one passage, thus: "[T]he reformed subjectivist principle [is] that apart from the experiences of subjects there is nothing, nothing, nothing, bare nothingness" (PR 167:26–28). Although this statement is clear enough in itself, it makes the *reformed* subjectivist principle difficult to distinguish from the (unqualified) subjectivist principle of Definition 2, as both seem to affirm panexperientialism. The reader can wonder, therefore, whether there is a subtle difference between them or whether Whitehead sometimes equated "the subjectivist principle" and "the reformed subjectivist principle." This difficulty is aggravated by the fact that the paragraph containing Definition 2 is introduced by a discussion of the *reformed* subjectivist principle (PR 166:27).

A similar problem arises, moreover, with regard to a third definition of the subjectivist principle. (Although this definition speaks of the subjectivist *doctrine*, instead of *principle*, it seems to be simply using an alternative expression for the same idea.)

> Definition 3: The consideration of experiential togetherness raises the final metaphysical question: whether there is any other meaning of 'togetherness.' The denial of any alternative meaning, that is to say, of any meaning not abstracted from the experiential meaning, is the 'subjectivist' doctrine. (PR 189:38–41)

This definition seems to affirm the same doctrine as Definition 2, because both definitions affirm a panexperientialist metaphysics. Right after this third definition of the subjectivist principle, however, the text says: "This reformed version of the subjectivist doctrine is the doctrine of the philosophy of organism" (PR 189:42–43). This text thereby seems to obliterate any distinction between the subjectivist doctrine and the reformed version thereof. The mystery of the subjectivist principle, therefore, includes the difficulty of understanding exactly what Whitehead meant by the *reformed* subjectivist principle.

The difficulty with regard to the reformed subjectivist principle is compounded by Whitehead's introduction of another ambiguity. Although the definition at PR 167:27–28—"that apart from the experiences of subjects there is nothing, nothing, nothing, bare nothingness"—seems clearly to say that the reformed subjectivist principle is, like the subjectivist principle of Definition 2, a statement about the nature of reality, Whitehead elsewhere indicates that the reformed subjectivist principle, like the subjectivist principle of Definition 1, concerns the datum of experience. That is, whereas the subjectivist principle of Definition 1 says that the datum consists wholly of universals, thereby implying solipsism, the reformed subjectivist principle says that the datum of experience involves the objectification of other *actualities* (PR 160:20–30). Is the reformed subjectivist principle about the nature of reality as a whole, the nature of the datum of experience, or somehow both?

As if all of this were not confusing enough, Whitehead then gives a *fourth* definition of the (unqualified) subjectivist principle—one that deals neither with the datum of experience nor with the nature of reality, but with the primary data of, and hence proper method for, philosophy:

> Definition 4: "Descartes...laid down the principle, that those sub-stances which are the subjects enjoying conscious experiences provide the primary data for philosophy, namely, themselves as in the enjoy-ment of such experience. This is the famous subjectivist bias which entered into modern philosophy through Descartes. In this doctrine Descartes undoubtedly made the greatest philosophical discovery since the age of Plato and Aristotle. (PR 159:9–16)

Although this subjectivist *bias* has not usually been considered another state-ment of the subjectivist *principle*, Whitehead clearly calls it a "principle" in the first sentence (as well as a "doctrine" in the final one). Also, the same implica-tions that are here said to follow from the subjectivist bias are said at PR 167:12–26 to follow from "the subjectivist principle." This passage on page 167—assuming that it says what Whitehead meant to say—shows beyond any doubt that the description of the subjectivist bias constitutes a definition of the subjectivist principle. I will, in fact, refer to this passage as "the key passage," because it provided Smith and me with our primary clue for solving the mystery of the subjectivist principle.

   To summarize the major elements of this mystery: there are four definitions of the subjectivist principle, which deal with three different issues. The first def-inition deals with an *epistemological* point (about the datum of experience); the second and third definitions deal with a *metaphysical* point (about the nature of reality); and the fourth definition deals with a *methodological* point (about the proper procedure for philosophy). Besides having these very different principles all sharing the same name, we have the fact that Whitehead rejects the first one while affirming the second, third, and fourth. We have, moreover, a *reformed* subjectivist principle, which, in one formulation, contradicts the first (epistemo-logical) subjectivist principle but, in another formulation, is hard to distinguish from the second and third (metaphysical) subjectivist principles. Finally, "the reformed subjectivist principle," like "the subjectivist principle," seems to be applied to distinct principles that Whitehead affirms.

   Is it possible to provide an interpretation of Whitehead's position that rec-onciles all these elements? Can the mystery of the subjectivist principle be solved? After looking at Lindsey's attempt ("Interpretation L") and then at my earlier effort (Interpretation G), I will offer the interpretation I worked out with Olav Smith (Interpretation SG). Although, as I will show, Interpretations L and G both fall short, the new interpretation suggested here will incorporate insights contained in each of them. Surprisingly, however, this new interpretation turns out to agree most fully, at least in regard to Whitehead's positive doctrine, with yet another view, that of Richard Rorty (Interpretation R), a criticism of which provided the starting point of Lindsey's essay.

INTERPRETATIONS R AND L

Rorty's essay was titled "The Subjectivist Principle and the Linguistic Turn." One problem with this essay, says Lindsey, is that although Rorty said that "to understand the needs *Process and Reality* was intended to satisfy, one must understand Whitehead's diagnosis of the state of modern philosophy,"[3] Rorty's account of that diagnosis is incomplete.[4] This incompleteness is said to be based in part on the fact that Rorty imperfectly understood what Whitehead calls "the subjectivist principle." That is, Rorty uses "the *subjectivist*[5] *principle* . . . as if it had the same meaning as the term *subjectivist bias*, which Rorty in turn confuses with the *reformed subjectivist principle*." But the truth, Lindsey holds, is that these three concepts are "clearly defined and distinguished by Whitehead."[6] Rorty's imperfect understanding is due partly to the fact that he "overlooks or ignores those texts which explicitly define the *subjectivist*[7] *principle*" and partly to the fact that "some portions of the text of *Process and Reality* which Rorty quotes need editorial correction." Lindsey's contention is that although these three concepts were clearly distinguished in Whitehead's thinking, they "do not stand out as so distinguished" in *Process and Reality* "due to the state of the text," which requires editorial correction.[8]

Lindsey's complaint that Rorty fails to deal with Whitehead's explicit definition of the subjectivist principle presupposes that this definition is given in, and only in, what is here called "Definition 1," according to which "the datum in the act of experience can be adequately analysed purely in terms of universals" (PR 157:25–26). Because this is a principle that Whitehead rejects, Lindsey infers that an editorial correction is needed in any passages in which the text has Whitehead endorsing the subjectivist principle. One such passage—our "key passage"—says: "The difficulties of all schools of modern philosophy lie in the fact that, having accepted the subjectivist principle, they continue to use philosophical categories derived from another point of view" (PR 167:12–14). This passage goes on to say that although these categories, which generate the concept of "quality inherent in substance," are of "the utmost pragmatic use," they nevertheless "deal with high abstractions unsuitable for metaphysical use."

This discussion, Lindsey points out, is substantially the same as Whitehead's earlier discussion of the implications of the subjectivist bias. In that discussion, after defining the subjectivist bias as the principle "that those substances which are the subjects enjoying conscious experiences provide the primary data for philosophy, namely, themselves as in the enjoyment of such experience," Whitehead continued:

> In this doctrine Descartes undoubtedly made the greatest philosophical discovery since the age of Plato and Aristotle. For his doctrine directly traversed the notion that the proposition, "This stone is grey," expresses a primary form of known fact from which metaphysics can start its generalizations.... Primitive men were not metaphysicians.... Their language merely expressed useful abstractions, such as "greyness of the stone." But... Descartes missed the full sweep of his own discovery, and he and his successors, Locke and Hume, continued to construe the functionings of the subjective enjoyment of experience according to the substance-quality categories. Yet if the enjoyment of experience be the constitutive fact, these categories have lost all claim to any fundamental character in metaphysics. (PR 159:13–28)

On this basis—that the points made at PR 159 in relation to the subjectivist *bias* are made at PR 167 in relation to the subjectivist *principle*—Lindsey rightly concludes that both passages are about the same doctrine.

He also rightly says that, if this subjectivist bias is called, as it is in the latter passage, the subjectivist "principle," a problem becomes obvious when we compare this passage with what, according to Lindsey,[9] is Whitehead's "formal definition" of the subjectivist principle, the one given at PR 157:25–26. For one thing, the subjectivist bias is *endorsed* by Whitehead, whereas the subjectivist principle as defined at PR 157—which says that the datum of experience consists only of universals—is *rejected*.[10] For another thing, the two doctrines completely differ with regard to the substance-quality concept of actuality: Whereas Whitehead says that the subjectivist principle about the datum *presupposes* "[t]he acceptance of the 'substance-quality' concept as expressing the ultimate ontological principle" (PR 157), the passage at PR 167—in which the subjectivist principle is identified with the subjectivist bias—says that accepting this principle makes it, in Lindsey's words, "not only unnecessary to continue to use [the substance-quality concept], but rather a mistake to do so."[11]

Having provided this analysis, Lindsey concludes that "something is amiss: either *subjectivist principle* has two distinct and incompatible meanings or Whitehead intended some other term in one of these passages."[12] Lindsey is clearly correct about this. But then he simply, without discussion, ignores the first alternative—that Whitehead might have used "subjectivist principle" in two, incompatible ways—moving quickly instead to the suggestion that in the passage at PR 167, "Whitehead intended to say *subjectivist bias*,"[13] so that the text there should be changed. Part of the problem with Rorty's analysis, Lindsey holds, is that because he did not realize that this editorial correction needed to be made, he was more easily able to assume, wrongly, that the subjectivist bias and the subjectivist principle embody the same, or at least compatible, doctrines.[14]

Another passage that helped mislead Rorty, according to Lindsey, is the one here called "Definition 2": "The subjectivist principle is that the whole universe consists of elements disclosed in the analysis of the experiences of subjects" (PR 166:36–38). The positions of Lindsey and Rorty are diametrically opposed with regard to this passage. Whereas Rorty evidently took it to be *the* definition of the subjectivist principle, Lindsey, not regarding it as even *a* definition of this principle, suggests that "reformed" should be inserted before "subjectivist principle."[15] Lindsey has three reasons for this suggested textual change. First, this definition states a doctrine that Whitehead endorses, whereas Whitehead, according to Lindsey, uses "the subjectivist principle" only for a doctrine that he rejects. Second, this definition, Lindsey points out, occurs "in a paragraph in which Whitehead is explaining the meaning of the *reformed subjectivist principle*."[16] And third, this definition indicates that the (unqualified) subjectivist principle is identical in meaning to the reformed subjectivist principle of 167:26-28, according to which it says "that apart from the experiences of subjects there is nothing, nothing, nothing, bare nothingness." The text should be changed, Lindsey concludes, to make clearer that Whitehead is speaking here of the *reformed* subjectivist principle.

Although Lindsey does not mention it, a passage creating a similar problem for his interpretation occurs at PR 189:39–43. After giving a definition of simply "the 'subjectivist' doctrine" (according to which there is no meaning to "togetherness" other than "experiential togetherness"), the text then refers to this definition as a "reformed version of the subjectivist doctrine." Lindsey, to be consistent, should have advocated that the text also be changed here, so that it would no longer suggest that Whitehead endorses "the subjectivist doctrine."[17]

Interpretations R and L, in sum, could hardly be further apart. According to Interpretation R, the *subjectivist principle*, the *subjectivist bias*, and the *reformed subjectivist principle* are, while perhaps not quite identical, at least compatible, together expressing a self-consistent position. But for Interpretation L, although the *subjectivist bias* and the *reformed subjectivist principle* are compatible, because the latter is "an extension" of the former,[18] these two doctrines, which Whitehead accepts, are incompatible with the *subjectivist principle*, which he rejects. Rorty can consider the subjectivist principle to be compatible with the other two doctrines, Lindsey holds, only because he ignores the passage in which Whitehead gives his formal definition of the subjectivist principle, instead understanding this principle on the basis of two other passages, one of which is really about the subjectivist bias, the other of which is really about the reformed subjectivist principle.

Interpretation L is obviously based on a more thorough examination of the relevant passages than Interpretation R—which could stand for "relaxed" as well as "Rorty"—the most obvious problem of which is that it simply ignores Definition 1, in spite of the fact that this definition is given on the first page of

Whitehead's chapter. However, whereas this definition is ignored by Interpretation R despite its prominence, its importance is exaggerated by Interpretation L, which assumes it to be the one and only definition of Whitehead's subjectivist principle. Interpretation L, because of this assumption, has seven problems that render it improbable:

1. It must maintain that, although such an error could not easily be explained as a typing or printing error, Whitehead meant "subjectivist bias" instead of "subjectivist principle" at PR 167:12–14.

2. It must maintain that "subjectivist principle" at PR 166:36, also being erroneous, should be changed to "reformed subjectivist principle."

3. It would, for the sake of consistency, also require a similar change at PR 189:42, which would be a third textual change.

4. More problematically, it must insist that Whitehead never uses alternate expressions, such as "subjectivism" or "subjectivist doctrine," as equivalents for "subjectivist principle," at least in passages in which the concept is endorsed, such as PR 190:34–35: "The philosophy of organism admits the subjectivist doctrine (as here stated), but rejects the sensationalist doctrine" (which contains the subjectivist principle of Definition 1, thought by Interpretation L to be *the* definition). Interpretation L would have to argue—improbably—that "the subjectivist doctrine" here is *not* simply a synonym for "subjectivist principle." Otherwise, this passage would have Whitehead accepting one subjectivist principle while rejecting another.

5. Worse, in assuming that "the subjectivist principle" refers only to the principle stated at PR 157:25–26, Interpretation L assumes that Whitehead, in entitling the chapter "The Subjectivist Principle," arbitrarily named it for what is only one of two subordinate doctrines in the Humean "sensationalist doctrine."

6. Worse yet, it implies that this chapter, unlike any other chapter, is named for a principle that Whitehead *rejects*. Interpretation L could overcome this anomaly only by suggesting that the chapter title be changed to "The Reformed Subjectivist Principle," which would be a fourth editorial change needed to bring the text into line with this interpretation.

7. Still worse, Interpretation L must maintain that "reformed subjectivist principle" is a misnomer, because this phrase does *not* refer to "a revised or reformed version of the *subjectivist*

principle" but a complete repudiation of it.[19] Whereas the previous claims would imply merely that Whitehead was occasionally careless in writing (which is certainly true), this one would imply that he was *conceptually* confused about one of his major points.

Given all these problems inherent in Interpretation L,[20] a better interpretation was needed.

INTERPRETATION G

Such an interpretation was offered in my 1977 essay, "The Subjectivist Principle and Its Reformed and Unreformed Versions." As this title indicates, I disagreed with Lindsey's assumption that Whitehead could not have used "the subjectivist principle" to refer to different, even incompatible, doctrines.

My thesis, in most general terms, was that "Whitehead uses the term 'subjectivist principle' in two ways: one use refers to a principle which he rejects, while the second refers to a more general principle which he accepts."[21] The first use was, of course, what is here called "Definition 1." Because it refers to the *datum* of an experience—saying that it "can be adequately analysed purely in terms of universals"—I called it "subjectivist principle$_D$."[22] As evidence that Whitehead was conscious that this doctrine was not his only subjectivist principle, I pointed out that he sometimes, after using "the subjectivist principle," added a qualifying phrase: "as to the datum" (PR 158:12), "as applying to the datum for experience" (PR 160:1–2), or "as here stated" (PR 158:19; 190:34–35). Whitehead's second way of using "the subjectivist principle," I suggested, is Definition 2. Because this principle—that "the whole universe consists of elements disclosed in the analysis of the experience of subjects" (PR 166:36–38)—refers to the nature of reality, I dubbed it "the subjectivist principle$_R$."[23] By virtue of saying that Whitehead had two ways of using or defining "the subjectivist principle," I could, unlike Lindsey, accept this definition as a definition of a subjectivist principle.

A second crucial feature of Interpretation G is that the two doctrines referred to by "the subjectivist principle" are not on the same level. One is a more general doctrine, whereas the other is a particular version of it. The title of Whitehead's chapter, I argued, refers to the more general doctrine, which he affirms. Then, as I indicated by the title of my essay, this more general subjectivist doctrine comes in two versions—reformed and unreformed, depending on how the datum of experience is analyzed.[24] The unreformed version was the subjectivist principle$_D$, according to which the datum consists exclusively of universals. This unreformed version has been characteristic of modern philosophy (illustrated inconsistently by Descartes and Locke, consistently by Hume and Kant). The reformed version, according to which the datum includes other actualities, not merely universals, is thereby a reformed version of a more general principle, which Whitehead shared with modern philosophy.

My earlier analysis, up to this point, agrees with my present analysis. But I then made a suggestion that took me off course. Whereas the weakness of Interpretation L is shown by its inability to accept Definition 2 without changing it, so that it no longer refers to the subjectivist principle, Interpretation G arguably errs in the opposite direction by regarding Definition 2 as stating *the* subjectivist principle—the one Whitehead's chapter was all about. That is, the *general* subjectivist principle, spoken of in the previous paragraph, was identified with the subjectivist principle$_R$.[25] My central claim—that the subjectivist principle$_R$ is a general doctrine that Whitehead shares with modern philosophers (although they fail to see its revolutionary implications)—depended crucially on my assumption at that time that what I now call the "key passage" about the subjectivist principle—which Lindsey had to change to make it refer instead to the subjectivist bias—was compatible with my thesis. Speaking of the subjectivist principle$_R$, I said: "It is *this* principle to which Whitehead refers when he says: 'The difficulties of all schools of modern philosophy lie in the fact that, having accepted the subjectivist principle, they continue to use philosophical categories derived from another point of view'" (PR 167:12-14).[26] I will return later to the question of whether this claim makes sense. For now, I will spell out the nature of Interpretation G more fully.

Interpretation G implied that "the subjectivist doctrine" has not merely two but three meanings. It could refer to (1) the subjectivist principle$_R$ as such (which would refer only to the nature of reality), (2) the unreformed version of the subjectivist principle$_R$ (which would be a compound doctrine having two parts: the subjectivist principle$_R$ plus the subjectivist principle$_D$), or (3) the reformed version of the subjectivist principle$_R$ (which would consist of the subjectivist principle$_R$ plus Whitehead's analysis of the datum of experience as involving other actualities, not merely universals). Evidently not quite seeing the full implications of my analysis, I did not realize that although this third doctrine is most clearly specified by speaking of "the reformed subjectivist doctrine," it could also justifiably be called simply "the subjectivist doctrine"— because the reformed version is a version of the subjectivist doctrine every bit as much as is the unreformed version. (My failure to see this led me to suggest a textual change, as we will see.) According to Interpretation G, in any case, the reformed subjectivist principle is a compound doctrine, having both a metaphysical and an epistemological dimension, being "a doctrine about *both* the nature of reality and the datum of experience."[27] As I also pointed out, but only in an endnote,[28] the same was true of what he called the "unreformed" subjectivist principle.

Having summarized my former treatment of the reformed subjectivist principle and Definitions 1 and 2 of the subjectivist principle, I turn now to my former treatment of the subjectivist *bias* (which I now, unlike my former self as well as Lindsey, see as constituting another definition of the subjectivist principle). I said:

> Since the 'subjectivist bias' deals with the data for philosophy, it is not strictly identical with the subjectivist principle$_R$.... But it is closely related, and logically *follows from it*. If... "the whole universe consists of elements disclosed in the analysis of the experience of subjects"..., it follows that the primary data for the philosopher should be the "subjects enjoying conscious experiences."[29]

As this statement shows, although the subjectivist bias was for me closely related to the subjectivist principle$_R$, it was, besides not being identical with this principle, also neither part of it nor another aspect of some more inclusive subjectivist principle.

My treatment of the relation of the subjectivist bias to the *reformed* subjectivist principle was similar, portraying it as related but distinct. Pointing out that "Whitehead first discusses the reformed subjectivist principle in the context of the subjectivist bias," I illustrated this point by quoting, among other passages, Whitehead's statement that "Descartes' discovery on the side of subjectivism requires balancing by an 'objectivist' principle as to the datum for experience." This statement shows, I said, that "the reform involved in the reformed subjectivist doctrine has to do with an objectivist view of the datum."[30] I failed to point out, however, that "Descartes' discovery on the side of subjectivism" is a reference to the subjectivist *bias*, not to the subjectivist principle$_R$. Ignoring that fact, I concluded that "the *reformed* subjectivist principle [is] a reformed version of... the subjectivist principle$_R$."[31] To make my present point in a different way: Although I then regarded the reformed subjectivist principle as twofold, having both a metaphysical and an epistemological dimension, I evidently saw no reason to think that it might be *tripartite*, having also a methodological dimension constituted by the subjectivist bias.

Interpretation G was a step forward. Evidence that it was closer to the truth than Interpretation L is provided by the fact that it had none of the latter's seven problems. That is, thanks to Interpretation G's recognition that there is a subjectivist principle that Whitehead accepts, it did not require textual changes in those passages in which Whitehead endorses this principle. It also did not entail that Whitehead named his chapter after a principle that, besides being merely a subordinate principle on par with Hume's sensationalist principle, was also rejected by Whitehead. Finally, by virtue of regarding the reformed subjectivist principle as a reformed version of a more general subjectivist principle that has been widely accepted by modern thought (albeit in an unreformed version), this interpretation avoided implying that Whitehead's "reformed subjectivist principle" was a misnomer.

Interpretation G, nevertheless, had its own problems. Four of these were pointed out by me at the end of my essay. The first two were stated thus:

> 1. If Whitehead did have in mind a distinction between two meanings of the subjectivist principle, one would expect him to have distinguished more clearly between them. I have shown that some of his language does give hints of a distinction, but one would have expected a clearer, terminological distinction.
> 2. If Whitehead indeed intended the chapter title, "The Subjectivist Principle," to refer to a principle which he endorsed, one would have expected the chapter to have begun somewhat differently.[32]

These two points are indeed problems. But they will probably remain problems for any plausible solution. They remain problems, at least, for my present proposal. They need not be considered serious problems, however, because it could well be that the chapter was simply composed in a rather careless, confusing way—a description that is true, if usually in less extreme form, about much of Whitehead's writing.

My third self-assessed problem was the fact that my interpretation required a textual change in the following passage:

> The consideration of experiential togetherness raises the final metaphysical question: whether there is any other meaning of 'togetherness.' The denial of any alternative meaning, that is to say, of any meaning not abstracted from the experiential meaning, is the 'subjectivist' doctrine. This reformed version of the subjectivist doctrine is the doctrine of the philosophy of organism. (PR 189:38–43)

I mentioned this passage earlier, pointing out that Whitehead uses both "subjectivist" and "reformed subjectivist" without making clear how they are related. I also argued earlier that Lindsey's interpretation, to remain consistent, would require a textual change in the next to final sentence so that it would clearly refer, as does the final sentence, to the *reformed* subjectivist principle (since otherwise Whitehead would be endorsing the [unqualified] subjectivist doctrine). Although Interpretation G does not require that change, it does, I argued, require a different one. Because the (unqualified) subjectivist doctrine can exist in an *unreformed* version, it has to be distinct from the reformed subjectivist doctrine. To preserve this distinction, "This" at the beginning of the final sentence, I argued, should have been "The."[33]

My argument had merit. In the first place, as I pointed out, additional reason to believe that Whitehead intended to distinguish between a general subjectivist doctrine and the reformed version of it is provided on the next page of Whitehead's text, where he said:

> The difficulties of the subjectivist doctrine arise when it is combined with the 'sensationalist' doctrine concerning the analysis of the components which are together in experience.... The philosophy or organism admits the subjectivist doctrine (as here stated), but rejects the sensationalist doctrine [by which Whitehead meant primarily the subjectivist principle of Definition 1, which is one component of the Humean "sensationalist doctrine"]: hence its doctrine of the objectification of one actual occasion in the experience of another actual occasion. (PR 190:16–37)

I was clearly right, therefore, to say that Whitehead had a general subjectivist doctrine, which could be embodied in either an unreformed or a reformed version. I was also right to suggest that the textual error I alleged, unlike the errors postulated by Lindsey, could be easily explained as a typist's misreading of Whitehead's handwriting.[34] After all, Whitehead did give the typist a handwritten copy, his handwriting was not always clear, and he was not a careful proofreader.

Nevertheless, the fact that Interpretation G required this textual change *was* a weakness. I will explain later, furthermore, why Whitehead could have written "This" instead of "The," even though he did, as Interpretation G said, affirm a general subjectivist doctrine that could be formulated in reformed and unreformed versions.

My fourth self-assessed problem also involved the relation between the unqualified and reformed subjectivist principles. I described this problem thus:

> Whitehead writes: "Finally, the reformed subjectivist principle must be repeated: that apart from the experiences of subjects there is nothing, nothing, nothing, bare nothingness" (PR 167:26–28).[35] The problem is that this seems to be merely a restatement of the subjectivist principle$_R$ ["The subjectivist principle is that the whole universe consists of elements disclosed in the analysis of the experiences of subjects" (PR 166:36–38)]; it seems to state nothing about the datum of a subject's experience, and hence seems not to be a restatement of the *reformed* subjectivist principle as I have interpreted it.[36]

Although I provided an interpretation of these two passages that allowed the distinction between the two principles to be maintained, this interpretation was, I admitted, "somewhat forced."[37]

I discussed this problem above, it will be recalled, in relation to the position of Lindsey, who provided another solution. No problem exists, argued Lindsey, once it is recognized that the statement at PR 166 occurs in a paragraph explaining the meaning of the *reformed* subjectivist principle. The fact that there is no problem, Lindsey further suggested, would be clearer if the text were emended so that it would say that "the reformed subjectivist principle is that the whole...." What I called the "subjectivist principle$_R$" (and I here call "Definition 2"), therefore, is really, according to Lindsey, a statement of the *reformed* subjectivist principle. In assessing this argument, we must remember that it was motivated by Lindsey's (false) belief that Whitehead could not have referred positively to the (unqualified) subjectivist principle. This consideration does not necessarily mean, however, that Lindsey was wrong about this passage, which does occur in a paragraph that begins by discussing the reformed subjectivist principle. My new interpretation, in any case, will suggest that although Lindsey was right to say that the entire paragraph is about the *reformed* subjectivist principle, the text is fine as it stands. With regard to my earlier interpretation, my present view can explain why, although I was right to say that there is a distinction in Whitehead's philosophy between the unqualified and the reformed subjectivist principles, this distinction need not be maintained, by means of a forced interpretation, in *this* passage.

Besides agreeing with my former self that two of the problems I saw in my own interpretation constitute real weaknesses in it, I have now discovered three additional problems—ones that are, moreover, even more serious than those I saw earlier.

One of these additional problems is that I did not, as I mentioned earlier, recognize that the definition of the subjectivist *bias*, which Whitehead also called both a "principle" and a "doctrine," should also be considered a definition of the subjectivist *principle* (or *doctrine*). Furthermore, given the fact that Whitehead called this doctrine "the greatest philosophical discovery since the age of Plato and Aristotle" (PR 159:13–15), should I not have suspected that it is this doctrine (or principle) to which the title of the chapter refers?

A second, closely related problem involves my earlier interpretation of the "key passage." According to this passage, "The difficulties of all schools of modern philosophy lie in the fact that, having accepted the subjectivist principle, they continue to use philosophical categories derived from another point of view" (PR 167:12-14). This passage is crucial for Interpretation SG, partly because all interpretations besides this one seem to have trouble accommodating it. Interpretation L had to assume that Whitehead meant to say "bias" here instead of "principle" (because otherwise Whitehead would be endorsing the subjectivist principle). According to Interpretation G, this passage would have Whitehead saying that all schools of modern philosophy have accepted the subjectivist principle$_R$, which, by asserting that "the whole universe consists of elements disclosed in the analysis of the experiences of subjects," is an affirmation of panexperientialism. Interpretation G is, therefore, clearly refuted by this passage.

A third problem with Interpretation G is that it took no account of the role played in the chapter's argument by the "sensationalist principle," which (falsely) says that "the primary activity in the act of experience is the bare subjective entertainment of the datum, devoid of any subjective form of reception" (PR 157:27–29). Although I did discuss this doctrine at some length, I did so only in my endnotes and only to correct Lindsey's misunderstanding of it. I did not show this doctrine to play an essential role in Whitehead's exposition of the subjectivist doctrine. But if the sensationalist principle—or rather, Whitehead's rejection of it—was not essential to this exposition, why would he have introduced it on the first page and then devoted much of sections 3 and 4 to it?[38]

Although I was not aware of these final three problems, I did conclude my essay by expressing "the hope that it will prod others to seek a better interpretation."[39] Such an interpretation is what Smith and I set out to provide.

INTERPRETATION SG

Most of the elements of our interpretation are implicit in the foregoing discussion—in the introductory summary of the mystery of the subjectivist principle combined with our critique of prior solutions. Much of what follows, accordingly, will simply involve showing how these elements fit together.

Advance Summary of Interpretation SG

According to the new interpretation offered here, the subjectivist principle referred to by Whitehead's chapter title is ambiguous. Whitehead sometimes used the expression in a minimal sense, sometimes in a middling sense, and sometimes in a maximal sense. In its *minimal* sense, this subjectivist principle is simply the subjectivist bias (here called "Definition 4"). Because the subjectivist principle in this minimal sense involves the proper method for philosophy, we can call it the subjectivist principle$_M$. In its *middling* sense, the subjectivist principle includes not only this methodological bias but also Whitehead's objectivist doctrine of the datum of experience. The subjectivist principle in this middling sense, having both the methodological and epistemological elements, can be called the "subjectivist principle$_{ME}$." In its *maximal* sense, the subjectivist principle also includes a panexperientialist metaphysics.

Given the addition of this metaphysical element, it can be called the "subjectivist principle$_{MEM}$."

By virtue of its latter two elements, the subjectivist principle in the maximal sense can also be called the "reformed subjectivist principle," because these two elements carry out the epistemological and metaphysical reforms that are implicit in the subjectivist bias—reforms that modern philosophy, while accepting this methodological revolution, failed to carry out. To put this point in the reverse way: *The reformed subjectivist principle can be considered simply the subjectivist principle in the maximal or full-fledged sense*, because the subjectivist bias, when fully thought through, implies an objectivist doctrine of the datum of experience (versus modern philosophy's subjectivist principle$_D$) and a panexperientialist metaphysic (versus modern philosophy's dualistic, materialistic and idealistic metaphysical positions or, alternatively, its positivistic refusal, rooted in a phenomenalist analysis of the datum of experience, to develop a metaphysical position).

Implicit in that point is another way of summarizing Interpretation SG. Whitehead's discussion of the subjectivist principle, as Rorty's essay emphasized, lies at the heart of his diagnosis of the problems of modern philosophy. At the root of this diagnosis is the fact that all schools of distinctively modern philosophy, besides accepting the subjectivist bias, retained old, alien philosophical categories that led them to a subjectivist (solipsistic) account of the datum of experience (the subjectivist principle$_D$) and to a false metaphysics (or else positivism). Whitehead's chapter involves a deconstruction of this *modern* subjectivist principle (which includes two elements: the subjectivist bias plus the subjectivist account of the datum) and a reconstruction of what could be called a "postmodern" subjectivist principle (with its three elements). This postmodern subjectivist principle is equivalent to the maximal subjectivist principle, which is in turn, as explained earlier, equivalent to the reformed subjectivist principle.

I believe that this interpretation, besides being illuminating of what Whitehead was up to, is also compatible with all the relevant passages. I will examine the difficult passages after explaining the bases for this interpretation.

From the Minimal to the Middling Subjectivist Principle

The key passage, as I have emphasized, is the one at PR 167:12–26, which begins: "The difficulties of all schools of modern philosophy lie in the fact that, having accepted the subjectivist principle, they continue to use philosophical categories derived from another point of view" (PR 167:12–14).

Although Lindsey wrongly thought that this passage should be altered, he rightly said that it concerns the subjectivist bias, as can be seen by comparing this passage with Whitehead's earlier discussion of that bias. In that earlier discussion, Whitehead said that Descartes, besides leading modern philosophy astray by increasing "the metaphysical emphasis on the substance-quality forms of thought," also did something positive of utmost importance. "He also laid down the [methodological] principle, that those substances which are the subjects enjoying conscious experiences provide the primary data for philosophy, namely, themselves as in the enjoyment of such experience. This is the famous subjectivist bias which entered into modern philosophy through Descartes" (PR 159:9–13).

Then, saying that although "[i]n this doctrine Descartes undoubtedly made the greatest philosophical discovery since the age of Plato and Aristotle," Whitehead added that Descartes, like Columbus, "missed the full sweep of his own discovery," because he "continued to construe the functionings of the subjective enjoyment of experience according to the substance-quality categories," failing to realize that "if the enjoyment of experience be the constitutive subjective fact, these categories have lost all claim to any fundamental character in metaphysics" (PR 159:13–27). As Lindsey emphasized, this way of evaluating the significance of the subjectivist bias is repeated at PR 167:12–26, but there as the implications of the subjectivist *principle*. The topic of the latter passage, therefore, must be identical with that of the former.

Lindsey's chief contribution was to point out this identification, thereby inadvertently revealing this latter passage to be the key to solving the mystery of the subjectivist principle. The positive importance[40] of this passage is twofold: It shows that Whitehead understood the subjectivist *principle*, at least partly, in terms of the subjectivist *bias*. And it shows that this subjectivist bias, which is a methodological point, is a principle that is shared by "all schools of modern philosophy."

Given this insight, we can see how to move beyond Interpretation G. That interpretation was correct to say that, in addition to the subordinate subjectivist principle that Whitehead introduces with disapproval on the first page of his chapter, he also had in mind a *general* subjectivist principle, which he shared with modern philosophy. But Interpretation G then misidentified this general principle, thinking it to be the one given in Definition 2, which endorses a pan-experientialist metaphysics. The key passage, besides showing this identification to be wrong, suggests that the general principle in question must be the methodological principle announced in the subjectivist bias, meaning that it is Definition 4 that states the general subjectivist principle.

This hypothesis is confirmed by a second crucial passage, in which Whitehead, discussing the doctrine he called the "reformed subjectivist principle," said that although "this doctrine fully accepts Descartes' discovery that subjective experiencing is the primary metaphysical situation which is presented to metaphysics for analysis . . . [,] Descartes' discovery on the side of subjectivism requires balancing by an 'objectivist' principle as to the datum for experience" (PR 160:23–35). The prior interpretations, not realizing that the subjectivist *bias* is also a subjectivist *principle*—let alone *the* subjectivist principle that Whitehead's chapter is all about[41]—assumed that the *reformed* subjectivist principle had to be a reformed version of something other than the subjectivist bias. This passage, however, shows that the reform Whitehead had in mind—which, everyone agrees, involves (at least) overcoming the subjectivist principle[D] by providing an "objectivist" analysis of the datum for experience—results in a reformed version of the subjectivist *bias*.

It is a reformed version because it contains the epistemological and metaphysical points that were implied by Descartes' methodological discovery from the outset, although Descartes, along with modern philosophy in general, failed to see these implications. Far from being a misnomer, then, "reformed subjectivist principle" expresses perfectly what Whitehead wanted to say. From his perspective, modern philosophy was malformed from the outset, because it had an epistemology and a metaphysics (or a positivistic refusal of metaphysics) that distorted the epistemological and metaphysical implications inherent in its subjectivist bias.

To explain: Descartes made a revolutionary discovery with regard to philosophical method, realizing that the primary data for philosophers are provided by their own subjective enjoyment of experience. According to this subjectivist principle, for example, when I see a grey stone, the primary fact is not "This stone is grey" but "my perception of this stone as grey" (PR 159:15–19). Implicit in this methodological subjectivism was a reform of the basic categories for providing an epistemological analysis of human experience and a metaphysical analysis of reality as a whole. This reform was implicit because the new methodological principle showed the inappropriateness of the substance-quality categories, which had dominated philosophical thought prior to Descartes' subjectivist turn. But Descartes and his modern followers, rather than carrying out this reform, retained those old categories, thereby developing an *unreformed* version of the subjectivist principle (bias). Whitehead reformed it, not only in the sense of reshaping it but also in the sense that this reshaping returned it to the form that was implicit in it from the outset. Because this reformed subjectivist principle involves a rejection of the version of the subjectivist bias (principle) that was integral to distinctively modern philosophy, this reformed version can be considered distinctively postmodern.

Why does the subjectivist bias imply this postmodern philosophy, with its epistemological and metaphysical elements? To begin with the epistemological element: the modern subjectivist principle, by virtue of its acceptance of the subjectivist bias, rightly says that philosophy should begin with an analysis of human experience as such, taking its primary elements as the starting points for generalization (PR 158–59). But modern philosophy wrongly held that the datum of experience—meaning that which is primary in the sense of being *given* to experience—consists entirely of universals. The basic reason why this analysis was accepted by the founding modern philosophers—Descartes and Locke inconsistently, Hume and Kant consistently[42]—was their retention of "the 'substance-quality' concept as expressing the ultimate ontological principle" so that "the final metaphysical fact is always to be expressed as a quality inhering in a substance" (PR 157–58). Descartes, therefore, defined substances, in the sense of actual things, as things that "required nothing but themselves in order to exist" (PR 159:7) so that the experiences of those substances that are human minds are merely their private qualities. And Hume "looked for a universal quality to function as qualifying the mind, by way of explanation of its perceptive enjoyment" (PR 159:29–30). Accordingly, "From the original fact of 'my perception of this stone as grey,' Hume extracts 'Awareness of sensation of greyness'; and puts it forward as the ultimate datum in this element of experience" (PR 159:37–39).

However, given the acceptance of the subjectivist bias, according to which "the enjoyment of experience [is] the constitutive subjective fact," the substance-quality category "has lost all claim to any fundamental character in metaphysics" (PR 159:25–27). In other words, "with the advent of Cartesian subjectivism, the substance-quality category has lost all claim to metaphysical primacy; and, with this deposition of substance-quality, we can reject the notion of individual substances, each with its private world of qualities and sensations" (PR 160:35–39). The philosopher is thereby freed to give an analysis of the datum of experience that corresponds to our common sense—in the sense of those beliefs that we inevitably presuppose in practice[43]—and "our common sense is inflexibly objectivist: We perceive other things which are in the world of actualities in the same sense as we are" (PR 158:23-24).

That is, once we are freed from distortion required by the substance-quality assumption, we are free to give an explicit analysis of the datum of experience that simply brings out our implicit presupposition, which is that we directly experience other actualities, not mere universals. We know that we experience blueness and roundness "with the eye." We know implicitly, in other words, that our experience of universals is derivative from our experience of actualities, such as our eyes. Therefore, once philosophers see that the subjectivist bias undermines the substance-quality categories, they will naturally combine this subjectivist principle as to philosophical method with "an 'objectivist' principle as to the datum for experience" (PR 160:34–35). They will thereby have a reformed subjectivist principle—at least with regard to the epistemological issue. By virtue of affirming the subjectivist principle$_{ME}$, they will have gone two-thirds of the way to the maximal, full-fledged subjectivist principle.

From the Middling to the Maximal Subjectivist Principle

To go all the way, they need to develop the metaphysical position that is implicit in the subjectivist principle$_{ME}$. Such a metaphysics, according to

Whitehead, would be what I call "panexperientialist" (but could equally well be called "pansubjectivist").

Whitehead made this point early in *Process and Reality*: saying that his philosophy repudiated the idea of "vacuous actuality"—understood as "a *res vera* devoid of subjective immediacy"—he added that the "notion of 'vacuous actuality' is very closely allied to the notion of the 'inherence of quality in substance'" (PR 29:1–6), referring ahead to the chapter entitled "The Subjectivist Principle" as the place where he would explain the basis for this repudiation. (Of course, as merely one chapter, it presupposes ideas developed more fully elsewhere in the book, several of which will, in fact, be mentioned in my exposition.)

In this chapter, just after the key passage—in which Whitehead complained about the retention of categories that have been undermined by the subjectivist principle$_M$—he referred specifically to these same two categories: "the concept of vacuous actuality, void of subjective experience; and . . . the concept of quality inherent in substance" (167:19–21).

He clearly held, therefore, that the subjectivist principle$_M$ leads to the subjectivist principle$_{MEM}$. We have seen how it leads to the subjectivist principle$_{ME}$. But how does it, or the subjectivist principle$_{ME}$, lead to a panexperientialist metaphysics and thereby to the subjectivist principle$_{MEM}$? There are two paths.

The first path involves an argument by analogy from the only actualities about which we have direct knowledge of what they are in themselves, because we know them from inside—namely, our own occasions of experience. Dualists and materialists, insofar as they claim to be basing their concept of 'vacuous (nonexperiencing) actualities' on primary elements in their own experience, assume that things such as grey rocks are such elements. As Whitehead points out, however, "This stone is grey" is *not* a primary element. It is, instead, a derivative abstraction from "my perception of this stone as grey" (PR 159).

The only thing we have direct, inside knowledge of is our own perceiving or, more generally, our own experiencing. This is our one and only inside knowledge of actual existence—of what it is like to be an actuality. We do know, as the subjectivist principle$_{ME}$ acknowledges, that our experience is the "self-enjoyment of being one among many, and of being one arising out of the composition of many" (versus Descartes, who took our experience to be the "self-enjoyment, by an individual substance, of its qualification by ideas," an idea that reflected his more general view that to be an "actuality" is "to be a substance with inhering qualities" [PR 145]). But if we are to have a meaningful idea of the other actual things constituting that "many," we can do so only if we think of them by analogy with an occasion of our own experience. Why is this? Because, if we accept the subjectivist principle$_M$, "the percipient occasion is its own standard of actuality" (PR 145). All actualities, therefore, must be thought of as occasions of experience.

The second path from the subjectivist principle_ME to panexperientialism involves the rejection of the "sensationalist principle," which was introduced by Whitehead on the first page of the chapter as the other half, along with the subjectivist principle as to the datum, of Hume's overall "sensationalist *doctrine*." The sensationalist *principle* is the false doctrine "that the primary activity in the act of experience is the bare subjective entertainment of the datum, devoid of any subjective form of reception" (PR 157). Whitehead's contrary doctrine is that the datum *from the very origination* of the experience evokes in it a *sympathetic* subjective form of response to itself, with this subjective form consisting most fundamentally of emotional and appetitive feelings (PR 162).

The way in which the subjectivist principle_ME leads to this view requires that we look more closely at Whitehead's account of the primary datum in human experience. Whitehead writes: "[C]ommon sense is inflexibly objectivist. We perceive other things which are in the world of actualities in the same sense as we are." Whitehead then adds that "our emotions are directed towards other things, including of course our bodily organs" (PR 158).

Far from being merely incidental, this mention of our bodily organs is central to Whitehead's position. Although Hume claimed in *theory* not to have direct perceptual knowledge of other actualities, he inadvertently revealed, Whitehead points out, that in practice he knew better. He revealed, for example, his awareness that he perceived colors *with his eyes* (PR 81, 122, 171–73). An even more complete description of our perception of a grey stone than that given earlier, therefore, would speak of *our perception of this stone as grey with (by means of) our eyes*. The part of this datum constituted by "this stone as grey" belongs to a derivative, high-level feeling (PR 160). A more primitive element in that occasion of experience is our feeling of our eyes, *with which* we see the stone. The generalization of this point is that we perceive the world external to our bodies *with* our bodies, so that our *most direct* perception of what we call "the physical world" is not our sensory perception of external things but *our reception of feelings from our bodies*.

Implicit in this recognition of the primacy of visceral feelings is a philosophical revolution. But modern philosophers, "concentrat[ing] on visual feelings" (meaning the *data* of visual perception), have "disdained the information about the universe obtained through their visceral feelings" (PR 121). That modern approach, however, is backward, because the "withness of the body," said Whitehead, "makes the body the starting point for our knowledge of the circumambient world" (PR 81; cf. 312). What information would we learn about the world in general if we would make our bodies—our *visceral* feelings—the starting point for knowledge about it?

The unique feature of my feelings of my own body, because of its "peculiarly intimate association with immediate experience," is that my bodily organs are "distinguishable data whose *formal constitutions are immediately felt* in the origination of experience" (PR 75; emphasis added). For Whitehead, the "formal" constitution of an actual entity—or what it is when considered "formally"—is what "the actual entity is in itself, for itself," which means "the experience enjoyed by [that] actual entity" (PR 51).[44]

Whitehead was not here violating his position that occasions of experience cannot prehend contemporary occasions, incidentally, because he did *not* mean that we feel the occasions of experience in our bodily organs while their feelings are still in the process of concrescence. Rather, "the eyes and the hands are in the past (the almost immediate past)" (PR 63). What he meant is that in feeling our bodily parts, we are aware that *they had their own feelings*, because we feel those feelings *sympathetically*. Describing the most fundamental dimension of our "physical experience," meaning our feeling of other actualities, Whitehead said: "The primitive form of physical experience is emotional—blind emotion—received as felt elsewhere in another occasion and conformally appropriated as a subjective passion. In the language appropriate to the higher stages of experience, the primitive element is *sympathy*, that is, feeling the feeling *in* another and feeling conformally *with* another" (PR 162). For present purposes, the most important ideas here are that we are aware of receiving emotion from "another occasion," an awareness that means that it must have its own emotion, and that in having sympathy with it we are "feeling the feeling *in* another," which means that this other thing had to have its *own* feeling.

About which other actualities are we directly aware, by virtue of being conscious of our sympathetic response to them, that they had their own experiences? We have this direct awareness, most clearly, about those actual entities constituting our own past occasions of experience (this kind of "feeling of feeling" is, of course, called "memory" [PR 120]). We also can have such awareness, albeit much less regularly and clearly, about the analogous occasions of experience constituting the psyches of other animals, especially other human beings.[45]

But what about lower grade actual entities, which have in modern thought been assumed to be vacuous actualities? With regard to such actualities, we are more or less consciously aware, most of our waking hours, of responding sympathetically to the *actualities constituting our bodily parts*. In fact, said Whitehead, a phenomenological survey of human perception "supports the view that the predominant basis of perception is perception of the various bodily organs, as passing on their experiences by channels of transmission and of enhancement" (PR 119). For present purposes, again, the central idea here is that in perceiving our bodily organs, we perceive them as passing on *their experiences*—which means that we are at least dimly aware they had their own experiences, out of which our experiences arose.

With regard to low-grade actualities *beyond* our bodies, we are not consciously aware of having sympathetic responses to them, at least ordinarily.[46]

This negative fact does not, however, mean that we should conclude that those more remote low-grade actualities are wholly devoid of feelings, or even that we should remain agnostic about them. Given the fact that "the animal body is only the more highly organized and immediate part of the general environment for its dominant actual occasion" (PR 119), there is surely no difference in kind between the actualities composing our bodies and those constituting nature beyond our bodies. We can reasonably conclude from the information about our bodily actualities derived from our visceral feelings, therefore, that the actualities beyond our bodies also have their own experiences. As Whitehead said in his most important statement on this point: "It is the accepted doctrine in physical science that a living body is to be interpreted according to what is known of other sections of the physical universe. This is a sound axiom; but it is double-edged. For it carries with it the converse deduction that other sections of the universe are to be interpreted in accordance with what we know of the human body" (PR 119). In other words, because we know that the actualities making up our bodies are experiential in character, we can reasonably infer that the remainder of the actualities in the universe are, in their formal constitutions, also experiential in character.[47] This is the final step in Whitehead's move from the subjectivist principle$_{ME}$ to panexperientialism and hence to the subjectivist principle$_{MEM}$.

EXPLAINING THE DIFFICULT PASSAGES

The main textual problems for Interpretation G, as we saw, involved its necessity for maintaining, in every passage, a distinction between the (unqualified) subjectivist principle and the reformed subjectivist principle. One passage that seemed to resist such a distinction is Definition 2: "The subjectivist principle is that the whole universe consists of elements disclosed in the analysis of the experiences of subjects" (PR 166: 36-38).

There are three reasons why Definition 2 seems to be a definition not only of the (unqualified) subjectivist principle but also of the reformed subjectivist principle. First, it occurs in a paragraph about that latter principle. Second the reformed subjectivist principle is, on the next page, defined as the doctrine that "apart from the experiences of subjects there is nothing, nothing, nothing, bare nothingness" (PR 167:26–28), and this definition is simply a reformulation of the same doctrine, panexperientialism, that is affirmed by Definition 2. Third, this definition of the reformed subjectivist principle is introduced by the statement that "the reformed subjectivist principle must be repeated," and the only candidate for a previous statement of it is Definition 2. These two definitions, therefore, seem to say that the (unqualified) subjectivist principle is identical with the reformed subjectivist doctrine.

Interpretation G—given its assumption that the subjectivist principle, being a general doctrine common to Whitehead and all modern philosophy, always had to be different from the reformed subjectivist principle—found this apparent identification troubling. According to the new interpretation, by contrast, the general subjectivist principle, which in its minimal form is the subjectivist bias (the subjectivist principle$_M$), can also exist in its middling form, which affirms an objectivist principle of the datum of experience (the subjectivist principle$_{ME}$), and in its maximal form, which also affirms a panexperientialist metaphysics (the subjectivist principle$_{MEM}$). Either of these latter two forms— the middling or the maximal—is also a *reformed* subjectivist principle. By virtue of affirming a panexperientialist metaphysics, Definition 2 states the subjectivist principle in the maximal sense. In terms of my subscripts, therefore, Definition 2 would read: "The subjectivist principle$_{MEM}$ is that the whole universe consists of elements disclosed in the analysis of the experiences of subjects." Thus understood, this passage, by virtue of affirming the identity of the (full-fledged or maximal) subjectivist principle with the reformed subjectivist principle, is, far from being a problem, the summary statement of the metaphysical point of Whitehead's chapter.

Interpretation G also had trouble with the fact that any distinction between the reformed and unreformed versions of the subjectivist principle seems to be obliterated by Definition 3, which says: "The denial of any alternative meaning [of "togetherness" other than "experiential togetherness"], that is to say, of any meaning not abstracted from the experiential meaning, is the 'subjectivist' doctrine. This reformed version of the subjectivist doctrine is the doctrine of the philosophy of organism" (PR 189:39-43). Interpretation G, as we saw, held that "This" in the final sentence needed to be changed to "The" in order to preserve a distinction between the general subjectivist doctrine (or principle) and the reformed version of it. My present interpretation requires no such change, because I now regard the reference in the next to final sentence to refer to the subjectivist doctrine in the maximal sense, which *is* the reformed version of the subjectivist doctrine. With subscripts, this definition would read: "The denial of any alternative meaning [of "togetherness" other than "experiential togetherness"], that is to say, of any meaning not abstracted from the experiential meaning, is the 'subjectivist' principle$_{MEM}$. This reformed version of the subjectivist principle$_M$ is the doctrine of the philosophy of organism." Interpretation SG, therefore, has no problem with the definitions of the subjectivist principle that were problematic from the perspective of prior interpretations.

This new interpretation, however, might seem to leave a problem with regard to the reformed subjectivist principle. According to the identifications made above, the reformed subjectivist doctrine can be equated with Definition 2 of the subjectivist principle, according to which "the whole universe consists of elements disclosed in the analysis of the experiences of subjects" (PR 166–36–38), and with Definition 3, "[t]he denial of any alternative meaning [of 'togetherness' other than 'experiential togetherness'], that is to say, of any meaning not abstracted from the experiential meaning" (PR 189:40–42).

The problem, discussed in relation to Interpretation G, is that these statements can seem to affirm no "reform" other than panexperientialism. I myself made this point about the latter one, saying that "it seems to state nothing about the datum of a subject's experience, and hence seems not to be a restatement of the *reformed* subjectivist principle as I have interpreted it."[48] I attempted, in what I admitted to be a "somewhat forced" interpretation, to explain how this latter definition could nevertheless be regarded, unlike the first one, as implicitly affirming an objectivist doctrine of the datum. From the perspective of the new interpretation, however, no forced distinction is needed, because *both* definitions are seen as referring to the reformed subjectivist principle.

To explain: just as Whitehead has minimal, middling, and maximal versions of the subjectivist principle, he has minimal and maximal versions of the reformed subjectivist principle. The minimal version simply balances the subjectivist bias with an objectivist doctrine of the datum of experience (with this version being illustrated in the two paragraphs at PR 160:20–39, in which the "reformed subjectivist principle" is limited to having "Descartes' discovery on the side of subjectivism [balanced] by an 'objectivist' principle as to the datum for experience").[49] The maximal version adds panexperientialist metaphysics.

It is natural that, when Whitehead is focusing on the maximal version, he would tend to emphasize the panexperientialist, metaphysical dimension of it, while simply presupposing the epistemological dimension. And this epistemological dimension, with its insistence that "the experiences of subjects" always involve the experiences of *other* subjects, *is* presupposed in the two passages in question. It is most clearly presupposed in Definition 3, which speaks of "experiential togetherness." But it can also be seen as presupposed in Definition 2, given Whitehead's view of the implications of the subjectivist principle$_M$ (the subjectivist bias), which we summarized above. That is, once philosophers have given up the substance-quality analysis of actuality (which they clearly have if they have affirmed Whitehead's panexperientialism, according to which the actual world consists exclusively of occasions of experience), nothing stands in their way of affirming the obvious fact—obvious because "our common sense is inflexibly objectivist"—that the datum of our experience always includes other actualities. Given panexperientialism, furthermore, these other actualities would be the experiences of other subjects. Accordingly, Definitions 2 and 3, besides being maximal versions of the subjectivist principle, are also maximal versions of the reformed subjectivist principle.[50]

CONCLUSION

The discussion of the subjectivist principle has come full circle. It began with Rorty's essay, which seemed simply to assume, uncritically, that Whitehead used "subjectivist principle," "subjectivist bias," and "reformed subjectivist principle" interchangeably. Lindsey then argued that this could not be true, because the subjectivist principle, as defined on the first page of the chapter, was a principle that Whitehead rejected. Lindsey rightly pointed out that Rorty's interpretation could not do justice to that passage and similar ones. But then Lindsey, assuming this passage to have provided *the* definition of Whitehead's subjectivist principle, himself could not accommodate a number of other passages.

My interpretation then made an advance by showing that Lindsey's preferred definition, being a definition of a principle Whitehead rejected, had to be distinguished from a more general subjectivist principle, which Whitehead accepted and to which the chapter title referred. But my identification of this more general principle with Definition 2, which affirms panexperientialism, meant that my interpretation, in turn, could not accommodate all the relevant passages.

My present interpretation, while being much more complex than Rorty's, essentially returns to his view. Part of the added complexity of this new view is that it distinguishes between a subjectivist principle that Whitehead rejected and one that he accepted. Having made that distinction, furthermore, it then makes a threefold distinction with respect to the subjectivist principle that Whitehead accepted, showing that it can be expressed in a minimal, a middling, or a maximal form. The new interpretation then adds that this subjectivist principle in its minimal sense can be equated with the subjectivist bias; that in its middling sense it can be equated with the reformed subjectivist principle in *its* minimal sense; and that the subjectivist principle in its maximal sense can be equated with the reformed subjectivist principle in *its* maximal sense. Accordingly, although Rorty's relaxed assumption—that all three terms pointed to a single doctrine—was essentially correct, it was far *too* relaxed.

Given Rorty's emphasis on the fact that Whitehead's analysis of the subjectivist principle was at the heart of his critique of the difficulties of distinctively modern philosophy, Rorty also recognized, without using the term, that Whitehead was proposing a type of *postmodern* philosophy. However, aside from this recognition and the vague agreement explained in the previous paragraph, I would disassociate myself from Rorty's essay. His presentation of Whitehead's analysis of the difficulties of modern philosophy involves a great simplification, as Lindsey complained, and even a distortion. I do not believe, moreover, that philosophers can, simply by taking the "linguistic turn," be justified in ignoring Whitehead's "panexperientialist turn."

But I do agree with Rorty's apparent assumption that, if the linguistic turn cannot solve the problems of modern philosophy, Whitehead's proposal would need to be taken seriously. In light of the fact that the linguistic turn has *not* turned out to be the universal solvent it was once widely anticipated to be, it is time for Whitehead's version of postmodern philosophy, based on carrying through the revolution implicit in Descartes' subjectivist turn, to be seriously explored. Previous chapters in this book have shown some ways in which Whitehead's panexperientialist turn allows us to overcome distinctively modern philosophical problems, which were created precisely by the fact that this turn was *not* taken by Descartes and modern philosophers in general.

Notes

1. WHITEHEAD'S PHILOSOPHY AS POSTMODERN PHILOSOPHY

1. The symbols for the works of Whitehead are given in the front of the book.

2. Cobb, "From Crisis Theology to the Post-Modern World."

3. Cobb, *God and the World*, 135, 138; "The Possibility of Theism Today," 105.

4. Cobb, *Christ in a Pluralistic Age*, 15, 25–27.

5. Griffin, "Post-Modern Theology for a New Christian Existence." Although the volume in which this essay was contained was not published because of numerous delays until 1977, my essay, which was written partly as a background essay for the other contributors, was written in 1972.

6. Matson, *The Broken Image*, vi, 139, 228.

7. Schilling, *The New Consciousness in Science and Religion*, 44–47, 73–74, 91, 183, 244–53.

8. Altieri, "From Symbolist Thought to Immanence: The Ground of Postmodern American Poetics."

9. Ferré, *Shaping the Future: Resources for the Post-Modern World*, 100, 106–07.

10. Randall, "The Nature of Naturalism," 367–69.

11. Bové, ed., *Early Postmodernism*.

12. Cobb, *Postmodernism and Public Policy*, introduction.

13. See Beardslee, "Stories in the Postmodern World: Orienting and Disorienting," and "Christ in the Postmodern Age: Reflections Inspired by Jean-François Lyotard."

14. See Jay, "The Debate over Performative Contradiction."

15. Passmore, *Philosophical Reasoning*, 60.

16. Santayana, *Scepticism and Animal Faith*, 14–15.

17. See Thomas McCarthy's critique of this mode of dealing with self-contradictions in his *Ideals and Illusions*.

18. James, *Some Problems of Philosophy*, 194.

19. Searle, *Minds, Brains and Science*, 85–86, 92–98.

20. See Marcus Ford, *William James's Philosophy* and "William James."

21. Griffin, *Reenchantment without Supernaturalism*, 6; *Unsnarling the World-Knot*, chs. 7, 9.

22. See Marcus Ford, "James's Psychical Research and Its Philosophical Implications."

23. See also Cobb, "Alfred North Whitehead," 181–87, and Griffin, *Reenchantment without Supernaturalism*, ch. 9.

24. Griffin, introduction to SUNY Series in Constructive Postmodern Thought (included in all the volumes in the series).

25. Gamwell, *The Divine Good*, 3–4.

2. WHITEHEAD'S PHILOSOPHY AND THE ENLIGHTENMENT

1. Hartshorne, *The Zero Fallacy*, 91.

2. Cassirer, *The Philosophy of the Enlightenment*; Gay, *The Enlightenment: The Rise of Modern Paganism*, and *The Enlightenment: The Science of Human Freedom*.

3. To say that they were common does not, of course, mean that they were universal. The romantic movement around the beginning of the nineteenth century was already a protest against certain aspects of the enlightenment. And it and Hegelianism fed a profoundly antimodern, antienlightenment sensibility reflected in National Socialism, Zionism, and Heidegger's philosophy. See Sternell, *The Founding Myths of Israel*, Finkelstein, *Image and Reality of the Israel-Palestine Conflict*, and Zimmerman, *Heidegger's Confrontation with Modernity*.

4. Easlea, *Witch Hunting, Magic, and the New Philosophy*, 89.

5. This summary is based on ch. 5 of my *Religion and Scientific Naturalism*, "Religion and the Rise of the Modern Scientific Worldview."

6. Klaaren, *The Religious Origins of Modern Science*, 147–48, 38, 165.

7. Ibid., 99–100, 158–59.

8. Ibid., 132, 149, 162–63, 166.

9. Ibid., 166–77, 171–72, 178.

10. Ibid., 147, 165, 177, 189.

11. Quoted in Koyré, *From the Closed World to the Infinite Universe*, 225.

12. Quoted in Easlea, *Witch Hunting, Magic and the New Philosophy*, 121.

13. Ibid., 111.

14. Westfall, *Never at Rest*, 381.

15. Klaaren, *Religious Origins of Modern Science*, 102–03, 132, 150–51.

16. Easlea, *Witch Hunting*, 89–90.

17. See Hill, *The World Turned Upside Down*.

18. Easlea, *Witch Hunting*, 109.

19. Berman, *The Reenchantment of the World*, 123.

20. Klaaren, *Religious Origins of Modern Science*, 163.

21. Cassirer, Kristeller, and Randall, *The Renaissance Philosophy of Man*, 177.

22. See Jacob, "Boyle's Atomism and the Restoration Assault on Pagan Naturalism," 218–19, and Mosse, "Puritan Radicalism and the Enlightenment."

23. *The Works of the Honourable Robert Boyle*, IV: 394.

24. Quoted in Koyré, *From the Closed World*, 216, 219, 217.

25. See Jacob, *Robert Boyle and the English Revolution*, 161–76.

26. Easlea, *Witch Hunting*, 135.

27. Cottingham, Stoothoff, and Murdoch, eds., *The Philosophical Writings of Descartes*, 46.

28. Easlea, *Witch Hunting*, 94–95.

29. Lenoble, *Mersenne ou la naissance du méchanisme*, 9, 120, 157.

30. Quoted in Crombie, "Mersenne," 317.

31. Easlea, *Witch Hunting*, 108.

32. Lenoble, *Mersenne*, 133, 157–58, 375, 381.

33. Jacob, "Boyle's Atomism," 218–19.

34. *The Works of the Honourable Robert Boyle*, III: 453, 457; IV: 416.

35. Quoted in Koyré, *From the Closed World*, 183, 184.

36. See Thomas, *Religion and the Decline of Magic*, 438–39, 578–79, and Trevor-Roper, *The European Witch Craze of the Sixteenth and Seventeenth Centuries*, 116, 132, 143–49.

37. Thomas, *Religion and the Decline of Magic*, 437; Easlea, *Witch Hunting*, 56.

38. Thomas, *Religion and the Decline of Magic*, 571–79; Trevor-Roper, *The European Witch Craze*, 180–81.

39. Kant, *Religion within the Limits of Reason Alone*, 163.

40. For this use of the term *semideism*, see Plantinga, "Evolution, Neutrality, and Antecedent Probability," 90.

41. Quoted in Hooykaas, *Natural Law and Divine Miracle*, 114.

42. Francis Darwin, ed., *The Life and Letters of Charles Darwin*, vol. 2: 6–7.

43. Lewontin, "Billions and Billions of Demons," 31.

44. The symbols for the works of Whitehead are given in the front of the book.

45. Recent calculations put the beginning of our universe at about 13.7 billion years ago.

46. On Hartshorne's use of "panentheism" and "world soul," see Hartshorne and Reese, eds., *Philosophers Speak of God*, vii, 1–57, and Hartshorne, *Omnipotence and Other Theological Mistakes*, 59, 134–35.

47. "The initial aim is the best for that *impasse*" (PR 244). This idea means that reference to God's regular, sustaining providence would be necessary to give a complete account of the whatness as well as the thatness of all events.

48. Griffin, *Religion and Scientific Naturalism*, ch. 8, "Creation and Evolution."

49. Harman, *The Nature of Morality*, 17, 381; Johnson, *Reason in the Balance*, 38n.

50. James, *Varieties of Religious Experience*, 520.

51. Ibid., 520–22.

52. Mackie, *The Miracle of Theism*, 13, 182.

53. In relation to naturalism understood as naturalism$_{nati}$, Whiteheadian panentheism could be called "supernaturalism$_{da}$," with "da" indicating that God is a *distinct actuality* or a *distinct agent*. Using this terminology, however, would surely lead to the same confusion as did James's "piecemeal supernaturalism." No matter how carefully one might try to make clear that God is a supernatural being only in the sense of being distinct from the totality of finite events and processes, the term *supernaturalism* would inevitably suggest that these natural processes could be interrupted.

54. Gamwell, *The Divine Good*, 3–4.

55. Ibid., 5 (quoting AI 162).

56. Ibid., 7–8.

57. My first book, *A Process Christology*, most of which I still endorse, contains my own attempt.

58. See my discussion in *Parapsychology, Philosophy, and Spirituality*.

59. Whitehead is here quoting Hume's *Treatise on Human Nature*, part 3, section 2.

60. Reid, *An Inquiry into the Human Mind*, 33.

61. Plantinga, *God and Other Minds*, xii; "Advice to Christian Philosophers," 24; Wolterstorff, *Reason within the Bounds of Religion*, 71, 79.

62. In this sense it was not true that either Descartes' substances or Leibniz's monads were completely independent, requiring nothing but themselves. They were dependent on God. Only God exemplified the ideal of being an individual in the sense of being absolutely independent of everything else.

63. Whitehead also used "events" more broadly, so that "[o]ne actual occasion is a limiting type of event" (PR 80).

64. Whitehead, unfortunately, violated this principle with regard to God. As a result, he implied that God was an exception to several metaphysical principles, even though he said that "God is not to be treated as an exception to all metaphysical principles" but as "their chief exemplification" (PR 343). Whitehead thereby threatened the coherence of his whole system. He should have consistently applied his dictum that although the "notion of an actual entity which...remains numerically one amidst the changes of accidental relations" is useful for some purposes, "in metaphysics [it] is sheer error" (PR 79). I discuss this issue in chapter 8.

65. Of course, influence between any two *enduring* individuals, such as two electrons, or two minds, or a mind and a brain cell, is mutual. This can occur because of the doctrine that all enduring individuals are temporally ordered societies, composed of rapidly repeating actual occasions. Two such enduring individuals influence each other many times per second. The doctrine that "contemporaries" cannot influence each other applies only to contemporaries in the strictest sense, meaning two occasions of experience that are concrescing at the same time. This issue is discussed further in chapter 8.

66. Hartshorne, *Creative Synthesis and Philosophic Method*, 191, 198.

67. Daly and Cobb's *For the Common Good* has developed the implications of Whitehead's view for socioeconomic theory.

68. See Cobb, *Process Theology as Political Theology*.

69. See Gould's "On Replacing the Idea of Progress with an Operational Notion of Directionality." But also see other essays in the same volume—*Evolutionary Progress*, edited by Matthew Nitecki—that argue against Gould's view.

70. Ayala, "Can 'Progress' Be Defined as a Biological Concept?" 80, 84, 90. I have discussed Ayala's criterion in *Religion and Scientific Naturalism*, 301–02.

71. See Ospovat, *The Development of Darwin's Theory*, 72, 210–28.

72. Griffin, *Evil Revisited*, ch. 1.

3. CONSCIOUSNESS AS A SUBJECTIVE FORM: INTERACTIONISM WITHOUT DUALISM

1. See McCarthy, *Ideals and Illusions*, 102–03.

2. John Passmore's statement as to why such an assertion is "absolutely self-refuting," quoted in chapter 1, bears repeating: "The proposition *p* is absolutely self-refuting, if to assert *p* is equivalent to asserting *both p and not-p*" (*Philosophical Reasoning*, 60).

3. See Jay, "The Debate over Performative Contradiction."

4. Hintikka, "Cogito, Ergo Sum," 32.

5. Seager, *Metaphysics of Consciousness*, 188.

6. Honderich, "Mind, Brain, and Self-Conscious Mind," 447.

7. Kim, *Supervenience and Mind*, 104.

8. Ibid., 286.

9. Searle, *The Rediscovery of the Mind*, 54, 48.

10. Searle, *Minds, Brains and Science*, 97.

11. Nagel, *The View from Nowhere*, 110–17, 123.

12. Lycan, *Consciousness*, 113–14.

13. Nagel, *The View from Nowhere*, 110–17; Searle, *Minds, Brains and Science*, 87, 92, 95.

14. Kim, *Supervenience and Mind*, xv.

15. Larmore, *The Morals of Modernity*, 87.

16. See Popper and Eccles, *The Self and Its Brain*, 105, and Lewis, *The Elusive Mind*, 26.

17. Madell, *Mind and Materialism*, 140–41.

18. Smart, "Materialism," 165, 168–69.

19. McGinn, *The Problem of Consciousness*, 45.

20. Swinburne, *The Evolution of the Soul*, 198–99. Swinburne is a dualist, but he sees that this problem is the same whether one is a dualist or a materialist.

21. McGinn, *The Problem of Consciousness*, 47.

22. Ibid., 1.

23. Nagel, *Mortal Questions*, 188–89.

24. Madell, *Mind and Materialism*, 2.

25. For an interpretation of Descartes as an occasionalist, see Baker and Morris, *Descartes' Dualism*, 153–54, 167–70. On Malebranche and Geulincx, see Copleston, *Descartes to Leibniz*, 117–19, 188–90.

26. James, *Some Problems of Philosophy*, 194.

27. Campbell, *Body and Mind*, 132, 131.

28. Ibid., 38, 48, 105–09.

29. Ibid., 125.

30. Kim, *Supervenience and Mind*, 367.

31. Searle, *Minds, Brains and Science*, 92.

32. Ibid., 86.

33. Ibid., 93.

34. Ibid., 87.

35. Ibid., 5, 94, 98.

36. Ibid., 86.

37. McGinn, *The Problem of Consciousness*, 17n; Nagel, *The View from Nowhere*, 110–23; Dennett, *Elbow Room*.

38. Taube, *Causation, Freedom and Determinism*, 17.

39. Searle, *Minds, Brains and Science*, 87. Explicitly denying that we have a mind that is distinct from the brain, Searle says, referring to the human head, that "the brain is the only thing in there" (*The Rediscovery of the Mind*, 248).

40. Searle, *The Rediscovery of the Mind*, 63.

41. Searle, *Minds, Brains and Science*, 117.

42. McGinn, *The Problem of Consciousness*, 23n.

43. Ibid., 55.

44. Ibid., 55, 53.

45. See, for example, Beloff 1962.

46. For example, in rejecting vitalism, Whitehead pointed out that it "involves an essential dualism somewhere" (SMW 79).

47. Hartshorne, "The Compound Individual."

48. I have included this doctrine in a list of ten core doctrines of process philosophy (*Reenchantment without Supernaturalism*, 6).

49. Johnson, "Whitehead as Teacher and Philosopher," 354.

50. 'Panexperientialism' was coined after Whitehead's time. As far as I know, I coined it and first used it in print in Cobb and Griffin, *Mind in Nature*, 98. But Charles Hartshorne commented favorably on it, saying that this term had advantages over both *panpsychism* and the alternative he had proposed, *psychicalism* ("General Remarks," 181).

51. McGinn, *The Character of Mind*, 32.

52. This fact does not, to be sure, deter some hostile critics who are determined to portray all versions of panexperientialism as unintelligible. For example, Paul Edwards, in an encyclopedia article on panpsychism, criticizes the doctrine as unintelligible for attributing experience to stars and stones, even while pointing out that Whitehead, the twentieth century's "most distinguished champion of panpsychism," held the experiencing units to be "not stars and stones but the events out of which stars and stones are constituted" (Edwards, "Panpsychism," 31). I have criticized Edwards for this treatment in Griffin, *Unsnarling the World-Knot*, 96–97.

53. Nagel, *Mortal Questions*, 168.

54. Donald R. Griffin, *Animal Minds*.

55. Hameroff, "Quantum Coherence in Microtubules," 97–99.

56. Adler and Tse, "Decision-Making in Bacteria"; Goldbeter and Koshland, "Simple Molecular Model for Sensing and Adaptation."

57. Keller, *A Feeling for the Organism*.

58. See Čapek, *The New Aspects of Time*, 54, 135, 205, 211.

59. Bohm and Hiley, *The Undivided Universe*, 384–87; Seager, *Metaphysics of Consciousness*, 282–83.

60. Griffin, *Parapsychology, Philosophy, and Spirituality*, 251–61; *Unsnarling the World-Knot*, 89–92; *Reenchantment without Supernaturalism*, 97–109.

61. By an aggregational event I mean simply the occurrence of something such as a rock at a particular moment—that is, the occurrence of all the molecular events that constitute the rock at that moment.

62. The term *perpetual oscillation*, I have suggested (Griffin, *Reenchantment without Supernaturalism*, 115–16), is more helpful than Whitehead's term *perpetual perishing*, which has proved to be perpetually confusing. (Many interpreters have taken the statement that an actual entity "perishes" after it reaches satisfaction to mean that it is no longer actual—which would mean that, by the ontological principle that only actualities can act, it would not be able to exert causation. But this is the exact opposite of Whitehead's meaning, as the following quotation makes clear: "[A]ctual entities 'perpetually perish' subjectively, but are immortal objectively. Actuality in perishing acquires objectivity, while it loses subjective immediacy. It loses the final causation...and it acquires efficient causation" [PR 29].)

63. This has been conclusively shown in Marcus Ford, *William James's Philosophy* and "William James."

64. McGinn, *The Problem of Consciousness*, 28n. McGinn even quotes a passage showing that Kant realized that panexperientialism, which he knew in its Leibnizian-Wolffian form, could overcome the chief difficulty in understanding the communion of body and soul. "The difficulty peculiar to the problem consists," suggested Kant, "in the assumed heterogeneity of the object of inner sense (the soul) and the objects of the outer senses.... But if we consider that the two kinds of objects thus differ from each other, not inwardly but only in so far as one appears outwardly to another, and that what, as thing in itself, underlies the appearances of matter, perhaps after all may not be so heterogeneous in character, this difficulty vanishes" (Kant, *Critique of Pure Reason*, 381 [B428]; quoted in McGinn, *The Problem of Consciousness*, 81). McGinn, however, is unable to incorporate this solution because of his conviction that panexperientialism is absurd.

65. Hartshorne, *The Logic of Perfection*, 229.

66. "[I]f we hold," said Whitehead, "that all final individual actualities have the metaphysical character of occasions of experience, then...the connectedness of one's immediate present occasion of experience with one's immediately past occasions, can be validly used to suggest categories applying to the connectedness of all occasions in nature" (AI 221). Indeed, he argued, we must do this if we are to use the notion of "causation" meaningfully. Since "we can only understand causation in terms of our observations of [our own occasions of experience]," then "in so far as we apply notions of causation to the understanding of events in nature, we must conceive these events under the general notions which apply to occasions of experience" (AI 184).

67. For James and Peirce on this issue, see Ochs, "Charles Sanders Pierce," 67–68.

68. In this statement of the way in which Whiteheadian panexperientialism agrees with dualism, I have restricted the discussion to *human* minds, because some dualists, including Descartes himself, do not attribute minds to nonhuman animals.

69. There has been a pervasive tendency, among both dualists and materialists, to conflate the two theses, as if affirming numerical distinctness were ipso facto to affirm ontological difference. I have discussed this tendency in *Religion and Scientific Naturalism*, 173–75.

70. On this view, the mind or soul is not, in Gilbert Ryle's pejorative phrase, a "ghost in the machine" because the body is no machine but a vast society of less sophisticated experiences.

71. These norms can be understood, in Whitehead's technical language, as either "eternal objects" or "propositions." In either case, they exist in God—in what Whitehead calls "the primordial nature of God," which is God's primordial envisagement of all pure possibilities, or eternal objects, with the appetition that they be realized in due season. Understanding Whitehead's psychology, accordingly, finally requires an understanding of his theology. But this dimension of his thought lies beyond the scope of the present discussion. It suffices here to point out that we apprehend norms by apprehending God, in whom

they exist. By virtue of this doctrine, Whitehead avoids McGinn's criticism that the causal effect of norms on our conscious experience would be a "funny" kind of causation because it would involve the exercise of efficient causation on the mind by abstract (non-actual) entities. In Whitehead's views, because the norms are in God, understood as the dominant member of the universe as a whole, our normative experience can be understood by analogy with the relation between our minds and our bodily cells.

72. It is, incidentally, not only dualists who have thought of consciousness as the stuff of the mind. Colin McGinn has said: "Logically, 'consciousness' is a stuff term, as 'matter' is; and I see nothing wrong, metaphysically, with recognizing that consciousness *is* a kind of stuff" (*The Problem of Consciousness*, 60n).

73. Insofar as Whitehead equates sense perception with perception in the mode of causal efficacy, he agrees with those "direct realists" who maintain, contrary to Hume, that sensory perception is not solipsistic but gives us direct knowledge of the existence of an external world. Whitehead differs from them, however, insofar as they fail to regard sense perception as a mixed mode of perception involving a nonsensory mode.

74. See Mackie's *Ethics*, the subtitle of which is *Inventing Right and Wrong*.

75. See Griffin, *Reenchantment without Supernaturalism*, 285–87; Griffin, ed., *Spirituality and Society*, 9–10;

76. See Griffin, "Morality and Scientific Naturalism," and *Reenchantment without Supernaturalism*, ch. 8.

4. WHITEHEAD'S DEEPLY ECOLOGICAL WORLDVIEW: EGALITARIANISM WITHOUT IRRELEVANCE

1. For a history of the term and controversies surrounding it, see Fox, *Toward a Transpersonal Ecology*.

2. Ibid., 75.

3. As Fox points out (ibid., 65, 66), George Sessions, in working out a classification scheme, listed the animal liberation movement as a form of shallow, rather than deep, ecology.

4. Fox, after having long been an advocate of deep ecology, decided that the term should be dropped. In his helpful discussion, he distinguishes three meanings of 'deep ecology': the formal, the philosophical, and the popular. The formal meaning refers to asking ever deeper questions until one gets down to fundamental assumptions (ibid., 92, 125–27). Fox rightly argues that this meaning is untenable (131–41). The popular sense involves a biocentric approach, according to which all forms of life are respected as having value in themselves, and in which some kind of biospherical egalitarianism is accepted (114–17). While pointing out that this popular meaning is "the one by which the term *deep ecology* is by far the most widely known," Fox believes that it contains nothing distinctive in relation to most other ecophilosophies (118). This leaves the philosophical meaning, which refers

to "Self-realization," and which involves "the realization of a more and more expansive sense of self" so that one identifies with more and more of the world (106). Fox believes that this "constitutes the essence of what is tenable and distinctive about the deep ecology approach to ecophilosophy" (118). On this basis, Fox suggests replacing the term with *transpersonal ecology*. My decision to use 'deep ecology' positively reflects a different assessment of the "popular" meaning of the term. In my view, the term *deep* popularly connotes the idea that intrinsic value goes all the way down, that there is no line below which we can rightly treat things as simply means to human ends. This point (which I have called "deep ecology$_b$") does distinguish this approach from that of many ecophilosophies. And the insistence on biospherical egalitarianism (deep ecology$_e$), especially as interpreted by Devall and Sessions, has even more clearly set deep ecology apart. Because I consider these two points both distinctive and—as reinterpreted in the present essay—true and valuable, I am happy to associate the Whiteheadian approach with the term.

5. This platform was first published in Sessions, *Ecophilosophy VI* (1984). It has been republished in Devall and Sessions, *Deep Ecology*, 70, and in Fox, *Toward a Transpersonal Ecology*, 114–15.

6. Daly and Cobb, *For the Common Good*, 384–85. See also Cobb, "Ecology, Science, and Religion," for a somewhat less confrontational contrast between Whiteheadian philosophy and (Naessian) deep ecology.

7. Devall and Sessions, *Deep Ecology*, 236.

8. See Naess, *Ecology, Community, and Lifestyle*.

9. Devall and Sessions, *Deep Ecology*, 225.

10. Griffin, *Reenchantment without Supernaturalism*, 6.

11. See Hartshorne, "The Compound Individual."

12. On panentheism, see Hartshorne and Reese, eds., *Philosophers Speak of God*, vii, 1–57, 233–334, 499–514, and Griffin, "Panentheism: A Postmodern Revelation." On God as "World Soul," see Hartshorne, *Omnipotence and Other Theological Mistakes*, 59, 134–35. Whitehead said that God "is not the world, but the valuation of the world" (RM 159).

13. Thomas Berry, *The Dream of the Earth*.

14. Naess, *Ecology, Community, and Lifestyle*, 33, 173, 174, 173, 168, 184.

15. See note 5.

5. TRUTH AS CORRESPONDENCE, KNOWLEDGE AS DIALOGICAL: PLURALISM WITHOUT RELATIVISM

1. Swidler, "Interreligious and Interideological Dialogue: The Matrix for All Systematic Reflection Today," in Swidler, ed., *Toward a Universal Theology of Religion*,

5–50, at 7. Swidler's tendency to equate truth and knowledge, or at least to assume that they are not categorically distinct issues, is illustrated by his statement that today "all truth, all knowledge, is seen as interpreted truth and knowledge" (7).

2. See Alston, *A Realist Conception of Truth*. Having pointed out that his "minimal-realist conception of truth" can be considered a minimalist correspondence theory (33, 39), Alston says that "it seems overwhelmingly obvious that the realist conception is the one we express with 'true,' when that predicate is applied to propositions, statements, and beliefs" (188).

3. Rorty, *Contingency, Irony, and Solidarity*, 5.

4. Rorty says that "the claim that an 'adequate' philosophical doctrine must make room for our intuitions," which is a claim I endorse about our hard-core commonsense intuitions, is a "reactionary slogan" (*Contingency*, 21).

5. O'Connor, *The Correspondence Theory of Truth*, 17.

6. Horwich, *Truth*, 1. The fact that correspondence is the standard view is also shown by Marian David's statement, in her discussion of the deflationary view of truth known as "disquotation," that correspondence is "the theory it wants to deflate" (*Correspondence and Disquotation*, 6).

7. Searle, *The Rediscovery of the Mind*, 17–18.

8. For example, Nicholas Rescher, in response to a claim that common sense places a constraint on philosophers, replies: "Stuff and nonsense. The philosophical land-scape is littered with theories that tread common sense underfoot. There are no sacred cows in philosophy—common sense least of all" (*The Strife of Systems*, 19).

9. Rorty, *Consequences of Pragmatism*, xxix–xxx.

10. Thomas McCarthy, besides suggesting that Jacques Derrida considered such ideas as transcendental illusions in Kant's sense, mentions the idea of truth as one of these ideas (*Ideals and Illusions*, 102–03).

11. Rorty, *Consequences of Pragmatism*, xxix–xxx.

12. Searle, *Minds, Brains, and Science*, 98.

13. Rescher's reply in note 8, above, was to John Kekes, who had said: "No philo-sophical, or any other, theory can provide a view which violates common sense *and remain logically consistent*. For the truth of common sense is assumed by all theories.... This necessity to conform to common sense establishes a constraint upon the interpretations philosophical theories can offer" (*The Nature of Philosophy*, 196; emphasis added). Rescher's "stuff and nonsense" reply simply ignores Kekes's main point, which is about avoiding inconsistency.

14. See note 6, above.

15. Rorty, *Contingency*, 3, 8.

16. Ibid., 7.

17. Marcus Ford has argued convincingly that James continued to presuppose the notion of truth as correspondence even after he developed his so-called pragmatic theory of truth, although he did make many statements that were inconsistent with this fact. See Ford, *William James's Philosophy*, 59–74, or "William James," 117–22. The main reason for thinking that Peirce rejected correspondence is his famous statement that truth is "the opinion which is fated to be ultimately agreed to by all who investigate" (Peirce, *Collected Papers of Charles Sanders Peirce*, 5: 268), which is usually taken to mean that he held an epistemic conception of truth. But some interpreters argue that Peirce's statement was merely a prediction, not a definition.

18. Rorty, *Consequences of Pragmatism*, xxix–xxx.

19. Rorty, *Philosophy and the Mirror of Nature*.

20. Rorty, *Contingency*, 68. Rorty also credits this definition in part to Peirce, but, as note 17 suggests, this may reflect a misunderstanding.

21. Putnam, *Reason, Truth, and History*, 55.

22. Alston, *A Realist Conception of Truth*, 189–90.

23. West, "Dispensing with Metaphysics in Religious Thought," 55; "Afterword: The Politics of American Neo-Pragmatism," 263–64. I have shown that West's Rortian criticism of truth as correspondence does not apply to Whitehead's correspondence theory of truth in my "Liberation Theology and Postmodern Theology: A Response to Cornel West," 133–41. The writings to which I was responding, I should add, were written many years ago. I do not mean to imply that West, with whom I agree on most issues, would still endorse the statements with which I took issue.

24. Davidson, "The Structure and Content of Truth," 302.

25. Putnam, *Words and Life*, v, 297.

26. Alston, *A Realist Conception of Truth*, 9–17; Horwich, *Truth*, 89–93; David, *Correspondence and Disquotation*, 45.

27. Alston (*A Realist Conception of Truth*, 9, 13), Horwich (*Truth*, 92), and David (*Correspondence and Disquotation*, 54–55) all agree that the primary reason for the rejection of propositions by contemporary philosophers is the nominalist rejection of "abstract entities" on the basis of a materialistic view of reality.

28. Rorty, *Contingency, Irony, and Solidarity*, 5.

29. Putnam, *Words and Life*, 302.

30. Putnam, "Replies," 368.

31. Although Putnam now says that he rejects materialism—which he sometimes calls "scientistic," "reductionist," or "disenchanted" naturalism (*Words and Life*, xxii, lxxiv n. 58, 312)—he still accepts this feature of materialism.

32. See my *Reenchantment without Supernaturalism,* especially ch. 1.

33. This is, obviously, a huge topic. In a chapter of *Reenchantment without Supernaturalism* entitled "Natural Theology Based on Naturalistic Theism," I have discussed thirteen features of the world to which atheism, I argue, cannot do justice.

34. See my chapter on "Religious Language and Truth" in *Reenchantment without Supernaturalism.*

35. See *Reenchantment without Supernaturalism,* ch. 7, and chs. 1 and 2 of Griffin, ed., *Deep Religious Pluralism.*

36. To say that truth is absolute "in this sense" does not rule out its being relative in other senses. I believe, for example, that all truths are relative in the sense that they are all ultimately related to each other in a self-consistent way (knowable by omniscience). But the idea that truth is relative in this sense, which would better be called its "relationality," is not contrary to its absoluteness vis-à-vis our cognitive processes.

37. Quine, "Two Dogmas of Empiricism," in Quine, *From a Logical Point of View.*

38. Larmore, *The Morals of Modernity,* 87.

39. Putnam, *Realism and Reason,* 1983.

40. Sellars, "Empiricism and the Philosophy of Mind," in Sellars, *Science, Perception, and Reality.*

41. Williams, *Groundless Belief,* 45–46.

42. *Reenchantment without Supernaturalism,* 54–68, 76–77, 338–42.

43. The reality of time is implied by the reality of the past combined with the distinction between the past and the future implied by our freedom, which presupposes that, although the past is fully settled, the future is not.

44. I am here quoting my own statement from *Reenchantment without Supernaturalism,* 362–63.

45. Hartshorne, *Man's Vision of God,* 80.

46. This way of thinking of the relations among the religions is suggested abstractly in Cobb and Griffin, *Process Theology,* ch. 2, "Doctrinal Beliefs and Christian Existence" (of which I was the primary author). It is applied to the relation between Christianity and Buddhism in ch. 8, "The Church in Creative Transformation" (of which Cobb was the primary author), esp. 136–42, and in Cobb, *Beyond Dialogue* and *Transforming Christianity and the World.*

47. In giving these illustrations, I must, of course, simply presuppose what I consider true and false.

48. Although it had long been believed that the doctrine of creation out of absolute nothingness came from the Bible, it has now been shown to be a postbiblical doctrine. See Levenson, *Creation and the Persistence of Evil,* and May, *Creatio Ex Nihilo,* which are

both heavily employed in my "Creation out of Nothing, Creation out of Chaos, and the Problem of Evil."

49. I have examined numerous attempts by traditional theists to develop an adequate theodicy in *God, Power, and Evil* and *Evil Revisited*.

50. See, for example, Cobb, *God and the World*, esp. chs. 1–3; Ogden, *The Reality of God*, esp. the title essay; and my *Reenchantment without Supernaturalism*, 129–48. On grace and free will, see Cobb, *Grace and Responsibility*.

51. On the Christian side, see Cobb, *Beyond Dialogue* and *Transforming Christianity and the World*. On the Buddhist side, see Yokota, "A Call to Compassion: Process Thought and the Conceptualization of Amida Buddhism," and "Where beyond Dialogue? Reconsiderations of a Buddhist Pluralist."

52. Lochhead, *The Dialogical Imperative*.

53. Knitter, *Jesus and the Other Names*, 31.

6. TIME IN PHYSICS AND THE TIME OF OUR LIVES: OVERCOMING MISPLACED CONCRETENESS

1. Capra, *The Tao of Physics*, 179.

2. Ibid., 183, 185.

3. De Broglie, "A General Survey of the Scientific Work of Albert Einstein," 113.

4. Zukav, *The Dancing Wu Li Masters*, 236, 237, 238.

5. Dossey, *Space, Time and Medicine*, 31; Gold, *The Nature of Time*, 100; Davies, *The Physics of Time Asymmetry*, 2.

6. Dossey, *Space, Time and Medicine*, 151.

7. Weyl, *Philosophy of Mathematics and Natural Science*, 166; Dossey, *Space, Time and Medicine*, 152, 153. I should add that, although I am critical of Dossey's endorsement of the dominant position on physics and time in this early book, I am highly supportive of his later books, which have performed a great service in bringing empirical studies in psychosomatic medicine to the attention of a wide audience.

8. It should be emphasized that not all religious visions in the East regard time as illusory. Most, in fact, do not. Illustrations are provided by Berthrong, "The Trouble with Time," and Reeves, "The Lotus Sutra and Process Thought." The relation between Whiteheadian process thought and those Buddhist schools that do think of the relations of the present to the past and the future as symmetrical is discussed in Berthrong's article and in Odin, *Process Metaphysics and Hua-Yen Buddhism*.

9. Ferré, "On the Ultimate Significance of Time for Truth, Goodness, and the Sacred," 314.

10. Dossey, *Space, Time, and Medicine*, 34.

11. It is important to note that this doctrine involves two types of *actual* entities. (Temporal-nontemporal dualism is *not* entailed by doctrines that distinguish between temporal actual entities and nontemporal *ideal* entities—such as Whitehead's "eternal objects.")

12. Davies, *The Physics of Time Asymmetry*, 12–13. This view, that the behavior of physical particles provides no basis for "anisotropy" (with the merely possible and minor exception of K mesons), was the consensus of the physics community when all the writers I am discussing were writing. Later, however, two sets of independent experiments revealed the existence of time asymmetry at the most fundamental levels. One physicist involved is quoted as saying, "It's really the first time in which we could distinguish an arrow of time" (Weiss, "Time Proves Not Reversible at Deepest Level," 277). This discovery should be taken as an empirical confirmation of a prediction by process philosophy. As Hartshorne said long ago, if the world consists of experiencing events all the way down, "science will tend more and more to reveal the fact" (*Beyond Humanism*, 260). Hartshorne's prediction is now being fulfilled more thoroughly by Reginald T. Cahill. See his *Process Physics: From Information Theory to Quantum Space and Matter* and "Process Physics: Self-Referential Information and Experiential Reality."

13. Quoted in Hoffman, *Albert Einstein*, 258.

14. De Beauregard, "Time in Relativity Theory: Arguments for a Philosophy of Being," 429.

15. Grünbaum, *Philosophical Problems of Space and Time*, 388.

16. Russell, *Mysticism and Logic*, 21.

17. Russell, *Our Knowledge of the External World*, 23.

18. Reichenbach, *The Direction of Time*, 16.

19. Mehlberg, *Time, Causality, and the Quantum Theory*, I: 207.

20. Denbigh, *Three Concepts of Time*, 167.

21. Davies, *The Physics of Time Asymmetry*, 4.

22. Feynman, *The Character of Physical Law*, 112.

23. Davies, *The Physics of Time Asymmetry*, 19–22; Feynman, *The Character of Physical Law*, 121.

24. Zwart, "The Flow of Time," 144.

25. Denbigh, *An Inventive Universe*, 39.

26. Ibid., 41.

27. Whitrow, *The Natural Philosophy of Time*, 338.

28. Davies, *The Physics of Time Asymmetry*, 22.

29. Chisholm, *Person and Object*, 15, 18.

30. I have argued this point in *Unsnarling the World-Knot*, ch. 3, and *Reenchantment without Supernaturalism*, ch. 1. Jürgen Habermas and Karl-Otto Apel employ, as part of their "critical theory," a similar argument in terms of the notion of "performative self-contradictions." Such self-contradictions arise, explains Martin Jay, "when whatever is being claimed is at odds with the presuppositions or implications of the act of claiming it" (Jay, "The Debate over Performative Contradiction," 29).

31. Gale, *The Language of Time*, 103–04.

32. Ibid., 5.

33. Dossey, *Space, Time and Medicine*, 152.

34. Cleugh, *Time and Its Importance in Modern Thought*, 49.

35. Ibid., 51.

36. Merrill, "The *t* of Physics," 240.

37. Cleugh, *Time and Its Importance in Modern Thought*, 50.

38. Nathaniel Lawrence argued similarly, addressing "the vanity which holds that abstract considerations of material science provide an adequate framework for understanding our experience of temporality" (Lawrence, "Time Represented as Space," 123–24). Physics, he pointed out, is a mode of practice focused upon measurement. For this purpose, it abstracts from time's passage, its additive or cumulative character, its absolute difference from spatiality, and its qualitative aspects. The result is time represented as space (which Bergson had criticized as "the spatialization of time"). There is justification for this abstract representation in the need for measurement, said Lawrence, but there is also danger, especially because in certain respects physics has been so successful: "The great danger in these restricted enterprises is success. Success in one's own particular practice convinces him that he has got his hands on the primary reality. And therefore the more he will argue that other visions of reality are best tested by one's own particular discipline" (123). But the truth, Lawrence said, is that "[t]here is no mode of practice whose presuppositions are adequate for generating a total philosophy.... Measurement is almost as hopelessly partial as an approach to reality as is the marketing of peas" (123, 129).

39. Eddington, *The Nature of the Physical World*, 22.

40. Ibid., 18.

41. Capra, *The Tao of Physics*, 183, 185.

42. Meyerson, "Various Interpretations of Relativistic Time," 356.

43. Cleugh, *Time and Its Importance in Modern Thought*, 69.

44. Einstein, *The Meaning of Relativity*, 31.

45. Quoted in Čapek, *The Concepts of Space and Time*, 366–67.

46. Frank, "Is the Future Already Here?" 388.

47 Ibid., 387, 389.

48. Čapek, *The Concepts of Space and Time*, 506, 507, 511.

49. Ibid., 514, 515, 518–19.

50. Ibid., 519, 521.

51. Prigogine and Stengers, *Order Out of Chaos*, 17.

52. Zwart, *About Time*, 155–59.

53. Čapek, *The Concepts of Space and Time*, 517.

54. Ibid., xxxiv–xxxv; "The Unreality and Indeterminacy of the Future in the Light of Contemporary Physics," 301.

55. From this point of view, of course, the existence of God means that either a nontemporal or a temporal actuality has existed from all eternity, depending upon whether one assumes God to be nontemporal, with Descartes, or temporal, with Newton. We are here, however, considering only finite, nondivine actualities.

56. Fraser, "Out of Plato's Cave," 143.

57. Ibid., 159.

58. Ibid., 143.

59. Fraser, *The Genesis and Evolution of Time*, 10.

60. Ibid., 34, 32.

61. Ibid., 37, 69.

62. Ibid., 34.

63. Ibid., 154.

64. Ibid., 34.

65. Ibid., 166.

66. Fraser, "Out of Plato's Cave," 143.

67. *The Genesis and Evolution of Time*, 32.

68. "Out of Plato's Cave," 147.

69. *The Genesis and Evolution of Time*, 66.

70. Ibid., 132.

71. Ibid., 135.

72. Ibid., 37.

73. "Out of Plato's Cave," 156.

74. Grünbaum, "The Anisotropy of Time," 152, 179–80.

75. Hartshorne, *Creative Synthesis and Philosophic Method*, 9, 27.

7. WHITEHEAD AND THE CRISIS IN MORAL THEORY: THEISTIC ETHICS WITHOUT HETERONOMY

1. Gamwell, *The Divine Good*, 3–4.

2. Ibid., 8, 1.

3. Larmore, *The Morals of Modernity*, 43, 44.

4. Benacerraf, "Mathematical Truth."

5. See page 24, above.

6. Gödel, "What Is Cantor's Continuum Problem?" 268.

7. Putnam, *Words and Life*, 503.

8. Chihara, "A Gödelian Thesis Regarding Mathematical Objects," 217.

9. Mackie, *Ethics*, 24.

10. Ibid., 79–80.

11. Ibid., 24.

12. Ibid., 38, 40.

13. Ibid., 48.

14. Ibid., 38–39.

15. Ibid., 15.

16. Ibid., 35, 299n.

17. Harman, "Is There a Single True Morality?" 366.

18. *The Nature of Morality*, 34.

19. Ibid., 11–13.

20. Ibid., 131–32.

21. Ibid., 90.

22. Harman, "Is There a Single True Morality?" 365, 366; emphases added.

23. Ibid., 366; *The Nature of Morality*, 17.

24. "Is There a Single True Morality?" 381.

25. *The Nature of Morality*, 8.

26. Ibid., 66.

27. Ibid., 9–10. Harman's reference to Benacerraf is in his "note on further reading" on that same page (10).

28. Ibid., 10.

29. Williams, *Ethics and the Limits of Philosophy*, 136, 151–52.

30. Ibid., 142–43, 149.

31. Ibid., 94.

32. Ibid., 152.

33. Ibid., 53, 128.

34. Ibid., 53.

35. Ibid., 128–29.

36. Williams, "Ethics and the Fabric of the World," 205.

37. Ibid., 191.

38. Ibid., 128.

39. Hare, "Ontology in Ethics," 53, 42.

40. Rawls, "Kantian Constructivism in Moral Theory," 519.

41. Rawls, *Political Liberalism*, 97.

42. Geertz, *Islam Observed*, 97.

43. Geertz, *Interpretation of Cultures*, 126–27.

44. Williams, *Ethics and the Limits of Philosophy*, 22.

45. Ibid., 182.

46. Ibid., 70, 69.

47. Habermas, *Justification and Application*, 39.

48. Ibid., 146.

49. Ibid., 71, 146.

50. Ibid., 79; *Postmetaphysical Thinking*, 51; "Transcendence from Within, Transcendence in this World," 239.

51. Habermas, *Justification and Application*, 137.

52. MacIntyre, *After Virtue*, 67.

53. Ibid., 65. This project, incidentally, should not be called simply "the enlightenment project," because, as mentioned earlier, it was not accepted by some of the enlightenment's leading moralists, such as Ferguson and Hutcheson.

54. Goldsworthy, "God or Mackie?" 45, 76.

55. Murphy, "Constitutionalism, Moral Skepticism, and Religious Belief," 241.

56. Ibid., 247.

57. Murphy, *Evolution, Morality, and the Meaning of Life*, 16.

58. "Constitutionalism, Moral Skepticism, and Religious Belief," 244.

59. Mitchell, *Morality: Religious and Secular*, 90.

60. Ibid., 91, 92.

61. "Constitutionalism, Moral Skepticism, and Religious Belief," 248.

62. Habermas, *Justification and Application*, 146.

63. Mackie, *The Miracle of Theism*, 1.

64. Ibid., 151.

65. Griffin, *Reenchantment without Supernaturalism*, chs. 4–5.

66. Ibid., 203.

67. Hersh, *What Is Mathematics, Really?* 12.

68. Quine, *From a Logical Point of View*, 41.

69. Quine, "Replies," 663–65.

70. Quine, *From Stimulus to Science*, 14.

71. Quine, *Theories and Things*, 14–15.

72. Putnam, *Words and Life*, 153.

73. Maddy, *Realism in Mathematics*, 37.

74. Lycan, *Consciousness*, 90.

75. Field, *Science without Numbers*; Hellman, *Mathematics without Numbers*.

76. For similar statements from a number of other philosophers and mathematicians, see Maddy, *Realism in Mathematics*, 2–3, and Hersh, *What Is Mathematics, Really?* 7.

77. Moschovakis, *Descriptive Set Theory*, 605. What is violated here is what mathematicians presuppose when they are actually engaged with problems. As Moschovakis points out, "most mathematicians claim to be formalists (when pressed)," because of the embarrassment created by the Platonic and Benacerraf problems, "while they spend their working hours behaving as if they were unabashed realists" (605–06).

78. Maddy, *Realism in Mathematics*, 44, 59, 78.

79. Larmore, *The Morals of Modernity*, 8, 86–89.

80. Ibid., 91–96.

81. Ibid., 86, 89, 114.

82. Ibid., 87, 99.

83. Ibid., 87.

84. Ibid., 100–02.

85. See page 141, above.

86. Larmore, *The Morals of Modernity*, 92–93, 96–97.

87. Ibid., 96–98.

88. Ibid., 116.

89. Ibid., 96–97, 114.

90. Ibid., 8, 96.

91. Ibid., 114–17.

92. Ibid., 53.

93. Ibid., 31–32, 40, 57, 62–63.

94. This passage reflects Whitehead's position when he delivered the 1925 Lowell Lectures, before he had developed his first doctrine of God, which is reflected in chapters 10 and 11 of *Science and the Modern World*.

95. Mackie, *Ethics*, 38–39.

96. Larmore, *The Morals of Modernity*, 96–97; Williams, *Ethics and the Limits of Philosophy*, 94.

97. See the section titled "Ontological Naturalism" in chapter 2, above.

98. In evaluating this rational defense, one would, of course, need to examine the entire, thirteen-part cumulative case (see *Reenchantment without Supernaturalism*, ch. 5), not simply the two parts discussed here.

8. RELATIVITY PHYSICS AND WHITEHEADIAN THEISM: OVERCOMING THE APPARENT CONFLICTS

1. Lucas, *The Future* and "The Temporality of God"; Isham and Polkinghorne, "The Debate over the Block Universe."

2. Hartshorne, "A Reply to My Critics," 616.

3. Ibid., 642.

4. Fost, "Relativity Theory and Hartshorne's Dipolar Theism."

5. Wilcox, "A Question from Physics for Certain Theists"; Ford, "Is Process Theism Compatible with Relativity Theory?"; Fitzgerald, "Relativity Physics and the God of Process Philosophy."

6. Gruenler, *The Inexhaustible God*, 16, 75.

7. Hartshorne, "Bell's Theorem and Stapp's Revised View of Space-Time," 187.

8. Wilcox, "A Question," 294–97.

9. Fitzgerald, "Relativity Physics," 251.

10. Wilcox, "A Question," 294.

11. Hartshorne, "Interrogation of Charles Hartshorne," 324–25.

12. Fitzgerald, "Relativity Physics," 258.

13. Johnson, "Some Conversations with Whitehead concerning God and Creativity," 9–10. I have discussed this and other ways in which Whitehead's doctrine of God as a single actual entity violates his metaphysical principles in *Reenchantment without Supernaturalism*, ch. 4.

14. Ford, "Is Process Theism," 128, 130.

15. Ford, "The Divine Activity of the Future," 171.

16. Ibid., 170.

17. Ford, "Hartshorne's Interpretation of Whitehead," 315.

18. Hartshorne, *Creative Synthesis and Philosophic Method*, 124.

19. Hartshorne, *Whitehead's Philosophy*, 117.

20. Fost, "Relativity Theory," 91.

21. Fitzgerald, "Relativity Physics," 273.

22. Ibid., 254.

23. Hartshorne, *Creative Synthesis*, 124–25.

24. Fitzgerald, "Relativity Physics," 254.

25. Lucas, *The Future*, 298.

26. Devlin, "Hartshorne's Metaphysical Asymmetry," 283.

27. John B. Bennett has argued that Whitehead's statements on this topic are inconsistent. He cites most of the passages that refer to direct, unmediated prehensions

of noncontiguous occasions (PR 63, 226, 284, and 307–08) but believes that they contradict Whitehead's comments at PR 120, which, he believes, "rather clearly suggest that there is prehension of the past only through the mediation of contiguous occasions.... Objectification of noncontiguous occasions is effected only through the mediating occasions" ("Unmediated Prehensions: Some Observations," 222). This interpretation, however, involves misreading. In this latter passage, Whitehead is dealing with the way in which data are transmitted from outside the animal body to the ultimate percipient within the body through chains of contiguous occasions. The issue of whether or not there is also a direct perception of external events, so that the percipient receives data from them that are not transmitted through a chain of contiguous occasions, simply does not come up. Accordingly, no "reconciliation" of this passage with the other is needed. (The position Bennett offers as a reconciliation, however, is one that I consider not only correct but also important.)

28. Henry Stapp, in a personal letter of April 16, 1992, said in support of this statement: "In quantum theory, interpreted in terms of Heisenberg's ideas of objective potentia and actual events, the influences are not normally transmitted via contiguous actual events.... [Rather], the influences between actual events are normally transmitted via 'potentia,' which are represented in quantum theory by the local quantum fields." This different view does not, however, mean that action at a distance is thereby implied: "In physics the normal causal interactions are carried by [local fields], and such causal connections are not considered to be action at a distance, since they are transmitted in a continuous way by a local process involving local quantum fields."

29. Lucas, *The Future*, 237–38.

30. Ibid., 239.

31. Wilcox, "A Question," 294.

32. Ford, *The Emergence of Whitehead's Metaphysics*.

33. The statement that pure physical causation is more powerful than hybrid physical causation requires qualification. The statement refers to the causal influence of a single event on another. Viewed in this light, the effect of hybrid physical causation is, in comparison with pure physical causation, probably vanishingly small, especially in the low-grade actual entities studied by physics, which have trivial mental poles. The pure physical causation is so much more powerful in terms of one event's influence upon another because the physical energy of an actual occasion (i.e., the creativity embodied in its physical pole) has a compulsive power that is not exerted by its mental energy (i.e., the creativity as distinctively embodied in its mental pole). The statement that pure physical causation is far more powerful needs to be qualified, however, by the recognition that hybrid physical causation, while very weak in itself (i.e., in terms of the influence of one event on other), can have powerful cumulative effects. Whereas pure physical causation is evidently exhausted, at least normally, on contiguous subsequent events, hybrid physical causation can influence remote events as well. Accordingly, when looking at the physical causation upon a present event from the entire past, the influence of the hybrid physical causation from the past may be as great as, or greater than, that of the pure.

That is, trillions of events in the past in which the same form was actualized could reinforce each other by directly, as well as indirectly, impressing that form upon the present event. This cumulative effect of a form of causation that is in itself very weak is, incidentally, at the core of Rupert Sheldrake's hypothesis of "formative causation," as developed in *A New Science of Life* (which I reviewed in *Process Studies* 12/1 [Spring, 1982], 38–40) and *The Presence of the Past*. It can also be used to explain Jungian archetypes, which Jung himself sometimes accounted for in terms of innumerable repetitions in the past of a particular form (see the introduction to Griffin, ed., *Archetypal Process*).

34. Suchocki, *The End of Evil*, 171.

35. Hartshorne, "Whitehead's Idea of God," 546.

36. Hartshorne, "Interrogation of Charles Hartshorne," 324–25.

37. Cobb, *A Christian Natural Theology*, 192.

38. Bergson, *Matter and Memory*, 178, 276, 279.

39. Ibid., 274–75, 279–80, 332.

40. Bergson, *Creative Mind*, 220–21.

41. Hartshorne, "The Compound Individual."

42. Baker, "Omniscience and Divine Synchronization," 203–04.

43. Griffin, *God, Power, and Evil*, 291–300; *Evil Revisited*, 26–31.

44. Cahill, "Process Physics."

CHAPTER 9: WHITEHEADIAN THEISM: A RESPONSE TO ROBERT NEVILLE'S CRITIQUE

1. This alternative is presented most systematically in Neville's three-volume work, *Axiology of Thinking*, the individual titles of which are *Reconstruction of Thinking* (1981), *Recovery of the Measure* (1989), and *Normative Cultures* (1995). From among Neville's many other works, I would especially lift up his 1974 book, *The Cosmology of Freedom*. Of primary importance for the development of his idea of God is his 1968 book, *God the Creator* (a new edition of which was published in 1992). Neville's growing importance as a Christian theologian, especially since he became dean of the School of Theology at Boston University, is signaled by the fact that Donald Musser and Joseph Price chose to include a chapter on him in their 1996 edited volume, *A New Handbook of Christian Theologians*.

2. Neville, *Creativity and God*, 146 n. 1. For Donald Sherburne's views, see his "Whitehead without God"; "The 'Whitehead without God' Debate: The Rejoinder" (which is a reply to a critique by John Cobb); and "Decentering Whitehead." Unfortunately, Sherburne has not yet written the kind of full-scale reconstruction of process philosophy that would be required to show that it could shed its theism while

retaining its adequacy and coherence. My argument in *Reenchantment without Supernaturalism,* especially chapter 5, implies that this could not be done.

3. *Creativity and God,* 6.

4. Ibid., 142. I also need to acknowledge that my critique of Neville's criticism of, and alternative to, process theology is not based on a complete examination of his works but primarily on *Creativity and God* and two essays: "Concerning *Creativity and God:* A Response" and "Contributions and Limitations of Process Philosophy." With regard to Neville's criticism of process theism, this limitation is not significant, as Neville's comments about process theism in later works reflect the same understanding expressed in these three publications. Any overall evaluation of the viability of Neville's own constructive position, however, would obviously have to be based on a much broader examination of his works, which deal with many issues not even intimated here. My critique of Neville's constructive position is limited to the argument that his alternative to process theism is open to criticisms at least as serious as those he has leveled at process theism.

5. Ibid., 37; Neville, "Contributions and Limitations of Process Philosophy," 284.

6. *Creativity and God,* 13, 38, 63; "Contributions and Limitations," 285–86.

7. *Creativity and God,* 38, 39, 41, 43.

8. Ibid., 13, 138.

9. Ibid., 38, 39–40, 45–47.

10. Neville, "Concerning *Creativity and* God: A Response," 4.

11. "Contributions and Limitations," 296.

12. Ibid., 286.

13. *Creativity and God,* 14.

14. Ibid., 38.

15. Ibid., 39.

16. Ibid., 42.

17. Quoted by Neville in *Creativity and God,* 12.

18. *Creativity and God,* 12–13.

19. "Concerning *Creativity and God,*" 4; "Contributions and Limitations," 285 (the reference is to PR 344).

20. *Creativity and God,* 8, 12–13.

21. Neville, *Soldier, Sage, Saint,* 107.

22. "Contributions and Limitations," 285.

23. This formulation reads: "That every condition to which the process of becoming conforms in any particular instance has its reason *either* in the character of some actual

entity in the actual world of that concrescence, *or* in the character of the subject which is in process of concrescence. This category of explanation is termed the 'ontological principle.' It could also be termed the 'principle of efficient, and final, causation.' This ontological principle means that actual entities are the only *reasons*; so that to search for a *reason* is to search for one or more actual entities. It follows that any condition to be satisfied by one actual entity in its process expresses a fact either about the 'real internal constitutions' of some other actual entities, or about the 'subjective aim' conditioning that process" (*Process and Reality,* 24).

24. Ibid., 19.

25. Griffin, *God, Power, and Evil,* 299.

26. *Creativity and God,* 37.

27. Ibid., 37.

28. Ibid., 43.

29. Ibid., 43–44.

30. Ibid., 44.

31. Ibid.

32. *Creativity and God,* 46._

33. Ibid., 47.

34. Ibid.

35. Ibid., 61.

36. Hartshorne, "Response to Neville's *Creativity and God,*" 97.

37. *Creativity and God,* 73; *Soldier,* 104.

38. *Creativity and God,* 63.

39. Ibid.

40. Ibid., 41, 43, 139.

41. Rescher, *The Riddle of Existence.* I have reviewed Rescher's book in *Canadian Philosophical Reviews,* December 1986: 531–32.

42. *Creativity and God,* 45.

43. *Soldier, Sage, Saint,* 108.

44. *Creativity and God,* 45.

45. Ibid.

46. Ibid.

47. I have been unable to locate the reference for this point.

48. *Creativity and God*, 13.

49. Ibid., 14.

50. Ibid.

51. Ibid., 9.

52. Ibid., 11.

53. Ibid., 10.

54. Ibid., 141.

55. Ibid., ix.

56. "Contributions and Limitations," 297, n. 24.

57. *Creativity and God*, 9, 10.

58. "Concerning *Creativity and God*," 6.

59. *Creativity and God*, 11.

60. *Soldier, Sage, Saint*, 110.

61. Neville, "Can God Create Men and Address Them Too?" 603, 610.

62. *Soldier, Sage, Saint*, 105.

63. "Contributions and Limitations," 290.

64. *Soldier, Sage, Saint*, 106.

65. Ibid., 109.

66. "Concerning *Creativity and God*," 5.

67. *Soldier, Sage, Saint*, 111, 113.

68. *Creativity and God*, 135. For an excellent volume of essays (dedicated to Cobb and Ogden) dealing with the relation of Wesleyan theology to process theology, see Stone and Oord, eds., *Thy Nature and Thy Name Is Love*.

69. *Creativity and God*, 11.

70. Cobb, "Response to Neville's Creativity and God," 97.

71. Cobb, "The Finality of Christ in a Whiteheadian Perspective" and "A Whiteheadian Christology."

72. Griffin, *A Process Christology*; "Schubert Ogden's Christology and the Possibilities of Process Philosophy"; "Is Revelation Coherent?"; and "The Essential Elements of a Contemporary Christology."

73. *Creativity and God*, 18, 20.

74. Cobb, "Response," 100.

75. *Creativity and God*, 18.

76. Ibid., 10.

77. *Soldier, Sage, Saint*, 106.

78. *Creativity and God*, 20.

79. Cobb, *Christ in a Pluralistic Age*, 139–42.

80. "Concerning *Creativity and God*," 15.

81. *Soldier, Sage, Saint*, 99, 105.

82. Ibid., 106.

83. "Concerning *Creativity and God*," 2; *Creativity and God*, 4.

84. *Creativity and God*, 8, 12.

85. "Concerning *Creativity and God*," 12.

86. *Creativity and God*, 90.

87. Ibid., 14.

88. Neville, "Hegel and Whitehead on Totality: The Failure of a Conception of System," 103.

89. *Creativity and God*, 90–91.

90. Ibid., 90.

91. Ibid., 15.

92. Ibid., 141.

93. Ibid, 95.

94. Ibid., 34.

95. *Soldier, Sage, Saint*, 108.

96. *Creativity and God*, 83–84.

97. Ibid., 85.

98. Ibid.

99. Ibid.

100. *Creativity and God*, 85.

101. Ibid.

102. Ibid., 83.

103. Ibid., 96.

104. Ibid., 68.

105. Griffin, "The Holy, Necessary Goodness, and Morality." I have made this argument more recently in *Reenchantment without Supernaturalism*, ch. 8.

106. *Creativity and God*, 21–22, 29, 34.

107. See *Creativity and God*, chap. 2. I have published two critiques of Lewis Ford's project: a review article of *The Emergence of Whitehead's Metaphysics*, which appeared in *Process Studies* 15/3 (Fall, 1986), 194–207, and a brief review of Ford's *Transforming Process Theism*, which appeared in the *Journal of Religion* 81/4 (October 2001), 668–70.

108. I have more recently made this argument at considerable length in ch. 4 of *Reenchantment without Supernaturalism*, in which I argue against Palmyre Oomen's contention in "The Prehensibility of God's Consequent Nature" that Whitehead's idea of God as a single, everlasting actual entity can be made consistent with the remainder of his position.

109. Cobb, *A Christian Natural Theology*, 176–91. In chapter 4 of *Reenchantment without Supernaturalism*, I have argued that the view of God as a single actual entity makes God an exception to five of Whitehead's metaphysical categories.

110. *Creativity and God*, 71, 137.

111. Ibid., 139.

112. Ibid., 33.

113. Ibid., 89.

114. Ibid., 137.

115. Ibid., 66.

116. Ibid., 140.

117. Ibid., 75. The words in single quotation marks are those of David Pailin.

APPENDIX: WHITEHEAD'S SUBJECTIVIST PRINCIPLE: FROM DESCARTES TO PANEXPERIENTIALISM

1. That essay, coauthored with Olav Bryant Smith, was entitled "The Mystery of the Subjectivist Principle." The basic insight on which this essay was based came from Smith, who developed it while writing his dissertation (a revised version of which has been published as *Myths of the Self: Narrative Identity and Postmodern Metaphysics* [Lanham, Md.: Lexington Books, 2004].) Smith also wrote a first draft of that essay. The final draft, almost completely different, was written almost entirely by me. In the present version, I remind the reader throughout of Smith's original inspiration and coauthorship by continuing to call the interpretation presented here "Interpretation SG." The present

chapter also involves revisions of three other types: the addition of the prefatory note; minor revisions throughout the essay; and, for reasons of length, the deletion of a section devoted to Lewis Ford's interpretation of "the reformed subjectivist principle" (which I had written).

2. All citations to *Process and Reality* are, of course, to the corrected edition. Readers who go back to examine the essays by Lindsey, Rorty, and myself are reminded that they used the pagination of the 1929 Macmillan edition (which is given in square brackets in the corrected edition).

3. Rorty, "The Subjectivist Principle and the Linguistic Turn," 134.

4. Lindsey, "The Subjectivist Principle and the Linguistic Turn Revisited," 97.

5. Lindsey's text actually has "subjective" (instead of "subjectivist") here, but I assume this simply to have been a typing or printing error.

6. Ibid., 99, 97.

7. See note 5, above, which refers to the same passage.

8. Lindsey, "The Subjectivist Principle," 99, 97.

9. Ibid., 97.

10. Ibid., 98.

11. Ibid., 97.

12. Ibid., 98.

13. Ibid.

14. Ibid., 99.

15. Although Lindsey does not explicitly say that a change is needed here, the fact that he implies it is shown not only by his final two paragraphs but also by the fact that earlier, in saying that the text of *Process and Reality* needs changing, he used the plural, speaking of "some *portions* of the text" (ibid., 97; emphasis added). If Lindsey were not suggesting that the passage on PR 166 should be changed, he would be advocating only a single change.

16. Ibid., 101.

17. The fact that Whitehead in this text uses "doctrine" instead of "principle" would not provide a legitimate basis for Lindsey to claim that, because this passage does not have Whitehead explicitly endorsing the subjectivist *principle*, it need not be changed. There is no reason to believe that Whitehead intended these alternative wordings to point to a substantive distinction.

18. Lindsey, "The Subjectivist Principle," 101.

19. Ibid., 101.

20. A list of problems with Lindsey's interpretation given in my 1977 essay differs from the present list in two respects: it did not have the third and fourth problems, and it failed to point out that some of the problems were more serious than others.

21. Griffin, "The Subjectivist Principle and Its Reformed and Unreformed Versions," 27.

22. Ibid., 28.

23. Ibid.

24. Ibid., 29.

25. Ibid.

26. Ibid., 28–29. Although the page reference to PR was included in the quoted material, it has here been changed to that of the corrected edition.

27. Ibid., 30.

28. Ibid., 35n3.

29. Ibid., 30.

30. Ibid.

31. Ibid., 31.

32. Ibid., 33.

33. Ibid., 31.

34. Ibid.

35. Again, the page reference to PR has been changed to that of the corrected edition.

36. Ibid., 32.

37. Ibid., 33.

38. The mere fact that this principle is said to be one of the two principles constituting Hume's sensationalist *doctrine* would surely not have provided a sufficient reason.

39. Ibid., 33.

40. I discussed earlier the negative importance of this passage, namely, that it rules out the prior interpretations (except perhaps Interpretation R, which was not worked out in sufficient detail for a judgment to be made).

41. I have to admit that when Olav Smith first proposed this identification in his dissertation, I responded by saying that although the subjectivist principle around which the chapter revolves is closely related to the subjectivist bias, the two concepts could not simply be equated. Now that this equation has come to seem obvious, I find my initial

response, besides somewhat embarrassing, also revealing, given the fact that I had surely worked with the relevant texts as much as anyone. The main reason why students of Whitehead have had such difficulty with this chapter, I believe, is the number of factors in it that obscure this equation (perhaps the most important of which is the fact, which threw Lindsey off course, that the chapter begins by seeming to identify the subjectivist principle with a [Humean] principle that Whitehead rejected).

42. "Consistently" here means in their theoretical analyses. In practice, as Whitehead pointed out, they inevitably presupposed the direct perception of other actualities ("because common sense is inflexibly objectivist" [PR 158]), and this presupposition was often expressed inadvertently in their writings (as when Hume acknowledged that he knew that we see colors *with our eyes* [PR 171–73]).

43. The locus classicus for Whitehead's commonsensism is his statement, expressed just before the chapter on "The Subjectivist Principle," that "the metaphysical rule of evidence" is "that we must bow to those presumptions, which, in despite of criticism, we still employ for the regulation of our lives" (PR 151). In place of the phrase "for the regulation of our lives," Whitehead sometimes simply said "in practice," thereby criticizing what he called Hume's "anti-rationalist" appeal to "practice" to justify various beliefs that could find no place in his theory (PR 153; cf. 81, 133, 242–43). In his most direct attack on this aspect of Hume's philosophy, Whitehead said: "Whatever is found in 'practice' must lie within the scope of the metaphysical description.... There can be no appeal to practice to supplement metaphysics" (PR 13). That Whitehead understood "common sense" in this strong sense, so that he was a "commonsense philosopher," is obscured, unfortunately, by the fact that he sometimes, both in *Process and Reality* (9, 17) and in other books, used the term in the derogatory sense, which is currently prevalent, to refer to false beliefs that are widely accepted at a particular time and place. However, there are many other passages in *Process and Reality*, besides the one quoted in the text, in which Whitehead uses "common sense" in the strong sense (PR 40, 51, 52, 128).

44. Whitehead's "formally" is derived from Descartes' *"formaliter"* (PR 219).

45. The most dramatic type of experience of this sort is that called "telepathy" (which literally means "feeling at a distance"), the reality of which Whitehead accepted (PR 253, 308). But telepathy—at least in the sense of the *conscious* awareness of the thoughts of another human being—is a rare experience. A more common experience, Whitehead suggested, is the "instinctive apprehension of a tone of feeling in ordinary social intercourse" (PR 308).

46. Charles Hartshorne reported a once-in-a-lifetime experience of becoming aware of all of nature as alive and as expressing feelings (see Griffin, "Charles Hartshorne," 202). Other people have, of course, reported experiences of this type, sometimes classified under "nature mysticism." But such experiences always seem to be reported as extraordinary ones.

47. Whitehead's argument to this conclusion is explained in more detail, and with reference to his other books, in Griffin, *Unsnarling the World-Knot*, ch. 8.

48. Griffin, "The Subjectivist Principle," 32.

49. Although this passage also says that "with the advent of Cartesian subjectivism, the substance-quality category has lost all claim to metaphysical primacy," the metaphysical implication is limited to the rejection of "individual substances, each with its private world of qualities." The rejection of "vacuous actuality" is not mentioned.

50. Alternatively, if one were not convinced that the objectivist principle of the datum is implicit in Definition 2, one could say that in it Whitehead had in mind merely the subjectivist principle$_{MM}$ and thereby merely the panexperientialist part of the reformed subjectivist principle.

Bibliography

Adler, Julius, and Wing-Wai Tse. "Decision-Making in Bacteria." *Science* 184 (1974): 1292-94.

Alston, William P. *A Realist Conception of Truth.* Ithaca: Cornell University Press, 1996.

Altieri, Charles. "From Symbolist Thought to Immanence: The Ground of Postmodern American Poetics." *Boundary* 2 1 (1973): 605–42.

Ayala, Francisco J. "Can 'Progress' Be Defined as a Biological Concept?" In Matthew H. Nitecki, ed., *Evolutionary Progress.* Chicago and London: University of Chicago Press, 1988: 75–96.

Baker, Gordon, and Katherine J. Morris. *Descartes' Dualism.* London and New York: Routledge, 1996.

Baker, John Robert. "Omniscience and Divine Synchronization." *Process Studies* 2/3 (Fall 1972): 201–08.

Beardslee, William A. "Stories in the Postmodern World: Orienting and Disorienting." In Griffin, ed., *Sacred Interconnections,* 163–76.

———. "Christ in the Postmodern Age: Reflections Inspired by Jean-François Lyotard." In Griffin, Beardslee, and Holland, *Varieties of Postmodern Theology,* 63–80.

Beloff, John. *The Existence of Mind.* London: MacGibbon and Kee, 1962.

———. "Minds and Machines: A Radical Dualist Perspective." *Journal of Consciousness Studies* 1 (1994): 32–37.

Benacerraf, Paul. "Mathematical Truth." In Paul Benacerraf and Hilary Putnam, eds., *Philosophy of Mathematics,* 2nd ed. Cambridge: Cambridge University Press, 1983: 402–20. (Originally published in 1973.)

Bennett, John B. "Unmediated Prehensions: Some Observations." *Process Studies* 2/3 (Fall 1972): 222–25.

Bergson, Henri. *Creative Mind*. New York: Philosophical Library, 1946.

———. *Matter and Memory*. London: Allen and Unwin, 1929.

Berman, Morris. *The Reenchantment of the World*. Ithaca: Cornell University Press, 1981.

Berthrong, John. "The Trouble with Time." *Process Studies* 23/2 (Summer 1994): 134–48.

Bohm, David. "Postmodern Science and a Postmodern World." In Griffin, ed., *The Reenchantment of Science*, 57–68.

Bohm, David, and B. J. Hiley. *The Undivided Universe: An Ontological Interpretation of Quantum Theory*. London and New York: Routledge, 1993.

Bové, Paul A., ed. *Early Postmodernism: Foundational Essays*. Durham, N.C.: Duke University, 1995.

Boyle, Robert. *The Works of the Honourable Robert Boyle*. London: Millar, 1744.

Brown, Delwin, Ralph E. James, and Gene Reeves, eds. *Process Philosophy and Christian Thought*. Indianapolis: Bobbs-Merrill, 1971.

Cahill, Reginald T. *Process Physics: From Information Theory to Quantum Space and Matter*. New York: Nova Science Publishers, 2005.

———. "Process Physics: Self-Referential Information and Experiential Reality." Forthcoming.

Campbell, Keith. *Body and Mind*, 2nd ed. Notre Dame: University of Notre Dame Press, 1984.

Čapek, Milič. "The Unreality and Indeterminacy of the Future in the Light of Contemporary Physics." In Griffin, ed., *Physics and the Ultimate Significance of Time*, 297–308.

———. *The New Aspects of Time: Its Continuity and Novelties*. Dordrecht and Boston: Kluwer Academic, 1991.

———, ed. *The Concepts of Space and Time* (Boston Studies in the Philosophy of Science, Vol. 22). Dordrecht: Reidel, 1976.

Capra, Fritjof. *The Tao of Physics: An Exploration of the Parallels between Modern Physics and Eastern Mysticism*. Boulder: Shambhala, 1975.

Cassirer, Ernst. *The Philosophy of the Enlightenment*. Princeton: Princeton University Press, 1968.

————, Paul O. Kristeller, and John H. Randall, Jr. *The Renaissance Philosophy of Man*. Chicago: University of Chicago Press, 1948.

Chalmers, David. "Facing Up to the Problem of Consciousness." *Journal of Consciousness Studies* 2 (1995): 200–19.

Chihara, Charles. "A Gödelian Thesis Regarding Mathematical Objects: Do They Exist? And Can We Perceive Them?" *Philosophical Review* 91 (1982): 211–17.

Chisholm, Roderick. *Person and Object*. La Salle: Open Court, 1976.

Cleugh, Mary F. *Time and Its Importance in Modern Thought*. London: Methuen, 1937.

Cobb, John B., Jr. *A Christian Natural Theology: Based on the Philosophy of Alfred North Whitehead*. Philadelphia: Westminster, 1965.

————. "The Finality of Christ in a Whiteheadian Perspective." In Dow Kirkpatrick, ed., *The Finality of Christ*. Nashville: Abingdon, 1966: 122–54.

————. "From Crisis Theology to the Post-Modern World." *Centennial Review* 8 (Spring 1964): 209–20. Reprinted in *Toward a New Christianity: Readings in the Death of God Theology*, ed. Thomas J. J. Altizer. New York: Harcourt, Brace, and World, 1967: 241–52.

————. "The Possibility of Theism Today." In Edward H. Madden, Robert Handy, and Marvin Farber, eds., *The Idea of God: Philosophical Perspectives*. New York: Thomas, 1968: 98–123.

————. *God and the World*. Philadelphia: Westminster, 1969.

————. "A Whiteheadian Christology." In Brown, James, and Reeves, eds., *Process Philosophy and Christian Thought*, 382–98.

————. *Christ in a Pluralistic Age*. Philadelphia: Westminster, 1975.

————. "Response to Neville's *Creativity and God*." *Process Studies* 10/3–4 (Fall–Winter 1980): 97–105.

————. *Beyond Dialogue: Toward a Mutual Transformation of Buddhism and Christianity*. Philadelphia: Fortress, 1982.

————. *Process Theology as Political Theology*. Philadelphia: Westminster, 1982.

————. "The Resurrection of the Soul." *Harvard Theological Review* 80/2 (1987): 213–27.

———. "Ecology, Science, and Religion: Toward a Postmodern Worldview." In Griffin, ed., *The Reenchantment of Science*, 99–114.

———. "Alfred North Whitehead." In Griffin et al., *Founders of Constructive Postmodern Philosophy*, 165–95.

———. *Grace and Responsibility: A Wesleyan Theology for Today*. Nashville: Abingdon, 1995.

———. *Transforming Christianity and the World: A Way beyond Absolutism and Relativism*, ed. Paul F. Knitter. Maryknoll: Orbis, 1999.

———. *Postmodernism and Public Policy: Reframing Religion, Culture, Education, Sexuality, Class, Race, Politics, and the Economy*. Albany: State University of New York Press, 2001.

———, and David Ray Griffin. *Process Theology: An Introductory Exposition*. Philadelphia: Westminster, 1976.

———, and David Ray Griffin, eds. *Mind in Nature: Essays on the Interface of Science and Philosophy*. Washington, D.C.: University Press of America, 1977.

Copleston, F. C. *A History of Philosophy*, vol. 4: *Descartes to Leibniz*. London: Burns Oates, 1960.

Cottingham, John G., Robert Stoothoff, and Dugald Murdoch, eds. *The Philosophical Writings of Descartes*, vol. 1. Cambridge: Cambridge University Press, 1985.

Crombie, A. C. "Mersenne." In C. G. Gillespie, ed., *Dictionary of Scientific Biography*. New York: Scribner, 1970–1976: vol. 9: 317.

Daly, Herman E., and John B. Cobb Jr. *For the Common Good: Redirecting the Economy toward Community, the Environment, and a Sustainable Future*, 2nd ed. Boston: Beacon, 1994.

Darwin, Francis, ed. *The Life and Letters of Charles Darwin*, 2 vols. New York: D. Appleton, 1896.

David, Marian. *Correspondence and Disquotation: An Essay on the Nature of Truth*. Oxford and New York: Oxford University Press, 1994.

Davidson, Donald. "The Structure and Content of Truth." *Journal of Philosophy* 87/6 (June 1990): 279–328.

Davies, Paul C. W. *The Physics of Time Asymmetry*. Berkeley: University of California Press, 1976.

Dawkins, Richard. *The Blind Watchmaker: Why the Evidence of Evolution Reveals a Universe without Design*. New York and London: Norton, 1987.

De Beauregard, Costa. "Time in Relativity Theory: Arguments for a Philosophy of Being." In Fraser, ed., *The Voices of Time*, 417–33.

De Broglie, Louis. "A General Survey of the Scientific Work of Albert Einstein." In P. A. Schilpp, ed., *Albert Einstein: Philosopher-Scientist*. La Salle: Open Court, 1949: 107–27.

Denbigh, Kenneth G. *An Inventive Universe*. New York: Braziller, 1975.

———. *Three Concepts of Time*. New York: Springer, 1981.

Dennett, Daniel E. *Elbow Room: The Varieties of Free Will Worth Wanting*. Cambridge: MIT Press, 1984.

Devall, Bill, and George Sessions. *Deep Ecology: Living as if Nature Mattered*. Salt Lake City, UT: Peregrine Smith, 1985.

Devlin, James P. "Hartshorne's Metaphysical Asymmetry." In Hahn, ed., *The Philosophy of Charles Hartshorne*, 275–90.

Dossey, Larry. *Space, Time and Medicine*. Boulder: Shambhala, 1982.

———. *Healing Words: The Power of Prayer and the Practice of Medicine*. San Francisco: HarperSanFrancisco, 1993.

Easlea, Brian. *Witch Hunting, Magic and the New Philosophy: An Introduction to Debates of the Scientific Revolution 1450–1750*. Atlantic Highlands, N.J.: Humanities, 1980.

Eddington, Arthur. *The Nature of the Physical World*. Ann Arbor: University of Michigan Press, 1968.

Edwards, Paul. "Panpsychism." In Edwards, *Encyclopedia of Philosophy*. New York: Macmillan, 1972, vol. 6: 23–31.

Einstein, Albert. *The Meaning of Relativity*, 3rd ed. Princeton: Princeton University Press, 1950.

Ferré, Frederick. *Shaping the Future: Resources for the Post-Modern World*. New York: Harper and Row, 1976.

———. "On the Ultimate Significance of Time for Truth, Goodness, and the Sacred." In Griffin, ed., *Physics and the Ultimate Significance of Time*: 309–17.

Feynman, Richard. *The Character of Physical Law*. Cambridge: MIT Press, 1965.

Field, Hartry. *Science without Numbers.* Princeton: Princeton University Press, 1980.

Finkelstein, Norman G. *Image and Reality of the Israel-Palestine Conflict.* London: Verso, 1995.

Fitzgerald, Paul. "Relativity Physics and the God of Process Philosophy." *Process Studies* 2/4 (Winter 1971): 251–73.

Ford, Lewis S. "Is Process Theism Compatible with Relativity Theory?" *Journal of Religion* 48/2 (April 1968): 124–35.

———. "The Divine Activity of the Future." *Process Studies* 11/3 (Fall 1981): 169–79.

———. *The Emergence of Whitehead's Philosophy, 1925–29.* Albany: State University of New York Press, 1984.

———. "Hartshorne's Interpretation of Whitehead." In Hahn, ed., *The Philosophy of Charles Hartshorne*: 313–37.

———. *Transforming Process Theism.* Albany: State University of New York Press, 2001.

———, ed., *Two Process Philosophers: Hartshorne's Encounter with Whitehead.* Tallahassee: American Academy of Religion, 1973.

Ford, Marcus P. *William James's Philosophy: A New Perspective.* Amherst: University of Massachusetts Press, 1982.

———. "William James." In Griffin et al., *Founders of Constructive Postmodern Philosophy*, 89–132.

———. "James's Psychical Research and Its Philosophical Implications." *Transactions of the Charles S. Peirce Society* 34 (1998): 605–26.

Fost, Frederic F. "Relativity Theory and Hartshorne's Dipolar Theism." Lewis S. Ford, ed., *Two Process Philosophers: Hartshorne's Encounter with Whitehead.* Tallahassee: American Academy of Religion, 1973: 89–99.

Fox, Warwick. *Toward a Transpersonal Ecology: Developing New Foundations for Environmentalism.* Boston: Shambhala, 1990.

Frank, Phillip. "Is the Future Already Here?" Čapek, ed., *The Concepts of Space and Time*: 387–95.

Fraser, J. T. "Out of Plato's Cave: The Natural History of Time." *Kenyon Review* 2 (Winter 1980): 143–62.

————. *The Genesis and Evolution of Time: A Critique of Interpretation in Physics.* Amherst: University of Massachusetts Press, 1982.

————, ed. *The Voices of Time.* New York: Braziller, 1966.

Gale, Richard M. *The Language of Time.* New York: Humanities, 1968.

Gamwell, Franklin I. *The Divine Good: Modern Moral Theory and the Necessity of God.* Dallas: Southern Methodist University, 1996.

Gay, Peter. *The Enlightenment: The Rise of Modern Paganism,* 2nd ed. New York: Norton, 1995.

————. *The Enlightenment: The Science of Human Freedom,* reissue, New York: Norton, 1996.

Geertz, Clifford. *Islam Observed: Religious Development in Morocco and Indonesia.* New Haven: Yale University Press, 1968.

————. *Interpretation of Cultures: Selected Essays.* New York: Basic Books, 1973.

Gödel, Kurt. "What Is Cantor's Continuum Problem? Supplement to the Second [1964] Edition." Reprinted in Kurt Gödel, *Collected Works,* vol. 2, ed. Solomon Feferman et al. New York: Oxford University Press, 1990: 266–69.

Gold, Thomas, ed. *The Nature of Time.* Ithaca: Cornell University Press, 1967.

Goldbeter, A., and D. E. Koshland Jr. "Simple Molecular Model for Sensing and Adaptation Based on Receptor Modification with Application to Bacterial Chemotaxis." *Journal of Molecular Biology* 161 (1982): 395–416.

Goldsworthy, J. D. "God or Mackie? The Dilemma of Secular Moral Philosophy." *American Journal of Jurisprudence* 30 (1985): 43–78.

Gould, Stephen Jay. "On Replacing the Idea of Progress with an Operational Notion of Directionality." Matthew Nitecki, ed., *Evolutionary Progress.* London and Chicago: University of Chicago Press, 1988: 319–38.

Griffin, David Ray. "Schubert Ogden's Christology and the Possibilities of Process Philosophy." *The Christian Scholar* 50 (Fall, 1967): 290–303, reprinted in Brown, James, and Reeves, eds., *Process Philosophy and Christian Thought,* 347–61.

————. "Is Revelation Coherent?" *Theology Today* 28 (October 1971): 278–94.

————. "The Essential Elements of a Contemporary Christology," *Encounter* 33 (Spring 1972): 170–84.

————. "Hartshorne's Differences from Whitehead." In Lewis Ford, ed., *Two Process Philosophers*: 35–57.

————. *A Process Christology.* Philadelphia: Westminster, 1973; reprinted with new preface, Lanham, Md.: University Press of America, 1990.

————. *God, Power, and Evil: A Process Theodicy.* Philadelphia: Westminster, 1976; reprinted with a new preface, Westminster John Knox, 2004.

————. "Post-Modern Theology for a New Christian Existence." In David Ray Griffin and Thomas J. J. Altizer, ed., *John Cobb's Theology in Process.* Philadelphia: Westminster, 1977: 5–24.

————. "The Subjectivist Principle and Its Reformed and Unreformed Versions." *Process Studies* 7/1 (1977): 27–36.

————. "The Holy, Necessary Goodness, and Morality." *Journal of Religious Ethics* 8/2 (Fall, 1980): 330–49.

————. "Liberation Theology and Postmodern Theology: A Response to Cornel West." In Griffin, Beardslee, and Holland, *Varieties of Postmodern Theology*: 129–49.

————. *Evil Revisited: Responses and Reconsiderations.* Albany: State University of New York Press, 1991.

————. "Charles Hartshorne." In Donald W. Musser and Joseph L. Price, eds., *A New Handbook of Christian Theologians.* Nashville: Abingdon, 1996: 200–13.

————. "Panexperientialist Physicalism and the Mind-Body Problem." *Journal of Consciousness Studies* 4/3 (1997): 248–68.

————. *Parapsychology, Philosophy, and Spirituality: Postmodern Explorations.* Albany: State University of New York Press, 1997.

————. *Unsnarling the World-Knot: Consciousness, Freedom, and the Mind-Body Problem.* Berkeley and Los Angeles: University of California Press, 1998.

————. *Religion and Scientific Naturalism: Overcoming the Conflicts.* Albany: State University of New York Press, 2000.

————. "Creation out of Nothing, Creation out of Chaos, and the Problem of Evil." In Stephen T. Davis, ed., *Encountering Evil: Live Options in Theodicy*, 2nd ed. Philadelphia: Westminster John Knox, 2001: 108–25.

————. *Reenchantment without Supernaturalism: A Process Philosophy of Religion.* Ithaca: Cornell University Press, 2001.

———. "Time in Process Philosophy." *KronoScope: Journal for the Study of Time* 1 (2001): 75–99.

———. "Morality and Scientific Naturalism: Overcoming the Conflicts." In Jerald T. Wallulis and Jeremiah Hackett, eds., *Philosophy of Religion for a New Century*. Dordrecht: Kluwer, 2003.

———. "Panentheism: A Postmodern Revelation." In Philip Clayton and Arthur Peacocke, eds., *In Whom We Live and Move and Have Our Being: Reflections on Panentheism for a Scientific Age*. Grand Rapids: Eerdmans, 2003.

———, ed. *Physics and the Ultimate Significance of Time: Bohm, Prigogine, and Process Philosophy*. Albany: State University of New York Press, 1986.

———, ed. *The Reenchantment of Science: Postmodern Proposals*. Albany: State University of New York Press, 1988.

———, ed. *Spirituality and Society: Postmodern Visions*. Albany: State University of New York Press, 1988.

———, ed. *Archetypal Process: Self and Divine in Whitehead, Jung, and Hillman*. Evanston: Northwestern University Press, 1989.

———, ed. *Deep Religious Pluralism*. Louisville: Westminster John Knox, 2005.

———, and Huston Smith. *Primordial Truth and Postmodern Theology*. Albany: State University of New York Press, 1989.

———, William A. Beardslee, and Joe Holland. *Varieties of Postmodern Theology*. Albany: State University of New York Press, 1989.

———, John B. Cobb Jr., Peter Ochs, Marcus P. Ford, and Pete A. Y. Gunter. *Founders of Constructive Postmodern Philosophy: Peirce, James, Bergson, Whitehead, and Hartshorne*. Albany: State University of New York Press, 1993.

Griffin, Donald R. *Animal Minds*. Chicago: University of Chicago Press, 1992.

Gruenler, Royce Gordon. *The Inexhaustible God: Biblical Faith and the Challenge of Process Theism*. Grand Rapids: Baker Book House, 1983.

Grünbaum, Adolf. *Philosophical Problems of Space and Time*. New York: Knopf, 1963.

———. "The Anisotropy of Time." In Gold, ed., *The Nature of Time*: 149–86.

Habermas, Jürgen. *Postmetaphysical Thinking: Philosophical Essays*, trans. William Mark Hohengarten. Cambridge: MIT Press, 1992.

————. "Transcendence from Within, Transcendence in this World." In Don Browning and Francis Schüssler Fiorenza, eds., *Habermas, Modernity, and Public Theology*. New York: Crossroad, 1992: 226–50.

————. *Justification and Application: Remarks on Discourse Ethics*, trans. Ciaran Cronin. Cambridge: Polity, 1993.

Hahn, Lewis Edwin, ed. *The Philosophy of Charles Hartshorne* (Library of Living Philosophers, Vol. 20). La Salle: Open Court, 1991.

Hameroff, Stuart R. "Quantum Coherence in Microtubules: A Neural Basis for Emergent Consciousness?" *Journal of Consciousness Studies* 1 (1994): 91–118.

Hare, R. M. "Ontology in Ethics." In Ted Honderich, ed., *Morality and Objectivity: A Tribute to J. L. Mackie*. London: Routledge and Kegan Paul, 1985: 39–53.

Harman, Gilbert. *The Nature of Morality: An Introduction to Ethics*. New York: Oxford University Press, 1977.

————. "Is There a Single True Morality?" In Michael Krausz, ed., *Relativism: Interpretation and Confrontation*. Notre Dame: University of Notre Dame Press, 1989: 363–86.

Hartshorne, Charles. "The Compound Individual." In Otis H. Lee, ed., *Philosophical Essays for Alfred North Whitehead*. New York: Longmans Green, 1936. Reprinted in Hartshorne, *Whitehead's Philosophy*: 41–61.

————. *Beyond Humanism: Essays in the New Philosophy of Nature*. New York: Willett, Clark, 1937.

————. *Man's Vision of God and the Logic of Theism*. New York: Harper and Row, 1941.

————. "Whitehead's Idea of God." In Paul Arthur Schilpp, ed., *The Philosophy of Alfred North Whitehead* (Library of Living Philosophers, Vol. 3), 2nd ed. New York: Tudor, 1951 (orig. 1941): 513–59.

————. *The Logic of Perfection and Other Essays in Neoclassical Metaphysics*. LaSalle: Open Court, 1962.

————. " Interrogation of Charles Hartshorne." In Sydney and Beatrice Rome, eds., *Philosophical Interrogations*. New York: Holt, Rinehart, and Winston, 1964: 321–54.

————. *Creative Synthesis and Philosophic Method*. London: SCM Press and LaSalle: Open Court, 1970; reprint, Lanham, Md.: University Press of America, 1983.

————. *Whitehead's Philosophy: Selected Essays, 1935–1970.* Lincoln: University of Nebraska Press, 1972.

————. *Born to Sing: An Interpretation and World Survey of Bird Song.* Bloomington: Indiana University Press, 1973.

————. "Bell's Theorem and Stapp's Revised View of Space-Time." *Process Studies* 7/4 (Winter 1977): 183–91.

————. "Physics and Psychics: The Place of Mind in Nature." In Cobb and Griffin, eds., *Mind in Nature:* 89–96.

————. "Response to Neville's *Creativity and God*." *Process Studies* 10/3–4 (Fall–Winter 1980).

————. *Omnipotence and Other Theological Mistakes.* Albany: State University of New York Press, 1984.

————. "General Remarks." In Robert Kane and Stephen H. Phillips, eds., *Hartshorne, Process Philosophy and Theology.* Albany: State University of New York Press, 1989.

————. "A Reply to My Critics." In Hahn, ed., *The Philosophy of Charles Hartshorne:* 569–731.

————. "Some Causes of My Intellectual Growth." In Hahn, ed., *The Philosophy of Charles Hartshorne:* 3–45.

————. *The Zero Fallacy and Other Essays in Neoclassical Philosophy,* ed. Mohammed Valady. Peru, Ill.: Open Court, 1997.

————, and William L. Reese, eds. *Philosophers Speak of God.* Chicago: University of Chicago Press, 1953.

Hellman, G. *Mathematics without Numbers.* Oxford: Oxford University Press, 1989.

Hesse, Mary. *Forces and Fields: The Concept of Action at a Distance in the History of Physics.* Totowa, N.J.: Littlefield, Adams, 1965.

Hill, Christopher. *The World Turned Upside Down.* London: Temple Smith, 1972.

Hintikka, Jaakko. "Cogito, Ergo Sum: Inference or Performance." *Philosophical Review* 71 (1962): 3–32.

Hoffman, Banesh, with Helen Dukas. *Albert Einstein: Creator and Rebel.* New York: Viking, 1972.

Honderich, Ted. "Mind, Brain, and Self-Conscious Mind." In Colin Blakemore and Susan Greenfield, eds., *Mindwaves: Thoughts on Intelligence, Identity, and Consciousness.* Oxford: Blackwell, 1987: 445–58.

————. *How Free Are You? The Determinism Problem.* Oxford: Oxford University Press, 1993.

Hooykaas, R. *Natural Law and Divine Miracle: A Historical-Critical Study of the Principle of Uniformity in Geology, Biology, and Theology.* Leiden: Brill, 1959.

Horwich, Paul. *Truth.* Oxford: Blackwell, 1990.

Isham, C. J., and John C. Polkinghorne. "The Debate over the Block Universe." In Robert John Russell, Nancey Murphy, and C. J. Isham, eds., *Quantum Cosmology and the Laws of Nature: Scientific Perspectives on Divine Action.* Vatican City: Vatican Observatory Publications, 1993: 135–44.

Jacob, James. "Boyle's Atomism and the Restoration Assault on Pagan Naturalism." *Social Studies of Science* 8 (1978): 211–33.

————. *Robert Boyle and the English Revolution.* New York: Franklin, 1978.

James, William. *Varieties of Religious Experience.* New York: Longmans, Green, 1902 (reprinted by Penguin Books, 1985).

————. "Does Consciousness Exist?" *Journal of Philosophy, Psychology and Scientific Methods,* 1, 18 (September 1, 1904). Reprinted in James, *Essays in Radical Empiricism,* ed. Ralph Barton Perry (1912). This volume republished along with James, *A Pluralistic Universe*: New York: Dutton, 1971.

————. *Some Problems of Philosophy.* London: Longmans, Green, 1911.

Jay, Martin. "The Debate over Performative Contradiction: Habermas versus the Poststructuralists." In Jay, *Force Fields: Between Intellectual History and Cultural Critique.* New York: Routledge, 1993: 25–37.

Johnson, A. H. "Whitehead as Teacher and Philosopher." *Philosophy and Phenomenological Research* 29 (1969): 351–76.

————. "Some Conversations with Whitehead concerning God and Creativity." In Lewis S. Ford and George W. Kline, eds., *Explorations in Whitehead's Philosophy.* New York: Fordham University Press, 1983: 3–13.

Johnson, Phillip E. *Darwin on Trial,* 2nd ed. Downers Grove, Ill.: InterVarsity Press, 1993.

————. *Reason in the Balance: The Case against Naturalism in Science, Law, and Education.* Downers Grove, Ill.: Intervarsity Press, 1993.

Jones, William B. "Bell's Theorem, H. P. Stapp, and Process Theism." *Process Studies* 7/4 (Winter 1977): 250–61.

Kant, Immanuel. *Religion within the Limits of Reason Alone*, trans. Theodore M. Greene and Hoyt H. Hudson. New York: Harper and Row, 1960.

———. *Critique of Pure Reason*, trans. Norman Kemp Smith. New York: St. Martin's, 1965.

Kekes, John. *The Nature of Philosophy*. Totowa, N.J.: Rowman and Littlefield, 1980.

Keller, Evelyn Fox. *A Feeling for the Organism: The Life and Work of Barbara McClintock*. New York: Freeman, 1983.

Kim, Jaegwon. *Supervenience and Mind: Selected Philosophical Essays*. Cambridge: Cambridge University Press, 1993.

Klaaren, Eugene. *Religious Origins of Modern Science: Belief in Creation in Seventeenth-Century Thought*. Grand Rapids: Eerdmans, 1977.

Knitter, Paul F. *Jesus and the Other Names: Christian Mission and Global Responsibility*. Maryknoll, N.Y.: Orbis, 1996.

Koyré, Alexandre. *From the Closed World to the Infinite Universe*. Baltimore: Johns Hopkins Press, 1957.

Larmore, Charles. *The Morals of Modernity*. Cambridge: Cambridge University Press, 1996.

Lawrence, Nathaniel. "Time Represented as Space." In Eugene Freeman and Wilfrid Sellars, eds., *Basic Issues in the Philosophy of Time*. La Salle: Open Court, 1971: 123–32.

Lenoble, Robert. *Mersenne ou la naissance du méchanisme*. Paris: Librairie Philosophique J. Vrin, 1943.

Levenson, Jon D. *Creation and the Persistence of Evil: The Jewish Drama of Divine Omnipotence*. San Francisco: Harper and Row, 1988.

Lewis, H. D. *The Elusive Mind*. London: Allen and Unwin, 1969.

———. *The Elusive Self*. London: Macmillan, 1982.

Lewontin, Richard. "Billions and Billions of Demons" (review of Carl Sagan, *The Demon-Haunted World: Science as a Candle in the Dark*). *New York Review of Books*, January 9, 1997: 28–32.

Lindsey, James E., Jr. "The Subjectivist Principle and the Linguistic Turn Revisited." *Process Studies* 6/2 (1976): 97–102.

Lochhead, David. *The Dialogical Imperative: A Christian Reflection on Interfaith Encounter*. Maryknoll: Orbis, 1988.

Lowe, E. J. "There Are No Easy Problems of Consciousness." *Journal of Consciousness Studies* 2 (1995): 266–71.

Lucas, John Randolph. *The Future: An Essay on God, Temporality, and Truth*. Cambridge, Mass., and Oxford: Blackwell, 1989.

———. "The Temporality of God." In Robert John Russell, Nancey Murphy, and C. J. Isham, eds., *Quantum Cosmology and the Laws of Nature: Scientific Perspectives on Divine Action*. Vatican City: Vatican Observatory Publications, 1993: 235–46.

Lycan, William G. *Consciousness*. Cambridge: MIT Press, 1987.

MacIntyre, Alasdair. *After Virtue: A Study in Moral Theory*. Notre Dame: University of Notre Dame, 1981.

Mackie, John. *Ethics: Inventing Right and Wrong*. New York: Penguin, 1977.

———. *The Miracle of Theism: Arguments for and against the Existence of God*. Oxford: Clarendon, 1982.

Maddy, Penelope. *Realism in Mathematics*. Oxford: Clarendon, 1990.

Madell, Geoffrey. *Mind and Materialism*. Edinburgh: University Press, 1988.

Matson, Floyd W. *The Broken Image: Man, Science and Society*, 1964; Garden City: Doubleday, 1966.

May, Gerhard. *Creatio Ex Nihilo: The Doctrine of "Creation out of Nothing" in Early Christian Thought*, trans. A. S. Worrall. Edinburgh: Clark, 1994.

McCarthy, Thomas. *Ideals and Illusions: On Reconstruction and Deconstruction in Contemporary Critical Theory*. Cambridge and London: MIT Press, 1993.

McGinn, Colin. *The Character of Mind*. Oxford: Oxford University Press, 1982.

———. *The Problem of Consciousness: Essays towards a Resolution*. Oxford: Blackwell, 1991.

Mehlberg, Henry. *Time, Causality, and the Quantum Theory*, vol. 1: *Essay on the Causal Theory of Time*, ed. Robert S. Cohen. Dordrecht: Reidel, 1980.

Merrill, A. A. "The *t* of Physics." *Journal of Philosophy* 19/9 (April 1922): 238–41.

Meyerson, Emile. "Various Interpretations of Relativistic Time." In Čapek, ed., *The Concepts of Space and Time*: 353–62.

Moschovakis, Y. N. *Descriptive Set Theory*. Amsterdam: North Holland, 1980.

Mosse, George L. "Puritan Radicalism and the Enlightenment." *Church History* 29 (1960): 424–39.

Murphy, Jeffrie G. *Evolution, Morality, and the Meaning of Life*. Totowa, N.J.: Rowman and Littlefield, 1982.

———. "Constitutionalism, Moral Skepticism, and Religious Belief." In Alan S. Rosenbaum, ed., *Constitutionalism: The Philosophical Dimension*. New York: Greenwood, 1988: 239–49.

Naess, Arne. *Ecology, Community, and Lifestyle: Outline of an Ecosophy*. Cambridge: Cambridge University Press, 1989.

Nagel, Thomas. *Mortal Questions*. London: Cambridge University Press, 1979.

———. *The View from Nowhere*. New York: Oxford University Press. 1986.

Neville, Robert Cummings. "Can God Create Men and Address Them Too?" *Harvard Theological Review* 61 (1968): 603–23.

———. *God the Creator: On the Transcendence and Presence of God* (orig. 1968). Albany: State University of New York Press, 1992.

———. *The Cosmology of Freedom*. New Haven: Yale University Press, 1974; reprint, Albany: State University of New York Press, 1996.

———. *Soldier, Sage, Saint*. New York: Fordham University Press, 1978.

———. *Creativity and God: A Challenge to Process Theology*. New York: Seabury, 1980.

———. "Concerning Creativity and God: A Response." *Process Studies* 11/1 (Spring, 1981): 1–10.

———. *Reconstruction of Thinking* (vol. 1 of *Axiology of Thinking*). Albany: State University of New York Press, 1981.

———. "Hegel and Whitehead on Totality: The Failure of a Conception of System." In George R. Lucas, Jr. ed., *Hegel and Whitehead: Contemporary Perspectives on Systematic Philosophy*. Albany: State University of New York Press, 1986: 86–108.

———. "Contributions and Limitations of Process Philosophy." *Process Studies* 16/4 (Winter 1987), 283–98.

———. *Recovery of the Measure: Interpretation and Nature* (vol. 2 of *Axiology of Thinking*). Albany: State University of New York Press, 1989.

————. *Normative Cultures* (vol. 3 of *Axiology of Thinking*). Albany: State University of New York Press, 1995.

Nitecki, Matthew, ed. *Evolutionary Progress*. London and Chicago: University of Chicago Press, 1988.

Nobo, Jorge. *Whitehead's Metaphysics of Extension and Solidarity*. Albany: State University of New York Press, 1986.

Ochs, Peter. "Charles Sanders Pierce." In Griffin et al., *Founders of Constructive Postmodern Philosophy*: 43–87.

O'Connor, D. J. *The Correspondence Theory of Truth*. London: Hutchison University Library, 1975.

Odin, Steve. *Process Metaphysics and Hua-Yen Buddhism*. Albany: State University of New York Press, 1982.

Ogden, Schubert M. *The Reality of God and Other Essays*. New York: Harper and Row, 1964.

Oomen, Palmyre. "The Prehensibility of God's Consequent Nature." *Process Studies* 27/1–2 (Spring–Summer 1998): 108–33.

Ospovat, Dov. *The Development of Darwin's Theory: Natural History, Natural Theology and Natural Selection 1838–1859*. Cambridge and New York: Cambridge University Press, 1981.

Passmore, John. *Philosophical Reasoning* (orig. 1961). New York: Basic Books, 1969.

Peirce, Charles Sanders. *Collected Papers of Charles Sanders Peirce*, ed. Charles Hartshorne and Paul Weiss. Cambridge: Harvard University Press, 1931–35.

Penrose, Roger. "Interview" (with Jane Clark). *Journal of Consciousness Studies* 1 (1994): 17–24.

Plantinga, Alvin. "Advice to Christian Philosophers." *Faith and Philosophy* 1/2 (July 1984): 253–71.

————. *God and Other Minds: A Study of the Rational Justification of Belief in God*, 2nd ed. Ithaca, N.Y.: Cornell University Press, 1990.

————. "Evolution, Neutrality, and Antecedent Probability: A Reply to McMullin and Van Till." *Christian Scholar's Review* 21/1 (1991): 80–109.

————. "When Faith and Reason Clash: Evolution and the Bible." *Christian Scholar's Review* 21/1 (1991): 8–32.

Popper, Karl, and John C. Eccles. *The Self and Its Brain: An Argument for Interactionism*. Heidelberg: Springer-Verlag, 1977.

Prigogine, Ilya, and Isabelle Stengers. *Order Out of Chaos: Man's New Dialogue with Nature*. New York: Bantam Books, 1984.

Putnam, Hilary. *Reason, Truth, and History*. Cambridge: Cambridge University Press, 1981.

———. *Realism and Reason*. New York: Cambridge University Press, 1983.

———. "Replies." *Philosophical Topics* 20/1 (Spring 1992): 347–408.

———. *Words and Life*, ed. James Conant. Cambridge: Harvard University Press, 1994.

Quine, Willard Van. *From a Logical Point of View*. Cambridge: Harvard University Press, 1953.

———. *Theories and Things*. Cambridge: Harvard University Press, 1981.

———. "Replies." In Lewis Edwin Hahn and Paul Arthur Schilpp, eds., *The Philosophy of W. V. Quine* (Library of Living Philosophers, vol. 18). LaSalle, Ill.: Open Court, 1986: 663–65.

———. *From Stimulus to Science*. Cambridge: Harvard University Press, 1995.

Randall, John Herman, Jr. "The Nature of Naturalism." In Yervant H. Krikorian, ed., *Naturalism and the Human Spirit*. New York: Columbia University Press, 1944: 354–82.

Rawls, John. "Kantian Constructivism in Moral Theory." *Journal of Philosophy* 77 (September, 1980): 515–72.

———. *Political Liberalism* (with a new introduction and the "Reply to Habermas"). New York: Columbia University Press, 1996.

Reese, William L. "The 'Trouble' with Panentheism—and the Divine Event." In Hahn, ed., *The Philosophy of Charles Hartshorne*: 187–202.

Reeves, Gene. "The Lotus Sutra and Process Thought." *Process Studies* 23/2 (Summer 1994): 98–118.

Reichenbach, Hans. *The Direction of Time*. Berkeley: University of California Press, 1956.

Reid, Thomas. *An Inquiry into the Human Mind on the Principles of Common Sense* (1764), critical edition, ed. Derek R. Brookes. University Park: Pennsylvania State University Press, 1997.

Rensch, Bernard. *Evolution above the Species Level.* New York: Columbia University Press, 1960.

———. "Arguments for Panpsychistic Identism." In Cobb and Griffin, eds., *Mind and Nature*: 70–78.

Rescher, Nicholas. *The Riddle of Existence: An Essay in Idealistic Metaphysics.* Lanham, Md.: University Press of America, 1985.

———. *The Strife of Systems: An Essay on the Grounds and Implications of Philosophical Diversity.* Pittsburgh: University of Pittsburgh Press, 1985.

Robinson, William S. *Brains and People: An Essay on Mentality and Its Causal Conditions.* Philadelphia: Temple University Press, 1988.

Rorty, Richard M. "The Subjectivist Principle and the Linguistic Turn." In George L. Kline, ed., *Alfred North Whitehead: Essays on His Philosophy.* Englewood Cliffs, N.J., 1963; Lanham, Md.: University Press of America, 1989: 134–57.

———. *Philosophy and the Mirror of Nature.* Princeton: Princeton University Press, 1979.

———. *Consequences of Pragmatism.* Minneapolis: University of Minneapolis Press, 1982.

———. *Contingency, Irony, and Solidarity.* Cambridge: Cambridge University Press, 1989.

Russell, Bertrand. *Mysticism and Logic.* London: Allen and Unwin, 1917.

———. *Our Knowledge of the External World.* London: Allen and Unwin, 1921.

Santayana, George. *Scepticism and Animal Faith.* New York: Dover, 1955.

Schilling, Harold K. *The New Consciousness in Science and Religion.* Philadelphia: United Church Press, 1973.

Seager, William. *Metaphysics of Consciousness.* London and New York: Routledge, 1991.

———. "Consciousness, Information, and Panpsychism." *Journal of Consciousness Studies* 2 (1995): 272–88.

Searle, John R. *Minds, Brains and Science: The 1984 Reith Lectures.* London: British Broadcasting Corporation, 1984.

———. *The Rediscovery of the Mind.* Cambridge: MIT Press, 1992.

Sellars, Wilfrid. *Science, Perception, and Reality.* New York: Humanities, 1963.

Sheldrake, Rupert. *A New Science of Life: The Hypothesis of Formative* Causation. London: Blond and Briggs, 1981.

———. *The Presence of the Past: Morphic Resonance and the Habits of Nature.* New York: Times Books, 1988.

Sherburne, Donald W. "Whitehead without God" (orig. 1967). In Brown, James, and Reeves, eds., *Process Philosophy and Christian Thought*: 305–28.

———. "The 'Whitehead without God' Debate: The Rejoinder." *Process Studies* 1/2 (1971): 101–13.

———. "Decentering Whitehead." *Process Studies* 15/2 (Summer 1986): 83–94.

Smart, J. J. C. "Materialism." In C. V. Borst, ed., *The Mind-Brain Identity Theory.* London: Macmillan, 1979: 159–70.

Smith, Olav Bryant. "Myths of the Self: Narrative Identity and Postmodern Metaphysics." Dissertation. Claremont Graduate University, Claremont, California, 2001; published as *Myths of the Self: Narrative Identity and Postmodern Metaphysics*. Lanham, Md.: Lexington Books, 2004.

Stapp, Henry P. "Quantum Mechanics, Local Causality, and Process Philosophy," ed. William B. Jones. *Process Studies* 7/3 (Fall 1977): 173–82.

———. "Einstein Time and Process Time." In Griffin, ed., *Physics and the Ultimate Significance of Time*: 264–70.

Sternhell, Zeev. *The Founding Myths of Israel: National Socialism and the Making of the Jewish State*, trans. David Maisel. Princeton: Princeton University Press, 1998.

Stone, Bryan P., and Thomas Jay Oord, eds. *Thy Nature and Thy Name Is Love: Wesleyan and Process Theologies in Dialogue*. Nashville: Abingdon, 2001.

Strawson, Galen. *Mental Reality*. Cambridge: MIT Press, 1994.

Suchocki, Marjorie Hewitt. *The End of Evil: Process Eschatology in Historical Context*. Albany: State University of New York Press, 1988.

Swinburne, Richard. *The Existence of God*. Oxford: Clarendon, 1979.

———. *The Evolution of the Soul*. Oxford: Clarendon, 1986.

Taube, Mortimer. *Causation, Freedom and Determinism*. London: Allen and Unwin, 1936.

Thomas, Keith. *Religion and the Decline of Magic*. New York: Charles Scribner's Sons, 1971.

Trevor-Roper, H. R. *The European Witch Craze of the Sixteenth and Seventeenth Centuries and Other Essays.* New York: Harper, 1969.

Weinberg, Steven. *Dreams of a Final Theory: The Scientist's Search for the Ultimate Laws of Nature,* 2nd ed. New York: Vintage Books, 1994.

Weiss, P. "Time Proves Not Reversible at Deepest Level." *Science News* 154 (October 31, 1998): 277.

West, Cornel. "Afterword: The Politics of American Neo-Pragmatism." In John Rajchman and Cornel West, eds. *Post-Analytic Philosophy.* New York: Columbia University Press, 1985: 259–75.

————. "Dispensing with Metaphysics in Religious Thought." *Religion and Intellectual Life* 3/10 (Spring 1986): 53–56.

Westfall, Richard. *Never at Rest: A Biography of Isaac Newton.* Cambridge: Cambridge University Press, 1980.

Weyl, Herman. *Philosophy of Mathematics and Natural Science.* Princeton: Princeton University Press, 1979.

Whitehead, Alfred North. *Essays in Science and Philosophy.* New York: Philosophical Library, 1947.

————. *Symbolism: Its Meaning and Effect* (orig. 1927). New York: Capricorn, 1959.

————. *Adventures of Ideas* (orig. 1933). New York: Free Press, 1967.

————. *Science and the Modern World* (orig. 1925). New York: Free Press 1967.

————. *The Function of Reason* (orig. 1929). Boston: Beacon, 1968.

————. *Modes of Thought* (orig. 1938). New York: Free Press 1968.

————. *Process and Reality: An Essay in Cosmology* (orig. 1929), corrected edition, ed. David Ray Griffin and Donald W. Sherburne. New York: Free Press, 1978.

————. *Religion in the Making.* New York: Fordham University Press, 1996 (reprint of 1926 edition).

Whitrow, G. J. *The Natural Philosophy of Time,* 2nd ed. Oxford: Clarendon, 1980.

Wilcox, John. "A Question from Physics for Certain Theists." *Journal of Religion* 40/4 (October 1961): 293–300.

Williams, Bernard. "Ethics and the Fabric of the World." In Ted Honderich, ed., *Morality and Objectivity: A Tribute to J. L. Mackie.* London: Routledge and Kegan Paul, 1985: 203–14.

————. *Ethics and the Limits of Philosophy.* Cambridge: Harvard University Press, 1985.

Williams, Michael. *Groundless Belief: An Essay on the Possibility of Epistemology.* Oxford: Blackwell, 1977.

Wills, Garry. *Inventing America: Jefferson's Declaration of Independence.* New York: Vintage, 1978.

Wolterstorff, Nicholas. *Reason within the Bounds of Religion,* 2nd ed. Grand Rapids: Eerdmans, 1984.

Yokota, John Shunji. "A Call to Compassion: Process Thought and the Conceptualization of Amida Buddhism." *Process Studies* 23/2 (Summer 1994): 87–97.

————. "Where beyond Dialogue? Reconsiderations of a Buddhist Pluralist." In Griffin, ed., *Deep Religious Pluralism:* 91–107.

Zimmerman, Michael E. *Heidegger's Confrontation with Modernity: Technology, Politics, and Art.* Bloomington: Indiana University Press, 1990.

Zukav, Gary. *The Dancing Wu Li Masters: An Overview of the New Physics.* London: Rider/Hutchinson, 1979.

Zwart, P. J. "The Flow of Time." In Patrick Suppes, ed., *Space, Time, and Geometry.* Dordrecht, Holland: Reidel, 1973: 131–56.

————. *About Time: A Philosophical Inquiry into the Origin and Nature of Time.* Amsterdam: North-Holland, 1976.

Index

actual entities, 10, 40
  as actual occasions, 133–34
  as substances, 10
actual occasions, 10, 12, 40, 133–34,
  246n63
  contemporary, 40, 137, 177, 204–08,
  211, 246n65
  as occasions of experience, 12, 61, 134
  physical and mental poles of, 42, 60
  as subject and superject (object), 61,
  206–08
Alston, William P., 90–91, 92, 253n2,
  254n27
Altieri, Charles, 4, 5
anisotropy, 113, 114, 136, 257n12
anticipation, 41
antirationalism, 7, 36
Apel, Karl-Otto, 7, 52, 258n30
appetition, 134–35
Aquinas. See Thomas Aquinas
Aristotle, Aristotelian, 16–19, 23, 95, 195,
  220
atheism, 25, 94–95, 155–56. See also natu-
  ralism_sam; naturalism_nati; Nietzsche
Augustine, 154
autonomy, 31, 139–42. See also heteronomy
Ayala, Francisco J., 46

Bacon, Francis, 19
Baker, John Robert, 182
Beardslee, William A., 242n13
Benacerraf, Paul, 143
Benacerraf problem, 143, 157–60, 161–62,
  262n77

Bennett, John B., 264–65n27
Bentley, Richard, 23
Bergson, Henri, 122, 123, 182, 258n78
Berkeley, Bishop, 143, 157
Berman, Morris, 19
Berthrong, John, 256n8
Bohm, David, 60, 179–81
Bové, Paul A., 5
Boyle, Robert, 17–18, 19, 21, 63
Bruno, Giordano, 22
Buddhism, 10, 107, 112, 205, 255n46

Cahill, Reginald T., 185, 257n12
Calvin, John, 17, 154, 204
Campbell, Keith, 56
Čapek, Milič, 123, 124, 125
Capra, Fritjof, 107–08, 109, 113, 122
Carroll, Lewis, 113, 157
Cassirer, Ernst, 15
category of the ultimate, 187–88
causation
  efficient and final, 42–43, 61, 63–64,
  249n62
  experience of, 37 (see also perception in
  the mode of causal efficacy)
  Hume on, 8, 10, 68
  panexperientialist view of, 62, 78,
  250n66
  primary and secondary, 25, 199, 203
Charleton, Walter, 21
Chihara, Charles, 144
Chisholm, Roderick, 119
christology, 202–03
Cleugh, Mary F., 121, 122

Cobb, John B., Jr., 4, 72, 73, 181, 202, 211, 246n67, 255n46, 256n51, 269n68
common sense
  hard-core and soft-core, 7, 52–53, 54, 61–65, 88, 119–29, 233, 235
  philosophical school of, 37, 52
compatibilism, 11, 53–54, 199
compound individuals, 58–59, 76
concrescence, 40, 204–05
consciousness, 51–69
  as high-level form of experience, 59, 79
  as subjective form, 51, 65–67
contemporaries, 40, 137, 177, 204–08, 211, 246n65
contradiction
  law of non-, 7, 52, 89, 99–100
  performative, 7, 13, 52, 89, 258n30
creation ex nihilo, 27, 255n49
creation out of chaos, 27
creative synthesis, 196
creativity, 28, 187–98

Daly, Herman E., 72, 73, 246n67
Darwin, Charles, 26, 46, 163
Darwinism
  neo-, 45, 46
  Social, 42
David, Marian, 92, 253n6, 254n27
Davidson, Donald, 91–92
Davies, Paul C. W., 108, 113, 115, 116
de Beauregard, Costa, 113
de Broglie, Louis, 10, 110, 113
deconstruction, 9, 12
deism, 25, 26
Denbigh, Kenneth G., 114–15, 116
Dennett, Daniel E., 57
Derrida, Jacques, 253n10
Descartes, 274n44
  dualism of, ix, 3–4, 11, 21, 51, 54–58, 59, 61, 74, 76, 131, 215
  mechanism of, 18, 23
  as occasionalist, 248n25
  on substance, 39, 77, 234, 246n62
  subjectivist bias (principle) of, 14, 51, 215–41, 275n49
  supernaturalism of, ix, 54, 55, 154, 259n55

Devall, Bill, 73, 252n4
Devlin, James P., 172
divine influence, 25–31
  variable, 25, 28. See also initial aim
Dossey, Larry, 108, 110, 120
dualism
  Cartesian, vii, ix, 3–4, 11, 51, 54–58 (see also Descartes, dualism of)
  crypto-, 133
  temporal-nontemporal, 111–12, 124–33, 257n11
  of theory and practice, 7–8, 36–37, 52, 68, 235, 274n43
  vitalism as, 248n46
Dummett, Michael, 90

Easlea, Brain, 16–17, 19
ecology, ecological, 4, 13
  deep, 70–85
Eddington, Arthur, 121
Edwards, Paul, 249n52
efficient and final causation, 42–43, 61, 63–64, 249n62
egalitarianism (biological), 71–73, 81–83
Einstein, Albert, 113, 118, 120, 122, 171, 172, 185
empiricism, 7
  conceptual, 32–33, 194
  Humean, 8, 33, 68–69, 224, 273n38, 274n42
  sensationist, 8–9
enduring individuals, 10, 137
  as societies, 40, 41, 60, 63–64, 77, 134, 246n65
enlightenment, 15–48
  project, 152, 262n53
  reason, 24
epiphenomenalism, 11, 53, 56, 117
eternal objects, 161, 250n71, 257n11
ethics. See moral theory
events, 60, 246n63
  aggregational, 249n61
evil, problem of, 81, 203–04
evolution, 12, 29, 45

feelings, 65–68, 134
  conceptual (mental), 65–66 (see also mental pole)

intellectual, 66–68
physical, 65 (*see also* physical pole)
propositional, 66
See also prehensions
Ferguson, Adam, 140, 262n53
Ferré, Frederick, 4, 110
Feynman, Richard, 115, 124
Field, Hartry, 262n75
Fitzgerald, Paul, 167, 168, 169, 171
Fludd, Thomas, 22
Ford, Lewis S., 167, 168, 170, 176, 211,
    271n107, 272n1
Ford, Marcus P., 243nn20,22, 250n63,
    254n17
Fost, Frederick F., 167
foundationalism, 6, 12, 38, 101–02
Frank, Phillip, 122–23
Fraser, J. T., 126–33, 134, 135, 137
freedom, 11–12, 63, 109–10, 198–203,
    255n43
functionalism, 51, 62, 65, 117

Gale, Richard, 119
Galileo, 22
Gamwell, Franklin I., 13, 31–32, 140, 164
Gassendi, Pierre, 22
Gay, Peter, 15
Geertz, Clifford, 149–50
genus-species fallacy, vii-viii, 154–55
Geulincx, Arnold, 55
Gilbert, William, 18
God
    consequent nature of, 44–45, 95,
        204–11
    creativity and, 188–98
    love (compassion) of, 206–08, 210
    as omniscient, 205–08
    as personally ordered society, 170,
        181–82, 187, 211–14
    primordial nature of, 44, 161–62,
        189–92, 250n71
    as single actual entity, 170, 264n13,
        271n109
See also panentheism; theism
Gödel, Kurt, 144, 179
Gödel problem, 143–44, 157–60, 162–63
Gold, Thomas, 108, 113

Goldsworthy, J. D., 152
Griffin, David Ray, 223–29, 245n57,
    247nn46–47, 248n48, 249n62, 250n69,
    251nn75–76, 255nn33–35,44,46,
    256nn48–50, 258n30, 263n98, 267n2,
    268n41, 271nn105–09

Habermas, Jürgen, 13, 45, 52, 76, 90,
    151–52, 154, 155, 164, 258n30
hard-core common sense. *See under*
    common sense
Hare, R. M., 149
Harman, Gilbert, 30, 144, 145–47, 148,
    152, 157, 159
Hartshorne, Charles, 97, 180, 194, 274n46
    on bottom layer of human thought, 102
    on compound individuals, 58–59, 76
    on cryptodualism, 133
    on enduring individuals, 41
    on God as personally ordered society,
        170, 181–85, 187, 205, 211, 214
    on mind-brain interaction, 56
    on necessary existence, 195
    on new enlightenment, 15, 48
    panentheism of, 27, 245n46
    on panexperientialism, 12, 249n50,
        257n12
    on relativity physics, 167–71
    temporalistic (dipolar) theism of,
        166–71, 186, 192, 198, 204, 212–14
Hegel(ian), 30, 39, 46, 243n3
Heidegger, Martin, 4, 6, 187, 243n3
Hellman, G., 262n75
Hersh, Reuben, 156, 161, 262n76
heteronomy, 31, 140–41, 142, 156, 160,
    164. *See also* autonomy
Hintikka, Jaakko, 53
Holy, the, 150–51
Honderich, Ted, 53
Horwich, Paul, 88, 89, 92, 254n27
Hume, David, 7, 8, 220, 224
    on causation, 8, 10, 68
    on metaphysics, 8
    on morality, 150, 163
    on perception, 33, 68–69, 224, 273n38,
        274n42

Hume, David, *Cont'd*
    sensationalist doctrine of, 216, 235
    sensationalist principle of, 216, 225–26,
        229, 235–37
    on theism, 140
    on theory and practice, 7, 36–37, 52,
        68, 235, 274n43
Hutcheson, Francis, 9, 140, 262n53

identism, 117, 248n39

Jacob, James, 244nn22,25
James, William, 11
    on consciousness, 61–62, 65
    on evidence, 6
    on laws of nature as habits, 63
    nondualism of, 3–4, 12, 61–62
    nonsupernaturalism of, 30, 55, 245n53
    panexperientialism (panpsychism) of,
        12, 62–63
    pragmatism of, 88, 89, 118, 254n17
    psychical research of, 12
    radical empiricism of, 9
    theism of, 30
    on truth, 254n17
Jay, Martin, 258n30
Jeans, James, 123
Jefferson, Thomas, 140
Johnson, A. H., 170
Johnson, Phillip, 30

Kant(ian), 5–6, 8, 9, 24, 52, 75, 140, 144,
    149, 151, 155–56, 160, 250n64
Kekes, John, 253n13
Kim, Jaegwon, 53, 54, 56
Klaaren, Eugene, 17
Knowledge, 86–87, 97–109, 141
    mathematical, 143, 156–59
    moral, 143–48

Larmore, Charles, 54, 99–100, 141, 147,
    159–60, 163
Lawrence, Nathaniel, 258n38
laws of nature
    as habits, 63
    legal-mechanical view of, 17–23
Leibniz, Gottfried, 39, 143, 157, 246n62

Levenson, Jon, 255n48
Lewis, H. D., 54
Lewontin, Richard, 26
liberation, 13, 45, 164
Lindsey, James E., Jr., 216, 218, 219–23,
    225, 240, 272n15, 274n41
linguistic turn, 219, 240–41
Lochhead, David, 104
Locke, John, 9, 18, 220, 224
Lucas, John, 171, 175
Luther, Martin, 154
Lycan, William G., 53, 158
Lyell, Charles, 26

MacIntyre, Alasdair, 152
Mackie, John, 31, 140, 144–45, 148–49,
    152, 154–55, 159, 163, 251n74
Maddy, Penelope, 158, 262n75
Madell, Geoffrey, 54, 57
magical tradition, 16–24
Magnus, Bernd, vii
Malebranche, Nicolas, 11, 55
Marx, Karl, 46
materialism, 4, 16, 51, 54–58, 92–94. *See
    also* naturalism$_{sam}$
mathematics, philosophy of, 156–60
Matson, Floyd, 4
May, Gerhard, 255n48
McCarthy, Thomas, 243n17, 253n10
McTaggart, J. M. E., 128
mechanism, 11–12, 16–17
Mehlberg, Henry, 114
mental (conceptual) pole, 42, 60
Merrill, A. A., 121
Mersenne, Fr. Marin, 22, 23
metaphysical principles, 28, 191, 195–96,
    246n64
metaphysics, 5–6, 121
Michelson-Morley experiment, 185
mind (psyche), 64
mind-body relation, vii, ix, 51–69. *See also*
    dualism; nondualistic interaction; iden-
    tism
miracles, 22
misplaced concreteness, 111, 175
Mitchell, Basil, 153
modern commitment, 13, 31–32, 140, 164
modern philosophy, viii, 13

modernism
  as antirational, 9
  postmodern, 13, 32, 45, 48, 164
monads, 39–40, 246n62
moral experience (intuition), 14, 36, 145,
  147–48, 160, 163
moral realism, 141, 142–49
moral theory (ethics)
  as autonomous, 140
  and theism, 140, 164
  and atheism, 145, 148
  and sensationism, art, 147–48
  Kantian, 144, 149, 151, 152
morality, 9, 13, 14, 44, 109–11, 139–64,
  197–98
  motivation for, 142, 149–53, 163–64
  point of view of, 151–52
Moschovakis, Y. N., 158, 262n77
Murphy, Jeffrie, 152–54

Naess, Arne, 71–72, 74, 82–83
Nagel, Thomas, 53, 54, 55, 57, 59
natural theology, 154–62, 255n33
naturalism, 29–31
  atheistic, 29, 30, 141
  disenchanted, 59, 254n31
  epistemic, 31–38
  nonreductionistic, 65
  ontological, 24–31
  reductionistic, 5, 254n31
naturalism$_{nati}$, 30–31, 146, 245n53
naturalism$_{ppp}$, 29, 163. *See also* panentheism; panexperientialism; prehensive
  doctrine of perception
naturalism$_{sam}$, 29. *See also* sensationist
  doctrine of perception; atheism; materialism
naturalistic theism, 26–31, 163, 255n33
Neoplatonism, 16–17
Neville, Robert Cummings, ix, 166,
  186–214, 266n1, 267n4
Newton, Isaac, 18, 21, 125, 154, 255n55
Nietzsche, Friedrich, vii, 45, 94, 99, 153,
  203
nominalism, 254n27. *See also* Platonic
  problem
noncontradiction, law of, 7, 52, 89,
  99–100

nondualistic interaction, 64
nonsensory perception, 10, 12, 23, 65
nontemporalist syllogism, 112–13, 114,
  124
norms, normative values, 9, 13, 54, 64–65,
  141, 250n71, 251n71. *See also* morality)

objective immortality, 208–11
Occam, William, 17
occasionalism, 55, 248n25
occasions of experience, 12, 61, 134
O'Conner, D. J., 87–88
Odin, Steve, 256n8
Ogden, Schubert M., 208, 269n68
ontological principle, 38–39, 69, 95,
  161–62, 188–92, 267–68n23
ontotheology, 12
Oomen, Palmyre, 271n108
Oord, Thomas Jay, 269n68

Paley, William, 154
panentheism, ix, 14, 17, 20, 27, 29, 68,
  81, 84, 163, 166, 245n46, 252n12. *See
  also* naturalism$_{ppp}$
panexperientialism, ix, 29, 47, 59–61, 67,
  111, 133–38, 215, 234–41, 249nn50,52,
  250nn64,68
  with organizational duality, 12, 59,
  75–76
  See also naturalism$_{ppp}$
panpsychism, 12, 59, 249nn50,52
pansophism, 19, 47
pantemporalism, 112, 124, 133–38
pantheism, 17, 20, 25, 197
Paracelsus, 19
Passmore, John, 7, 247n2
perception
  in the mode of causal efficacy, 9–10, 34,
    37
  in the mode of presentational immedi-
    acy, 9, 33, 68
  in the mode of symbolic reference, 34,
    68
  nonsensory, 10, 12, 18, 34–35, 144, 162
  prehensive doctrine of, 29, 33, 35, 162
    (*see also* naturalism$_{ppp}$)
  sensationist doctrine of, 8, 23–24, 33,
    157, 273n38
  as sympathetic, 80, 236–37

perceptual law (Whitehead's), 67–68
performative contradiction, 7, 10, 52, 89, 258n30
perpetual oscillation (perishing), 42–43, 61, 63–64, 170, 249n62
physical causation (pure and hybrid), 175–76
physicalism, 157
physical pole, 42, 60
physical prehension, 68
  pure and hybrid, 174
physical purposes, 67
Plantinga, Alvin, 37, 245n40
Plato, 20, 43, 112, 220
Platonic forms, 126, 142–43, 145–47, 156–61. *See also* eternal objects
Platonic problem, 142–43, 156–57, 161–62, 262n77
pluralism
  ontological, 41
  of values, 43–44, 95–97
Popper, Karl, 54
postmodern
  dominant image of, 12–14
  Kant-based and Whitehead-based, 10–11
  science, 4, 14, 60
  theism, 139
  two types of, vii–viii
  Whitehead's philosophy as, vii–x, 3–43
postmodern modernism, 13, 32, 45, 48, 164
prehensions, 10, 33, 35, 78, 134
  conceptual, 35 (*see also* mental pole)
  intellectual, 68–69
  negative and positive, 134
  physical, 35 (*see also* physical pole)
  propositional, 35
  See also feelings
Prigogine, Ilya, 123
process philosophy, 15, 24–26, 248
process physics, 185
progress, 45–47
propositions, 35, 66, 86–87, 92, 250n71
Putnam, Hilary, 90, 91–92, 94, 99–100, 144, 158, 254n31

Quine, Willard Van, 99, 157, 158, 159

Randall, John Herman, Jr., 4–5
rationalism, 7, 35–38
Rawls, John, 149
reason, 24
Reese, William L., 167
Reeves, Gene, 256n8
reformed epistemology, 37
Reichenbach, Hans, 114
Reid, Thomas, 11, 37
relativism, 4, 43
  cognitive, 98–99
relativity
  Einsteinian, 121–23, 168–85
  Whiteheadian, 176
religion and science, 6, 14, 36, 109, 138
religious experience, 14, 36, 274n46
religious perspective, 149–50
Rescher, Nicholas, 196, 253nn8,13
Rorty, Richard M., 11, 87, 88, 89, 90, 91, 92, 94, 152, 219–22, 240–41, 253n4, 254n20
Russell, Bertrand, 113–14, 115
Ryle, Gilbert, 250n70

Schilling, Harold, 4
science and religion, 6, 14, 36, 109, 138
scientism, 10–11
Scotus, Duns, 17, 196
Seager, William, 53, 60
Searle, John R., 53, 54, 56–57, 62, 64, 88
Sellars, Wilfrid, 100
sensationalist doctrine, 216, 235
sensationalist principle, 216, 225–26, 229, 235–37
sensationist doctrine of perception (sensationism), 8, 23, 33, 157, 216, 273n38
sensory perception, 79
  deconstruction of, 9
  full-fledged, 34
  three elements of, 9
Sessions, George, 71–72, 251–52nn3–4
Shankara, 195
Sheldrake, Ruppert, 266n33
Sherburne, Donald W., 186, 226n2
Smart, J. J. C., 54
Smith, Huston, 112
Smith, Olav Bryant, 215, 218, 271n1, 273n41

Social Darwinism, 42
Solipsism, 7, 8, 34, 217
special theory of relativity, 121–23,
    168–85
Spinoza, 25, 112
Stapp, Henry P., 179
Stendahl, 154
Stengers, Isabelle, 123
Stone, Bryan P., 269n68
Stubbe, Henry, 21, 22
subjective bias, 14, 218, 219, 225, 273n41
subjective form, 51, 60, 66–67
subjectivist principle, 14, 215–41
    minimal, middling, and maximal,
        229–39
    reformed, 216–17, 218, 219
Suchocki, Marjorie Hewitt, 181
supernaturalism, 22, 25, 30–31, 245n53
Swidler, Leonard, 252–53n1
Swinburne, Richard, 181

Taube, Mortimer, 57, 64
telepathy, 12, 175, 274n45
theism
    classical, 166
    dipolar, 44, 198
    naturalistic (nonsupernaturalistic),
        26–31, 58, 163, 255n33
    postmodern, 129
    process, 166–67
    temporalistic, 166–67
    traditional and nontraditional, vii–viii,
        154–56
    Whiteheadian, 13–14, 155, 186–214
    Whitehead's turn to, 58, 139–40,
        160–63, 263n94
theory and practice, 7, 36–37, 52, 274n43
Thomas Aquinas, 25, 43, 154, 205
Thomism, 17, 18–19, 196
Tillich, Paul, 187
time, 8, 10, 106–38
    arrow of, 114–15
    asymmetry of, 106–07, 257n12
    atomic, 136–37
    chaotic, 137

dualistic view of, 124–33
    as experience-dependent, 131–33
    irreversibility of, 107, 115, 135
    materialism and, 135–36
    nontemporalist view of, 111–24
    reality of, 255n43
    relational (vs. absolute) view of, 125
    spatialization of, 122–24
transcendental illusions, 9, 88
truth, 86–105
    absoluteness of, 255n35
    atheism and, 94–95
    as correspondence, vii, 86–97
    correspondence theories of, 89–90
    epistemic conception of, 90–92
    as hard-core commonsense idea, 87–88
    materialism and, 92–94
    pluralism and, 85–86

uniformitarianism, 24, 28

vacuous actuality, ix, 58, 74–75, 234–37,
    275n49
vitalism, 248n46

Weber, Max, 69
Weiss, P., 257n12
Wesley, Charles, 204
Wesley, John, 201
West, Cornel, 254n23
Westfall, Richard, 18
Weyl, Herman, 108, 113, 120
White Queen, 113, 115
Whitehead, Alfred North, passim
Whitrow, G. J., 116
Wilcox, John T., 167, 168, 169, 175
Williams, Bernard, 144, 147–49, 150–51,
    152, 163
Williams, Michael, 100
Wolterstorff, Nicholas, 37

Yokota, John Shunji, 256n51

Zukav, Gary, 108, 109
Zwart, P. J., 115–16, 124